# The Language of Riddles, Humor and Literature

Six essays by John M. Dienhart

*John M. Dienhart*
*August 12, 1939 - April 4, 2004*

# The Language of Riddles, Humor and Literature

Six essays by John M. Dienhart

*Nina Nørgaard (ed.)*

University Press of Southern Denmark 2010

© The author and University Press of Southern Denmark 2010
Printed by Grafisk Data Center
Cover Design by Donald Jensen
University of Southern Denmark Studies in Linguistics vol. 20

ISBN 978 87 7674 477 9
ISSN 1602 5113

This book has been published with generous support from:
The Hartvigson-Dienhart-Fund
The Faculty of the Humanities, University of Southern Denmark

*RASK Supplement Vol. 18*
RASK is an international scholarly journal which publishes articles and reviews pertaining to the field of language and communication. RASK is edited by members of the Institute of Language and Communication at the University of Southern Denmark in collaboration with an international Advisory Board.

University Press of Southern Denmark
Campusvej 55
DK-5230 Odense M
Phone: +45 6615 7999
Fax:    +45 6615 8126
www.universitypress.dk

Distribution in the United States and Canada:
International Specialized Book Services
5804 NE Hassalo Street
Portland, OR 97213-3644 USA
www.isbs.com

Distribution in the United Kingdom:
Gazelle
White Cross Mills
Hightown
Lancaster
LA1 4 XS
U.K.
www.gazellebooks.co.uk

# Contents

Introduction 7
*Nina Nørgaard*

Remembering John M. Dienhart 11
*Professor Emeritus Jacob Mey*

A linguistic look at riddles 13

Triggers and targets: a linguistic look at humor 49

Eudora Welty's "No Place for You, My Love" –
the pronominalization of a text 81

Adverbials, direct objects and the style of Carson McCullers 155

Adjectives ending in *-ly*: a study based on material
from modern English literature 167

Phonological ingenuity in "Five Songs" by W. H. Auden 247

# Acknowledgements

The author and publishers would like to thank the following for permission to reproduce the articles of the present collection:

John M. Dienhart, "A linguistic look at riddles", *Journal of Pragmatics* 31, 1998, pp. 95-125. Reprinted by permission of Elsevier.

John M. Dienhart, "Triggers and targets: a linguistic look at humor", *Pre-Publications of the English Department of Odense University* (PEO), 88, 1997. Reprinted by permission of *PEO*.

John M. Dienhart, "Eudora Welty's 'No Place for You, My Love' – the pronominalization of a text", Odense American Studies International Series (*OASIS*), 55, 2002. Reprinted by permission of *OASIS*.

John M. Dienhart, "Adverbials, direct objects and the style of Carson McCullers", *Publication On English Themes* (POET) 18, 1992, pp. 121-134. Reprinted by permission of *POET*.

John M. Dienhart, "Adjectives ending in *–ly*: a study based on material from modern English literature", *Pre-Publications of the English Department of Odense University* (PEO), 127, 2003. Reprinted by permission of *PEO*.

John M. Dienhart, "Phonological ingenuity in 'Five Songs' by W. H. Auden", *Pre-Publications of the English Department of Odense University* (PEO), special issue, 1994, pp. 63-104. Reprinted by permission of *PEO*.

# Introduction

In April 2004, the English Department at the University of Southern Denmark lost a dear and special colleague when John M. Dienhart was suddenly taken from us by a cruel illness. Dienhart was a dedicated linguist who loved his job and engaged in all his projects with great commitment. Celebrated, in particular, for his legendary enthusiasm as a teacher and as the leader of the research and development project *Visual Interactive Syntax Learning* (VISL), Dienhart was highly respected by colleagues and students alike. While Mayan languages and Internet-based grammar were Dienhart's major fields of research, he also produced a number of stylistics articles on the language of riddles, humor and literature in the course of his career. My conviction that these articles emphatically deserve to be collected and published has led me to put together this book.

The six articles presented here investigate a variety of linguistic aspects of texts from different genres. The focus of "A linguistic look at riddles" is the punning riddle (i.e. the conundrum) and the linguistic triggers which lie at the heart of the pun – and hence also the fun – of such riddles. Here Dienhart examines conundrums whose existence and meaning pivot on the similarity of phonetic form which is employed to link semantically rather different worlds or concepts as in "What is worse than raining cats and dogs? *Hailing* taxis." The riddles are described and classified according to the degree of phonetic similarity involved in the linguistic trigger, thus establishing a cline of categories from similarity at one end to dissimilarity at the other. While drawing on the well-known categories of *polysemy*, *homonymy* and *homophony* from semantic theory, the article points to the need for two additional categories if the linguistic nature of the punning riddle is to be described adequately. The term for one of these categories, *paraphony*, is appropriately borrowed from music. The other, my personal favourite, is Dienhart's own invention and itself a linguistic pun, namely *hahaphony* (hahafunny) which designates a pun created by "breaking a word (or phrase) into false parts" as in "What do ghosts eat for dinner? Spook-etti." (cf.

chapter 3). According to Dienhart, punning riddles, like art, may even be seen to counter habituation by creating a sense of newness through the bringing together of what are often quite disparate worlds.

"Triggers and targets: a linguistic look at humour" is a follow-up to the article just described in that here Dienhart demonstrates how the model he developed for the analysis of conundrums applies equally well to other kinds of humorous discourse. Deploying the five types of linguistic trigger set up in the previous article, Dienhart now analyses a broader corpus of texts such as jokes, limericks, graffiti, comic strips, advertising, newspaper and magazine headlines as well as the punning riddles for which he first developed his model. Interestingly, even visual-verbal puns can be captured and explained by the model as in the multimodal meaning-making of one of the examples which combines a verbal text about queuing and a visual representation of the backside of a cow in a brochure about automatic payment service (see chapter 4 for a coherent explanation of this phenomenon).

The remaining four articles of this collection all have literary texts as their data while their foci, aims and methods differ. The first of these sets out to examine a stylistic feature of Eudora Welty's short story "No Place for You, My Love": the extensive use of pronouns instead of proper names. The aim of this study is twofold: to give an account of the nature and complexity of pronominal reference in general, and to provide the reader with a deeper understanding of Welty's text and the role played by pronominalisation in this respect. In Welty's writing, names of people and places usually play a significant role, yet in "No Place for You, My Love" the main characters are unnamed from beginning to end and are referred to through pronominal reference only. Whether it is Welty who withholds the names from the readers, or the two characters who withhold them from each other, this particular linguistic choice clearly helps create a certain sense of anonymity which is absolutely central to the theme of a story in which two strangers from the North meet in a New Orleans restaurant, go for a ride in a rented car, eat, dance, embrace and kiss and then depart to their respective worlds. It is also, however, a linguistic choice which opens up a potential for ambiguity in that it may be difficult to distinguish between the protagonists and other characters in the story if all characters are referred to as "he", "she", "they" and related pronominal forms. Setting out the general conventions of pronominal reference tracking (i.e. the grammatical, logical and contextual principles which enable readers to decode pronouns), Dienhart demonstrates how Welty cleverly handles the challenge of avoiding ambiguity in a narrative which refrains from naming its protagonists and conveys much of its information in an indirect manner. The article is an exemplary illustration of how work in stylistics may simultaneously contribute to our understanding of aspects of a given text as well as of a particular linguistic phenomenon. Because of its clear structure and pedagogical style, the article is furthermore highly suitable for teaching students about pronominalisation.

"Adverbials, direct objects and the style of Carson McCullers" challenges the general understanding expressed by many grammars of English that PAO (i.e. Predicator-Adverbial-Object) constructions are uncommon (or even unacceptable, as claimed by some) in the English language. On the basis of examples from two novels by the American author, Carson McCullers, and cross checked against various English grammar books and two corpus-based studies of adverbials, a useful typological hierarchy of seven PAO constructions is proposed and a list of grammatical principles which are operative in these constructions is established. Altogether, a curiosity initially sparked by the style of McCullers' prose here leads to a well-qualified analysis of aspects of this style and to a much needed refinement of existing grammatical descriptions of a particular syntactic phenomenon. Predicator-Adverbial-Object constructions are, in fact, not quite as uncommon as many English grammars would seem to claim, though McCullers appears to rely rather heavily on the more marked types of these constructions which, it is argued, ties in nicely with the content and message of her fictional worlds.

The intentions of "Adjectives ending in -*ly*: a study based on material from modern English literature" differ slightly from those of the two previous articles. Where the stylistic analysis of Welty's short story and McCullers' novels aimed to say something about the style of the two authors as well as about a particular grammatical construction in general, the next article likewise takes its examples from narrative prose, but centres on investigating a particular grammatical phenomenon while leaving aside the style of the literary texts from which the examples are taken. The point of departure of this study is students' often rather simplified rules about adverbs and adjectives according to which the -*ly* suffix is frequently seen indiscriminately (and hence sometimes wrongly) as an adverbial marker. This misconception – which is often supported by the tendency of grammar books to virtually ignore adjectives in -*ly* – spurs Dienhart to examine the group of English adjectives which bear the -*ly* suffix, in order to provide the reader with a more nuanced view of this particular corner of English grammar. Based on a corpus of eight modern novels in English and a benchmark corpus of ten additional English prose texts, Dienhart illuminatingly accounts for the nature, distribution and history of adjectives ending in -*ly* – a not particularly productive adjectival suffix, as it turns out, though nor is it completely moribund, as illustrated, for instance, by the occurrence of "King Kongly" in a text from 1982.

In the last article of the present collection, Dienhart turns to the phonological side of poetry, examining five short poems by the twentieth-century poet W. H. Auden. The poems were not originally composed and intended as a poetic unit, but in later publications they were placed together and were referred to by Auden as "Five Songs". The crux of the analysis is clearly form rather than content – perhaps mirroring Auden's own interest in the former, but undoubtedly also reflecting Dienhart's enthusiasm and admiration for the phonological structure of the five poems. This article is best described as an eye-opening equilibristic display in the phonological analysis of Auden's intricate use of metre and rhyme, some of which is traced back to Anglo-Saxon and old Icelandic verse.

Characteristic of all the articles are a great enthusiasm and a thoroughness which command admiration and respect. "John didn't know how to write short articles", a colleague once said with a smile – an observation proved by Dienhart's careful attention to detail in the articles collected here, which may be smiled at by those of us in possession of less academic stamina, yet which first and foremost reflects the seriousness with which he approached his data and which informed all his work.

I would like to express my thanks to Professor David Nye, University of Southern Denmark, for suggesting that I should collect and edit Dienhart's articles for a publication, and to Karin Dienhart, who warmly supported the idea. Publication has been supported by the Faculty of the Humanities, University of Southern Denmark and by a very generous grant from the Hartvigson-Dienhart Fund, to whom I express my gratitude. I hope John would approve of the book – I will always remember him with respect and affection.

Nina Nørgaard
University of Southern Denmark, August 2009

# Remembering John M. Dienhart

*by Professor Emeritus, Jacob L. Mey*

Our good friend, colleague and collaborator John M. Dienhart, Associate Professor of English at the University of Southern Denmark and Head of the English Department for several years, passed away on April 4, 2004, after a brief, brave bout with cancer.

When I last saw John, he was in a wheelchair, but had kept his usual high spirits, joking about how we two should reinstate the "Night Shift" – his nickname for those who worked past the ordinary hours. Now, when I am in my office late at night, I sorely miss his cheerful presence and his helpful suggestions for solving some editorial puzzle that I had run into.

John was also a valued collaborator of the *Journal of Pragmatics.* Not only did he have several articles in print or in the making, he also offered his services as a reliable referee, whose reports were always fair, complete, and not least, on time. His latest work, "Triggers and targets: a linguistic look at humor", was still under revision when he was struck by his fatal illness.[1] In this work, he continued an earlier tradition, as exemplified in his 1999 article for *Journal of Pragmatics*, "A linguistic look at riddles" (*JOP* 31(1): 95-125),[2] a work that earned him much praise from his colleagues in various English departments.

John Dienhart was educated at Yale University (B.A., mathematics), Arizona State University (M.A., anthropology), and the University of Wisconsin-Madison (M.A., linguistics). He joined the faculty at Odense University (now: University of Southern Denmark) in 1971. His research and publications dealt with English grammar, phonetics, general linguistics, comparative syntax (English, Danish, German), the language of poetry, the language of humor, computers, and Mayan languages.

John was also intensely concerned about teaching, and his students were his life. Unrelentingly, he pushed them forward to greater excellency, always there with the helping hand, even where others would have thought it beneath their dignity to produce simple, but effective teaching aids. His teaching qualities were recognized by the University of Southern Denmark, Faculty of Humanities, in 1999, when he was awarded the Excellence in Teaching Prize for that year. On a more practical side, John organized the Book Sales in connection with the annual Hans Hartvigson Symposium at the University of Southern Denmark, thereby raising substantial funds toward providing scholarships for students in the English Department. For this, too, he will be remembered fondly, and missed. (The Book Sales will be continued and are still raising money, now for the Hartvigson-Dienhart Fund).

John Dienhart was one of the founding fathers of the Odense project "Visual Interactive Syntax Learning" (VISL). He was untiring in his efforts to further the project in every possible way: he wrote countless VISL applications, and as project coordinator, available almost around the clock, he ensured the smooth running of the VISL project from day to day for the benefit of users world wide. With the passing of John Dienhart, the VISL team has lost a very valuable and enthusiastic member.

I find it appropriate to end this obituary by quoting our Institute Chair, Steffen Nordahl Lund, who, in his message on the occasion of John's death, remarked that John, until the end, "as always, was full of the future". We want to remember him in this way, and live as he did, keeping our eyes on the road, while supporting and entertaining our fellow wayfarers.

Jacob L. Mey
Professor Emeritus of Linguistics
Editor-in-chief, *Journal of Pragmatics*
University of Southern Denmark, January, 2005

## Notes

1. Editor's note: Unfortunately this article has been lost, but an earlier version of it appears in chapter 4 of this book.
2. Editor's note: Chapter 3 of this book.

# A linguistic look at riddles

*John M. Dienhart*

Abstract

The riddle has been the subject of considerable interest among anthropologists and folklorists for some time. Recently, linguists, too, have begun to examine the riddle, perhaps as an offshoot of the burgeoning linguistic interest in humor in general. This paper offers a new look at one type of riddle, the so-called 'conundrum', or 'punning riddle'.

Adopting Arthur Koestler's notion of 'bisociation', linguistic triggers (the 'punch lines') in conundrums can be viewed as phonetic forms linking the semantics of two disparate worlds. Conundrums can then be classified according to the nature of these linguistic triggers.

Based on a variable which is termed the 'similarity factor', a 'similarity cline' is constructed, along which the triggers, and hence the conundrums, can be classified. One end of this cline marks maximal similarity of form, namely total identity, while the other end marks absolute dissimilarity of form. In between these poles are five stages – polysemy, homonymy, homophony, paraphony, and hahaphony – each stage being progressively further removed from the identity pole. These stages mark increasingly weaker degrees of phonetic similarity between the bisociated elements in the linguistic trigger. This classification serves to illuminate the nature of the conundrum itself, while at the same time accounting for a variety of subtypes which fertile minds have invented.

*Keywords:* Humor; Riddles; Similarity, phonetic: Puns; Semantics; Bisociation

## 1. Introduction

Riddles seem to be part of human culture in all areas and all ages. In the first major collection of English riddles, Taylor (1951) compares English riddling themes with those of riddlers from other cultures. His comparative data includes riddles from every continent – from Argentina in the west to Korea in the east, from Lapland in the north to Madagascar in the south.[1]

Since riddles typically describe one 'object' in terms of another, anthropologists and folklorists have often viewed riddles as one means of gaining insight into the nature of the mental relationships which members of a given society perceive among the elements of material and non-material culture. Riddles, it is argued, can provide a useful indication of cultural norms and world view. The 'outsider' looking in may sometimes be taken by surprise:

(1) A European standing on one leg.
(solution: 'a mushroom'; from the Akamba in Kenya, cited in Haring 1974: 203)

Often the 'outsider' needs to gain considerable insight into the culture being investigated if the comparison is to be illuminating:

(2) Lightning in the cow-peas.
(solution: 'a baldheaded old man'; also from the Akamba, cited in Haring 1974: 205)

From European culture a typical example is the following:

(3) Little Miss Etticoat
In a white petticoat
And a red nose;
The longer she sits
The shorter she grows.
(solution: 'a candle'; from Northern Ireland – Taylor 1951 : 221)

There is an immense literature dealing with the collection and classification of riddles of this type in various societies. Taylor's own bibliography of 'Collections of riddles cited' is 27 pages long (1951: 871-897).

In Taylor's view, riddles like (1)-(3) are "true riddles",[2] as opposed to "the conundrum or witty question" which "often plays with puns" (1951: 1). Excluded from his collection are therefore the more 'modern' English riddles such as the following:[3]

(4) What happened to Ray when he was stepped on by an elephant?
He became an X-Ray. (5001 : 119)

(5) What do you get if you cross a bear and a skunk?
Winnie the Pooh. (5001: 227)

For the sake of convenience, let us follow tradition and label riddles such as (4) and (5) 'conundrums'.[4] Other labels that can be found are 'joking riddles' or 'punning riddles' (Redfern 1984: 82-83; Raskin 1985: 26). In general, such riddles are examples of the larger subcategory of 'verbal humor' as opposed to 'conceptual humor' as described by Freud in 1905.

The word 'conundrum' tends to be shied away from in 'serious ' linguistic work on riddles. I fail to find it, for example, in Pepicello and Green's 1984 book which bears the title *The language of riddles*. Instead, they speak of riddles which make use of 'linguistic ambiguity' (our 'conundrums') as opposed to 'contextual ambiguity' (Taylor's 'true riddles'). If the label 'conundrum' is being consciously avoided by some linguists, it may be because the word is 'contaminated' by its association with the word 'pun', which is definitely not in favor, in many circles, as a subject for serious study. Augarde writes, for example, that "nowadays conundrums are considered childish, suitable only for the playground or for times when adults let their hair down" (1986: 10). Espy, in his book *The game of words*, prefaces his examples of 'riddles and conundrums' (1971: 208) with the remark that "anyone over ten years of age is invited to skip this section". In the same vein, Gruner (1978: 71) claims that

> ... losing to a conundrum is not the same thing as losing to a straight riddle. To be sure, the loser has been outsmarted, but *double meaning* was used! ... The riddle has turned from a 'real' contest of brains to a 'play' contest more like a game than a fight .... The 'duel' turns not upon wisdom and knowledge of the real world, but upon nonsensical symbolic manipulation of the 'unreal'.

I agree with Redfern (1984: 82), who cites this quotation, that Gruner is overstating the case. In the first place, language is certainly a 'real' part of culture; and in the second place, riddles of any variety (like humor in general) typically depend on 'double meaning'.

Admittedly, riddles like (4) and (5) are clearly aimed solely at amusement. But whether the riddle is intended to educate or to amuse, or to do both, 'double meaning' – in the sense of comparison of some sort – is at the heart of most riddles, 'traditional' or non-traditional.

Making comparisons is a very human occupation. We spend our lives comparing one thing to another, and behaving according to the categorizations we make. Patterns govern our lives, be they patterns of material culture, or patterns of language.

Growing up in any society involves, in large measure, discovering what categories are relevant in the particular culture in which we find ourselves. Within a few years after birth, we have established mental 'control' over many, if not most, of the 'objects' within our experience. 'Things' are classified as the same, similar or different, and we construct mental 'boxes' in which to put objects which 'match' in some way.

However, the number of new boxes we create diminishes rapidly as we grow older. We become 'fixed' in our perceptions, and the world, once fresh and new, loses its ability to surprise as we become increasingly familiar with the objects it contains, and increasingly adept at placing the objects encountered today into boxes created yesterday.

Artists of all kinds – poets, painters, playwrights, sculptors, architects – know this, and they work at creating new objects for us, establishing new relationships, challenging our view of the world.

It has been argued, convincingly in my opinion, that riddles, too, can provide for adults the sense of newness and exploration which otherwise diminishes in the growing-up process.[5] If the objects themselves are no longer new, we can amuse ourselves by creating new patterns, new relationships between old objects.

The relationships, of course, are established by the riddler. The riddler is in control, either because he himself has made up the riddle (this is the rare case) or because he proposes to share a riddle which he has heard (this is the common case) with his audience (the riddlee or riddlees). In either case the riddler 'challenges' the riddlee to discover the relationship he has in mind.

## 2. Towards a characterization of the riddle

How is the challenge presented? In other words, how do we know when we are dealing with a riddle? The answer to this question is not as easy as it may seem, and much has been written about riddle definition. Although this question is peripheral to my main interest in this paper (after all, we generally recognize a riddle when we see one, even if we can't define it), it seems reasonable to explore the nature of the riddle in general before focussing on that particular type of riddle – the conundrum – that I wish to examine in more detail.

It is tempting to start by stating that a riddle consists of two parts, a question and an answer. But we know that this is neither a necessary nor a sufficient condition. That the condition is not sufficient is at once obvious:

Q: 'How much is 2 plus 2?'
A: '4'.

This is not a riddle. Nor do question and answer games such as *Trivial Pursuit* consist of riddles. Note that it does not help if we make the (quite reasonable) standard addition that the riddler's 'question' is not really a request for an 'answer', since the riddler already knows the answer, and in fact, knows (or hopes) that the riddlee does not. Like riddlers, teachers generally know the answers to questions they ask their students. Nonetheless, such questions are still not riddles.[6] That the condition is not necessary is shown by the first three examples cited at the beginning of this paper (riddles (1)-(3)). Consider further:

(6) In spring I am gay,
In handsome array;
In summer more clothing I wear;
When colder it grows,
I fling off my clothes;
And in winter quite naked appear.
(from Canada, cited in Taylor 1951: 215; the solution is 'a tree')

This verse, too, is a riddle, though not stated in question form. A better known example is the following nursery rhyme:

(7) Humpty Dumpty sat on a wall,
Humpty Dumpty had a great fall,
All the king's horses and all the king's men
Couldn't put Humpty Dumpty together again.

This is actually a riddle, with 'an egg' as the 'solution'.

Though brevity is generally a common feature of riddles, it is not a necessary condition. Many of the Old English riddles from the Exeter Book,[7] for example, are quite long. Consider riddle number 39 (given here in one of its modern English translations – from Meyvaert 1976: 200-201):

(8) Writings say that the creature is
clear and visible among the race of men
on great occasions. It has special power,
greater by far than men may realize.
It will visit individually each
of the living; then it departs, continuing on its way.
It will never be there a second night,
but it must forever wander on an exile's path,
without a home; nor will it be more lowly for that.
It has neither foot nor hand, nor has it ever touched earth,
nor has it either of two eyes,
nor has it mouth, nor did it ever speak to men,

nor has it any mind; but writings say
that it is the poorest of all the creatures
that were brought forth according to their kinds.
It has neither soul nor life, but it is destined to endure journeys
far and wide throughout this wondrous world.
It has neither blood nor bone, yet has been a comfort
to many men throughout this earth.
Never has it touched heaven, nor may it go to hell,
but it must forever live by the teachings
of the king of glory. It takes long to say
how its destined existence will continue afterwards,
the devious shapings of the fates; that is a curious thing
to relate. True is everything
that offers guidance in words about this creature;
it has not any limb, but lives even so.
If you can solve riddles quickly,
in true words, say what it is called.

Whatever solution one accepts for this riddle, and many have been suggested ('day', 'death', 'moon', 'time', and most recently 'cloud'[8]), the point is that this riddle is not brief, nor is it, strictly speaking, a question.

Sometimes the riddler clearly announces that a riddle is on the way:

(9)  Riddlum, riddlum, raddy,
     All head and no body.
     (from West Virginia; cited in Taylor 1951: 10; the solution is 'a tadpole')

In Africa, the telling of riddles often follows a very definite pattern, with the riddler announcing his intention to tell a riddle and the riddlee announcing his willingness to listen to it. For example, the Lamba of South Africa invariably start their riddles with 'tyo' ('Guess the riddle') and the riddlee responds with 'Ka kesa' ('Let it come') (Harries 1971: 381).

Now, of course, it cannot be denied – despite the above examples – that the riddle is often given in question form, particularly today in the English-speaking world. More specifically, many 'modern' English riddles take the form of a *wh*-question (that is, a question introduced by such items as *why, when, where, what, how*):

(10) What do you call a person who puts you in touch with the spirit world?
     A bartender. (5001: 165)

(11) When is a door not a door?
    When it's ajar.

(12) Why did the football manager give his team a lighter?
    Because they kept losing their matches. (5001: 29)

Many of the openings tend to be rather formulaic, as in the last riddle above – 'Why did the ...?'. Other examples are e.g. 'How can you tell ...?' and 'What's the difference between ... ? '. Generalizing, we can say that all riddles (whether or not they are stated in question form) have in common a two-part structure: an initial 'text' ('$text_1$') in which the riddler supplies a series of clues (generally insufficient or misleading) from which a second 'text' ('$text_2$') is to be surmised by the riddlee. Harries (1971: 379) labels the former the 'precedent' and the latter the 'sequent'.

The riddle is thus one of the more interactive types of humor in that the riddler invites the riddlee to participate in the riddling process. Admittedly the riddlee, once he picks up the signal that a riddle is on the way, frequently replies simply 'I don't know'[9] since he wisely assumes that he hasn't got much chance of responding correctly to such questions as:

(13) What goes cluck-cluck bang?
    (I don't know.)
    A chicken in a minefield. (5001: 157)

Occasionally the riddler takes advantage of this automatic admission of ignorance on the part of the riddlee. Perhaps the best-known example is:

(14) Why did the chicken cross the street?
    (I don't know.)
    To get to the other side. [10]

Similarly, the 'What's the difference between ...?' type of riddle may also take this turn:

(15) What's the difference between an elephant and a watermelon?
    (I don't know.)
    You'd be a fine one to send to the store for a watermelon.

Here the riddler purposely misleads (and hence attempts to be doubly humorous) by adopting the riddle formula, though no riddle is intended.

Sometimes the riddler fools the riddlee by supplying an answer which treats as a focus some element in the precedent which the riddlee does not anticipate:

(16) Why did the elephant wear red socks?
   Because his green ones were being washed.

Returning now to the notion of a two-part structure, we note that this seems to be a necessary condition, but it is clearly not sufficient. As we observed earlier, typical question and answer situations (as in the classroom or in games like *Trivial Pursuit*) are not riddles; but they do consist of two-part structures. Something more is needed. What this 'something more' is has been the subject of many books and articles dealing with the nature not only of riddles but of humor in general.

One of the most widely cited works in this connection is Sigmund Freud's 1905 book, *Der Witz und seine Beziehung zum Unbewussten*, the most recent English translation of which is by James Strachey and entitled *Jokes and their relation to the unconscious* (1981).

In Chapter 2 ('The technique of jokes', 1981: 16-89) of his book, Freud works out his basic dichotomy between 'verbal jokes' and 'conceptual jokes'. The distinction rests on whether the nature of the joke is primarily linguistic or situational. Crucial to the technique of verbal jokes is the highly economical "multiple use of the same material", which is "nothing other than a word capable of multiple interpretation, which allows the hearer to find the transition from one thought to another" (1981: 54).

This notion of 'multiple use of the same material' is further developed, under the label 'bisociation', in Arthur Koestler's book *The act of creation*. In Koestler's words, 'bisociation' refers to "the perceiving of a situation or idea, L, in two selfconsistent but habitually incompatible frames of reference, M1 and M2" (Koestler 1971: 35; L stands presumably for 'link' and M for 'matrix'.) For Koestler, bisociation is not only a basic characteristic of humor in general, but of the creative act itself:

> I have coined the term 'bisociation' in order to make a distinction between the routine skills of thinking on a single 'plane', as it were, and the creative act, which ... always operates on more than one plane. The former may be called single-minded, the latter a double-minded, transitory state of unstable equilibrium where the balance of both emotion and thought is disturbed. (Koestler 1971: 35)

The image Koestler thus provides is of two intersecting 'planes' (or matrices). The intersection is the shared 'link', which belongs simultaneously to both planes. Where Koestler speaks of 'planes' or 'matrices' or 'frames of reference',

Norrick (1986) refers to 'schema conflict' and Raskin (1985) to 'semantic scripts'. Raskin (1985: 99) claims that a text can be characterized as a joke if both of the following conditions are satisfied:

(i) The text is compatible, fully or in part, with two different scripts.
(ii) The two scripts with which the text is compatible are opposite in a special sense.

Raskin's claim for oppositeness (even in 'a special sense') is too strong, at least for riddles, as we shall see, but his characterization of verbal humor as involving the use of one text to evoke two different 'worlds' ('semantic scripts') is clearly in line with the views expressed by Koestler and Freud before him.

Raskin's 'semantic scripts' are often linked by means of one or more 'triggering devices' which switch us from the one script to the other. His formal label (1985: 114) is the 'semantic script-switch trigger'. The trigger is that part of the text which figures in both scripts. It is the shared element by means of which (in Koestler's terms) the bisociation of the two scripts is effected.

Like Raskin, Nash (1985) refers to the "*trigger* [my emphasis] that detonates the humorous mass" (1985: 7). This trigger can be viewed as "a centre of energy, some word or phrase in which the whole matter of the joke is fused, and from which its powers radiate" (1985: 7). The place where this 'center of energy' is located is referred to by Nash as the 'locus'.

With the combined help of these earlier investigators, we are now in a position to provide a working characterization of the riddle. I propose the following formulation:

A riddle can be viewed as a discourse type involving a two-part structure: an initial 'text' (the 'precedent') in which the riddler supplies a series of clues (generally insufficient or misleading) from which a second 'text' (the 'sequent') is to be surmised by the riddlee. The precedent is often, but not necessarily, expressed in the form of a question. Together, the precedent and the sequent make up the riddling text as a whole. This text establishes a link (or 'bisociation') between two 'scripts' (or 'frames of reference'). The riddler, through the precedent, deliberately plays up one script and then, through the sequent, awakens the riddlee's awareness of a second script. When the link between the two scripts is 'verbal' (rather than 'conceptual' – to state the distinction in Freud's terminology), we can speak of a 'linguistic trigger' (or 'triggers'). The location(s) of the trigger(s) can be called the 'locus' (or 'loci') of the humor (or humorous attempt). [12]

Riddles involving only linguistic triggers form a subcategory of verbal humor, a subcategory which I would like to call 'language riddles', but which, as I have already indicated, I shall refer to, following tradition, as 'conundrums'.

If we consider the 16 riddles which have been cited so far, it should be apparent that riddles (4), (5), (10), (11) and (12) are conundrums. These five clearly have linguistic triggers (X, *Pooh*, *spirit*, *ajar*, and *matches*, respectively). The others do not.

The following two riddles are also conundrums. Let us employ some of the terminology presented above to analyze them in more detail:

(17) What is a *cloak*?
 The mating call of a Chinese frog. (5001: 154)

(18) What's the best cure for water on the brain?
 A *tap* on the head. (5001 : 20)

Both riddles make use of a 'linguistic trigger' (*cloak*, *tap*). Observe further that these examples illustrate that the 'locus' of a conundrum can occur either in the 'precedent' (as in (17)), or in the 'sequent' (as in (18)).

The form *tap* in riddle (18), with its two different interpretations ('a light blow', 'a spigot'), has us mentally juggling two 'scripts' once we pick up the clue in the answer. In one script we envision an action – a person being tapped on the head; in the other script we envision a curious state – a human head with a spigot protruding – where the 'water on the brain' can be drained off. (These are different scripts, but not – in any useful sense – 'opposite'.)

In (17), the word *cloak* starts us off in a script dealing with clothing. When the answer is supplied, we reinterpret *cloak* as the Chinese (mis)pronunciation of the word *croak*, and are thus taken into the second script, the world of the frog. Observe that the sequent lies totally within this second script (*mating call*, *frog*). In order to understand the riddle, of course, the riddlee must bring to its interpretation the background knowledge that the phonemic distinction which native English speakers make between /1/ and /r/ can cause problems for some non-native speakers of English. As Nash appropriately observes about jokes in general (1985: 9):

> ... before the joke can be discharged in all its swiftness[,] there is much to be apprehended about cultural and social facts, about shared beliefs and attitudes, about the pragmatic bases of communication. If that sounds laboured and obscure, let us try to put it another way. Humour is not for babes, Martians, or congenital idiots. We share our humour with those who have shared our history and who understand our way of interpreting experience. There is a fund of common knowledge and recollection, upon which all jokes draw with instantaneous effect[.]

Note that when the locus of the riddle is in the precedent, the 'trigger' is already present, waiting for the appropriate context (supplied by the sequent) to release it.

This is the case in the 'cloak' riddle. When the locus of the riddle is in the sequent (as in the 'tap' riddle), the trigger is both provided and released in the answer.

It seems obvious, now, that one meaningful way to analyze and classify conundrums (as well as other types of verbal humor) is to investigate the nature of the linguistic trigger. What types of linguistc devices are employed in the 'bisociation' of two 'scripts'? Before I offer my own answer to this question, let us examine some of the proposals found in the more recent literature.

## 3. Linguistic triggers as viewed by Pepicello, Green and Weisberg

Probably the most intensive work on the linguistic analysis of riddles is that resulting from the collaboration of Pepicello, Green and Weisberg. In a series of articles (Green and Pepicello 1978; Pepicello 1980: Pepicello and Weisberg 1983; Pepicello 1987) and a book (Pepicello and Green 1984), they have subjected the riddle to the searchlight of linguistic theory, more particularly to a variant of the 'standard' theory of transformational grammar. Since the 1984 book provides both a representative and detailed presentation of their theory, let us look briefly at the views expressed in it.

Pepicello and Green (1984) suggest that conundrums (though they do not use this term) can be classified into three basic linguistic types; these are (a) phonological, (b) morphological, and (c) syntactic. Furthermore, the morphological and syntactic categories can be subdivided. The following illustrative examples are taken from their book:

(a) 'phonological'
(19) What turns but does not move?
    Milk. (1984: 27)

(b) 'morphological'
(20) Why is coffee like the soil?
    It is ground. (1984: 37)

(21) What kind of cat do you find in the library'?
    A catalogue. (1984: 43; 'pseudomorpheme')

(c) 'syntactic'
(22) Why is a goose like an icicle?
    Both grow down. (1984: 45; 'phrase structure ambiguity')

(23) What do you call a man who marries another man?
    A minister. (1984: 48; 'transformational ambiguity')

Though Pepicello and Green might have chosen slightly more humorous examples, that is, of course, irrelevant for the linguistic principles involved. Let us see why they classify these riddles as they do.

In (19), the trigger is said to be 'phonological' because "two different lexical items have identical phonological form" (1984: 27). Riddle (20) has a 'morphological' trigger because "the lexical item /grawnd/, a noun, is homophonous with the past participle of the verb /graynd/" (1984: 38). Morphology is also said to trigger (21), but this time by means of a 'pseudomorpheme' (the 'cat' in 'catalogue' is not related to 'feline'; in fact it is not a morpheme at all). Riddle (22) allegedly involves syntactic ambiguity which is due solely to the underlying structure of the two readings: in the 'goose' reading, *down* is a noun functioning as direct object; in the 'icicle' reading, *down* is an adverb. Pepicello and Green call this 'phrase structure ambiguity'. Finally, the 'syntactic' trigger in (23) is an example of 'transformational ambiguity', because two different underlying syntactic structures are assumed to be involved ('X marries Y' vs. 'Z marries X to Y') and these two underlying structures are allegedly converted to identical surface structures by transformational rules (1984: 48-50).

The problem with Pepicello and Green's classification, in my view, is first of all that it is so closely linked to (a now outdated version of) transformational grammar. This is particularly noticeable in their division of syntactic ambiguity into the two types: 'phrase structure ambiguity' and 'transformational ambiguity'. As transformational theory changes (and it is changing all the time) the classification of these riddles must necessarily change.

In the second place, the logic of the classification is questionable. Consider, for example, their treatment of (19) (repeated here, for convenience, as (24)):

(24) What turns but does not move?
   Milk.

To argue that the linguistic trigger here is 'phonological' because "two different lexical items have identical phonological form", whereas it is 'morphological' or 'syntactic' in the other examples, is surely to miss the point. The trigger is, in a very basic sense, 'phonological' in all five of the riddles cited above from Pepicello and Green.

Whether we are dealing here with two different lexical items, $turn_1$ and $turn_2$ (as Pepicello and Green claim) or with a single lexical item, *turn* (as my copies of the *Longman Dictionary of Contemporary English* and *The American Heritage Dictionary of the English Language* suggest), what is clearly involved is identity of form and difference of meaning.

Pepicello and Green's model might even allow us to argue that this riddle involves 'syntax' as well, possibly even a 'transformation'. For example, the various senses of *turn* (whether it is one word or two) have clear, and different, syntactic correlations. In the sense of 'revolve', *turn* can combine with *around*. But in the sense of 'become sour' it cannot. Perhaps, even, the construction *The milk turned* is the result of a 'deletion transformation' (to use Pepicello and Green's terminology) applied to an 'underlying' string such as *The milk turned sour*.

A similar argument for the role of 'syntax' could be made for those triggers which Pepicello and Green classify as 'morphological'. Consider again (20) (repeated here as (25)):

(25) Why is coffee like the soil'?
    It is ground.

Granted, we are dealing here with different morphologies: in one case *ground* is a noun and in the other it is the past participle of *grind*. But probably different syntaxes are involved as well. In the 'coffee' reading we have (in one syntactic model) the structure S ('it') + P ('is ground'), while in the 'soil' reading we have S ('it') + P ('is') + Cs ('ground'). That is, we have two different syntactic patterns: S P vs. S P Cs. [13]

I think Pepicello and Green are confusing the means with the end. What (19)-(23) have in common is that the riddler has made use of various linguistic means in the English language to create a 'trigger' that relates to two different scripts. The 'trigger' is not phonology or morphology or syntax. The trigger is a phonetic form which lends itself to multiple interpretations. Linguistic triggers, as Nash (1985: 25) nicely puts it, match 'phonetic consonance' with 'semantic dissonance'.

The conundrum, like much verbal humor, is based on this similarity between linguistic forms (and a corresponding disparity of meaning). Such similarity is the central feature of the 'word-play' involved in this type of riddle. So let us take this as our starting point.

## 4. Linguistic triggers: A new point of view

I wish to propose that crucial to the nature of conundrums, and particularly useful for their classification, is a variable which I shall label the 'similarity factor'. This factor refers to the similarity between paired forms of linguistic signs.

Ever since Saussure, it has been customary to describe the linguistic sign as a combination of two parts: form (or expression) and meaning (or content). Since linguistic triggers match 'phonetic consonance' (similarity of form) with 'semantic dissonance' (difference in meaning), it is the form that our 'similarity factor' is concerned with. Note, however, that a form may be expressed in writing as well as in speech, so we will need to take into account both orthographic form and phonetic form.

This will be done on the cline which I am proposing here. 'Total identity' marks one end of the cline and 'total dissimilarity' marks the other. In between are a number of relationships which are well-known from semantic theory: polysemy, homonymy and homophony. To these, I wish to add two new terms: paraphony and hahaphony. I shall define these notions in a moment, but first let us look at the cline itself:

(TRUE IDENTITY)
POLYSEMY
HOMONYMY
HOMOPHONY
PARAPHONY
HAHAPHONY
(TRUE DISSIMILARITY)

What is important here is the relative ranking of the various degrees of similarity. Polysemy, for example, is nearer to true identity than is homonymy. In fact, polysemy is true identity from the point of view of form, since polysemy involves only one form with multiple meanings. Likewise, homonymy ranks higher on the similarity scale than does homophony. This is because homonyms are words which are pronounced *and* spelled alike, whereas homophones are pronounced the same but need not be spelled the same. So homonymic pairs are more similar than homophonic pairs. Let us now examine each of the categories in turn, from 'top' to 'bottom'.

**Polysemy** – one word with multiple meanings (for example, mouth meaning 'the body opening through which an animal takes its food', 'the part of a stream or river that empties into a larger body of water', or 'the opening through which any container is filled or emptied' – *The American Heritage Dictionary of the English Language*, 1970: 858). Here there is only one form, but more than one meaning.

**Homonymy** – two words with the same form (both orthographically and phonologically) and different meanings (for example, $tap_1$ meaning 'a light blow' vs. $tap_2$ meaning 'spigot'). Here there are two (identical) forms, each with its own meaning(s).

**Homophony** – two words with the same phonological form but different orthographic forms and different meanings (for example, *tale* vs. *tail*). Here there are two partially identical forms, each with its own meaning(s).

**Paraphony** (or 'near homophony') – two words which are similar but not identical in phonological form. They differ in meaning and orthography (for example, *gnawing* vs. *knowing*).[14]

**Hahaphony** (or **Hahafunny**) – I have coined this label to refer to an 'artificial' type of (near) homophony whereby similarity of sound is produced by means of a kind of pseudo-morphemic analysis. Examples are: 'Ewe-niform' vs. 'uniform', or 'spook-etti' vs. 'spaghetti' (more on these below). As the examples illustrate, hahaphony typically creates new 'words' or phrases, thus extending (*ad infinitum*) the linguistic possibilities for establishing 'relationships' that can form the basis for riddling (or humor in general). Although hahaphony produces pairs that are very similar (or even identical) in sound, I have nonetheless placed this device at the far end of the similarity scale because of the artificiality of the generated constructions. Both riddler and riddlee are fully conscious of this 'foreignness' with respect to the standard vocabulary of English.

We have now reached the end of the line. Beyond hahaphony lies 'dissimilarity'. The resulting scale is thus:

Identity ← Polysemy ← Homonymy ← Homophony ← Paraphony ← Hahaphony ← Dissimilarity

The rest of this paper will be devoted to an examination of the various types of conundrums as classified according to this cline.

## 5. The 'similarity cline' applied to conundrums

In applying the categories making up the similarity scale, it seems reasonable to start at the 'top', nearest identity, and move down, toward dissimilarity.

### 5.1 Polysemy

In general I think it is fair to say that conundrums do not normally involve polysemy as the sole linguistic trigger. This is probably because any two scripts connected only by a polysemic trigger would tend to be so closely related that their bisociation would not be considered very interesting or amusing.[15]

Suppose, for example, that we wish to create a conundrum using the polysemic form, *mouth*. We might come up with something like: 'What has a mouth but no nose?'. However, the solution, 'A river' (or 'a bottle', or 'a cave'), is not very striking (though small children might enjoy this riddle as they learn to extend the meaning of the word *mouth*).

Considerably more humor is packed into the following conundrum, which adds to the polysemic *mouth* a play on a homophonic pair:

(26) What has four eyes and a mouth'?
    The Mississippi. (5001: 270)

This riddle has two linguistic triggers, the form *mouth* with its multiple meanings, and the homophones *eyes/i's*.

The discussion of polysemy is made more complicated, however, by the wellknown fact that it is very difficult to draw a clear line between polysemy and homonymy.[16] Consider, for example, the following riddle:

(27) What did the python say to its victim?
   I've got a *crush* on you. (5001: 17)

This is an example of polysemy if we use *The American Heritage Dictionary of the English Language* (1970: 319) as our guide. There we find a single entry for *crush*: one of the meanings is given as 'to press between opposing bodies so as to break or injure: mash; squeeze', and another is given as '*informal*: an infatuation'.

On the other hand, we must view this as an example of homonymy if we follow the *Longman Dictionary of Contemporary English* (1978: 267-268), where we find two separate entries – one for the verb, $crush_1$, and one for the noun, $crush_2$. Under the verb entry we find 'to press with great force so as to break, hurt, or destroy the natural shape or condition'; under the noun entry we find (listed as 'informal') the meaning 'a strong foolish and short-lived liking or love for someone'.

Despite the difficulty involved in distinguishing clearly between the categories of polysemy and homonymy, I think we can already sense one of the advantages of the 'similarity' scale that I am proposing in this paper. The items compared in a conundrum must have some 'distance' between them. Too little distance, and the riddle does not have a sufficient element of 'surprise'.

Example (27) illustrates two features whereby such distance can be created, even when we are at the top end of the cline, near the 'identity' pole. One technique is to play on word class contrasts (*crush* as verb vs. *crush* as noun). Another is to create distance by using the given lexical item as part of an idiom, thereby shifting its meaning considerably. Thus *crush* as a noun figures in the larger construction, 'to have/get a crush on' = 'to be infatuated'.

The next two riddles create semantic 'distance' in a similar fashion, by playing off a literal reading against a more figurative one. This is often aided by the addition of an adverbial panicle:

(28) What did one tonsil say to the other?
   You'd better get dressed – the doctor's *taking* us *out* tonight. (5001 :

(29) What happened to the terrorist who tried to *blow up* a bus?
   He burnt his lips on the exhaust pipe. (5001: 132)

But it can also be created by other means:

(30) Why did the one-handed man cross the street'?
To get to the *second-hand* shop. (5001: 23)

Here polysemy is forced onto a phrase (*second-hand*) for the nonce, with surprising effect: it takes a figurative expression and urges us to examine it literally. The riddle also echoes the well-known line 'Why did the chicken cross the street?' cited earlier.

Let us now move a bit further down the similarity cline, a bit further away from the 'identity' end of the scale.

*5.2 Homonymy*

The following two riddles have (according to my dictionaries) homonymic triggers (rather than polysemic ones), in that the items in question, *spotted* (as adjective) and *dressing* (as noun), are given entries which are separate from the entries for the verbs *to spot* and *to dress*.

(31) Why couldn't the leopard escape from the zoo?
Because he was always *spotted*. (5001: 30)

The homonyms are (i) the past particple of the verb meaning 'to see' and (ii) the adjective 'having spots' (from the noun 'spot' + the adjective-forming suffix 'ed'). Note that the word-play on the two different readings of 'spotted' is facilitated by the double function of 'was': (i) auxiliary verb with past participle – that is, a complex predicator, here interrupted by an adverbial (P- A -P) – vs. (ii) copula verb with adjective – that is, a predicator with a subject complement (P A Cs). Thus the double reading is: (i) 'Because he was always seen', and (ii) 'Because he always had spots'.

(32) Why did the lobster blush'?
Because he saw the salad *dressing*. (5001: 27)

The play on 'dressing' (present participle of the verb *to dress* vs. noun meaning 'sauce') is here made possible by the double function of 'salad' (subject of the verb 'dressing' vs. first member of a compound noun). In the spoken form the potential ambiguity of 'dressing' is threatened by the fact that this word would normally be more heavily stressed as a verb than as a member of the compound.[17]

Though one might be able to make a case for polysemy (rather than homonymy) in (31) or (32), or in both, there seems to be no doubt that the next riddle makes use of pure homonymy. Polysemy would seem to be out of the question:

(33) What's worse than raining cats and dogs?
    *Hailing* taxis. (5001 : 22)

The homonymy here involves the verb meaning 'fall like hail' vs. the verb meaning 'signal to'. The sequent, 'hailing taxis', urges the riddlee to create a new script from the precedent by interpreting the idiom *raining cats and dogs* (that is, 'raining heavily'), in a literal sense. This coincides with a new interpretation of the phrase 'hailing taxis', so the two scripts ('rainy weather' and 'getting a cab') become bisociated by *hail*.

The next example makes use of linguistic triggers in both the question and the answer, but it is perhaps not, strictly speaking, a riddle, since it has the form of a yes/no-question:

(34) Have you ever seen a salad *bowl*?
    No, but I've seen a square *dance*. (5001: 30)

This clever little construction plays (twice) on the formal identity of a subject + (non-finite) verb construction and a compound noun construction. The ambiguity is based on the fact that an 'accusative with infinitive' can function in English as object of a transitive verb (cp. 'Have you ever seen *him bowl*? No, but I've seen *her dance*'), and hence can enter into an ambiguity relation with certain compound nouns – namely those whose second element (e.g. *bowl*, *dance*) can be both noun and verb. I would classify the first trigger (*bowl*) as a case of homonymy (despite stress differences), the second (*dance*) as polysemy.

At first glance, the next example seems fully parallel to the one above:

(35) Can a shoe *box*?
    No, but a tin *can*. (5001: 30)

Here we have two clear cases of homonymy. In the precedent we have $box_1$ as noun ('rectangular container') vs. $box_2$ as verb ('to hit with the hand') and in the sequent we find a parallel with $can_1$ as noun ('a metal container') vs. $can_2$ as auxiliary verb. Observe that the parallel between 'shoe box' and 'tin can' is made possible by the ellipsis of the implied main verb ('No, but a tin can box'). Note further that although this example (like (34)) is a yes/no-question, it does not, strictly speaking, involve a double reading (whereas (34) does). The only possible grammatical reading here is the one where *box* and *can* are interpreted as verbs. Structurally speaking the compound noun interpretation ('shoe box' and 'tin can') are not possible. Nonetheless, bisociation has been established because of our knowlege of the existence of these compound nouns.

*5.3 Homophony*

As we noted above, when two words sound the same but differ in meaning and orthography, we speak of homophony. By adding this device to his arsenal, the riddler increases immeasurably the possibilities for riddling. Riddles involving homophony are particularly well-suited to the spoken form. When written, the riddle loses some of its force, since the difference in spelling visually resolves the potential ambiguity, weakening the effect of the linguistic trigger:

(36) When is a boy like a pony?
    When he's a little *hoarse/horse*. (Butters 1987: 112)

The homophones here consist of an adjective (*hoarse*) vs. a noun (*horse*). Note the role of the copula verb ('s), which allows both an adjectival and a nominal complement. Note, too, the role played by the double function of *little*, which is an adverb in the first reading ('little hoarse') and an adjective in the second ('little horse'). It is particularly when so many linguistic devices play a role in contributing to the bisociation that Pepicello and Green's classification technique seems misguided. The basic linguistic trigger is clearly the homophonic pair, *hoarse/horse*, and this triggering is made possible by linguistic support from other aspects of the English grammatical system.

As example (36) illustrates, a sequent with a homophonic trigger is particularly well-suited for responding to a precedent which makes a direct comparison between two objects. One reading relates to the first object, the other reading to the second. This is very clearly saying two things at once, and hence, as Freud pointed out, true economy of expression.

The next example builds on a similar syntactic structure, though the homophones are here both nouns:

(37) How is a short story writer like a prostitute?
    They both sell a little *tale/tail*. (Butters 1987: 114)

Note here that again *little* has a double function. When modifying the countable noun *tale*, it is an adjective and means 'small'; as a modifier of the (here) uncountable *tail*, it combines with the indefinite article, *a*, to mean 'some' (contrast 'I've got a little money' with 'I've got a little dog').

The following riddle combines homonymy with homophony to create two otherwise parallel linguistic triggers. In both cases the triggering is abetted by reliance on ellipsis (cp. '[You should paint] the sun rose'):

(38) What colors should you paint the sun and the wind?
    The sun *rose* and the wind *blue/blew*. (5001: 31)

Sometimes the homophony is created by 'ignoring' word or morpheme boundaries:

(39) Why is a mouse like fresh hay?
    Because the *cattle/cat'll* eat it. (5001: 28)

Here we have homophony between a noun (*cattle*) and a contracted form of the string, *cat will*, which is reduced to *cat'll*. Observe further that the linguistic trigger in this example is made possible by the fact that the third person plural form of English present tense verbs ('The cattle *eat* it') is normally identical to the base, or infinitive form ('The cat will *eat* it').

A well-known conundrum which shows up in many riddle collections puts the homophony in the precedent rather than in the sequent:

(40) What's black and white and *red/read* all over?
    A newspaper.


*5.4 Paraphony*
Moving further down the similarity scale, we come now to the notion of 'near homophony' – that is, to similarity rather than identity on the phonological level. A riddle can become especially 'punny' when two near-homophones (paraphones) are mentally linked by using a word in the sequent whose semantic content ties in with an item in the precedent, while at the same time being phonetically similar to the word or phrase it 'replaces'. The 'replaced' form (which connects to the second script) is often mentally supplied from well-known collocations:

(41) What do cannibals have for lunch?
    Baked *beings*. (5001: 31)

*Baked beings* ties in cleverly with cannibals, while at the same time calling to mind that similar, and more normal lunch food, *baked beans*.

The next example makes use of two pairs of synonyms, but there would be no humor in this at all if it were not for the role of a paraphonic pair contrasting *serpent* with another noun which typically collocates with *civil*:

(42) What do you call a polite snake?
    A civil *serpent*.

The next three examples need no comment:

(43) What did the beaver say to the tree?
It's been nice *gnawing* you. (5001: 130)

(44) What did the judge say when he saw a skunk in the courtroom?
*Odour* in the court! (5001: 174)

(45) What should you try to avoid when it's raining cats and dogs?
Stepping in a *poodle*. (5001: 263)

Sometimes the paraphony involves well-known song titles or opening lines. Such textual allusion or echoing is sometimes referred to as 'intertextuality':[18]

(46) What did the clown sing at the end of the day?
*Jester* Song at Twilight. (5001: 21)

(47) What did the coke say to the coal?
What Kind of *Fuel* am I? (5001: 160)

A number of 'ghost' riddles are constructed on the basis of paraphony:

(48) Why was the ghost arrested?
Because he didn't have a *haunting* license. (5001: 26)

(49) What is the best way for a ghost-hunter to keep fit?
He must exorcise regularly. (5001: 144)

(50) Where does Dracula stay when he's in New York'?
In the *Vampire* State Building. (5001: 239)

(51) How does a ghoul start a letter'?
*Tomb* it may concern. (5001: 412)

In some riddles a trigger which is paraphonic in one dialect of English is homophonic in another:

(52) What did Cinderella say when her photographs were mislaid?
Some day my *prints* will come. (5001: 155)

(53) What animal can you never trust'?
A *cheetah*. (5001: 17)

Note that riddle (53) makes it clear that collocations (such as idioms, song titles, and other more or less fixed phrases), while useful for uncovering the 'missing' member of the paraphonic pair, are not a necessary feature of paraphony.

The following quite ingenious example, in which the complete sequent (a whole sentence) is the trigger, involves a pair which is paraphonic in slow speech but can become homophonic in fast speech:

(54) What did the electrician's wife say when he came home at 2 a.m.?
    *Wire you insulate*? (5001: 292)

Considerably less ingenious is one garden variety of this type of conundrum, a variety which by now, I hope, has wilted on the vine. I have in mind the 'grape' riddles, which were quite common in my school days:

(55) What is sweet and purple and lives in Monaco?
    Princess *Grape*.

(56) What is strong and purple and conquered Greece and Egypt?
    Alexander the *Grape*.

Riddlers who enjoyed this type of punning (*grape/Grace, grape/Great*) soon ran out of paraphones for *grape* and eventually dropped all pretence of constructing a riddle on paraphonic principles. The result was the abandonment of any kind of linguistic trigger (and audience) whatsoever:

(57) What is purple, has wheels and goes slam, slam, slam, slam?
    A four-door grape.

I shall conclude this category with a conundrum which skillfully links 'grape' and 'elephant' riddles. The linguistic trigger involves paraphony in my dialect, but would involve homophony in other dialects of English:

(58) What did the grape say when an elephant stepped on it?
    Not much – it just gave a little *whine/wine*. (5001: 119)

*5.5 Hahaphony*

A particularly productive type of riddle results from a pseudo-morphemic[19] analysis of a word in the sequent, whereby part of the word is replaced by a similar sounding element, creating a new 'word' which links up with some concept in the precedent. Needless to say, this increases boundlessly the range of options available to unrepentant riddlers, since they can now create, unendingly, new 'words' out of old ones. The resulting forms, though generally not part of the English vocabulary, often become endowed with a surprising element of meaning:

(59) If a buttercup is yellow what color is a hiccup?
*Burple*. (5001: 151)

(60) What weighs two thousand kilos and has a flower behind its ear?
A *hippy potamus*. (5001: 20)

(61) Where would you find a prehistoric cow?
In a *moo-seum*. (5001: 23)

(62) What do you get when you cross a dog with a chicken'?
A hen that lays *pooched eggs*. (5001: 8)

(63) How do you weigh a whale?
Take it to a *whale-weigh* station. (5001: 10)

Sometimes it requires considerable alertness (in the absence of visual clues) on the part of the riddlee to discern what pseudo-morphemic legerdemain the riddler is performing:

(64) What do lady sheep wear'?
*Ewe*-niforms. (5001: 30)

(65) What did the astronaut find in his stocking on Christmas Day?
*Missile*-toe. (5001: 8)

(66) What did they give the man who invented the door-knocker?
The *No-bell* prize. (5001: 162)

Not surprisingly, hahaphony allows riddlers to invest 'ghost' riddles with new spirits:

(67) What do ghosts eat for dinner'?
*Spook-etti*. (5001: 144)

(68) What do ghosts wear in the rain?
*Boo-ts* and *ghoul-oshes*. (5001: 144)

The next example exploits two instances of synonymy to provide an interpretation of three pseudo-morphemes:

(69) What is a happy tin in the United States?
   *A-merry-can.* (5001: 29)

Here the synonym pairs *happy/merry* and *tin/can* are employed in the construction of the hahaphonic pair *A merry can/American*.

One last example of this type involves a linguistic trigger which depends on a bilingual association:

(70) Why does a Frenchman have only one egg for breakfast?
   Because one egg is *an oeuf* (5001: 415)

*5.6 Combinations*

As we have seen, conundrums, short as they are, sometimes make multiple use of the linguistic devices we have examined above. That is, the triggering is muitilocative. For example, we found a combination of polysemy and homophony in (26), two cases of homonymy in (35), and a case of homonymy combined with homophony in (38). The next example makes use of double paraphony:

(71) What do you get if elephants trample Batman and Robin?
   *Flatman* and *Ribbon*. (5001: 118)

Note that in this example, unlike our earlier cases of multilocative triggering, both members of the trigger(s) actually appear in the riddle. The precedent contains the 'straight' members (*Batman* and *Robin*) and the sequent contains the paraphonic counterparts, one based on assonance (*Flatman*), the other on consonance (*Robin*). Now it is not unusual to find double triggering where all four words in the triggers are manifested in the text, but generally they all appear in the sequent. The following example is characteristic of the type:

(72) What's the difference between a jeweller and a jailer?
   One *sells watches* and the other *watches cells*. (5001: 107)

Note the pattern here. The standard formula for this kind of riddle is 'What's the difference between X and Y?'. This formula gives the riddler a chance to demonstrate how to link, linguistically, two apparently dissimilar objects named in the precedent. The linguistic trigger in the sequent involves metathesis – that is, the interchanging of sounds, letters, syllables, words or phrases.[20] In (72) whole words are interchanged.

As this example indicates, it is quite common in this type of riddling for one member of each pair to be a verb and the other to be a noun, thus making use of the basic English transitive verb pattern: S P O. The result is a riddle based on a double case of word-pairing taking the form of a chiasmus ('a crossing over') in the sequent:

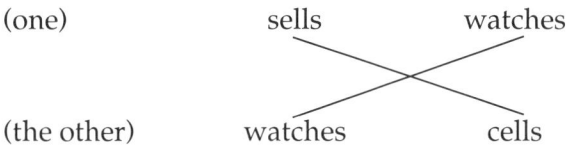

(one)              sells            watches

(the other)        watches          cells

The metathesis here links a homophonic pair (*sells* (verb)/*cells* (noun)) with a homonymic (or polysemic) pair (*watches* (verb)/*watches* (noun)). So here we have a combination of homophony and homonymy (or polysemy) linked by metathesis. Note, additionally, the paraphony in the X/Y pair of the precedent *jeweller*/*jailer*).

Another example of this type is:

(73) What's the difference between a railway guard and a teacher?
    One *minds* the *train* and the other *trains* the *mind*. (5001: 107)

Not all riddles in this category play on the S P O pattern, as the following examples indicate:

(74) What's the difference between a stubborn mule and a stamp?
    One you *lick* with a *stick* and the other you *stick* with a *lick*. (5001: 207)

(75) What's the difference between a Crown Prince and a tennis ball?
    One is *heir* to the *throne* and the other is *thrown* into the *air*. (5001: 207)

(76) What's the difference between a cat and a comma?
    A cat has *claws* at the end of its *paws* and a comma has a *pause* at the end of its *clause*.
    (5001: 207)

Note that riddles (75) and (76) each make double use of homophonic pairs. In (76) the pairs even rhyme. From the syntactic point of view, however, these two riddles are marginally flawed because of the variation in preposition usage in

*A linguistic look at riddles* · 37

the one example (75), and of article usage in the other (76): *heir to the throne/ thrown into the air; has claws/has a pause*. The 'flaw' is more noticeable in (75) since it occurs within the domain marked by the metathesis – that is, it occurs between the metathesized pairs.

Not surprisingly, this type of riddle also makes frequent use of paraphony. The simplest type involves the metathesis of the initial letter in a word pair:

(77) What's the difference between a forged pound note and an insane rabbit?
One is *bad money* and the other is a *mad bunny*. (5001: 107)

Sometimes more than one sound in each word is involved:

(78) What's the difference between a church bell and a pickpocket?
One *peals* from the *steeple*, the other *steals* from the *people*. (5001: 176)

In both (77) and (78), however, it is the syllable onset that undergoes metathesis. Occasionally, whole syllables are involved, in which case the metathesis can become more difficult to sense, especially when, as in the next example, we are also confronted with a whole array of synonyms (*tube/hollow cylinder, crazy/ silly, Dutchman/Hollander*):

(79) What's the difference between a tube and a crazy Dutchman?
One is a *hollow cyli-nder* and the other is a *silly Holla-nder*. (5001: 206)

When entire syllables are involved like this, one begins to sense a kind of ha-haphony, as though e.g. *cylinder* is to be interpreted as 'silly' + 'nder'. Another example of this type is (80), but in this case we find one word (of two syllables) being paired against two words (of one syllable each). This creates an even stronger feeling of hahaphony:

(80) What's the difference between a girl and a postage stamp?
One is a *female* and the other is a *mail fee*. (5001: 207)

Here the chiasmus strengthens the impression that pseudo-morphology is involved:

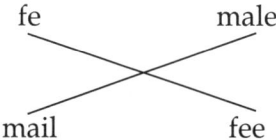

The final example of this type ingeniously employs three sets of pairs, two of them undergoing metathesis around the third:

(81) What's the difference between a hungry man and a glutton?
One *longs to eat*, the other *eats too long*. (Butters 1987:114)

Here the metathesis involving 'long' and 'eat' builds on the homonymy between *long* (verb) vs. *long* (adverb), and on the homophony (if we disregard stress differences) between *to* (infinitive marker) vs. *too* (adverb).

## 6. Riddles for the eye

To paraphrase an observation in Redfern (1984: 28), 'Riddles, unlike children, should be heard and not seen'. That is why one seldom discusses orthography when commenting on riddles. They are generally meant for the ear, not the eye. However, we have already seen that some of the riddles which rely on pseudo-morphemes (hahaphony), such as (64)-(66), are easier to comprehend when seen than heard. And I suspect that most listeners would not understand the following riddle at all unless they saw it in writing:

(82) Why did the *antelope*?
Nobody *gnu*. (5001: 271)

This riddle uses hahaphony in the precedent (*antelope* (n.) vs. *ant* (n.) + *elope* (v.)) and homophony in the sequent (*gnu/knew*). It is not likely that the listener will pick up the word-play on this last pair without orthographic help.

There is, however, a certain type of riddle which is quite common, even though it clearly plays on orthography. The basic idea is to let one of the two 'scripts' involved in the riddle be an orthographic one:

(83) Why is a naughty boy like the letter D?
Both make *ma mad*. (5001: 28)

(84) Why is the letter T like an island?
Because it's in the middle of *water*. (5001: 265)

What is going on here is that the linguistic trigger – for example, *water* in (84) – creates bisociation by being interpreted both as a referring form ('object-language') and as a thing in itself ('metalanguage'). As a referring form it can be an object surrounding an island; as a thing in itself, it is a string of five letters, the middle one being 't'. Note how much help the bisociation gets from the multiple interpretations of the noun *middle*. Similarly in (83), the conundrum is crucially aided by the resiliency of the verb *make*.

Of course the riddlee must be literate in order to understand the bisociation in riddles like these, since he has to be able to interpret the 'thing in itself' script, which involves orthography. But at least both riddles can be understood without visual aid by a literate listener. The next two riddles demand somewhat more orthographic awareness:

(85) What cheese is made backwards?
    Edam. (5001: 14)

(86) What occurs once in every minute, twice in every moment, but not once in a thousand years?
    The letter M. (5001: 148)

In each of these riddles the unsuspecting riddlee is misled into contemplating a script based on an object-language interpretation of the precedent. The sequent, however, introduces quite a different script – by focussing on a metalanguage interpretation. One has to appreciate the ingenuity that creates riddles like these. They begin to take on the quality of mathematical puzzles.

## 7. Conclusion

We have seen that riddles, like much humor, can be divided into two broad categories: those that involve linguistic triggers (conundrums) and those that do not. This paper has focussed on the analysis and classification of the conundrum. My basic argument has been that condundrums (and, I believe, humor of many varieties) can be illuminatingly viewed from the vantage point of a scale which ranks bisociated words and phrases according to the degree of similarity they display in their phonetic and orthographic forms. The scale ranges from identity at one end to dissimilarity at the other:

Identity ← Polysemy ← Homonymy ← Homophony ← Paraphony ← Hahaphony ← Dissimilarity

In the case of polysemy the bisociation is brought about by one and the same form which stands in both scripts and contributes one of its meanings to each.

With homonymy the bisociation is created by the fact that two identical forms, each with its own meaning(s), stand at the intersection of the two scripts. We have seen that it is particularly difficult to distinguish homonymy from polysemy, since we are faced with the challenge of deciding when we are dealing with one single form and when with two identical forms. The problem can be compared to trying to determine if we are dealing with one person or with identical twins if we see only one person at any given time. I have suggested that here is a case where humor might aid linguistics, since the use of particular forms as linguistic triggers in humorous texts might be taken as *prima facie* evidence for homonymy as opposed to polysemy (both twins being forced to appear on the scene at the same time).

When we reach homophony our problems of classification are greatly diminished since bisociation is based on the use of words that are only partially identical in form – though they sound alike, they are spelled differently, and hence they are easily recognized and distinguished.

Identity is further weakened in the case of paraphony, which forces bisociation on the basis of forms that are similar rather than identical in sound. At this point, the notion of intertextuality is particularly useful, since it is common for one of the scripts to call into play a 'similar' script which is well-known to the riddlee. With paraphony the riddler generally provides only one script, but standing as close as it does to a script shared by speakers sharing the same culture (a proverb, song title, etc.) it mentally creates the second script as a kind of echo.

In the case of hahaphony, the bisociation is manufactured by squeezing new meaning out of old words through the process of pseudo-morphemic 'analysis'. This creates nearly unlimited opportunities for the riddler, and further decreases the likelihood that the riddlee will come up with the required solution unaided.

We have also seen that many riddles make use of multiple triggering. One particularly common type of combination utilizes metathesis to link paired items, giving rise to the curious case of the riddler insisting on difference ('What's the difference between X and Y') in the precedent, and then stating the difference in terms of some linguistic similarity in the sequent.

Finally we have examined a series of riddles which in some sense can be said to be aimed at the eye as well as the ear, in that one of the two bisociated scripts involves observations on the orthographic form of given words, focussing on metalanguage rather than object-language.

This all goes to show that the riddler, like the poet, takes the whole world of 'objects', material as well as non-material, as the stuff out of which to create new combinations, to 'recycle'[21] the tired, worn out, overused detritus of our daily lives and hand back new products that sometimes generate groans and grimaces, but often delight and amuse with their irrepressible, at times ingenious, linking of phonetic consonance with semantic dissonance. Our experience and perceptions are constantly being altered as a result of such bye-sociations.

# Notes

1. A cursory perusal of Taylor's immense collection of riddles yields examples from: Argentina, Armenia, Barbados, Bermuda, Bulgaria, Canada, Chile, Cuba, Czechoslovakia, Denmark, Estonia, Finland, France, Germany, Greece, Hawaii, Hungary, Iceland, India, Indonesia, Iran, Ireland, Italy, Jamaica, Japan, Korea, Lapland. Letland, Lithuania, Madagascar, Malaysia, Mongolia, Norway, Poland, Portugal, Puerto Rico, Rumania, Russia, Samoa, Scotland, Spain, Surinam, Sweden, Switzerland, Turkey, Wales, Yugoslavia. For a very early riddle, and the dire consequences thereof, see Samson's challenge to the Philistines in the Old Testament (Judges 14: 1-20).

   American Indians were for some time wrongly assumed to constitute one group of people who were without riddles. This mistaken view apparently goes back to the early days of American anthropology. Thus Sapir (1932: 217) writes that "it is a well known fact, often stressed by Boas, that the American indians do not go in for riddles and proverbs". Despite the topic of his own short paper ('Two Navaho puns'), Sapir adds to the myth of the humorless Indian by remarking that "it begins to appear likely that the American Indian has a generalized lack of interest in light verbal fancy". This view has since been overturned. There are now a number of papers documenting the existence of riddles in various Indian tribes. Taylor (1944) contributed one of these papers himself. Some other examples are Scott (1963) and Cunningham and Lorenzo ( 1991 ).

2. Taylor (1951: 4-5) makes an interesting observation about the objects treated in 'true' riddles of European origin:

   > In European riddling ... the themes of riddles are found almost exclusively in the vicinity of the farmer's house. Earthworms, chickens, milk, and eggs, as well as household tools, are characteristic and popular themes. Yet even here the choice is extremely limited: dogs and horses are not often the answers to riddles, although often used as the means of comparison. Cats or mice are virtually never used in either sense. European riddlers rarely allude to wild animals. It would be hard to find riddles for a stork, a bear, a fox, or a wolf, frequent as these creatures are in folk story. Only a few fruits or vegetables occur as the themes of riddles: the carrot, the onion, the walnut, the blackberry, and the cherry comprise the list. Apples and pears are almost completely unknown to riddlers. The thistle, but not the rose, is the subject of riddles .... Provisionally at least, we can say that modern European traditional riddles deal with the objects in a woman's world or a world as seen from the windows of a house.

3. A large number of the riddles cited in this paper are taken from the collection *5001 jokes* (1992). References to this work are given as (5001: page number). Where a riddle is cited with no reference at all, it is too well-known to need one.

4. 'Conundrum' is described in *The Penguin Dictionary of Literary Terms and Literary Theory* (Cudden 1992: 192) as follows: "A word of very obscure origin, it denotes a form of riddle whose answer involves a pun". This follows very closely one of the descriptions in the *OED*. The first reference given there is from the year 1596, but the early meaning has been lost. By 1645, "'conundrum' had the general sense of "a pun or word-play depending on similarity of sound in words of different meaning"". By 1769 (sense 4) the word had taken on the meaning referred to above: "a riddle in the form of a question[,] the answer to which involves a pun or play on words" (*OED*, Vol. III, 1989: 857).

   Both the Penguin and the *OED* definitions are somewhat misleading, since they strongly imply that the pun is always in the answer to the riddle. More accurate (as we shall see) is Augarde's characterization in *The Oxford Guide to Word Games* (1986: 10): conundrums are "riddles which depend on a pun. The pun is usually in the answer ... but it may be in the question".

5. It has frequently been pointed out that conundrums (and word-play in general), being intimately linked to the form of vocabulary items in a language, are notoriously difficult to translate from one language to another. In this way such humor has much in common with poetry.

For an excellent discussion of this point (and many others), see Morreall's 1989 article 'Enjoying incongruity'.

6. Chiaro (1992: 68) is thus not providing an adequate characterization of the riddle (not even of the conundrum) when she writes that: "a riddle is a brief question and answer exchange between two people, but unlike most question and answer routines the riddle is always answered by the person who posed it in the first place."

   The observation that the riddler is not seeking information but providing it may be a fairly recent one. It is clearly stated in Harries (1971: 388), and Haring, writing three years later, praises Harries for this 'ingenious' insight, labelling it a 'major contribution' to the study of riddles (Haring 1974: 198).

7. *The Exeter Book* is a collection of Old English poetry given to the library at Exeter Cathedral by Exeter's first bishop, Leofric. The book includes 94 riddles, and is believed to date from the middle of the tenth century (Krapp and Dobbie 1966: ix-xvi). Of course, in comparing riddles of the Old English period with those of the present period, we must bear in mind that the riddle genre, like genres in general, is in large part culturally determined – and hence in a constant state of flux. As the genre changes, so, too, will the definintion of that genre.

8. See for example von Erhardt-Siebold 1946 ('death') and Meyvaert 1976 ('cloud'). Meyvaert boldly claims that his solution is definitive: "Although it may appear foolhardy to claim finality in any area of scholarly research, the present paper does pretend to settle once for all the problem of what the Anglo-Saxon poet had in mind when he wrote the verses quoted above." (Meyvaert 1976: 196). Hamnett 1967: 384) makes this point very nicely:

   > The clues provided in the descriptive element(s) seldom furnish enough evidence for the answer to be definitely gathered from them. This is the principal reason why people seldom spend much time thinking about a riddle, and why, when they do think about it, they are more likely to be trying to recall *a known but forgotten answer* [Hamnett's emphasis] than to be genuinely attempting to tackle a new problem. Their difficulties are aggravated by the fact that riddles are often 'objectively' susceptible of more than one reasonable and appropriate solution, but in fact only one solution 'counts' as correct.

   Or, in Nash's (1985: 49) succinct formulation: "[c]hallenged by the signal, the addressee obediently resigns himself to ignorance".

10. Like most 'texts', an 'old' riddle, once it enters the public domain, may form the basis for later riddles which refer to it either directly or indirectly. The riddle about the chicken crossing the street has led to such echoes as:

    (i) Why did the elephant cross the street'?
    Because it was the chicken's day off. (5001 : 117)
    (ii) Why did the germ walk across the microscope?
    To get to the other slide. (5001: 136)

11. Norrick is clearly indebted to Koestler, and cites him frequently in his work. The debt is also eminently clear from the title of his 1986 paper, "A frame-theoretical analysis of verbal humor: Bisociation as schema conflict'. Koestler also figures (as does Freud) in the bibliography of Norrick's newest linguistic contribution to the theory of humor, *Conversational joking: Humor in everyday talk* (1993). Raskin makes no mention of Koestler in *Semantic mechanisms of humor* (1985), but he states his indebtedness to Freud in no uncertain terms when he claims (1985: 43) that Freud's work is "the closest that humor research has ever come to the technical aspects of this [i.e. Raskin's] book".

    It should be pointed out that Koestler's *The act of creation* has not found favor in all circles. But Hamnett (1967: 379), I think, puts the work into proper perspective:

    > Koestler's book, it could be argued, was unkindly received by the academic world. Some criticism was informed and justified .... but many scholarly readers were so alienated

> by the infelicitous combination of journalism and pseudo-science [which] the study undoubtedly displays that the elements of value and interest in the central theme were lost sight of or taken for granted.

12. The reason for all the parentheses in this paragraph is that some riddles (like humorous texts in general) can have multiple triggers, and hence multiple loci ('multilocative'). This is the case, for example, when a riddle involves a chiasmus (as we shall see).
13. The following abbreviations for grammatical functions are used in this paper: A (Adverbial), S (Subject), P (Predicator), O (direct Object), C (Complement), Cs (subject Complement). Function labels which are followed and preceded by a hyphen represent discontinuous constituents. Thus P-...-P marks a discontinuous Predicator:
    (i) He was always spotted.
    S P-    A    -P
    This is the convention adopted in Bache et al. (1991).
14. I have borrowed the label 'paraphonic' (and 'paraphony') from music, and use it to refer to words that are similar ('para-') in sound rather than the same ('homo-'). Curiously, linguistics has borrowed 'homophonic' from music, but not (to my knowledge) 'paraphonic'. Apparently a related label, 'paronymic', has been used in linguistic circles. For example, Redfern (1984: 18, 91) speaks of paronyms when referring to 'quasi-homophones'. Strictly speaking, though, paronyms are apparently supposed to be etymologically related (see, for example, Cuddon 1992: 684). At any rate, the label 'paraphonic', focussing as it does on similarity of sound, suits my purposes better than 'paronymic'.
15. This is not to say that such riddles do not exist. I take the following to be an example of a polysemic trigger:

    > (i) What doesn't ask questions but must always be answered?
    > A telephone. (5001: 267)

    It can be argued that the solution to this riddle depends on different meanings of the verb, *answer*. But that, of course, depends on how the meaning of *answer* is defined. In the *Longman Dictionary of Contemporary English* (1978: 34) we do indeed find two different meanings listed (and hence polysemy). One meaning which is listed is 'to reply (to): *You didn't answer his question*'; another is 'to attend or act in reply to (a sign, such as a telephone ringing, a knock on the door, or a whistle): *I telephoned this afternoon, but nobody answered.*' In *The American Heritage Dictionary of the English Language* (1970: 55), however, both of these senses are covered in one entry (hence no polysemy): 'to reply to'.
16. One of the most thoughtful and thorough discussions of the problems involved in trying to distinguish between polysemy and homonymy can be found in Lyons (1977: 550-569). His discussion focusses on two criteria which would appear to be central to the problem: etymological relationship and relationship of meaning. Lyons clearly establishes, however, that neither criterion is as straightforward as one might assume. His considered opinion is that "it is preferable to leave the theoretical status of the distinction between homonymy and polysemy unresolved" (1977: 552). We should keep in mind that while the distinction may be a problem for linguists, riddlers get along quite nicely without worrying about it. One might even consider using riddles as 'data' in tackling the problem. Possibly the very fact that a particular item is made the linguistic trigger for a conundrum can be taken as an argument against a polysemic interpretation of the item in question.
17. The stress parameter further complicates the question of what constitutes homonymy. Though I am quite willing to allow the label 'homonymy' to cover the two types of 'dressing' here, some analysts would not be. Pepicello and Green, for example, take a stronger view. They criticize one investigator for misconstruing

    > the term 'homonym', apparently confusing it with 'homograph'. Specifically, he claims that the terms hot dog (a warm canine) and ho! dog (a wiener) are homonyms, when in

fact the pronunciations of these two phrases are distinguished in English by their stress patterns. In the latter case, primary stress is on hot, in the former case, on dog. Thus, although the two phrases are indeed spelled alike, they are not homonyms (Pepicello and Green 1984: 80).

For those sharing this view, the 'dressing' riddle might be said to involve a special case of paraphony rather than homonymy. The pair of 'hot dogs' would differ in sound and meaning, but not in orthography.

18. Norrick (1989: 117), for example, observes that "intertextuality occurs any time one text suggests or requires reference to some other identifiable text or stretch of discourse, spoken or written". Intertextuality is thus a form of allusion, and it therefore follows, says Norrick, that if "jokes and puns present little intelligence tests for hearers, then intertextual jokes amount to intelligence tests prefaced by quizzes in literary history" (Norrick 1989:118). Once again we see that the comprehension of humorous 'texts' generally demands a good deal of shared cultural experience.
19. As we have seen in (21), the label 'pseudo-morpheme' also figures in the work of Pepicello and Green (1984: 42-43). It is treated briefly in Nash as well (1985: 143).
20. Pepicello and Green (1984: 58-60) provide a good discussion of the use of metathesis in riddling. The reversal of sounds is a well-known phenomenon in word-play, intentional as well as non-intentional. It is, of course, involved in many tips of the slung, often referred to as Spoonerisms ('Please sew me to another sheet'; 'Our queer old dean'), discussed, for example in Hockett (1967), Espy (1971: 230), Chiaro (1992: 18-19). Since reversal on any level can be a comic device in itself, it should not surprise us to find metathesis used in riddling.
21. This connection between word-play and 'recycling' I owe to Redfern (1984: 157): "Ingenuity and the finding of new use for old objects are surely desirable civic qualities in an age of vanishing resources".

# References

*5001 jokes*, 1992. Manchester: World International Publishing.

*The American Heritage dictionary of the English language*, 1970 [1969]. New York: American Heritage.

Augarde, Tony, 1986. *The Oxford guide to word games*. Oxford: Oxford University Press.

Bache, Carl, Mike Davenport, John Dienhart and Fritz Larsen, 1991. *An introduction to English sentence analysis*. Copenhagen: Munksgaard.

Butters, Ronald, 1987. "Review of Pepicello and Green" 1984. *International Journal of the Sociology of Language* 65: 112-115.

Chiaro, Delia, 1992. *The language of jokes: Analysing verbal play*. London: Routledge.

Cuddon, J.A., 1992 [1977]. *The Penguin dictionary of literary terms and literary theory*. 3rd edition. London: Penguin.

Cunningham, Keith and Alfred K. Lorenzo, 1991. "'He just fell over dead?': Navajo humour, Navajo Hózhó". In: Gillian Bennett, ed., *Spoken in jest*, 15-28. Sheffield: Sheffield Academic Press.

Erhardt-Siebold & Erika von, 1946. "Old English riddle no. 39". *PMLA* 61: 910-915.

Espy, Willard, 1971. *The game of words*. Devon: Readers Union Group.
Freud, Sigmund, 1981 [1960]. *Jokes and their relation to the unconscious*. London: The Hogarth Press. (Translated by James Strachey from the German *Der Witz und seine Beziehung zum Unbewussten*, 1905.).
Green, Thomas A. and W.J. Pepicello, 1978. Wit in riddling: A linguistic perspective. Genre 11: 1-13.
Gruner, C., 1978. *Understanding laughter*. Chicago, IL: Nelson-Hall.
Hamnett, Ian. 1967. "Ambiguity, classification and change: The function of riddles". *Man* 2: 379-392.
Hating, Lee, 1974. "On knowing the answer". *Journal of American Folklore* 87: 197-207.
Harries, Lyndon, 1971. "The riddle in Africa". *Journal of American Folklore* 84: 377-393.
Hockett, Charles, 1967. "Where the tongue slips, there slip I". In: *To honor Roman Jakobson*, vol. 2, (= Janua Linguarum, Studia Memoriae, Series Major, No. 32), 910-936. The Hague: Mouton.
Koestler, Arthur, 1971 [1964]. *The act of creation*. New York: Macmillan.
Krapp, George Philip and Elliot van Kirk Dobbie, eds., 1966 [1936]. *The Exeter book*. Volume 3 of *The Anglo-Saxon poetic records*. New York: Columbia University Press.
*Longman Dictionary of Contemporary English*, 1978. London: Longman.
Lyons, John, 1977. *Semantics*, vol. 2. Cambridge: Cambridge University Press.
Meyvaert, Paul, 1976. "The solution to Old English riddle 39". *Speculum - A Journal of Medieval Studies* 61: 195-201.
Morreall, John, 1989. "Enjoying incongruity". *Humor* 2(1): 1-18.
Nash, Walter, 1985. *The language of humour*. London: Longman.
Norrick & Neal, 1986. "A frame-theoretical analysis of verbal humor: Bisociation as schema conflict". *Semiotica* 60: 225-245.
Norrick, Neal, 1989. "Intertextuality in humor". *Humor* 2(2): 117-139.
Norrick, Neal, 1993. *Conversational joking: Humor in everyday talk*. Bloomington, IN: Indiana University Press.
*The Oxford English Dictionary*, vol. Ill, 1989. Oxford: Clarendon.
Pepicello, W.J., 1980. "Linguistic strategies in riddling". *Western Folklore* 39: 1-16.
Pepicello, W.J., 1987. "Pragmatics of humorous language". *International Journal of the Sociology of Language* 65: 27-35.
Pepicello, W.J. and Thomas A. Green, 1984. *The language of riddles: New perspectives*. Columbus, OH: Ohio University Press.
Pepicello, W.J. and Robert W. Weisberg, 1983. "Linguistics and humor". In: P.E. McGhee and J.H. Goldstein, eds., *Handbook of humor research*, vol. 1, 59-83. New York: Springer.
Raskin, Victor, 1985. *Semantic mechanisms of humor*. Dordrecht: Reidel.

Redfern & Walter, 1984. *Puns*. Oxford: Blackwell.

Sapir, Edward, 1932. "Two Navaho puns". *Language* 8:217-219.

Scott, Charles, 1963. "New evidence of American Indian riddles". *Journal of American Folklore* 76: 236-241.

Taylor, Archer, 1944. "American Indian riddles". *Journal of American Folklore* 57: 1-15.

Taylor, Archer, 1951. *English riddles from oral tradition*. Berkeley, CA: University of California Press.

# Triggers and targets: a linguistic look at humor

*John M. Dienhart*

## 1. Introduction

In an earlier article (Dienhart 1993)* I proposed a theory of humor based on what I called the "similarity factor" to account for a wide range of linguistically triggered riddles. In the conclusion of that article, I observed that the model I presented there could be extended beyond the riddle to encompass many other types of humor.

In the present article, I want to take up that claim and apply the model to a representative selection of short humorous texts. These include – in addition to riddles – jokes, comic strips, limericks, and graffiti. I shall also provide a few examples from advertising and from newspaper and magazine headlines.

## 2. Two types of humor

There are, broadly speaking, two basic types of humor – that which is linguistically triggered, and that which is not. Linguistically triggered humor is based on some kind of play with language. Humor which is not linguistically triggered is not based on language play, but employs instead some other feature, or combination of features. These can be situational, cultural, logical, etc. This categorial distinction is not new. Freud, for example, in his book, *Der Witz und seine Beziehung zum Unbewussten* (1905), distinguished between "verbal" jokes and "conceptual" jokes.[1]

### 2.1 Examples of humor with no linguistic trigger

To get a feel for the difference between the two categories, let us start by looking briefly at three examples of humor which are not linguistically triggered. As illustrations I have selected a comic strip, a riddle, and a joke. First, the comic strip:

*Reprinted with permission from PIB Copenhagen*

In this clever strip, Ferd'nand is using a forked tree-branch (probably from a willow tree) to try to locate water. We all know that the branch is supposed to bend in the direction of water, which, typically, is to be found underground. But Ferd'nand is in for a surprise – as indicated in the second frame by the upward movement of the branch and by the single piece of 'text' (a question mark). In the final frame, we see that there is an unexpected but rather logical reason for the behavior of the branch. Clearly the humor in this strip in not linguistically triggered, since no language is used in the strip at all.

Consider next the following riddle, which makes fun of the inhabitants of a well-known Danish city:

Q: What does it say on the bottom of beer bottles in Aarhus?
A: Open other end.

Though we do indeed have a text here, the humor is not linguistically triggered. Instead the humor comes from the inference we are led to draw concerning the level of intelligence of the good folk in Aarhus.

My final example of humor which is not based on language play is the following joke:

Joe and Pete are having a drink at a bar. Joe says to Pete, "I know it's none of my business, but don't you think you ought to put up curtains on your bedroom window? I was going past your house last night and I couldn't help seeing you and your wife making mad, passionate love."
"The joke's on you", says Pete. "I wasn't even home last night!"

*Calvin and Hobbes © Bill Watterson. Distr. By Universal Press Syndicate. 2010 Reprinted with permission. Europa Press. All rights reserved.*

## 2.2 Examples of humor with a linguistic trigger

The three examples of humor provided above can now be contrasted with examples involving some kind of play on language – involving, that is, a linguistic trigger. First, a Danish comic strip – one with Sten and Stoffer, the Danish rendition of Calvin and Hobbes:

Hobbes's question in the final frame can be translated into English as "Are they biting today?" Clearly, the humor in this strip involves a play on the interpretation of the verb *bide*, 'to bite' – which functions as the linguistic trigger (note that the trigger works in English as well).

We see similar word-play in the following riddle:

Q: What's worse than raining cats and dogs?
A: Hailing taxis.

In this example the linguistic trigger is *hailing*, which here can mean either 'to come down like pellets of ice' or 'to call out to'.

Finally, to round out the contrast between the two types of humor, here is a joke with a linguistic trigger:

Little boy: Grandma, can you make a noise like a frog?
Grandma: I don't think so. Why do you ask?
Little boy: Well, Mom said we'll get $20,000 when you croak.

In this case, the double meaning of croak triggers the humor. As we can see, it is common (but not obligatory) for the trigger to appear at the end of the text – since this maintains the 'suspense'. We find a similar situation in the following limerick:

> A maiden at college called Breeze
> Weighed down by B.A.'s and Ph.D.'s
> Collapsed from the strain
> Alas, it was plain
> She was killing herself by degrees.

Here again, the linguistic trigger – *by degrees* – appears at the very end of the text. Since the basic rhyme scheme of a limerick (aabba) is generally known to the reader/hearer, the text provides, in lines one and two, a tiny clue to the phonological nature of the upcoming linguistic trigger (it is likely to rhyme with *Breeze* and *D's*). And once the trigger is pulled, the reader/hearer discovers that semantic clues, too, were provided earlier (B.A.'s and Ph.D.'s being types of degrees). The other reading, of course, is 'little by little'.

## 3. The nature of a linguistic trigger

Having seen several examples of a linguistic trigger in a humorous text, it is now appropriate to look more closely at the nature of a linguistic trigger and how it works. Dienhart (1993) provides a broad review of the literature dealing with the concept behind the label 'linguistic trigger'. For convenience and for the sake of the reader who may not be familiar with that article, I shall here briefly summarize this information.

Put very simply, a linguistic trigger (LT) is a word or a group of words which can be interpreted in more than one way. Thus, an LT is the place in a text where a double reading is made possible. This metaphorical use of the word 'trigger' has been around for awhile. Thus Raskin (1985: 114) speaks of "the semantic script-switch trigger" and Nash (1985: 7) refers to "the trigger that detonates the humorous mass". The trigger, says Nash, can be viewed as "a centre of energy, some word or phrase in which the whole matter of the joke is fused, and from which the powers radiate" (1985: 7). This is simply a modern statement of the view expressed much earlier by Freud.

### 3.1 The concept of bisociation

The fact that a linguistic trigger brings together two different readings or combines two 'worlds' is sometimes referred to as 'bisociation'. This term appears to have been coined by Arthur Koestler in his book, *The Act of Creation*, which was published in 1964. Koestler (1971: 35) offers the following diagram to help explain the concept:

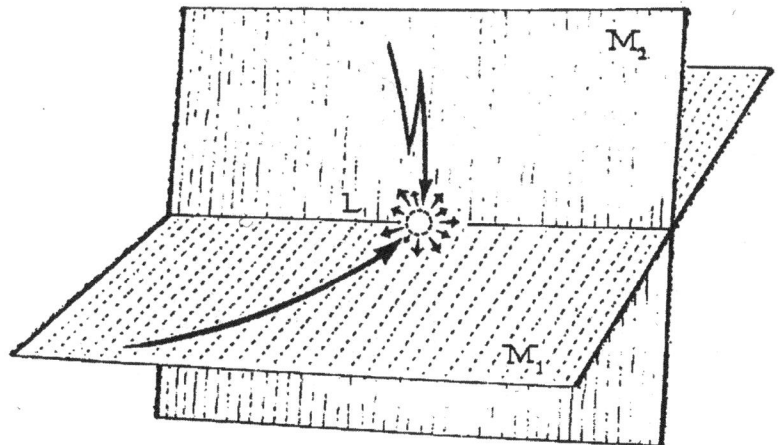

In Koestler's words, bisociation refers to "the perceiving of a situation or idea, L, in two self-consistent but habitually incompatible frames of reference, $M_1$ and $M_2$" (Koestler 1971: 35); L stands presumably for 'link' and M for 'matrix'). For Koestler, bisociation is not only a basic characteristic of humor in general, but of the creative act itself:

> I have coined the term 'bisociation' in order to make a distinction between the routine skills of thinking on a single 'plane', as it were, and the creative act, which . . . always operates on more than one plane. The former may be called single-minded, the latter a double-minded, transitory state of unstable equilibrium where the balance of both emotion and thought is disturbed. (Koestler 1971: 35)

Though the term is new,[2] the concept of bisociation is not. It is quite simply an illustration of the principle of economy. As Freud (1981: 54) puts it, we are dealing with "multiple use of the same material", which is "nothing other than a word capable of multiple interpretation, which allows the hearer to find the transition from one thought to another".

The phenomenon of bisociation is not limited to humor alone. Most of us have witnessed it in such 'double-minded' drawings as the following, which are clearly capable of producing Koestler's "transitory state of unstable equilibrium", as we see first one image, then another (I will not here reveal the nature of the double images in each of the diagrams, but leave this discovery to the reader; however, should the reader need help, 'solutions' are provided in note 3 at the end of this paper):

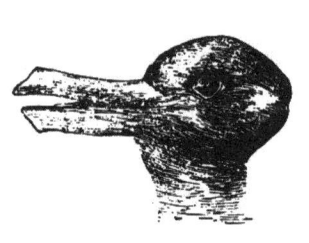  

Figure A                          Figure B                          Figure C

## 4. Five types of linguistic trigger

Returning now to our analysis of humor, I argued in Dienhart (1993) that there are five basic types of linguistic trigger and I illustrated how these could be used to classify riddles. I would now like to show that these five types work equally well when applied to a wide range of humorous texts. Once again I shall summarize from my earlier presentation (Dienhart 1993: 13-14).

The crucial variable at the heart of the classification is what I have called the 'similarity factor' – which refers to the degree of similarity between paired forms of linguistic signs.

Ever since Saussure, it has been customary to describe the linguistic sign as a combination of two parts: form (or expression) and meaning (or content). Linguistic triggers match phonetic consonance (similarity of form) with semantic dissonance (difference in meaning). Consequently, it is the form that our similarity factor is concerned with. We must bear in mind, however, that a form may be expressed in writing as well as in speech, so we need to take into account both orthographic form and phonetic form. The resulting system of types of linguistic trigger can then be viewed as a cline, with absolute identity and absolute dissimilarity representing the two poles.[4] In between are a number of relationships which are well-known from semantic theory: polysemy, homonymy and homophony.

To these I added (in 1993) two new terms: paraphony and hahaphony. The resulting cline is as follows:

(ABSOLUTE IDENTITY)
POLYSEMY
HOMONYMY
HOMOPHONY
PARAPHONY
HAHAPHONY
(ABSOLUTE DISSIMILARITY)

Each of these terms will be defined and illustrated below. What is important to note here is the relative ranking of the various degrees of similarity. This can be demonstrated visually in the form of a target, as in Figure D on the next page. The center of the target represents identity. Moving outward from the center, away from identity, we encounter weaker and weaker degrees of similarity: polysemy, homonymy, homophony (and homography, if we take the visual with the auditory), paraphony and hahaphony. Each of these types of linguistic trigger increases the opportunity for bisociation. Beyond the realm of hahaphony (that is, outside the target itself), lies absolute dissimilarity.

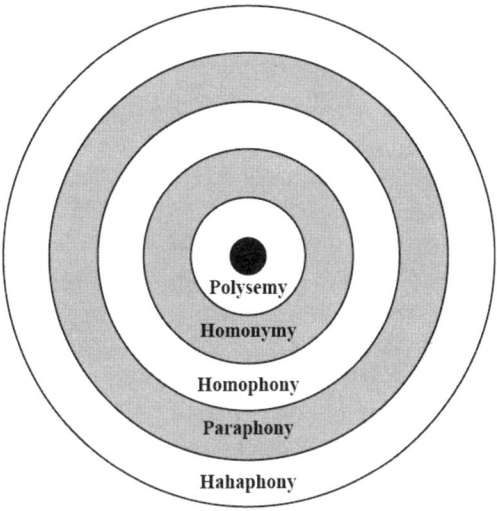

The rest of this paper will be devoted to examining and illustrating each of the five rings in this target – that is, each of the five types of linguistic trigger. As I mentioned at the outset, illustrative examples will be taken from a variety of different genres of humor.

## 5. Polysemy

The word *polysemy* means literally 'many' (*poly*) 'meanings' (*seme*). So polysemy refers to one word (or phrase) with multiple meanings. Thus polysemy appears to involve the smallest measure of difference which can be utilized to create bisociation. We find ourselves in the first ring in the target:

Let us consider some examples. First, a riddle:

> Q: What did one tonsil say to the other?
> A: You'd better get dressed – the doctor's taking us out tonight.

The linguistic trigger in this text is found in the answer: *taking out*. The two meanings involved are: 1) 'to invite someone to a restaurant, show, etc.', and 2) 'to remove'.

Sometimes the double meaning results not from the ambiguity of a single word or compound, but from a whole cluster of words. It is customary to distinguish terminologically between the two types by referring to the first as 'polysemy' and the second as 'syntactic ambiguity'. The principle involved is otherwise the same. Consider the following joke:

> A well-dressed man came out of a smart hotel and snapped to
> the doorman: "You there! Call me a taxi!"
> "Certainly, sir," said the doorman politely. "You're a taxi."

The linguistic trigger here is the whole imperative construction, *Call me a taxi!* As intended by the utterer of the command, the syntactic analysis is P Oi Od (equivalent in meaning to "Call a taxi for me"), whereas the doorman adopted the analysis P Od Co (equivalent in meaning to "Tell me that I am a taxi").[5]

The same type of syntactic ambiguity is at play in the next example:

> First Woman: "I just got a brand new set of golf clubs for my husband."
> Second Woman: "Excellent trade!"

In this case the linguistic trigger is *for my husband*, which can mean either a) 'as a present for my husband', or b) 'in exchange for my husband'. It is apparent that much linguistic humor is the result of someone having discovered or uncovered a latent meaning in a word or phrase – a meaning that would normally be overlooked (or, if spotted, then discarded as irrelevant), and then creating a context where the bisociation can come into play. The humor in the above example would disappear if the speaker had said instead: "I just got my husband a brand new set of golf clubs".

The cartoonist, Gary Larson, makes frequent use of the technique of polysemy/syntactic ambiguity by playing a figurative reading off against a literal one – as in the following cartoon.

Here Larson is forcing us to take the phrase *at the wheel* literally, thereby turning it into a linguistic trigger of the polysemic type. In the (normal) figurative reading, *wheel* is understood as a part standing in for the whole (that is, an example of synecdoche), so that *wheel* means 'steering wheel of a car', and *falling asleep at the wheel* means 'falling asleep while driving'. Observe that having removed the car from the scene, Larson must provide some other cause for

## THE FAR SIDE® By GARY LARSON

**Thag Anderson becomes the first fatality as a result of falling asleep at the wheel.**

the ensuing fatality – and hence a sabre-toothed tiger approaches from the left. Strictly speaking, this creates a double reading of *fatality* as well: a) killed in a car accident, b) eaten by a wild animal.

Playing the literal against the figurative is a very common technique in comic strip humor. Here is another example, this time from Mort Walker's well-known 'Beetle Bailey' strip:

© *King Features/Bulls*

*Trigger and targets: a linguistic look at humor* · 57

The double interpretation of the linguistic trigger, *step on it*, needs little discussion after this clever visualization of the bisociation. Note, by the way, the role of the second frame in the comic strip: Sarge's *Oh-oh* marks the moment of truth – the moment when the bisociation becomes apparent to him.

## 6. Homonymy

*Homonymy*, which derives from *homo* ('same') plus *onoma* ('name'), refers to two (or more) words which sound the same and are spelled the same, but differ in meaning. Thus, while polysemy involves one sign with multiple meanings, homonymy involves multiple signs – whose signifiers are identical, both orthographically and phonologically.[6] With homonymy we move one ring further from the center of the target, and the range of possible linguistic triggers becomes correspondingly greater:

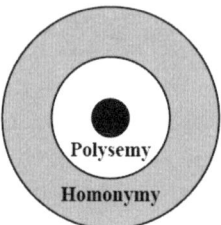

The following riddle provides an illustration of homonymy (but see note 6):

Q: Why couldn't the leopard escape from the zoo?
A: Because he was always spotted.

The linguistic trigger is the word *spotted*, which shows up at the very end of the answer – thus postponing the locus of the bisociation until the very last word of the riddle. The bisociation involves a) the adjective *spot*, formed from the noun *spot* by adding the denominalizing suffix *-ed* (cp. *soft-hearted, tight-fisted, left-handed*), and b) the past participle of the verb *to spot*. The trigger makes use of the fortunate coincidence that the English denominalizing suffix is identical to the past participle suffix, and that the verb *to be* (here realized as *was*) can function both as a copula verb and as an auxiliary in a passive construction. Thus the two instances of *spotted* participate in different syntactic constructions. The adjective reading is S P A Cs, while the verb reading is S P- A -P.

Consider next, the following graffito:

Some things happen only to women. Period.

Graffiti provides some of the shortest and most compact texts in any language. Like others before and since, Freud stressed the importance of brevity in wit, arguing that a swiftly delivered trigger packs the greatest wallop and releases the most energy – in the form of laughter. Perhaps this helps explain why graffiti is so hard to wipe out (bisociation intended). In this example, the stage is set with a six-word statement. Then comes the one-word trigger. Presumably most people would view this trigger as an illustration of homonymy (rather than polysemy), since the two meanings are so different: a) 'full stop', b) 'menstruation'.

The next example comes from a Danish comic strip entitled "Livets gang i Lidenlund":

In this example the trigger is the word *pæren*. The idiomatic phrase, *Brug da pæren*, means 'Use your head', but it could also mean 'Use the light bulb'. Of course, such an interpretation, in the given context, could only be made by a dimwit (or dim watt). But notice that the speaker in the strip is giving us all kinds of linguistic clues about the low voltage of Egon's brain power. He is described as a *to'sk*, *skrupskør*, and a *kløvning*.

Note, too, that the comic strip is an ideal medium for depicting an unexpected second meaning. Here a new meaning is revealed when Egon replaces the hammer with a light bulb. In this case the artist has chosen to let only the reader perceive the double meaning. The bisociation is not revealed to any of the characters in the strip. Egon fails to grasp the idiom – so he is aware of only the literal reading. The speaker, on the other hand, has turned his back in the final frame, so he is only aware of the figurative meaning – the one he intended.

## 7. Homophony

*Homophony* comes from *homo* ('same') plus *phone* ('sound'), and hence refers to words which sound the same but differ in meaning. Homophony is thus not the same as homonymy, though the two terms are often used interchangeably. Homonyms are identical in both spoken and written form, whereas homophones require identity only of the spoken forms. Thus, while it is true to say that all homonyms are also homophones, the reverse is not true. The words *tale* and *tail*, for example, are homophones, but they are not homonyms. So homophones, though they sound the same, do not have to look the same. By relaxing one of the conditions on signifier identity, we increase the range of vocabulary items which are available for use as linguistic triggers. We have moved outward to a new ring in the target:

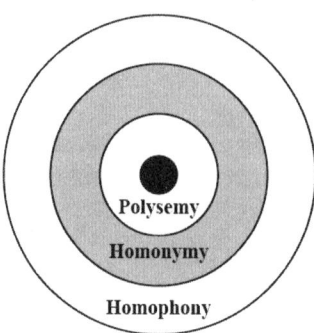

It follows, of course, that humor involving homophones should generally be heard but not seen. That is, homophonic linguistic triggers tend to be more successful in an oral presentation than in a written one. This is illustrated by the next example:

Q: What is black and white and red/read all over?
A: A newspaper.

In this riddle, the trigger is in the question. The homophones involved are the color, *red*, and the past participle of the verb *to read*. By introducing the terms *black* and *white* in the question, the riddler pushes the riddlee in the direction of the wrong homophone, thereby obscuring the answer. When the riddlee gives up, which is the typical response, the riddler supplies the answer, which then reveals the existence of the other homophone. Clearly, this riddle does not lend itself to an orthographic presentation. If it is presented as I did above, the linguistic trigger is immediately identified in the question itself. If we choose instead to write either red or read, we run into two problems: either we are guilty of lying (a newspaper is not red), or we immediately point the reader in the direction of the answer. Homophony, unlike children, should be heard and not seen.

It follows that graffiti, which relies heavily on the orthographic medium, does not make heavy use of homophony. The following is alleged to have appeared on some suitable Danish surface:

Jeg er også gået over til prins! – Margrethe

The linguistic trigger here is the word *prins*, which is a play on the Danish word for "prince" and the cigarette brand "Prince". Thus the text can be understood as either a) Queen Margrethe has chosen (for her husband) Prince (Henrik), or b) Queen Margrethe has switched cigarette brands and now prefers Prince. The latter reading echoes the advertising slogan for Prince, which for awhile was quite common in Danish newspaper ads and on Danish television. This Danish graffito works despite the visual display of only one of the two homophones, because the other one (*Prince*) is mentally supplied by any reader familiar with the advertising slogan. So the bisociation is provided by a kind of intertextuality, a concept to which I shall return.

Here is another example of a linguistic trigger which is based on homophony:

Chemistry teacher: Who can tell me the formula for water?
Debbie: HIJKLMNO!
Teacher: What in the world are you talking about, Debbie?
Debbie: Well, yesterday you told us it was H to O.

The homophones here are the numeral, *two*, as intended by the chemistry teacher (**H2O**), and the preposition, *to*, as understood by Debbie.

## 8. Paraphony

The label for the next ring in the target needs some explanation, since it is not a standard term in humor studies:

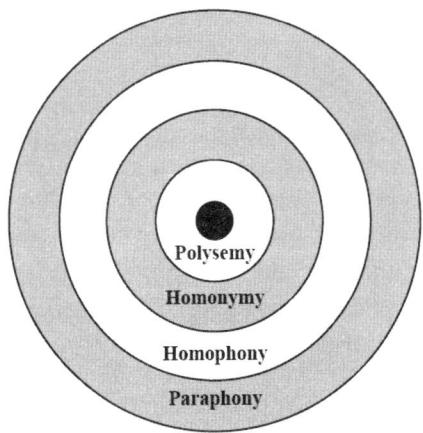

I shall repeat here the arguments which I gave in my 1993 article for adopting *paraphony* as the label for this new ring:

> I have borrowed the label 'paraphonic' (and 'paraphony') from music, and use it to refer to words that are *similar* ('para-') in sound ('phone-') rather than the same ('homo-'). Curiously, linguistics has borrowed 'homophonic' from music, but not (to my knowledge) 'paraphonic'.
> Apparently a related label, 'paronymic', has been used in linguistic circles. For example, Redfern (1984: 18, 91) speaks of *paronyms* when referring to 'quasi-homophones'. Strictly speaking, though, paronyms are apparently supposed to be etymologically related (see, for example, Cuddon 1992: 684). At any rate, the label, 'paraphonic', focusing as it does on similarity of sound, suits my purposes better than 'paronymic'.[7]

The magic of paraphony, as far as humor is concerned, is that it relaxes the condition on signifier identity to such an extent that a new range of possibilities for linguistic triggering is opened up – a range that is practically unlimited. As an illustration of the new possibilities, consider the following riddle:

Q: How does a ghost start a letter?
A: Tomb it may concern.

The linguistic trigger is clearly the word *tomb*, which plays against the formulaic opening of a certain type of letter, *To whom it may concern*. The similarity in pronunciation between the paraphonic pair *tomb* and *to whom* can best be appreciated in terms of a phonemic transcription: /tum/ vs. /tə hum/.[8] These forms are close enough to allow an easy bisociation. Observe how various elements in the text relate to and support each of the two readings. The word *tomb* in the answer belongs to a semantic field which includes the word *ghost* in the question. Similarly, *to whom* belongs to a semantic field which includes the word *letter* in the question; and idiomatically it is connected with the words *it may concern* in the answer.

Finally, we might note that in rapid speech, the paraphonic pair may even become homophonic. There are, in modern English, several fast-speech phenomena which produce what are sometimes referred to as 'weak forms'. One of these is vowel-deletion and another is *h*-dropping. Vowel-deletion is seen in such common instances as *What's he doing?* (instead of *What is he doing?*), and *h*-dropping is found, for example, in the pronunciation of *I should have gone*, which sounds like (and is sometimes informally written as) *I should of gone*. Thus, when spoken rapidly, /tə hum/ can easily become /tum/ as a result of the operation of these two processes.

Here is another example of paraphony in a riddle:

Q: How do you weigh a whale?
A: Take it to a whale-weigh station.

The members of the paraphonic pair *whale-weigh*, /welwe/, and *railway*, /relwe/, differ only in the pronunciation of the initial consonant: /w/ vs. /r/. And even this distinction is absent in the speech of some people, perhaps most notably in the case of the cartoon character, Elmer Fudd (who is always chasing that well-known wabbit, Bugs Bunny). So for speakers like Elmer Fudd this linguistic trigger involves homophony rather than paraphony.

Here is an example of paraphony in a joke:

1st Eskimo: Where's your ma from?
2nd Eskimo: Alaska.
1st Eskimo: Forget it, I'll ask her myself.

Here the members of the paraphonic pair are more dissimilar than in the previous two examples. But enough similarity exists between the spoken forms of *Alaska*, /əlæskər/, and *I'll ask her*, /aɪlæskhər/, to make the bisociation possible. As these bisociations become increasingly far-fetched, the response of the addressee is increasingly likely to be a groan of dismay rather than Laughter.[9] Note, once again, that in rapid speech the members of the bisociated pair become increasingly similar. In this case, h-dropping reduces the pronoun, *her*, to a vowel-initial form, and the initial diphthong, /aɪ/ can easily become schwa, /ə/. The result is that /aɪlæskhər/, can become /əlæskər/. For some speakers (British, for example), the reduction can proceed even further, with loss of the post-vocalic /r/. The result would be /əlæskə/, and once again paraphony will have become homophony.

Here is another example of a paraphonic linguistic trigger:

Bill: I'm going to have my appendix taken out.
Friend: Will you have a scar?
Bill: No thanks, I don't smoke.

The linguistic trigger here is supplied by the friend: *scar*. The word is part of the hospital script (*appendix, taken out*). But in Bill's response it moves into a new script by virtue of the paraphonic relation holding between *scar* and *cigar*: /skɑr/ vs. /sɪgɑr/. Again, rapid speech might reduce *cigar* to a one-syllable word by deleting the first vowel. If this were to happen, homophony would again result, since the distinction between /k/ and /g/ is neutralized after /s/. Note, by the way, that there is a tenuous link between the *scar* and the *cigar* scripts: in some American circles cigars are distributed by the proud father after the birth of a child. Since childbirth commonly takes place in a hospital, cigars can be linked to a hospital script.

Needless to say, paraphony is not restricted to riddles and jokes. Here is a limerick with a paraphonic trigger:

> Undressing a maiden called Sue,
> Her seducer exclaimed: "If it's true
> That a nipple a day
> Keeps the doctor away,
> How healthy you must be with two."

The linguistic trigger in this text is found in the third line: *a nipple*. Clearly this sequence finds its bisociated counterpart, *an apple*,[10] only for those readers or listeners who are familiar with the English proverb, "An apple a day keeps the doctor away." So the second text is supplied by cultural knowledge. Such textual allusion or echoing is commonly referred to as "intertextuality".

Norrick (1989: 117) observes that "intertextuality occurs any time one text suggests or requires reference to some other identifiable text or stretch of discourse, spoken or written". It follows, says Norrick (1989: 118), that if "jokes and puns present little intelligence tests for hearers, then intertextual jokes amount to intelligence tests prefaced by quizzes in literary history".

As we saw earlier (*Jeg er også gået over til prins*), graffiti, which relies on short, terse written texts, often, by necessity, demands that the second text be culturally supplied. Here is another example – from a men's toilet:

> To pee or not to pee.

The linguistic play on the voiceless vs. voiced stop (/p/ vs. /b/) is apparent only to those who are familiar with the opening line of Hamlet's famous monologue. For the reader who would like to test his or her ability to supply the culturally determined second script in several additional graffiti texts, here are three further examples (the 'solutions' are supplied in note 11):

1. Absinthe makes the heart grow fonder.
2. Carry me back to old virginity.
3. Genitals prefer blondes.

Cartoonists, too, often make use of paraphonic triggers, relying on the reader to supply the second text by drawing on shared cultural knowledge. Here are three examples. The first involves a short *yes/no*-question posed by a male dog,

Fido (clearly the canine on the left) to his lady-friend. The linguistic trigger is found at the very end of the text:

Won't you come in and see my itchings?

Fido is employing the age-old gimmick of inviting one's lady-friend inside on the pretence of showing off some material acquisition. In this instance there is linguistic play on *itchings* vs. *etchings*. The first item belongs to the dog script, the second to the human script. An invitation to view etchings is not a standard ploy, but it ties in with the semantic field of works of art – which includes other items such as paintings.

*Reprinted with permission from PIB Copenhagen*

In this "Peanuts" comic strip (Danish: "Radiserne"), the artist has, in fact, supplied both members of the bisociated pair: *Johannes Døberen* ('John the Baptist') and *Johannes Dobberman* ('John the Doberman'). Clearly, this linguistic trigger works in Danish but not in English – which raises the interesting question: What was the wording of the original English text from which this translation was made? Whatever the original text was, this is a masterful translation.

This political cartoon appeared in *Newsweek* shortly after a referendum in Quebec failed to establish a majority for secession from the rest of Canada. The text supplied by the cartoonist plays against the proverb, "If at first you don't succeed, try, try again". Note that the word *secede* is boldfaced, thereby providing the reader with a small clue about how to go about a mental search for the second text.

Linguistic triggers are quite common in *Newsweek*, and not just in the political cartoon section. Here is a different type of example (*Newsweek*, March 16, 1996, p. 41):

> MALAYSIA
>
> **Edifice Complex**
> Building the biggest, the best – and the costliest
>
> BY RON MOREAU
>
> Texans like to boast that everything in their state is a little bit bigger. Some day Malaysians may be known as the Texans of Southeast Asia. Determined to keep up with the country's 8 percent growth rate, Prime Minister Mahathir Mohamad has launched a series of massive infrastructure projects. A new airport, a huge dam and even a new capital city are on the drawing boards. Mahathir recently topped off the crowning symbol of his ambitions: the 452-meter twin office towers that will give Kuala Lumpur the world's tallest building . . .

The article describes the building boom that the Malaysian capital city, Kuala Lumpur, has been undergoing. So the heading, *Edifice Complex*, is certainly appropriate. But intertextuality is clearly also involved, since this text reminds the reader of the well-known expression, *Oedipus Complex*. There seems to be nothing particularly Freudian in the article (other than the sexual connotations of tall buildings in general), so the linguistic play is primarily intended as an eye (and mind) catcher – inviting the reader to stop turning the pages of the magazine and read the article. The trigger is quite clever, since in addition to the *Edifice/Oedipus* word-play, it makes use of the multiple meanings of the word 'complex' – one of which is clearly associated with buildings (cp. 'a building complex', or 'an apartment complex'). Looking briefly at the paraphonic pair, note that the spelling differences are far greater than the phonological ones – as with paraphonic pairs in general. In fact, the phonological difference is primarily in the contrast between the bilabial /p/ and the labio-dental /f/, though there is also a slight difference in the quality of the final vowel (/ɪ/ vs. /ə/) – a difference which is likely to disappear in rapid speech (unstressed vowels tend to reduce to schwa): /ɛdəfɪs/ vs. /ɛdəpəs/.

The reader may wonder why I continually place such emphasis on the phonological nature of these paraphonic linguistic triggers. The reason is that so much of our humor is based on the spoken word. Admittedly, we have seen examples of graphic humor, such as comic strips, graffiti, and magazine articles. But the principles at work in the linguistic triggering which I am discussing are fundamentally based on the spoken form. It is the phonological form of the signifier which typically creates the bisociation. And the addresser is typically striving for identity of form. In the case of polysemic, homonymic, and homophonic triggers, the phonological identity is assured – by definition. In the case of paraphonic triggering, however, the addresser is attempting to relate two phonologically *similar* but *different* forms. consequently, paraphonic linguistic triggers are most likely to 'work' – that is, to create the desired bisociation in the mind of the addressee – the more similar the phonological form of the two members of the bisociated pair are. If we keep the image of the similarity cline/target in mind, the addresser is attempting to come as close to the center of the target as possible, since the center marks the locus of maximum use of the same material. We must always bear in mind that the addresser is constantly aiming at identity of form.

I would like to conclude this section by looking at a particular genre of jokes which is solidly based on the paraphonic trigger. I have in mind that peculiarly American phenomenon known as the 'knock-knock' joke. Here is a typical example:

1st speaker: Knock knock.
2nd speaker: Who's there?
1st: Tarzan.
2nd: Tarzan who?
1st: Tarzan stripes forever.

The basic idea in this formulaic word-play is for the addresser (1st speaker) to find a proper name (since it is expected that the knocker on the door is a person) which can be used to introduce, or trigger, some phonologically related but semantically unrelated second text. The addressee (2nd speaker) is the selected victim whose participant role is fully ritualized (first response: "Who's there"; second response: "X who?"). In this particular example, the play involves the name of the American national anthem: "Stars and stripes forever". Phonologically, the first two words of this title (in an American English dialect) are /stɑrzən/, which is only one phoneme removed from the name of /tɑrzən/.

Occasionally the knock-knock joke involves a series of related names, such as the following:

1st : Knock knock.
2nd: Who's there?
1st: Amos.
2nd: Amos who?
1st: A mosquito bit me.

(Pause)

1st : Knock knock.
2nd: Who's there?
1st: Andy.
2nd: Andy who?
1st: Andy bit me again.

This sequence is a play on the name of an old American radio program: "Amos and Andy".

Sometimes the paraphonic ties in the knock-knock pairs can be extremely tenuous. One final example of the genre indicates how weak the link can be:

1st : Knock knock.
2nd: Who's there?
1st: Eskimos, Christians, and Italians.
2nd: Eskimos, Christians, and Italians who?
1st: Eskimos, Christians, and Italians no lies.

## 9. Hahaphony

This word, which I coined in my earlier article on riddles (Dienhart 1993: 14-15, 22-23) is based on word play between the suffix *-phony* and the word *funny* (cp.

*hahafunny*). As we shall see below, I use this term to refer to a type of paraphony or homophony which is created by breaking a word (or phrase) into false parts. The fastest way to illustrate my point is to take a simple example:

Q: What do ghosts eat for dinner?
A: Spook-etti.

The linguistic trigger, of course, is found in the answer to the riddle, *spook-etti*. This nonce construction is a play on a legitimate lexical item, *spaghetti*; but it plays on that word by breaking it into false parts, one of which bears a semantic relationship to the word ghosts in the question part of the riddle.

The process of dividing a word into its constituent parts is a legitimate linguistic activity. The process is part of what linguists refer to as 'morphology'. A morphological analysis of an English word such as *gentlemanly*, for example, would lead to the discovery of three meaningful parts, or morphemes – namely *gentle*, *man*, and *ly*. But, of course, no linguist would dream of analyzing *spaghetti* into *spook* and *etti*. This is something punsters do, not linguists. This punning process is what I am referring to with the label *hahaphony*. My label is equivalent to the terms 'pseudo-morpheme' and 'pseudomorphemic analysis', which can be found in some of the literature on the linguistic analysis of humor (for example, in Pepicello and Green 1984: 42-43, and in Nash 1985: 143).

This process creates unlimited possibilities for establishing new forms of bisociation, and hence for new linguistic triggers. The maker of humorous texts is free, within the bounds of comprehensibility, to take existing English words and phrases and create forms which no one has ever seen (or heard) before. Here are two more riddles based on the hahaphony principle:

Q: If a buttercup is yellow, what color is a hiccup.
A: Burple.

Q: Where would you find a prehistoric cow?
A: In a moo-seum.

We have now reached the outer ring (though it is a very large one) of our target:

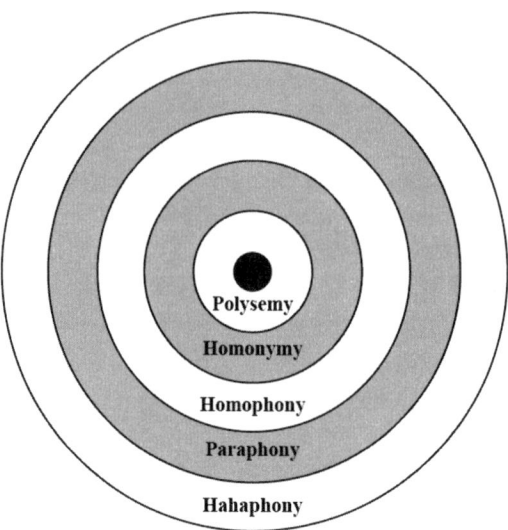

It should be added that hahaphony can also involve multilingual word play, as the following riddle makes clear:

Q: Why does a Frenchman have only one egg for breakfast?
A: Because one egg is an oeuf.

Of course, this means that the little quizzes Norrick refers to can also encompass knowledge of foreign languages. The following Danish graffito employs, in a sense, terms from three languages:

Ka' Anders And styre Libyen?
Ka' Daffy?

The first line asks if Donald Duck (Danish: *Anders And*) can govern Libya. The second line asks if Daffy can. The linguistic trigger is *Ka' Daffy*, which is bisociated with the name of Libya's ruler, Qaddafi (rendered as Kadaffi in Danish). An examination of the trigger reveals just how much ingenuity has gone into its creation. The pseudo-morphology involves the breaking up of Qaddafi's name into a Danish yes/no-question involving an auxiliary verb (*kan*) and a subject (*Daffy*). The verb is reduced from its full form by deleting the final consonant to produce *ka'*. This is, in fact, a common rapid-speech form in Danish, and is also found informally written with the apostrophe instead of the *n*. Observe that the reader is already introduced to the *ka'* form in the first question, thus simplifying the interpretation of the second one. The name *Daffy* refers to the English cartoon character, Daffy Duck. So Donald is linked to Daffy, who through hahaphony is linked to Qaddafi.

Less complicated, but still based on the hahaphony principle, is the dialogue in the following Calvin and Hobbes cartoon:

*Calvin and Hobbes © Bill Watterson. Distr. By Universal Press Syndicate. 2010 Reprinted with permission. Europa Press. All rights reserved.*

In this cartoon, Calvin uses a linguistic trigger to fool Hobbes. Like *Qaddafi*, the word *antelope* can be falsely cut into a noun (*ant*) and a verb (*elope*), though here the process is more elementary, since no real effort has to be made to create the bisociation: antelope can be cut into *ant + elope* without any orthographic juggling. This is still hahaphony, of course, since this is an improper morphemic analysis of the word antelope. Observe how Waterson, the cartoonist, moves gradually from the first script to the second. In the opening frame, Calvin's question includes the word *antelope*, spelled as one word. Like Hobbes, in the second frame, the reader starts out with the antelope script. The ambiguity, where we mentally supply the space between *ant* and *elope*, only becomes apparent later in the strip. In the third frame, Calvin introduces the second script by supplying a rough definition of the meaning of 'to elope'. The moment when this second script sinks into Hobbes's consciousness is captured by his facial expression in the same frame. His crossed arms and angry look in the last frame tie in with his comment, *It's not funny*, which is the equivalent of a verbal groan: Hobbes lets Calvin know that he understands the bisociation – he has passed the test – though he is not at all happy about being made fun of.

In the following newspaper clipping we have an example of hahaphony in a Danish headline:[13]

# Fyn er Z-plittet

Mindst tre af ni fynske kredse flytter med Pia Kjærsgaard til Dansk Folkeparti, og flere FRP-medlemmer følger efter.

Af
GITTE FØRBY og
HALLADOR HENRIKSEN

Engang var de venner. Men i dag er omkring 450 fynske medlemmer af Fremskridtspartiet delt i to lejre, som kan har hån og overbærende bemærkninger til overs for hinanden.

Understanding the bisociation in this example requires a few comments about Danish politics. Each duly registered political party in Denmark is symbolized by one of the letters of the alphabet. The very conservative "Fremskridtsparti" ('Progress Party') is denoted by the letter 'Z'. In 1995 there was a power struggle for the leadership of this party. The two contenders were Pia Kjærsgaard and Kim Behnke. When Pia lost to Kim, she left the Progress Party – along with a number of likeminded members – and founded a new party called "Dansk Folkeparti" ('Danish People's Party'). The result was that the old party was split (*splittet*). The newspaper headline has therefore modified the Danish past participle, *splittet*, replacing the initial *s* with a Z. This hahaphonic trigger thus bisociates the notion of 'splitting' and the Progress Party (Z). Note that the bisociation is continued in the drawing. The literal reading of the headline is "Funen is split". Funen is a Danish island which has provided the political base from which Pia Kjærsgaard was elected to Parliament. In the picture we see that the island is split by the Z, which itself is split into two halves clearly signifying lightning bolts. This is a lot of work for the letter Z to perform – a fine instance of maximal use of minimal material.

Here are two additional examples of hahaphony – both from the same Danish newspaper (*Fyens Stiftstidende*, summer 1996):

Vi Slo'venien

Det gik helt Portu-galt

Both headlines refer to soccer game results. In the first case, the newspaper is celebrating a Danish victory over the Slovenian team. In the second example, it is lamenting a loss to Portugal. The linguistic play in the first example involves the Danish verb *slå* 'to beat', whose past tense form is *slog*. The final *g* is silent and has been deleted in the headline (its former position being marked by the apostrophe). In this fashion, a pseudo-morphemic analysis of *Slovenien* (the Danish name for Slovenia) can yield a past tense verb form in the first syllable of the word.

In the second example, the playful element is *galt*, which means 'wrong' – as in *Det gik helt galt* ('Things went completely wrong'). By adding a final *t* to Portugal, and performing another pseudo-morphemic analysis, a new hahaphonic trigger is created.

With hahaphony, we have reached the outer ring in the target. Beyond this ring lies (in theory at least) phonological dissimilarity which is so great that no linguistic triggering is possible.

Having said that, however, I must immediately make the following qualification: the area beyond the hahaphony ring is probably empty. As I remarked earlier, the human mind is capable of quite remarkable associations, as our illustrations under paraphony and hahaphony have shown. It is no doubt possible to bring any potential 'outsiders' into the last two rings of the target (the areas of paraphony and hahaphony) by some form of mental gymnastics. If punsters can find "spook" in *spaghetti*, "moo" in *museum*, and "slog" in *Slovenia*, (not to mention "Eskimos, Christians, and Italians" in *Ask me no questions and I'll tell you no lies*) they are surely capable of anything.

Before concluding, however, there is one additional aspect we should investigate: any given humorous text, regardless of its length, can make use of more than one linguistic trigger at a time.

## 10. Multiple linguistic triggers

Here is a riddle which uses a multiple trigger (cited in Dienhart 1993: 23):

Q: What do you get if a herd of elephants tramples Batman and Robin?
A: Flatman and Ribbon.

Here we have two cases of paraphony: *Batman/Flatman* and *Robin/Ribbon*. Unlike so many cases of paraphonic triggers, intertextuality is not involved here. Both members of each pair are supplied in the riddle itself – one term in the question, the other in the answer.

Consider next a more complicated example. The following sign was found in the men's room of a restaurant. In this cleverly constructed message there are three different linguistic triggers, all co-operating to produce two sentences which are phonologically very nearly identical, though the elements in the sentences are semantically disparate:

> WE AIM TO PLEASE.
> YOU AIM TOO, PLEASE
>                 – The Management

The most disparate pair of all is *to/too*. The first member of the pair is an infinitive marker ('to please') while the second is an adverb. This trigger could be viewed as a homophonic one (/tu/ in both cases), though in actual speech there is a stress difference which results in the reduction to schwa of the vowel in the infinitive marker (yielding /tə/). Hence this is better viewed as an example of paraphony.

Another trigger in this text is the form please. In the first sentence it is used as a verb, in the second as an interjection. Since it is probably best to view this as one form with two different meanings (here reflected as different word classes), this trigger is a polysemic one.

The third trigger is also polysemic: the word *aim*. But this is polysemy which is nearer the center of the target. The word is a verb in both sentences, but in the first sentence it means 'try' or 'intend', whereas in the second it means 'point at something'.

The following Danish political slogan is also constructed out of three linguistic triggers:

SE TIL VENSTRE FØR DU KRYDSER.

The two meanings involved here are: 1) Check out (the political party) Venstre before you mark your vote (by putting an x in the appropriate box); 2) Look left before you cross (the street). The central element in the slogan is the name *Venstre*, which means 'left', and is also the name of a Danish political party. So this is one of the triggers – probably best viewed as an instance of homonymy (Venstre is not a left-leaning party, but is actually quite conservative). Observe that the slogan works best when capital letters are used for the whole text. This maximizes the effectiveness of this particular trigger by obviating the necessity of choosing between the written forms of "Venstre" and "venstre".

Another trigger is the word *krydser*. This should probably be seen as a case of polysemy, the two meanings being 1) 'make an x', and 2) 'cross over from one side to another'.

The third trigger is the polysemic reading of the word *se*. It can mean literally 'look' (as in 'look left'), or it can have the more figurative meaning of 'consider', or 'take into consideration'.

Multiple triggering is also at work in the following Danish advertisement:

This is taken from a brochure informing customers that they can get their bank to pay a particular annually recurring bill and thereby put an end (Danish *ende*) to the long lines (Danish *køerne*) that might be encountered by those who make their payment at the post office. But there is a second reading of the text, *Se en ende på køerne*, as intimated by the picture of the cow: køerne is a definite plural form meaning 'the cows' ("ko" = cow). And *ende* can be taken literally to mean the end or backside. This is manifested when the brochure is opened to reveal the next text and picture:

**Her ender køerne**

The new text, *Her ender køerne,* means either 1) 'Here is the end of the lines' or 2) 'Here is the end of the cows'.

One final example, this one from another Calvin and Hobbes comic strip, illustrates how extensive (and rather far-fetched) linguistic triggering can be:

Calvin and Hobbes © Bill Watterson. Distr. By Universal Press Syndicate. 2010 Reprinted with permission. Europa Press. All rights reserved.

There are several examples of paraphony in this strip, which is probably difficult to comprehend outside the United States, because of the cultural knowledge needed about practices in American schools. Note, however, that the artist, Waterson, gives the reader as much help as he can by keeping language play out of the first frame of the comic strip. The three words in this frame provide the clue to the other text which is being played against:

    I PLEDGE ALLEGIANCE
    to     the     flag
    TO  QUEEN  FRAGG

    of   the  United  States of  America
    AND HER MIGHTY STATE OF HYSTERIA

By virtue of the intertextual nature of the humor here, the writer can get away with 'matching' such otherwise very dissimilar pairs as *(United)/mighty* and *(America)/ hysteria*. Despite the weak phonological connections, the pairing of these items is ensured by the strict linearity of the two texts – guaranteeing that both texts have the same number of words, and that the words are paired item by item.

This comic strip of Waterson's illustrates my earlier point that the scope of paraphony and hahaphony is so large that new affiliations can be found for practically any word in the English language. The possibilities for bisociation appear to be limitless.

## 11. Conclusion

I believe I have shown that the model I developed for the linguistic analysis of riddles (Dienhart 1993) is widely applicable to all forms of humor where linguistic triggering is involved. In fact, it applies equally well also to texts, such as advertising and newspaper headlines, where the humor is minimal, but where the play with language is used as an attention-getter.

The basic point behind the theory is one described long ago by Freud and others: multiple use of the same material. What I have demonstrated is that 'sameness' can be viewed as a sliding scale, nicely visualized in terms of a target with concentric rings moving increasing outward from the central notion of 'identity'. Moving outward from the center, away from identity, we encounter weaker and weaker degrees of similarity:

| | |
|---|---|
| Homonymy | (*take out*) |
| Homophony | (*period*) |
| Homophony | (*red, read*) |
| Paraphony | (*Alaska, I'll ask her*) |
| Hahaphony | (*spaghetti, spook-etti*) |

My focus has been on degrees of *phonological* similarity (that is, similarity between pairs of 'signifiers'), since so much humor is orally delivered. And because it is orally delivered, there are various phonological devices, particularly various rapid-speech phenomena, which come into play – thus helping the author of the humorous text in his search for phonological similarities.

Some of the devices we have encountered are:

vowel deletion
vowel reduction (especially reduction to schwa)
*h*-dropping
neutralization of /k/ and /g/ after /s/
word-boundary movement involving *a* and *an*

We have also seen that intertextuality plays a major role in linguistic triggering – since one way to get multiple meanings out of a single text is to have a given text call up a phonologically related text. But in order for the addressee to have mental access to this second text, he must generally have a good knowledge of the culture as well as of the language. As Walter Nash has remarked (1985: 9):

> before the joke can be discharged in all its swiftness, there is much to be apprehended about cultural and social facts, about shared beliefs and attitudes, about the pragmatic

bases of communication. If that sounds laboured and obscure, let us try to put it another way. Humour is not for babes, Martians, or congenital idiots.

## Notes

*     Editor's note: The article referred to here was later published in *Journal of Pragmatics* and is the first article in the present publication.
1. An English translation of Freud's 1905 book was made by James Strachey and published in 1960. I have used the 1981 reprint. The relevant discussion of 'verbal' jokes vs. 'conceptual' jokes can be found in chapter two, "The Technique of Jokes" (see Strachey's 1981 translation, pp. 16-89).
2. "New" in a relative sense, since more than 30 years have elapsed since Koestler introduced the term. In general, Koestler's insights have been ignored by the scientific community. Hammett (1967: 379) argues that this is due to an "infelicitous combination of journalism and pseudo-science" in Koestler's writing style. "Pseudo-science" may be too harsh a label, but the fact remains that Koestler's works appear to have found a more enthusiastic audience outside academia than inside it. However, Koestler's contribution to the theory of humor has been graciously acknowledged in the work of at least one scholar, namely Neal Norrick (see in particular his 1986 paper).
3. Figure A: The feature to focus on is the parallel protuberances at the left; these can be seen either as the beak of a duck which is facing left, or as the ears of a rabbit which is facing right.
Figure B: Foregrounding the white space reveals a chalice; foregrounding the black area reveals two faces in profile looking at one another.
Figure C: The crucial element here is probably the leftmost curved line connecting the upper and lower black areas. In one view, this can be seen as the nose of an old woman who has her chin tucked down in a fur coat; in the other view it is the cheek bone and chin of a much younger woman in profile, facing left.
4. Since the human mind is very adept at establishing links between what at first glance might seem to be highly disparate entities, "absolute dissimilarity" is a rather nebulous concept. As we shall see, the two categories nearest the dissimilarity pole – namely, paraphony and hahaphony – provide a home for a surprising variety of creative bisociations – bisociations revealing linguistic similarities many of us would never have contemplated. This is the fond hunting ground of the punster, in particular.
5. The symbols employed in this paper are those used in the "Odense system", as illustrated in Bache, Davenport, Dienhart, and Larsen (1993): P = 'predicator', Oi = 'indirect object', Od = 'direct object', Co = 'object complement', Cs = 'subject complement', and A = 'adverbial'. Hyphens are used to mark discontinuous constituents. Thus a sentence such as *He has never visited Odense* would be analyzed as S P- A -P Od, where the adverbial, *never*, breaks up the predicator, *has visited*, making it discontinuous.
6. As many linguists have pointed out, it is difficult if not impossible to draw a clear distinction between polysemy and homonymy (see, for example, Lyons 1977: 550-569, Crystal 1997: 297). However, as I noted earlier (Dienhart 1993: 33, fn. 16), "while the distinction may be a problem for linguists, riddlers [and all other designers of linguistic triggers] get along quite nicely without worrying about it."
7. In his latest edition of *A Dictionary of Linguistics and Phonetics*, Crystal defines paronym(y) as follows: "A term sometimes used in semantic analysis to refer to the relationship between words derived from the same root. It is especially applied to a word formed from a word in another language with only a slight change: French *pont* and Latin *pons* are paronyms, and the relationship between them is one of paronymy" (Crystal 1997: 279). This is thus clearly not the term needed for the next ring, as will be apparent from the upcoming examples.
8. The phonemic symbols used in this paper conform to those found in Bauer, Dienhart, Hartvigson, and Jakobsen (1980). The consonant symbols are self-evident. The vowel sym-

bols are: /ɪ/ as in *tip*, /e/ as in *tail*, /ɛ/ as in *red*, /æ/ as in *bat*, /u/ as in *moon*, /ɑ/ as in *not*, /aɪ/ as in *light*, and /ə/. This last symbol is referred to as "schwa". It is the sound of the first vowel in e.g. *about*, and the last vowel in e.g. *sofa*.

9. As has been pointed out in the past, linguistically triggered humor is, to a large extent, confrontational. The addresser is supplying the addressee with a mental puzzle, and consequently the addressee is put in the unenviable position of being tested. The speed (and veracity) of the response can be seen as a measure of the knowledge and intelligence of the addressee. Genuine laughter means: I passed the test, and I find the joke (or riddle, or whatever) humorous. A genuine groan means: I passed the test, and I find the joke unfunny. The point is that the groan, like the laughter, signals understanding – it audibly announces that the addressee has passed the test.

10. Interestingly, the play between *a nipple* and *an apple*, which involves in part, the existence and interchange of two forms of the indefinite article (*a* vs. *an*), actually mirrors certain historical changes in the English language. Two concrete examples are: *an apron* and *a nickname*. The former derives from *a napron*, the latter from *an ekename* (*eke* meaning 'addition'; a nickname was hence 'an additional name'). What we see here is linguistic change brought about by confusion regarding the location of word boundaries.

11. The first example plays on the proverb "Absence makes the heart grow fonder". The second mirrors the title of a song by Stephen Foster, "Carry me back to old Virginy", and the third recalls the title of a book which was made into a movie starring Marilyn Monroe, "Gentlemen prefer blondes".

12. Not surprisingly, the second text may not leap readily to mind: "Ask me no questions and I'll tell you no lies".

13. The newspaper article is from *Fyens Stiftstidende*, October 7, 1995.

# References

Bauer, Laurie, John M. Dienhart, Hans H. Hartvigson, Leif Kvistgaard Jakobsen. 1980. *American English Pronunciation*. Copenhagen: Gyldendal.

Bache, Carl, Mike Davenport, John Dienhart, and Fritz Larsen. 1993. *An Introduction to English Sentence Analysis*, 2nd ed. (1st ed. 1991) Copenhagen: Munksgaard.

Crystal, David. 1997. *A Dictionary of Linguistics and Phonetics*, 4th ed. (1st ed. 1980). Oxford: Blackwell Publishers.

Cuddon, J. A. 1992. *The Penguin Dictionary of Literary Terms and Literary Theory*, 3rd ed. (1st ed. 1977). London: Penguin.

Dienhart, John. 1993. "A Linguistic Look at Riddles". *PEO* No. 71.

Freud, Sigmund. *Jokes and their Relation to the Unconscious*. London: The Hogarth Press, 1981. (Translated by James Strachey (and first published in 1960) from the German *Der Witz und seine Beziehung zum Unbewussten*, 1905).

Hammett, Ian. 1967. "Ambiguity, classification and change: the function of riddles". *Man* 2, 379-392.

Koestler, Arthur. 1971. *The Act of Creation*. New York: Macmillan (first published 1964).

Lyons, John. 1977. *Semantics*, vol. 2. Cambridge: Cambridge University Press.

Nash, Walter. 1985. *The Language of Humour*. London: Longman.

Norrick, Neal. 1986. "A frame-theoretical analysis of verbal humor: bisociation as schema conflict". *Semiotica*, 60, 225-245.

Norrick, Neal. 1989. "Intertextuality in humor", *Humor* 212, 117-139.

Pepicello, W. J. and Thomas A. Green. 1984. *The Language of Riddles: New Perspectives*. Columbus: Ohio University Press.

Raskin, Victor. 1985. *The Semantic Mechanisms of Humor*. Dordrecht, Holland: D. Reidel Publishing Co.

Redfern, Walter. 1984. *Puns*. Oxford: Basil Blackwell.

# Eudora Welty's "No Place for You, My Love" – the pronominalization of a text

*John M. Dienhart*

## 1. Introduction

This essay investigates a particular linguistic feature of one of Eudora Welty's more experimental short stories. The feature is the extended use of pronouns instead of proper names, and the story is "No Place for You, My Love".

The story was first published in 1952 in *The New Yorker*. Shortly thereafter it appeared, with minor revisions, as the opening story in *The Bride of the Innisfallen and Other Stories* (Welty 1955a: 3-27). Since the revised version of 1955 is the one that appears in subsequent collections of Welty's short stories, this is the version I have adopted here. Wherever differences between the 1955 and the 1952 versions may be significant to my argument, I point this out.

When this story appeared in 1955, it occasioned considerable confusion on the part of reviewers. One problem was that there seemed to be no plot to speak of; the story did not seem to go anywhere. It did not conform to the earlier Welty style. Another problem was the cognitive challenge posed by the text itself. It seemed to be vague, ambiguous, and generally hard to process. Pingatore (1996: 336) observes that early reviewers were uncomfortable with the 1955 collection as a whole. They allegedly had difficulty "penetrating these opaque, baffling stories". One such reviewer was Thomas Carter, who claimed – and he meant this negatively – that "the language pretty much *is* the story" (1955: 293). Later reviewers, says Pingatore, agreed with this characterization, but not with the verdict. She claims that it was Alun Jones who, in 1963, first made explicit the assertion that "the clue to coherence in this story resides in its experimental narrative technique". Here is how Pingatore summarizes Jones's argument:

> He proposes that the vagueness early readers complained of is deliberate as Welty moves away from the conventional methods of plot and characterization to experiment with an impressionistic style that provides the substance of the story; in other words, Jones uses Carter's dismissive criticism to build his own case for Welty's new approach (the language is the story). Jones maintains that the reader's unsettling experience corresponds

to that of the characters, which is the effect Welty aims for in "No Place for You, My Love". (Pingatore 1996: 336-337)

To the best of my knowledge, no one has yet explicitly investigated the linguistic nature of this "impressionistic style". It is my view that one of the most salient features of this style is Welty's general refusal to supply personal names for the protagonists, using instead the pronouns "he", "she", and "they" (and the corresponding forms, "him", "her", "them", etc.). It takes but little reflection to realize that such a device, if not handled carefully, can create confusion, even chaos, in a text, as the reader tries to keep track of the characters and their interaction. I hope to show in this essay how Welty manages to operate within these self-imposed restrictions, and how this device in fact enhances the story itself.

## 2. A penchant for proper names

Anyone familiar with Eudora Welty's work knows that the names of people and places are generally integral elements in her stories. As Elizabeth Evans (1981: 130) has remarked, "given names, surnames, nicknames, titles, and descriptive epithets are a significant part of the flavor of Miss Welty's fiction". Frequently a personal name constitutes the very first word(s) of a Welty story:

- "**R. J. Bowman**, who for fourteen years had traveled for a shoe company through Mississippi, drove his Ford along a rutted dirt path." ("Death of a Traveling Salesman" [1941]; Welty 1980: 119)
- "**Powerhouse** is playing!" ("Powerhouse" [1941]; Welty 1980: 131)
- "**William Wallace Jamieson's** wife **Hazel** was going to have a baby." ("The Wide Net" [1943]; Welty 1980: 169)
- "**Lorenzo Dow** rode the Old Natchez Trace at top speed upon a race horse, and the cry of the itinerant Man of God, 'I must have souls! And souls I must have!' rang in his own windy ears." ("A Still Moment" [1943]; Welty 1980: 189)
- "**Solomon** carried **Livvie** twenty-one miles away from her home when he married her." ("Livvie" [1943]; Welty 1980: 228)
- "**Loch** was in a tempest with his mother." ("June Recital" [1949]; Welty 1980: 275)
- "**Delilah** was dancing up to the front with a message; that was how she happened to be the one to see." ("The Burning" [1955]; Welty 1980: 482)

Sometimes there may, of course, be an epithet (e.g. Mr. or Mrs.) or a characterizing adjective immediately in front of the name:

- "**Mrs. Watts** and **Mrs. Carson** were both in the post office in Victory when

the letter came from the Ellisville Institute for the Feeble-Minded of Mississippi." ("Lily Daw and the Three Ladies" [1941]; Welty 1980: 3)
- "**Old Mr. Marblehall** never did anything, never got married until he was sixty." ("Old Mr. Marblehall" [1941]; Welty 1980: 91)

There may be some additional text preceding the personal name, but even though this preceding text may run from a single word to more than a dozen, the name itself is still generally found somewhere in the opening sentence:

- "When **Josie** first woke up in the night she thought the big girls of the town were having a hay-ride." ("The Winds" [1943]; Welty 1980: 209)
- "That was **Miss Snowdie Maclain**." ("Shower of Gold" [1949]; Welty 1980: 263)
- "One morning at breakfast **Eugene Maclain** was opening his paper and without the least idea of why he did it, when his wife said some innocent thing to him – 'Crumb on your chin' or the like – he leaned across the table and slapped her face." ("Music from Spain" [1949]; Welty 1980: 393)
- "I was getting along fine with **Mama**, **Papa-Daddy** and **Uncle Rondo** until my sister **Stella-Rondo** just separated from her husband and came back home again." ("Why I Live at the P.O." [1941]; Welty 1980: 46)
- "'How come you weren't here yesterday?' **old Mrs. Stark** asked her maid, looking up from her solitaire board – inlaid wood that gave off pistol-like reports under the blows of her shuffling cards." ("The Wanderers" [1949]; Welty 1980: 427)
- "One morning in summertime, when all his sons and daughters were off picking plums and **Little Lee Roy** was all alone, sitting on the porch and only listening to the screech owls away down in the woods, he had a surprise". ("Keela, the Outcast Indian Maiden" [1941]; Welty 1980: 38)
- "'Reach in my purse and git me a cigarette without no powder in it if you kin, **Mrs. Fletcher**, honey,' said **Leota** to her ten o'clock shampoo and set customer." ("Petrified Man" [1941]; Welty 1980: 17)

In all these cases, no matter how far down in the opening sentence it appears, the name of one or more of the major characters is established at the very beginning of the story. "No Place for You, My Love" departs radically from this pattern. One of the most striking characteristics of this Welty story is the fact that the two main characters start out nameless and remain nameless throughout the narrative. The story opens in the following way:

> They were strangers to each other, both fairly well strangers to the place, now seated side by side at luncheon – a party combined in a free-and-easy way when the friends he and she were with recognized each other across Galatoire's. The time was a Sunday in summer – those hours of afternoon that seem Time Out in New Orleans. (1955a: 3)

Throughout the story, the two main characters are referred to simply as "he" and "she", or jointly as "they". I shall follow Welty's example and refer to them in the same fashion in this paper, although for reasons which will become apparent, I shall use capital letters to identify the protagonists. This applies to the basic forms – HE, SHE, THEY – as well as to the related pronominal forms – HIM, HER, THEM; HIS, HERS, THEIRS; HIMSELF, HERSELF, THEMSELVES.

This absence of names for the two main characters raises two interesting questions. The first is of a general nature: Why does Welty choose not to name these two people? The second is of a linguistic nature: In the absence of personal names, how does Welty manage to distinguish HIM and HER (and THEM) from the other people in the story?

The two questions are interconnected, as we shall see. I shall investigate the general question first, after a brief summary of the story itself.

## 3. The basic plot

"No Place for You, My Love", as we have it in its published version, is considerably different from Welty's original manuscript, which was entitled "The Gorgon's Head" (Pingatore 1996: 334). In a short essay which Welty wrote about the development of this story, she provides us with some insight into the type of modifications that were involved in the major revision. The essay in question is entitled "How I Write", and appeared in *The Virginia Quarterly Review* in 1955. Here are two relevant paragraphs from that essay (1955b: 246-247):

> What happened was that I was invited to drive with a friend down south of New Orleans one summer day, to see that country for the first (and only) time, and when I got back home I realized that without being aware of it at the time I had treated a story, which I was working on then, to my ride, and it had come into my head in an altogether new form. I set to work and wrote the new version from scratch, which resulted in my throwing away the first and using the second. I learned all the specific detail of this story from the ride, though I should add that the story in neither version had any personal connection with myself and there was no conscious "gathering of material" on a pleasant holiday.
>
> As first written, the story told, from the inside, of a girl in a claustrophobic predicament: she was caught fast in the over-familiar, monotonous life of her small town, and immobilized further by a hopeless and inarticulate love, which she had to pretend was something else. This happens all the time. As a result of my ride I extracted her. But she had been well sealed inside her world, by nature and circumstance both, and even more closely by my knowing her too well (the story had gone on too long) and too confidently. Before I could prize her loose, I had to take a primary step of getting outside her mind. I made her a girl from the Middle West – she'd been what I knew best, a Southerner, before. I kept outside her by taking glimpses of her through the curious eyes of a stranger:

instead of the half-dozen characters (I knew them too well too) from the first version, I put in one single new one – a man whom I brought into the story to be a stranger.

As we shall see, throwing away the girl's southernness and introducing the stranger as her companion had important ramifications for the narrative, both linguistically and thematically.

The basic plot of the revised story can be outlined as follows. HE and SHE, both Northerners, meet in a New Orleans restaurant. After lunch HE invites HER to go for a drive, south of New Orleans, in his rented convertible. SHE accepts. Undaunted by excruciating heat and hordes of mosquitoes THEY race through increasingly desolate territory until THEY reach a small ferry. THEY drive on board and cross the Mississippi River. On the other side THEY continue THEIR journey along a road which gradually changes from pavement to shells and ultimately comes to a dead-end at Baba's Place, a local beer hall. Here THEY get a beer and a bite to eat and eventually dance to the music of a jukebox. After that THEY drive back in the evening heat to New Orleans. On the return journey there is a kiss and an embrace which is encumbered by the heat and the mosquitoes. Back in New Orleans HE drops HER off at HER hotel and then heads back to HIS.

There can be no denying that the plot of this story is deceptively simple. Anyone reading it for the first time will probably be disappointed by the fact that very little seems to happen. However, as early as 1955, one critic, Walter Elder, sensed that there was something deeper to this story – that Welty, despite, or perhaps because of, her new style was once again saying something vital and universal about the human condition:

> So nothing happens . . . and they have that afternoon of being separated together, and they have it whole. They kept their Yankee heads among swamps, heat, reptiles, strange people, music, and unhappy loneliness. They gain Miss Welty's prize, the sense of what might have been and cannot be, to hold during what is and shall be. She had a bruise on her temple; his wife was entertaining unmarried college friends. They have driven to the end of the world and returned. In Miss Welty's world, no one does anything more, – or seldom less. (Elder 1955: 662)

Several years later, Joyce Carol Oates (1969: 57) made a similar observation:

> It is an outstanding characteristic of Miss Welty's genius that she can write a story that seems to me, in a way, about 'nothing' – Flaubert's ideal, a masterpiece of style – and make it mean very nearly everything.

If "nothing happens", if "the language is the story", then there is every reason to look closely at the language, and at the reasons behind Welty's linguistic decisions. The use of pronouns instead of proper names for the protagonists is one of the key decisions that she makes.

## 4. The general question: Why?

With the background now in place, we are in a position to investigate the first, and more general, question: Why does Welty choose not to name the two main characters?

Part of the answer to this question is related to the fact that the story deals with a meeting between two strangers. That THEY are strangers, in a strange place, is established in the first line of the story itself (p. 3):

- "THEY were *strangers* to each other, both fairly well *strangers* to the place" (unless otherwise noted, all italics in this and the following citations are mine).

Curiously, however, THEY not only start out as strangers, but end the day still strangers – despite having spent the whole afternoon and evening in one another's company. At the end of the story, we are told (p. 25):

- "For THEIR different reasons, HE thought, neither of THEM would tell this (unless something dragged it out of THEM), that, *strangers*, THEY had ridden down into a *strange* land together and were getting safely back – by a slight margin, perhaps, but margin enough." (p. 25)

Note the strong parallels between these two quotations, the first at the beginning of the story, the second at the end of the story. In the first passage we are told that THEY are strangers to one another and to the place. In the second passage, we are reminded that this is the case. What happens in between the two passages? That, of course, is the story, but the overriding fact is that THEY remain strangers to one another.

How can this be? For one thing, HE and SHE say very little to one another, and what THEY do say reveals almost nothing about THEMSELVES:

- "THEY rode mostly in *silence*." (p. 7)
- "THEY danced on still as the record changed, after standing *wordless* and motionless, linked together in the middle of the room, for the moment between." (p. 22)
- "Going back, the ride was *wordless*, *quiet* except for the motor and the insects driving themselves against the car." (p. 23)

*4.1 Point of view*

It is not only that THEY do not converse much on THEIR journey – even when THEY do speak, there is very little real communication – about THEMSELVES or about anything else. The fact that THEY restrict THEIR exchange of information with one another means that the flow of information to the reader is also restricted. This is because Welty has chosen to tell the story from three intermingled points of view: 1) HIS, 2) HERS, and 3) an omnipresent but less than omniscient narrator. Let me illustrate these three points of view with excerpts from the narrative:

1. HIS: "The moment HE saw HER little blunt, fair face, HE *thought* that here was a woman who was having an affair.... With a married man, most likely, HE *supposed*" (p. 3)
2. HERS: "It must stick out all over me, SHE *thought*, so people think they can love me or hate me just by looking at me." (p. 3)
3. NARRATOR'S: "THEY settled into the car – a faded-red Ford convertible with a rather threadbare canvas top" (p. 6)

The alternation of the voices is one of the features that contributes to the density of Welty's text. It is an integral part of her narrative style. As she herself has remarked (1979: 128), "point of view is hardly a single, unalterable vision, but a profound and developing one of great complexity. The vision itself may move in and out of its material, shuttle-fashion, instead of being simply turned on it, like a telescope on the moon."

Of the three points of view in this story, the narrator's is the predominant one. However, this is not the voice of an all-knowing author, but rather a somewhat curious combination of what HE and SHE, jointly, might perceive. This will become more apparent as we progress with our analysis.

*4.1.1 HIS voice and HER voice*

Of the two personal points of view, HIS predominates over HERS. This would seem in large part to be due to the nature of the original manuscript and the major reversal taken by the revision. Recall Welty's remark that "as first written, the story told, from the inside, of a girl in a claustrophobic predicament", whereas in the revision Welty "had to take a primary step of getting outside her mind" and that Welty "kept outside her by taking glimpses of her through the eyes of a stranger" (1955b: 246-247).

Consequently, what little we learn about HER comes primarily from HIM, and as we will see below, HIS observations are not always to be trusted. Through HIM we learn that SHE has "a little blunt, fair face" (p. 3) – a "naive face" (p. 4), and a "straw-colored head" (p. 12). HE guesses that SHE is thirty-two years old (p. 4). SHE is wearing an "exasperating hat" which was "more than frivolous, it was conspicuous, with some sort of glitter or flitter tied in a band around the straw and hanging down" (p. 5). And SHE is wearing earrings in the form of "a little metal ball set with small pale stones" that "danced beside each square, faintly downy cheek" (p. 12). That is all we learn about HER physical appearance, though we do learn (p. 10) that on the ferry a bag of some sort hung from HER wrist.

If HE tells us little about HER, HE also tells us little about anything or anybody else. Welty allows us to peer into HIS mind, but by qualifying his observations in various ways she creates a voice which is tentative rather than highly informative. This is a reflection of the fact that HE does not ask for information, but instead hypothesizes about it. Consider first the excerpt which was cited earlier:

- "The moment HE saw HER little blunt, fair face, HE *thought* that here was a woman who was having an affair. . . . With a married man, *most likely*, HE *supposed*" (p. 3)

Note how Welty's choice of the verbs "thought" and "supposed", as well as the adverbial modification, "most likely", keeps the reader somewhat off-balance. We are allowed to know no more about HER than HE is able to deduce or infer. Here are some additional instances:

- "Something, though, HE *decided*, had been settled about HER predicament – for the time being anyway; the parties to it were all still alive, *no doubt*." (p. 4)
- "HE *guessed* HER age, as HE could not *guess* theirs: thirty-two." (p. 4)
- "HE informed HER, 'In there's your oil, I *think*.'"
- "Had SHE felt a wish for someone else to be riding with THEM? HE *thought* it was *more likely* that SHE would wish for HER husband *if SHE had one* (HIS wife's voice) than for the lover in whom HE *believed*." (p. 12)
- "SHE *appeared* to be sound asleep" (p. 25)
- "SHE disappeared through the revolving door, with a gesture of smoothing her hair, and HE *thought* a figure in the lobby strolled to meet HER." (p. 26)

All the words and phrases which I have italicized in the above citations have the effect of qualifying the information to such an extent that the reader is unable to determine whether it is factual or not. As if this information were not vague enough, additional doubts are sometimes created by a narrative voice which seems to comment, negatively, on the accuracy of HIS intuitions:

- "It was the wrong hat for HER, thought this Eastern businessman *who had no interest whatever in women's clothes and no eye for them*" (p. 3)
- "SHE had that naive face that HE associated, *for no good reason*, with the Middle West – because it said 'Show me,' *perhaps*." (p. 4)

Here, the italicized phrases seem to be cautionary admonitions warning the reader not to accept at face value HIS views about HER, tentative as those views may be in the first place.

HER "voice" is not as frequent as HIS, since SHE is more passive than HE, being more the observed than the observer. Consequently, we get even less information about HIM from HER than we get about HER from HIM. We learn that HE is wearing a tie (p. 7), that HIS hands are "manicured" (p. 14), that HE occasionally lights up a cigarette (pp. 14, 26), and that HE has "black hair" which "in the wind looked unreasonably long and rippling" (p. 28). As is the case with HIS voice, HERS, when it is heard at all, may have some qualifying word or phrase:

- "SHE could not feel a thing in the skin of HER face; *perhaps* SHE was crying and not knowing it." (p. 10)

In addition to the various types of qualification which accompany the information HE and SHE relay, the reader's understanding is hampered by THEIR very reticence and apparent reluctance to engage in any meaningful dialogue with one another. During the journey, THEY do ask a few questions of one another, but consider what type of response these questions occasion:

First instance (p. 5):
HE: "Have you ever driven down south of here?"
SHE: "South of New Orleans? I didn't know there was any south to *here*? Does it just go on and on?"
HE: "That's what I'm going to show you."
SHE: "Oh – you've been there?"
HE: "No!"

Second instance (p. 8):
HE: "Shall we cross here?" HE asked politely.
(SHE: No response)

Third instance (p. 14):
SHE: "What is your wife like?"
(HE: No verbal answer is given)

Fourth instance (p. 15):
HE:     "If we go any further, it'll have to be by water – is that it?"
SHE:    "You know better than I do"

Fifth instance (p. 21):
SHE:    "I wonder what he called me"
HE:     "Who?"
SHE:    "The one who apologized to you."
(HE:    No response)

Sixth instance (p. 23):
HE:     "Ready to go?"
(SHE:   No response)

From these examples (and this is the complete list of question and "answer" type dialogue between THEM), it is evident that even direct questions, when posed at all, do not elicit much information.

This inability on THEIR part to share any interesting and relevant information with one another is not limited to THEIR own interaction. There is, in fact, very little verbal communication between THEM and any other characters in the story. The two occasions where this does take place are both quite ineffective. At one point in Baba's Place, HE is called over by an old man in a palm tree shirt to receive an apology from his companion. But the exact conversation that takes place on this brief occasion is never shared with the reader, and when SHE cautiously inquires about it ("'I wonder what he called me,' SHE whispered in HIS ear", p. 21), no answer is supplied. The other instance involves the interaction between Baba and HER, when Baba comes to take THEIR order (p. 18):

> When he got ready to wait on THEM, Baba strolled out to the counter, young, black-headed, and in very good humor.
> "Coldest beer you've got. And food – What will you have?"
> "Nothing for me, thank you," SHE said. "I'm not sure I could eat, after all."
> "Well, I could," HE said, shoving HIS jaw out. Baba smiled. "I want a good solid ham sandwich."
> "I could have asked him for some water," SHE said, after he had gone.

What is of particular interest here is the fact that SHE regrets not having asked for water. When Baba returns, bringing HIM the beer and sandwich which HE ordered, SHE asks "Could I have some water?" (p. 19). Instead of the water Baba brings HER "an opened, frosted brown bottle" and "a thick sandwich". Much later, when HE drops HER off at HER hotel after returning to New Orleans, SHE remarks (p. 26): "I never got any water". Contained in this seemingly trivial event, I think, is additional evidence that SHE, particularly, has difficulty interacting with HER environment.

So HIS voice and HER voice reveal very little to the reader about THEMSELVES or about one another. As Jones (1969: 42) has insightfully remarked, dialogue, in Welty's hands, "often becomes a means of evading contact and communication".

*4.1.2 The third voice*

This voice, too, when it takes over, can be frustratingly circumspect in supplying information. Here are a few examples:

- "THEY were threading through the narrow and one-way streets, past . . . the balcony with the live and *probably* famous black monkey dipping along the railing as over a ballroom floor." (p. 7)
- "THEY did not risk going on to HER husband – *if SHE had one*." (p. 14)
- "Then HE *might* have cocked HIS dark city head down at her; SHE did not look up at HIM, only turned when HE did." (p. 17)
- "A massive back, *presumably* female, with a twist of gray hair on top, stood with a ladle akimbo." (p. 18)
- "And suddenly SHE made a move to slide down from HER stool, *maybe* wishing to walk out into that nowhere down the front steps to be cool a moment." (p. 21)

These are curious remarks, given that the author could supply the requisite information at any time (the story is, after all, the author's creation). Here are Welty's own remarks (1955b: 247-248) about this curious voice – a voice which came into being as she revised the original manuscript:

> ... the vital thing that happened to the story came from writing, as I began the work. My first realization of what it was came when I looked back and recognized that country (the once-submerged, strange land of "south from South" that had so stamped itself upon my imagination) as the image to me of the story's predicament come to life. This pointed out to me, as I wrote into the story, where the real point of view belonged. Once I was outside, I saw it was outside – suspended, hung in the air between the two people, fished alive from the surrounding scene, where as it carried the story along it revealed itself (I hoped) as more real, more essential, than the characters were or had any cause to be. In effect there'd come to be a sort of third character present – an identity rather: the relationship between the two and between the two and the world. It was what grew up between them meeting as strangers, went on the trip with them, nodded back and forth from one to the other – listening, watching, persuading or denying them, enlarging or diminishing them,

forgetful sometimes of who they were or what they were doing here, helping or betraying them along. Its rôle was that of hypnosis – it was what a relationship does, be it however brief, tentative, potential, happy or sinister, ordinary or extraordinary. I wanted to suggest that its being took shape as the strange, compulsive journey itself, was palpable as its climate and mood, the heat of the day – but was its spirit too, a spirit that held territory – what's seen fleeting past by two vulnerable people who might seize hands on the run. There are times in the story when I say neither "she felt" nor "he felt" but "they felt."

This passage gives us additional insight into Welty's reasons for keeping the two main characters nameless: she has chosen to downplay the individuals while highlighting the relationship and its exposure to the unfolding Southern setting THEY encounter – to subordinate THEIR voices, and thereby also THEM, to this third voice.

However, Welty gets carried away a bit here in her enthusiasm for describing and defending the nature of this third voice. The last sentence in the above quotation implies that this voice is capable of getting inside THEIR collective heads. Such instances are in fact practically non-existent in the narrative. Consider, for example, Welty's explicit claim that "there are times" when she writes "they felt". The plural form "times" is unjustified. There is only a single instance where "they felt" occurs:

- "When THEY reached the other side, **THEY felt** that THEY had been racing around an arena in THEIR chariot, among lions." (p. 12)

Significantly, even this instance is not found in the *New Yorker* version. There the text reads "SHE felt" (1952: 39) rather than "THEY felt". So Welty was still developing that "third character" in the years between 1952 and 1955. The only other example I can find where there is even a hint of a shared emotion is this one:

- "THEY had *grown fond* of all the selections by now" (p. 23)

In other words, despite Welty's characterization of this voice, it is much more of an "outside" observer than an "inside" one. This is clearly established by considering the types of verbs which accompany the subject pronoun THEY. Here are some examples:

- "THEY *looked* with grateful dignity at each other" (p. 5)
- "THEY *settled* into the car" (p. 6)
- "THEY *rode* mostly in silence" (p. 7)
- "THEY *stood* pat up there riding the river" (p. 11)
- "THEY *bolted* over a cattle guard" (p. 13)

- "THEY *caught up* with an old man walking in a sprightly way in THEIR direction" (p. 15)
- "THEY *crossed* the floor and sat, alone there, on wooden stools" (p. 18)
- "THEY *danced* on still as the record changed" (p. 22)
- "THEY *had driven* down into a strange land together" (p. 25)
- "THEY *shook* hands" (p. 26)

All of these verbs describe actions which can be perceived by an outside observer. None of them describe any kind of mental or emotional state.

It is my personal opinion that Welty's goals for the story are in fact better served by keeping this third voice completely outside HIM and HER. During my reading of the story, and long before I had come across Welty's own description of this third voice, I was bothered by the single phrase, "they felt", in the text. It seemed out of place and out of sense. Similarly the phrase, "she felt", in the *New Yorker* version also seemed inappropriate, since it focussed too much on HER. At the risk of being accused of trying to improve on a remarkable story, I would suggest that Welty ought to have written something like the following:

- "When THEY reached the other side, **THEY no doubt felt** that THEY had been racing around an arena in THEIR chariot, among lions."

A revision along these lines would allow that third voice to make a qualified guess about THEIR emotional state – *hence remaining on the outside*. Such a comment would be much better in tune with other third voice remarks such as:

- "**Perhaps** HER measuring coolness was to HIM what HIS bodily shade was to HER, while THEY stood pat up there riding the river" (p. 11)
- "And suddenly SHE made a move to slide down from HER stool, **maybe** wishing to walk out into that nowhere down the front steps to be cool a moment." (p. 21)

Be that as it may, Welty has succeeded in distancing herself from the story by establishing a trio of voices whose combined communication still leaves the reader in something of a fog regarding the two protagonists. The reader's perception of THEM, THEIR journey, and the landscape THEY travel through is determined to a large extent by what THEY say and see, by how THEY interpret what THEY see, and by what the third voice can reveal to us from the outside. THEIR overriding silence is thus what is largely responsible for us knowing so little about THEM. In particular, supplying names for these protagonists, if the names are not somehow naturally forthcoming in and through the story itself, would be an act of author intrusion.

Of course, the very fact that THEY do not inquire after each other's name at any time during the long journey is very odd in itself. While we can better understand now why Welty has chosen to keep THEM anonymous, and how she accomplishes this, nonetheless most readers will no doubt have a nagging suspicion that in real life such anonymity between two people who spend so many hours in each other's company would be strange indeed. On the other hand, the fact that Welty has "withdrawn" herself from the telling of the story means that it is not Welty who is withholding the names, but THEY THEMSELVES. Consequently, THEIR namelessness is further evidence of THEIR inability, THEIR reluctance, to communicate.

*4.2 A general absence of personal names*

But namelessness is not limited to THEM in this story. Names of people in general are studiously avoided throughout the narrative. Given the nature of the points of view involved, we need no longer be surprised by this fact. Since THEY are strangers to the place, THEY know no one. Whatever characters the story brings into view are introduced to us primarily through THEIR eyes, and these characters are nameless for the simple reason that THEY do not know the names of the people THEY meet – unless THEY can see the names in print in some fashion or other.

The only personal name that plays any role in the story is "Baba", the owner of the beer shack where THEY eat and dance. How do THEY get to know his name? THEY see it in neon lights:

- "A narrow neon sign, the lone sign, had come out in bright blush on the beer shack's roof: 'Baba's Place'". (p. 17).

Baba is the name of a person; but in the genitive ("Baba's") it is also the name of a place.

HE and SHE do come across a few other personal names in the story, but these, too, are intimately connected with place. For example, THEIR car journey takes THEM through a churchyard, where

- "A paved track ran between two short rows of raised tombs, all neatly white-washed and now brilliant as faces against the vast flushed sky. The track was the width of the car with a few inches to spare. HE passed between the tombs slowly in the manner of a feat. *Names took their places on the walls* slowly at a level with the eye, names as near the eyes of a person stopping in conversation, and as far away in origin, and in all their music and dead longing, as Spain." (pp. 13-14)

Like Baba's name "in bright blush" on the neon sign, these names of people long departed appear on "white-washed" tombs "brilliant as faces". The names, observed in passing by HIM and HER, but not made known to the reader, are engraved in stone. Like Baba's name in neon lights, they have become part of the place, part of the landscape.

In a rather similar vein, HE and SHE spot a name on the wall at Baba's Place:

- "One of the written messages tacked before THEM [on the overhang above the counter at Baba's Place] read: 'Joe! At the boyy!!' It looked very yellow, older than Baba's Place." (pp. 18-19)

This name, too, is of someone presumably no longer present, possibly dead. The paper is very old, and therefore so is "Joe". Like the names in the churchyard, Joe's name is divorced from the person and affixed to a place.

Another, minor instance of a name made somewhat visible occurs just as THEY drive THEIR car onto the ferry:

- "Another boy drew his affectionate initials in the dust of the door on HER side." (p. 9)

This image of the initials of a living being inscribed on a dusty car door is a significant precursor of the scene THEY encounter later, where the names of the dead are inscribed on stone. With this simple but powerful device, a sense of human mortality enters the story.

Before looking briefly at how we are introduced to the other, relatively few, nameless human characters in the story, it should be pointed out that two proper names are mentioned in passing at the very end of the narrative, after HE has said good-bye to HER at HER hotel:

- "In **Dickie Grogan's**, as HE passed, the well-known **Josefina** at her organ was charging up and down with *Clair de Lune*." (pp. 26-27)

The parallel between Baba's Place and Dickie Grogan's – both cited as place names in the genitive – provides an interesting symmetry for the two endpoints of the journey. As for Josefina, apparently Welty allows this name into the story without any visual concomitant because it is so "well-known" that even HE, a stranger, presumably is familiar with her name.

In the absence of names for the people THEY encounter on THEIR journey, people move in and out of our vision as they move in and out of THEIRS, and are identified and characterized by some prominent visible feature:

- "*One red-haired man* in a burst of wildness even tried to give away his truck-load of shrimp" (p. 9)
- "One of the four cardplayers at a table in the middle of the floor was *the newspaper reader*" (pp. 17-18)
- "*A massive back, presumably female, with a twist of gray hair on top*, stood with a ladle akimbo. *A young man* joined her" (p. 18)
- "[O]ne of the men who had come in beckoned from across the room. It was *the old man in the palm-tree shirt*." (p. 19)
- "At the side of the room *a man with a cap on his white thatch* was trying his best to open a side screen door" (p. 20)
- "*The old thatched man* was again drunkenly trying to get out by the stuck side door" (p. 23)

We see, then, that Welty employs a number of devices which in effect limit the amount of information that is revealed to the reader. The most striking instance of this is the fact that the two protagonists are, and basically remain, strangers – not only to each other, but also to us. But it is true on a broader scale as well. People move in and out of the story, nameless unless identified in some written form which can be seen by the protagonists. In this way, the people are transients, individually backgrounded, while the relationship and the physical setting are foregrounded.

*4.3 Place names*

In a very real sense, then, place is as important in this story as the characters. Gretlund, whose 1994 book is dedicated to a discussion of Welty's "Aesthetics of Place", asked Welty the following pertinent question in his 1978 interview with her (Gretlund 1994: 387):

> In 1951 you said that "in a story, character and place have almost equal, or even interchangeable, contributions to make." Do you still feel that this is true?

to which Welty responded as follows:

> Now I wouldn't say "interchangeable"; but I think that place can almost be a character in a story. Place can have really important and even dramatic significance.

There can be no doubt that the landscape which comes to light in "No Place for You, My Love" made a very strong impression on Welty. In her discussion of this story she writes (1955b: 248): "Anyone who has visited the actual scene of this story has a chance of recognizing it when he meets it here, for the story is visual and the place is out of the ordinary". Jones (1969: 45) goes so far as to argue that Welty identifies less with her characters than with "the landscape through which they drive". Certainly we learn more about the landscape than we do about the characters travelling through it. Nonetheless, the landscape is revealed to us through the eyes of the characters as well as through the third voice, the third voice being the most poetic of the three:

> More and more crayfish and other shell creatures littered THEIR path, scuttling or dragging. These little samples, little jokes of creation, persisted and sometimes perished, the more of them the deeper down the road went. Terrapins and turtles came up steadily over the horizons of the ditches. Back there in the margins were worse – crawling hides you could not penetrate with bullets or quite believe, grins that had come down from the primeval mud. (p. 8)

Here is one of HER perceptions:

> When SHE looked clear around, thinking they had a fire burning somewhere now, out of the heat had risen the full moon. Just beyond the trees, enormous, tangerine-colored, it was going solidly up. Other lights just striking into view, looking farther distant, showed moss shapes hanging, or slipped and broke matchlike on the water that so encroached upon the rim of ground THEY were standing on. (p. 16)

And here is one of HIS:

> He stopped the car and got out to clean the windshield thoroughly with HIS brisk, angry motions of driving. Dust lay thick and cratered on the roadside scrub. Under the now ash-white moon, the world travelled through very faint stars – very many slow stars, very high, very low. It was a strange land, amphibious – and whether water-covered or grown with jungle or robbed entirely of water and trees, as now, it had the same loneliness. HE regarded the great sweep – like steppes, like moors, like deserts (all of which were imaginary to HIM); but more than it was like any likeness, it was South. The vast, thin, wide-thrown, pale, unfocused star-sky, with its veils of lightning adrift, hung over this land as it hung over the open sea. Standing out in the night alone, HE was struck as powerfully with recognition of the extremity of this place as if all other bearings had vanished – as if snow had suddenly started to fall. (pp. 23-24)

Together, the three voices give us an ongoing description of the strange and wondrous territory THEY are traveling through. And unlike the case with personal names, proper names of places are frequent in the story. In order of appearance we find the following places identified by name: Galatoire's, Arabi, Venice, Baba's Place, and Dickie Grogan's. It should be borne in mind, of course, that the names of all these places can be visually identified, and hence their occurrence in the story does not conflict with the point of view that fails to reveal the names of persons. We have already seen that Baba's Place is identified in neon lights. No doubt the same is true for the other eating places as well, namely Galatoire's and Dickie Grogan's. As for Arabi and Venice, here is how these place names are introduced:

- "Driving, HE spread HIS new map and put HIS finger down on it. At the intersection marked **Arabi**, where THEIR road led out of the tangle and HE took it, a small Negro seated beneath a black umbrella astride a box chalked 'Shou Shine' lifted his pink-and-black hand and waved THEM languidly good-by." (p. 6)
- "'**Venice**,' SHE heard HIM announce, and HE dropped the crackling map in HER lap." (p. 16)

Arabi and Venice are integral parts of the territory THEY are traversing. The names are made visible on road signs and on the map which HE regularly consults as THEY drive south. This map, which is a necessary accouterment for THEIR journey, serves as a constant reminder to the reader that THEY are "both fairly well strangers to the place" (p. 3).

There is at least one place name which is visible to THEIR eyes, but which Welty chooses not to reveal to the reader:

- "SHE gave HIM the name of HER hotel, HE drove her there, and HE said good night on the sidewalk." (p. 26)

The hotel, being simply a temporary residence for one of the transient strangers, is important only as a dropping-off point at the end of the story. It does not warrant further identification.

*4.4 North vs. South*

Since THEY are strangers to the South, it would be reasonable to inquire where THEY are from. Knowing what we now know about the nature of THEIR dialogue, it will come as no surprise to learn that neither of THEM ever asks the other for this information. Let us see how Welty passes this information on to the reader. In the early stages of the story we are supplied with some very general pointers in the form of locative descriptors:

- "It was the wrong hat for her, thought *this Eastern businessman* who had no interest whatever in women's clothes and no eye for them" (p. 3)

- "What THEY amounted to was two *Northerners* keeping each other company." (p. 4)
- "SHE had that naive face that HE associated, for no good reason, with *the Middle West*" (p. 4)

So we learn that both of THEM are Northerners. More specifically, HE is from the Northeast, SHE from the Midwest. As the story progresses, we are given further details, but primarily in the form of allusions:

- "'I find the heat down here depressing,' SHE said, *with the heart of Ohio in her voice*." (p. 5)
- "'Wake up.' HER *Northern* nudge was very timely on HIS arm." (p. 8)
- "'It's never anything like this in *Syracuse*,' HE said." (p. 13)
- "'Or in *Toledo* either,' SHE replied with dry lips." (p. 13)
- "Then HE might have cocked HIS dark *city* head down at HER" (p. 17)
- "HE was not leaving for *Syracuse* until early in the morning." (p. 26)
- "As HE drove the little Ford safely to its garage, HE remembered for the first time in years when HE was young and brash, a student in *New York*, and the shriek and horror and unholy smother of the subway had its original meaning for HIM as the lilt and expectation of love." (p. 27)

In this roundabout way, Welty identifies HIM as a visitor from Syracuse, New York and HER as a visitor from Toledo, Ohio. THEIR strangeness to the place brings THEM together despite THEIR strangeness to one another. THEIR very Northernness unites THEM. THEY are foreigners in foreign territory – the South. Quite naturally, therefore, references to the North and to Northerners are counterbalanced by references to the South and Southerners:

- "It was a serious, now-watch-out-everybody face, which orphaned HER entirely in the company of these *Southerners*." (p. 4)
- "The *Southern* look – *southern* mask – of life-is-a-dream irony, which could turn to pure challenge at the drop of a hat, he could well wish away." (p. 5)
- "It was a strange land, amphibious – and whether water-covered or grown with jungle or robbed entirely of water and trees, as now, it had the same loneliness. HE regarded the great sweep – like steppes, like moors, like deserts (all of which were imaginary to HIM); but more than it was like any likeness, it was *South*." (p. 24)

Note that Welty writes "South", not "the South". Without the article in front of it, "South" becomes a concept rather than a geographical region. For Jones (1969: 45), this Southern landscape "takes on the atmosphere of a dream as if all roads going South from New Orleans led to the edge of the world, to the very borders of consciousness". Note the various connotations the word "south" takes on:

- "'Have you ever driven down *south* of here?'
- Out on Bourbon Street, in the bath of July, SHE asked at his shoulder, '*South* of New Orleans? I didn't know there was any *south* to *here*. Does it just go on and on?'" (p. 5; "here" is italicized in the original text)
- "After backing out between the tombs HE drove on still *south*, in the sunset." (p. 15)
- "In its eyes and open mouth were those fires THEY had had glimpses of, where the cattle had drawn together: a face, a head, far down here in the *South – south* of *South*, below it." (p. 25)

Jones (1949: 46) elaborates eloquently on his vision of the deeper meaning lurking in this journey of two Northerners into this metaphorical South:

> The journey of these two is like the journey of Conrad's hero into the heart of darkness, a voyage into the interior world where the trappings of social life fall away and leave the individual naked in an elemental landscape confronting the deeper realities of self and of the heart of the mystery we call life.

But there is even more to Welty's vision than this. A counterpart to this nakedness "in an elemental landscape" is the protective shell that each of the travelers brings to the journey, and which remains nearly impenetrable throughout the trip – keeping THEM strangers to one another.

*4.5 Separateness and imperviousness*

THEIR willful separateness despite THEIR togetherness is one of the basic themes in Welty's story, as is made clear early in the narrative (1955a: 4-5):

> Of all human moods, deliberate imperviousness may be the most quickly communicated – it may be the most successful, most fatal signal of all. And two people can indulge in imperviousness as well as in anything else.

One of the clearest examples of this deliberate imperviousness is HIS response when SHE asks about HIS wife. We have already seen that HE responds with total silence. But this is only part of the picture, as the fuller context (1955a: 14) makes clear:

> "What is your wife like?" SHE asked. HIS right hand came up and spread – iron, wooden, manicured. SHE lifted HER eyes to HIS face. HE looked at HER like that hand. Then HE lit a cigarette, and the portrait, and the right-hand testimonial it made, were blown away. SHE smiled, HERSELF as unaffected as by some stage performance.

The upraised hand means "No Trespassing". It is a visible deterrent, effectively blocking any access to information about his personal affairs. Though we are told that SHE is "as unaffected" by this rebuff "as by some stage performance", SHE did not forget it. Later, while THEY are dancing in Baba's, it is SHE who becomes impervious (1955a: 21-22):

> If THEY had ever been going to overstep THEMSELVES, it would be now as HE held HER closer and turned HER, when SHE became aware that HE could not help but see the bruise at HER temple. It would not be six inches from HIS eyes. SHE felt it come out like an evil star. (Let it pay HIM back, then, for the hand HE had stuck in HER face when SHE'd tried once to be sympathetic, when SHE'd asked about HIS wife.)

Here the bruise itself is the only communication to HIM (and the reader) about HER personal state. HE (and we) may conclude, like Binding (1994: 214), that it is the result of "a passionate quarrel". But even if that assumption is made, it is an open question whether this is the result of a falling out with "HER husband if SHE had one" or "the lover in whom HE believed" (1955a: 12). As Mortimer (1994: 121-122) remarks, "both protagonists have secrets and no intention of revealing them". As with so much of the narrative, the reader, like the protagonists, sees through a glass darkly.

While we are on the subject of the upraised hand, it is important to correct a misconception in an otherwise reasonably insightful paragraph by Binding (1994: 214):

> There is contact, both physical and psychological, between them: they dance together at the Shrimp Dance at Bab's [sic] Place, he puts a silencing hand on her when she attempts to ask him about his private life; he sees the bruise at her temple (the scar, presumably, of a passionate quarrel); they kiss when he stops the car on the long, dark way back. But this is not the beginning of a new relationship; it was never envisaged as such by either person; instead it is an experience deeper than that word can normally encompass, a drive into the southern land that is a drive into deep recesses of being, where neither joy nor sorrow, neither desire nor need, can be separated. (Binding, 1994: 214)

It is definitely not the case that HE "puts a silencing hand on HER". The hand is upraised but does not touch HER. Touching at this point would be a direct violation of the imperviousness that characterizes THEM and THEIR relationship. As Welty herself has remarked in her comments on this story (1955b: 249), "the only time they will yield or touch is while they are dancing in the crowd that to them is comically unlikely (hence insulating, non-conducting) or taking a kiss outside time". Welty's insistence on this point is apparently behind one of the small but significant revisions she made in the story after it appeared in *The New Yorker* in 1952. As THEY are dancing, SHE remarks (1955a: 21):

> "I get to thinking this is what we get – what you and I deserve," SHE whispered, looking past HIS shoulder into the room. "And all the time, it's real. It's a real place – away off down here . . ."

*The New Yorker* version (1952: 42) followed this up with the remark: "HE patted her between the shoulder blades." I think we can concur with Welty's decision to delete this line in the 1955 version. Such uncharacteristically tender, even paternalistic, contact is out of place in the story.

There is one place, still, in the narrative where HE touches HER prior to the dance scene, but this contact is fully in keeping with the theme. The incident occurs just after THEY have parked the car and are preparing to enter Baba's. It is now dusk and a full moon has come up:

> There was a touch at HER arm – HIS, accidental. "We're at the jumping-off place," HE said. SHE laughed, having thought HIS hand was a bat (1955a: 16).

This accidental touch is thematically appropriate, particularly since HER reaction (believing the hand to be a bat) indicates that SHE had no expectation whatsoever of there being any deliberate physical contact between THEM.

Note that the lack of physical contact mirrors the lack of verbal contact. These people are sealed into THEMSELVES. They are travelling inside shells. In case the "shell" image might elude us, Welty provides numerous comparisons from the animal kingdom. The most prominent example is the alligator which THEY encounter on the ferry (1955a: 11):

> The boys had a surprise – an alligator on board. One of them pulled it by a chain around the deck, between the cars and trucks, like a toy – a hide that could walk. HE thought, Well they had to catch one sometime. It's Sunday afternoon. So they have him on board now, riding him across the Mississippi River . . . The playfulness of it beset everybody on the ferry. The hoarseness of the boat whistle, commenting briefly, seemed part of the general appreciation. "Who want to rassle him? Who want to, eh?" two boys cried, looking up. A boy with shrimp-colored arms capered from side to side, pretending to have been bitten.
> What was there so hilarious about jaws that could bite? And what danger was there once in this repulsiveness – so that the last worldly evidence of some old heroic horror of the dragon had to be paraded in capture before the eyes of country clowns?

This alligator, though hauled around on a leash like a domestic pet, is characterized physically by a highly impervious exterior. Furthermore, Welty's characterization of the alligator as "the last worldly evidence of some old heroic horror of the dragon" conjures up a mythical counterpart that is even more redoubtable.

When the ferry lands at the other side of the Mississippi, the alligator puts in one final appearance (1955a: 12), though its fearsomeness has been even further reduced:

> The cars and trucks, then the foot passengers and the alligator, waddling like a child to school, all disembarked and wound up the weed-sprung levee.
> Both respectable and merciful, their hides, SHE thought, forcing HERSELF to dwell on the alligator as SHE looked back.

Moving down the evolutionary ladder, Welty throws other creatures in THEIR path – most of which, like the alligator, have a protective covering:

- "SHE watched the road. Crayfish constantly crossed in front of the wheels, looking grim and bonneted, in a great hurry." (p. 7)
- "More and more crayfish and other shell creatures littered THEIR path, scuttling or dragging. These little samples, little jokes of creation, persisted and sometimes perished, the more of them the deeper down the road went. Terrapins and turtles came up steadily over the horizons of the ditches." (p. 8)

An alligator, crayfish and "other shell creatures", terrapins and turtles – all are protected by tough exteriors. Even more encased are animals which are not even visible – animals which challenge the very imagination:

- "Back there in the margins were worse – crawling hides you could not penetrate with bullets or quite believe, grins that had come down from the primeval mud." (p. 8)

And, of course, there is a direct link to the encased creatures that are the staple of the region THEY are traversing, namely shrimp. Here is a description of one of Baba's activities:

- "He was counting over the platters the old woman now set out on the counter, each heaped with shrimp in their shells boiled to iridescence, like mounds of honeysuckle flowers" (p. 22).

In Welty's imagination, the hide imagery extends even to inanimate objects:

- "The flaked-off, colored houses were spotted like the hides of beasts faded and shy" (pp. 5-6).

This theme of impenetrability provides an insight into another role played by the use of pronouns instead of names: The pronouns mask THEIR identity, thereby adding to the general sense of imperviousness. We can push this argument even further. By a curious orthographic coincidence the words "HE" and "SHE" are each contained in the word "SHELL": *s-HE-ll*, *SHE-ll*. HE and SHE are thus literally enshelled. But perhaps this is not a coincidence. With Welty one can never be certain where creative imagination stops and coincidence begins. (Anyone familiar with the tongue-twister "She sells sea shells by the seashore" has a pre-existing mental link between "she" and "shell".)

Despite this imperviousness, however, THEY do come together in what is the high point in Welty's story – THEY dance:

> Then, THEY were like a matched team – like professional Spanish dancers wearing masks – while the slow piece was playing.
> Surely even those immune from the world, for the time being, need the touch of one another, or all is lost. THEIR arms encircling each other, THEIR bodies circling the odorous, just-nailed down floor, THEY were, at last, imperviousness in motion. THEY had found it, and had almost missed it; THEY had had to dance. THEY were what THEIR separate hearts desired that day, for THEMSELVES and each other. (p. 22)

The nearly total absence of physical contact prior to this scene dramatically heightens the effect of THEIR togetherness (with masks still in place) when THEY dance at Baba's. The resulting "imperviousness in motion" – separate connectedness, or connected separateness – is the culmination of the journey. It is, as Carson (1992: 31) observes, "the perfect image of the dynamic tension between union and separateness". We might note that there is also a grammatical union in this excerpt: the third person singular pronouns, "he" and "she", are joined by the remaining member of the set, "it": "THEY had found *it* and almost missed *it*".

Ultimately, then, THEIR journey together does affect THEIR lives in a small but immeasurable fashion. In the view of Alun Jones (1969: 43), "No Place for You, My Love" is an attempt by Welty

> to define what Philip Larkin, the English poet, calls a 'frail travelling coincidence'; the accident of being at the same place at the same time and sharing intensely for a brief period the lives of others. There is a strong feeling also that travelling exists between places in a kind of nowhere; that travelling is something that happens outside of time somewhere between departure and arrival.

We have seen now that Welty's decision to keep the protagonists nameless is an ingenious device for developing and enhancing this theme – in a multitude of ways.

At the same time her decision imposes a heavy burden on the personal pronouns – those little grammatical words that take the place of the absentee labels. It also forces the reader to be constantly alert in applying the grammatical conventions and decoding the clues which help determine the referent for each individual pronoun.

## 5. The linguistic question: How?

Having investigated the question of why Welty has chosen to keep HIM and HER nameless throughout the story, we turn our attention now to an examination of the linguistic question: Given the absence of personal names, how does Welty manage to distinguish HIM and HER from the other people in the story? In order to answer this question reasonably, it is appropriate to consider first the general conventions – both grammatical and logical – of pronominal reference itself. We shall then be in a better position to understand and appreciate Welty's wizardry in helping the reader through the pronominal maze.

### 5.1 Some general features of pronominal reference

Pronouns play a major role in any linguistic text. Though they generally function as markers of known information, having in themselves little or no semantic content, their contribution to the flow and coherence of a text is immense. As writers and readers, speakers and hearers, however, our use and interpretation of pronouns is so automatic that their fundamental role in written and spoken texts generally escapes our conscious attention – until a writer like Welty chooses to make special use of these grammatical forms.

To get a sense of the role played by pronouns, let us start with a little experiment. The following paragraph is taken from the very first page of the first story in *The Collected Stories of Eudora Welty* (1980: 3). It displays a natural harmonious interplay between pronouns and personal names:

> Version 1 (original text):
> Mrs. Watts and Mrs. Carson were both in the post office in Victory when the letter came from the Ellisville Institute for the Feeble-Minded of Mississippi. Aimee Slocum, with her hand still full of mail, ran out in front and handed it straight to Mrs. Watts, and they all three read it together. Mrs. Watts held it taut between her pink hands, and Mrs. Carson underscored each line slowly with her thimbled finger. Everybody else in the post office wondered what was up now.

This short text contains a large number of pronouns, among which are "her", "they", "both", "it", and "all". These small and seemingly unimportant pronominal forms play a vital role in textual cohesion and in the reduction of unnecessary repetition of referents. To get a sense of their role, let us replace a mere four of these, namely the personal pronouns "her" (three times) and "they" (once) with the proper nouns for which they stand:

> Version 2:
> Mrs. Watts and Mrs. Carson were both in the post office in Victory when the letter came from the Ellisville Institute for the Feeble-Minded of Mississippi. Aimee Slocum, with Aimee Slocum's hand still full of mail, ran out in front and handed it straight to Mrs. Watts, and Mrs. Watts, Mrs. Carson, and Aimee Slocum all three read it together. Mrs. Watts held it taut between Mrs. Watts's pink hands, and Mrs. Carson underscored each line slowly with Mrs. Carson's thimbled finger. Everybody else in the post office wondered what was up now.

Without the pronouns, the text is not only cumbersome but unacceptable as English – though there is no problem at all understanding who did what. The text would be even more cumbersome if we had replaced all of the pronouns with the appropriate nouns. Nobody writes like that.

What happens if we take the opposite approach, replacing the personal names (Mrs. Watts, Mrs. Carson and Aimee Slocum) with personal pronouns?

> Version 3:
> She and she were both in the post office in Victory when the letter came from the Ellisville Institute for the Feeble-Minded of Mississippi. She, with her hand still full of mail, ran out in front and handed it straight to her, and they all three read it together. She held it taut between her pink hands, and she underscored each line slowly with her thimbled finger. Everybody else in the post office wondered what was up now.

This text feels more grammatical than the previous version, with the exception of the odd opening ("She and she"), but the text has become referentially opaque – we do not know who did what. This, then, is the problem which Welty faces when she chooses not to use personal names. Of course, the problem is particularly acute in this particular excerpt, because all three individuals involved are female. Since English personal pronouns can differentiate between male and female referents (e.g. "he" vs. "she"), we can help this particular text along by changing the sex of Mrs. Watts, so that instead of three females, there are two females and one male:

Version 4:
He and she were both in the post office in Victory when the letter came from the Ellisville Institute for the Feeble-Minded of Mississippi. She, with her hand still full of mail, ran out in front and handed it straight to him, and they all three read it together. He held it taut between his pink hands, and she underscored each line slowly with her thimbled finger. Everybody else in the post office wondered what was up now.

This is rapidly approaching the style of Welty's "No Place for You, My Love", but we need to make one more revision: We must distinguish in some way between the two remaining females. Let us therefore characterize one of them as "the postmistress":

Version 5:
He and she were both in the post office in Victory when the letter came from the Ellisville Institute for the Feeble-Minded of Mississippi. The postmistress, with her hand still full of mail, ran out in front and handed it straight to him, and they all three read it together. He held it taut between his pink hands, and she underscored each line slowly with her thimbled finger. Everybody else in the post office wondered what was up now.

And there we have it – Welty's chosen format for dealing with the protagonists and the people THEY encounter in "No Place for You, My Love". There remains a bit of ambiguity in the clause "she underscored each line slowly with her thimbled finger", since "she" and "her" could refer to either of the two females. But if we had learned earlier that the female protagonist had a thimble on her finger, we could disambiguate both the "she" and the "her" in this clause, the reference being to the main character, rather than to the postmistress. Note, too, that once we determine that it is the main female character who has the thimbled finger, it follows by the normal – but unconscious – application of logic on the part of the reader that "she" in this clause must also refer to that person. The alternative reading, corresponding to "Mrs. Carson underscored each line slowly with Aimee Slocum's finger" would suggest either a highly macabre scene in which Aimee Slocum's finger has been severed from her hand, or that Aimee Slocum is so blind or otherwise handicapped that she needs help moving her finger across the page.

If I have gone on at some length here to highlight what in retrospect may seem fairly obvious, it is simply to make clear the linguistic challenge that Welty has set herself, and at the same time to prepare the way for a discussion of some of the devices which English grammar makes available to Welty to help her meet this self-imposed challenge.

*5.1.1 Some of the linguistic devices available*

The English language provides a number of linguistic devices which directly or indirectly contribute to the establishment of the appropriate links between pronouns and their referents. Both writer and reader continuously make use of these devices – the former during the process of encoding, the latter during decoding.

*5.1.1.1 Semantic similarity*

One of the most obvious facts about pronominal reference is that the pronoun and its referent must be semantically similar – that is, the two must have the same number and gender (e.g. a singular masculine pronoun such as "he" must refer to a single masculine entity). This point can be illustrated by the following two excerpts from "No Place for You, My Love":

- "Another boy drew **his** affectionate initials in the dust on **her** side." (p. 9)
- "a small Negro seated beneath a black umbrella astride a box chalked 'Shou Shine' lifted his pink-and-black hand and waved **them** languidly good-by." (p. 6)

At the risk of overstating the obvious, the fundamental rule of semantic similarity informs us that an interpretation of the first sentence allows the masculine "his" but not the feminine "her" to refer to "another boy", while in the second sentence the plural "they" cannot possibly refer to the singular "pink-and-black hand". Observe, however, that the feature of semantic similarity alone will not allow us to infer that "his" refers to "another boy" rather than to HIM in the first sentence. To ensure the assignment of the proper masculine referent in this case, some other devices must be at play. One of these is anaphoric proximity.

*5.1.1.2 Anaphoric proximity*

In the original version (Version 1) of our experimental text, it is worth noting that the pronoun "her" appears three times, and each time the form refers to a different person:

- "Aimee Slocum, with **her** hand still full of mail, ran out in front and handed it straight to Mrs. Watts"
- "Mrs. Watts held it taut between **her** pink hands"
- "Mrs. Carson underscored each line slowly with **her** thimbled finger"

What is it that allows us, with no help from Welty, to correctly identify the reference of these three identical forms ("her") as, respectively, Aimee Slocum, Mrs.

Watts, and Mrs. Carson? A closer examination of each of the contexts provides the answer: we look to the left for the nearest possible referent. This establishes our next basic principle of pronominal reference: in general, pronouns refer backwards (that is, the reference is anaphoric) and the referent is likely to be found in the noun or noun phrase which is closest to the pronoun, providing that the referent and the pronoun are semantically similar.

It should be pointed out that though pronominal reference is typically anaphoric, as in the above three cases, occasionally the reference can be forwards (that is, the reference is cataphoric). In such cases the pronoun is usually found in a subordinate clause and the referent is identified in the same sentence in a following clause, as in the next example from "No Place for You, My Love":

- "When **he** got ready to wait on THEM, <u>Baba</u> strolled out to the counter, young, black-headed, and in very good humor". (p. 18)

Here the most natural, and contextually appropriate, interpretation of the pronoun "he" is that it refers cataphorically to Baba. (It is of course logically possible, but fully out of context in the actual story, to assume that "he" refers to someone other than Baba, and that as this other person got ready to wait on THEM, Baba just happened to stroll out to the counter.)

*5.1.1.3 Reflexive pronouns*

The use of a reflexive pronoun (such as "himself", "herself", "themselves") typically imposes a grammatical obligation on the pronoun to refer to an entity identified inside the sentence itself, thus establishing intra-sentential co-reference. Most commonly the reflexive pronoun functions as an object, and the co-referent as the subject. Thus in the following excerpt from "No Place for You, My Love", the reflexive pronoun, "themselves" (object), can only refer to "A family of eight or nine people" (subject):

- "<u>A family of eight or nine people</u> on foot strung along the road in the same direction the car was going, beating **themselves** with the wild palmettos." (p. 8)

Had a non-reflexive pronoun (e.g. "them") been used instead, the reference could not have been to "A family of eight or nine people", but instead would have had to be to some other plural entity (such as THEM).

*5.1.1.4 Topic continuity*

It is often the case that the referent for a given pronoun is not to be found inside the given sentence itself. Consider the following excerpts from "No Place for You, My Love":

- "<u>The passengers</u> walking and jostling and jostling about there appeared oddly amateurish too – amateur travelers. **They** were having such a good time." (p. 9)
- "<u>Baba</u> was smiling. **He** had set an opened frosted brown bottle before HER on the counter, and a thick sandwich, and stood looking at HER. " (pp. 19-20)

In cases like these, an additional principle is often operative – namely the principle of "topic continuity" (Givón 1984: 137):

> While human discourse may have loftier, more abstract themes, we would consider it as being prototypically about the fate, affairs, doings, trials and tribulations of individual – most commonly nominal – topics.

Normal discourse typically involves topic continuation rather than topic disruption. One of the most common grammatical means for maintaining topic continuity is for a subject pronoun to mark a continuation of the subject of the preceding clause or sentence (Givón 1993, vol. I: 237). In our two examples above, it is therefore most natural to assume that "They" is linked to "the passengers", and "He" to "Baba".

But topic continuity also commonly applies to other grammatical constructions as well. After the subject, the object is the most common:

- "The boys had a surprise – <u>an alligator</u> on board. One of them pulled it by a chain around the deck, between the cars and trucks, like a toy – a hide that could walk. HE thought, Well they had to catch one sometime. It's Sunday afternoon. So they have **him** on board now, riding **him** across the Mississippi River ... 'Who want to rassle **him**? Who want to, eh?' two boys cried, looking up." (p. 11)

Here the most natural interpretation of the three object pronouns, "him", is that they all continue the topic of the first sentence in the excerpt – they refer to the alligator.

*5.1.2 The "open file" analogy*
Adapting a metaphor from Givón (1990: 894), referent identifiers such as nouns (e.g. "Baba") and noun phrases (e.g. "your wife") can be viewed as "file labels" identifying the files where information about the intended referent is stored in the mind. The first introduction of a noun or noun phrase typically creates

a new "file" ready to receive information about the referent as it accumulates in the text. Existing files can be viewed as either "open" or "closed". A file is "open" if the given referent is currently "activated" (that is, topical in some sense) and hence mentally easily accessible. It is "closed" if the given referent is no longer in short term memory (that is, forgotten in some sense). Pronouns are typically used to refer to open files.

As the reader moves through a text, files are opened and closed according to the likely longevity of the entities introduced. It follows that the files for main characters (and other persistent entities) in a text are open for much longer periods than those for minor characters and transient entities. To illustrate, consider the following two excerpts from "No Place for You, My Love":

- "One red-haired man in a burst of wildness even tried to give away **his** truckload of shrimp to a man on the other side of the boat" (p. 9)
- "Once the car lights picked out two people – a Negro couple, sitting on two facing chairs in the yard outside **their** lonely cabin" (p. 24)

As readers, we mentally create a "file" for both the red-haired man and the Negro couple, thus allowing us (briefly) to refer to the former with the pronoun "his" and the latter with the pronoun "their". But at the same time we are aware that these are bit players in the wider context of the narrative, and consequently any future occurrence of "his" or "their" is not likely to point to either of these entities. In other words, we "close" these two files almost as quickly as we create them. In fact, we close them as soon as the given sentence comes to a close.

On the other hand, the files for HIM and HER are open for nearly the whole narrative. Only after HE drops HER off at the hotel near the end of the story, are we likely to close HER file, thus freeing the feminine pronouns for other use in the short remainder of the narrative.

Because the files for HIM and HER are open nearly the whole time, however, these files run the risk of competing with open files for other entities in the story, no matter how briefly these other files remain open. It is because Welty has chosen not to provide personal names for the HIM and HER files that she must carefully and continually consider the ability of the reader to correctly link the pronominal pointers to the appropriate file. Wherever the normal linguistic devices supplied by English grammar are insufficient to ensure an unambiguous decoding of the reference, normal logic and narrative context take on important roles.

## 5.1.3 Logic and context

Ambiguity is an important and inherent feature of human language. Without the ability to construct texts with multiple meanings, our language capacity would be severely impoverished. Humor, poetry, and irony would obviously suffer. Consequently, it is comforting to learn that grammatical rules do not uniquely govern the interpretation of texts. There are many cases of pronominal usage which leave a wide margin for interpretation, despite the adherence to grammatical norms. But in many cases, logic and context can be decisive in ruling out readings which, from a purely grammatical point of view, are potentially ambiguous. Consider the following constructed example:

- Andrew put on his coat and raced out of the room.

Strictly speaking, there is referential ambiguity in the interpretation of the pronoun "his" in this sentence. The most natural interpretation would invoke the principle of anaphoric proximity to assign "Andrew" as the referent. In other words, Andrew put on his own coat. But another reading is theoretically possible: Andrew might have put on some other male person's coat and then raced out of the room. This could be an inadvertent act, or Andrew might have been stealing the coat. Unless such a sentence is created to be intentionally ambiguous, it should be possible on the basis of simple logic and wider context to establish exactly which meaning is intended.

Some languages avoid such ambiguity by using two different pronouns – one meaning e.g. "his own" and the other meaning e.g. "someone else's". One such language is Danish, where the distinction can be captured by "sin" (his own) vs. "hans" (some other male person's). The above sentence can thus be rendered in Danish in two different ways:

- Andrew tog **sin** frakke på og løb ud af værelset.
- Andrew tog **hans** frakke på og løb ud af værelset.

Of course, English could make it clear that the coat belonged to Andrew by adding the word "own":

- Andrew put on his own coat and raced out of the room.

But this is highly marked (it highlights the possibility that Andrew had a choice of coats and that he decided to forego theft in this case). Instead of "his own", the natural English construction would be "his", and the unmarked reading would be "his own", a reading which would be overruled in favor of "someone else's" only if context dictated it. It is this same principle that is operative in the sentence we examined earlier:

- "Mrs. Carson underscored each line slowly with **her** thimbled finger" where the unmarked reading is that "her" means "her own", and not someone else's. In "No Place for You, My Love", we shall see that potential ambiguity in pronominal reference can often be resolved by direct appeal to logic and context.

## 5.1.4 Pronoun tracking

We have now examined a variety of principles which are used by writer and reader, speaker and hearer, to facilitate the encoding and decoding of pronominal reference – that is, to facilitate what is known as "pronoun tracking". Failure to abide by these principles can cause pronoun tracking to become difficult and sometimes (in the case of poor writing or deliberate ambiguity) impossible. In summary, the basic conditions for felicitous pronoun tracking are:

- The referent and the pronoun must be semantically similar – in particular, they should agree in gender and in number.
- The original referent should be clearly identified prior to the use of the pronoun – or immediately after the use of the pronoun. In general, pronouns refer *backwards* (anaphoric reference), though occasionally the reference can be forwards (cataphoric reference), in which case the pronoun is typically in a subordinate clause and the referent is identified in the same sentence in a following clause.
- The use of reflexive pronouns typically imposes a grammatical obligation on the pronoun to refer to an entity identified inside the sentence itself. Often the reflexive pronoun functions as object in the clause, while the co-referent functions as subject.
- In the case of referential competition, it is common for a pronoun to continue to refer to the current topic, topic continuity being more prototypical than topic disruption. In particular a subject pronoun in one clause tends to refer to the subject of the preceding clause or sentence.
- The original referent should be available in the reader/hearer's short-term memory (the "file" should be "open").
- Where rules of grammar fail to remove potential ambiguity, common logic and contextual information often prove to be useful supplements.

So natural and so rapid is the interaction of grammar, context, and logic in the mind of the reader (and hearer) that there is little, if any, awareness that these mental activities are being performed in the process of pronoun tracking – a process that is performed in connection with every referential pronoun encountered in the text. It is only when someone like Eudora Welty pushes our faculties to the limit that we become cognizant of what is involved.

*5.1.5 Some statistics*

We are now ready to undertake a detailed examination of the personal pronouns in "No Place for You, My Love". My purpose in doing so is two-fold. In the first place I wish to explore how Welty keeps HIM and HER (and THEM) distinct from the other entities in the narrative. Secondly, I wish to illuminate the range and application of the strategies described above – strategies we so unconsciously and effectively employ in working out the intricacies of pronoun tracking.

Let us begin with a statistical overview of the third person personal pronouns in Welty's text. The following table enumerates the occurrences of a) female pronouns, b) male pronouns, and c) plural pronouns. The first column identifies the relevant pronoun, the second indicates the number of occurrences which refer to the two protagonists, the third displays the corresponding number for all non-protagonists, while the final column provides the totals for all categories:

|  | Protagonists |  | Other |  | Totals |
|---|---|---|---|---|---|
| **She** | 86 | (97.7%) | 2 | (2.3%) | 88 |
| **Her** | 103 | (97.2%) | 3 | (2.8%) | 106 |
| **Hers** | 1 | (100%) | 0 | (0%) | 1 |
| **Herself** | 4 | (100%) | 0 | (0%) | 4 |
| **Totals** | 194 | (97.5%) | 5 | (2.5%) | 199 |
|  |  |  |  |  |  |
| **He** | 113 | (88.3%) | 15 | (11.7%) | 128 |
| **Him** | 20 | (69%) | 9 | (31%) | 29 |
| **His** | 40 | (64.5%) | 22 | (35.5%) | 62 |
| **Himself** | 4 | (57.1%) | 3 | (42.9%) | 7 |
| **Totals** | 177 | (78.3%) | 49 | (21.7%) | 226 |
|  |  |  |  |  |  |
| **They** | 62 | (69.7%) | 27 | (30.3%) | 89 |
| **Them** | 23 | (71.9%) | 9 | (28.1%) | 32 |
| **Their** | 20 | (50%) | 20 | (50%) | 40 |
| **Theirs** | 0 | (0%) | 1 | (100%) | 1 |
| **Themselves** | 4 | (44.4%) | 5 | (55.6%) | 9 |
| **Totals** | 109 | (63.7%) | 62 | (36.3%) | 171 |
|  |  |  |  |  |  |
| **Grand totals** | 480 | (80.5%) | 116 | (19.5%) | 596 |

*Table 1: Instances of third person personal pronouns*

We see that the story contains a total of 596 occurrences of third person personal pronouns. Of these, 480 (80.5%) relate to the protagonists, while 116 (19.5%) do not. On the basis of these statistics alone, we can see that, as readers, one basic strategy we could adopt would be to assume that all third person personal pronouns refer to the protagonists. We would be right about 80% of the time. Indeed, I believe that this is the basic strategy that any reader of this story ultimately adopts. Since HE and SHE (and, therefore, THEY) are the story's main characters, the "files" relating to these characters are always "open". The reader would thus be justified in assuming that the "default" reference for all third person personal pronouns is these two people.

It is reasonable, therefore, for us to focus our analytical attention on the 20% of the cases where these pronouns do not refer to the protagonists – that is, we shall concern ourselves primarily with the instances summarized in the next-to-last column in Table 1. A full listing of these instances, in their appropriate contexts, can be found in Appendix 1 ("non-SHE": 5 instances), Appendix 2 ("non-HE": 49 instances) and Appendix 3 ("non-THEY": 62 instances). (It should be noted that except for "non-SHE", the number of instances is greater than the number of sentences listed in the Appendices, since many sentences contain more than one instance.) We shall begin with the smallest set: "non-SHE".

*5.2 "non-SHE" (instances of **she** and **her** which do not refer to HER)*

The use of the feminine pronouns in English is limited primarily to female human beings. It is, of course possible, particularly for males, to use the feminine pronouns to refer to such inanimate objects as cars and boats – particularly if they are objects of beauty. Now there are indeed both a car and a ferry which figure strongly in Welty's story, but Welty is not about to increase the pronoun tracking problem by treating these as feminine objects. The car which takes THEM on THEIR journey is a rented one that is described as "a faded-red Ford convertible with a rather threadbare canvas top" (p. 6). It is therefore not surprising that the car is referred to only with the neuter pronoun (e.g. "'**It's** rented,' HE explained", p. 6). Likewise, the boat which takes THEM across the Mississippi is rather nondescript. It is described as a "tiny ferry" (p. 8), a "small, amateurish-looking boat" (p. 9) with a "rusty rim" (p. 9). It comes as no surprise, therefore, that the boat, too, is referred to only in the neuter (e.g. "the boat still delayed in what seemed a trance – as if **it** were too full to attempt the start", p. 9).

So in this story the feminine pronoun is used only to refer to female persons, and since there are very few of these other than HER, the use of "she" and "her" as pointers to the female protagonist is considerably less problematic than the corresponding cases for "he" and "they".

As depicted in Table 1, there are 199 instances in all of the feminine personal pronoun. 194 of these refer to HER, while only 5 do not. They are as follows:

1. "HIS wife would not be at **her** most charitable if HE came bringing malaria home to the family." (p. 8)
2. "THEY caught up with an old man walking in a sprightly way in THEIR direction, all by himself, wearing a clean bright shirt printed with a pair of palm trees fanning green over his chest. It might better be <u>a big colored woman's</u> shirt, but **she** didn't have it." (p. 15)
3. "<u>A massive back, presumably female, with a twist of gray hair on top</u>, stood with a ladle akimbo. A young man joined **her** and with his fingers stole something out of the pot and ate it." (p. 18)
4. "<u>HIS wife</u> had recommended that HE stay where HE was this extra day so that **she** could entertain some old, unmarried college friends without HIM underfoot." (p. 26)
5. "In Dickie Grogan's, as HE passed, <u>the well-known Josefina</u> at **her** organ was charging up and down with *Clair de Lune*." (pp. 26-27)

The conventions I have adopted here are as follows: as indicated earlier, capitalized pronouns refer to the protagonists; boldfaced pronouns refer to entities other than the protagonists; and underlined items identify the referents for the boldfaced pronouns.

Consider first instances #1 and #4. Both sentences involve HIS wife, who, though not in New Orleans at all, enters HIS mind twice in the story, once near the beginning (#1), and again at the very end (#4). In #1 there is grammatically no other option than to identify the referent of "her" as HIS wife. Anaphoric proximity is all that is needed to establish the referent. In #4 the principles of both anaphoric proximity and subject continuity again point to HIS wife as the referent. Of course it is grammatically possible for "she" to refer to HER rather than to HIS wife, but this interpretation can be ruled out on logical grounds: in the first place, we can assume that HIS wife is unacquainted with HER, so HIS wife would not be making any recommendations regarding HER, and secondly SHE in fact has HIM "underfoot" in the sense that THEY are indeed together.

Anaphoric proximity also identifies the referent in #5, where "her" tracks "the well-known Josefina", the organ player in Dickie Grogan's. Of course, we are not forced, grammatically, to rule out a reference to HER in this case, but again logic plays a vital role – it would be nonsensical to assume that SHE possesses an organ which is housed in Dickie Grogan's, and that this is the instrument which Josefina is playing.

In #2 the situation is a bit more complicated, since the sentence itself is quite unusual: "It **might** better <u>a big colored woman's</u> shirt, but **she** didn't have it". Grammatically **speaking**, the reference here could be either to (an imagined) "big colored **woman**" or to HER. Since the clause containing the pronoun makes a negative **claim**, it makes no difference, strictly speaking, who does not have the shirt in question. But logically, of course, the reference must be to the colored woman, since it makes no sense in the context of the story to speak about "a big colored woman's shirt" which SHE does not have. Also, the use of the conjunction "but" ties the two clauses together, linking "she" in the second clause with the colored woman in the first. Note, incidentally, that the reference here is still anaphoric, but this time it is not to the item which is subject of the preceding sentence, which is the shirt, but rather to a genitive modifier of the word "shirt". It is this, in part, which makes the sentence itself seem rather unusual.

The final instance of the use of the feminine pronoun for non-SHE is #3. This, again, is an unusual example. Grammatically speaking, the pronoun "her" could refer either to HER or to "a massive back, presumably female, with a twist of gray hair on top". That it refers to the latter is established in large part by the wider context describing THEIR entrance to Baba's Place:

> The barnlike interior was brightly lit and unpainted, looking not quite finished, with a partition dividing this room from what lay behind . . . Midway along the partition was a bar, in the form of a pass-through to the other room, with a varnished, second-hand fretwork overhang. THEY crossed the floor and sat, alone there, on wooden stools. An eruption of humorous signs, newspaper cutouts and cartoons, razor-blade cards, and personal messages of significance to the owner or his friends decorated the overhang, framing where Baba should have been but wasn't.
> Through there came a smell of garlic and cloves and red pepper, a blast of hot cloud escaped from a cauldron THEY could see now on a stove at the back of the other room. A massive back, presumably female, with a twist of gray hair on top, stood with a ladle akimbo. A young man joined **her** and with his fingers stole something out of the pot and ate it. At Baba's they were boiling shrimp.
> When he got ready to wait on THEM, Baba strolled out to the counter, young, black-headed, and in very good humor.
> "Coldest beer you've got. And food – What will you have?"
> "Nothing for me, thank you," SHE said. "I'm not sure I could eat, after all." (pp. 17-18)

We now have enough information to determine the referent of "her". The setting involves two rooms – the one THEY are seated in and the back room THEY are looking into. In the back room THEY see "a massive back", which THEY presume is female, standing near a cauldron on a stove. The young man "stole something out of a pot and ate it". The reader must now make the logical assumption that "cauldron" and "pot" refer to the same object. Once that link is made, it follows that the young man, the pot, and the "massive back" must all be in the same room. SHE is not in that room. Consequently "her" can only refer to the "massive back, presumably female, with a twist of gray hair on top" and not to HER. Welty is not making it easy for the reader here, but we see that she has planted enough clues to establish the appropriate referent.

Note that in this example (#3), as in #2, the use of the feminine pronoun is rather unusual. The direct antecedent for the pronoun is the word "back", which is neither male nor female. Here we have an instance of *pars pro toto*, the word "back" standing in for the whole person. Note further the progression in definiteness as THEY acquire more knowledge about the place THEY find THEMSELVES in. First, the back is "presumably female". Then the pronoun "her" establishes the back as belonging to a female. The presumption has become a certainty. A few lines later, SHE makes another inference: "SHE decided the woman back there must be Baba's mother". Shortly thereafter, the definitive step is taken – the person is stated to be Baba's mother:

> The original pair of little boys ran in once more, with the hyphenated bang. They got nickels this time, then were brushed away from the table like mosquitoes, and they rushed under the counter and on to the cauldron behind, clinging to **Baba's mother** there. (pp. 20-21)

We have now seen that there are four female characters who compete with HER for the use of the feminine pronouns. Significantly, two of them are not even "physically" present in the story. HIS wife (#1, #4) appears in HIS mind only, and a "big colored woman" (#2) is introduced only as a hypothetical owner of a "clean bright shirt printed with a pair of palm trees". Their presence is thus fleeting and insubstantial. As for Josefina, she does not put in an appearance until the very last paragraph of the story, after HE has deposited HER back at HER hotel. Furthermore, it is quite likely that HE did not even see Josefina, but simply heard her "charging up and down with *Clair de Lune*", "as HE passed". So the only character that (albeit briefly) physically occupies the same general space as SHE does is Baba's mother – who first appears simply as "a massive back, presumably female". Linguistically speaking, then, the only real challenge for Welty as regards the use of the feminine personal pronouns is how to distinguish HER from Baba's mother while THEY are in Baba's Place. And this she accomplishes by contextual clues.

As something of an aside, I think it may be instructive to look at another example of the type of misreading which can occur if the reader does not pay careful attention to Welty's text. We have already noted the erroneous interpretation of HIS upraised hand given by Binding (1994). Another case involves a misrepresentation of the person in the back room whom we have now decoded as Baba's mother. Carson (1992: 31) lets her imagination run away with her when she reads the text as "the massive black of indefinite sex". We have seen that the slow revelation of the sex of this person is a direct result of Welty's narrative technique, where we learn as THEY learn. The indefiniteness disappears as THEY learn more and reveal more to us. But Carson's reading of "back" as "black" cannot be attributed to any difficulty due to the Welty style. This is a misreading which, unfortunately, contributes significantly to Carson's feeling that Baba's Place seems "at first glance a surrealistic inferno" filled with "grotesque people" (Carson 1992: 31).

As a transition to the next section, which deals with the masculine pronouns, let us examine more carefully how Welty introduces Baba, along with his mother. The scene-setting starts with the information that Baba was not behind the bar when THEY entered. This is conveyed indirectly by the rather curious description of "the overhang, framing where Baba should have been but wasn't" (p. 18). If he was not behind the bar, where was he? We are led by Welty to draw the conclusion that he was in the back room with his mother. This is not stated directly. We are told that "a young man joined her and with his fingers stole something out of the pot and ate it." And then we are told that "Baba strolled out to the counter, young, black-headed and in very good humor". The use of the adjective "young" links these two passages and makes it likely that "the young man" is Baba himself. But, as in the case of Baba's mother, Welty forces us to make these inferences bit by bit, so that we struggle through the same recognition process that THEY go through as THEY gather information after entering Baba's place. We are not told directly who the two people in the back room are. Only by sifting the information meagerly provided in the larger context do we come to the conclusion that the "massive back" really is female, that it belongs to Baba's mother, and that the "young man" is presumably that mother's son, Baba.

Once this identification is made, we have an additional clue that the pronoun "her" in example #3 must refer to Baba's mother and not to HER: the young man cannot be in two places at once. At first he is stealing something out of a pot in one room, and then (as Baba) he strolls into the other room (note that he strolled "*out to the counter*") to wait on THEM. Thus movement is added to place as devices used by Welty to aid the reader in establishing the appropriate pronoun reference. In fact, movement and place are vital in the present instance in preparing us, quite unconsciously, for a significant switch in pronoun tracking. Consider once again the opening scene in Baba's Place which is described in the excerpt above. There are two feminine pronouns in this text: "her" ("a young man joined **her**") and "she" ("'Nothing for me, thank you,' SHE said"). The first pronoun ("her"), as we have just seen, tracks Baba's mother, while the second ("she") tracks HER. Consequently, without any clear textual indicators at all, the feminine pronoun has switched its reference from one female to another. What are the factors which help us make this switch?. The first is the fact that Baba has moved. He leaves the room his mother is in, and comes out to where THEY are sitting. Next, the fact that "he got ready to wait on THEM" prepares us for the referential switch, since SHE is included in the reference to THEM. Another factor involves simple logic.

Baba remarks: "Coldest beer you've got. And food – What will you have?". Baba is not likely to inform his mother that Baba's Place serves beer and food, and thereafter ask her what she would like to eat and drink. Lastly, since SHE is the main character and the only female who has done any speaking in the story so far, it is natural to assume that it is SHE who responds to Baba's question. As the narrative unfolds, we learn that Baba's mother remains as silent in the remainder of THEIR visit to Baba's Place as she does in this scene.

*5.3 "non-HE" (instances of **he/him/his/himself** which do not refer to HIM)*

There are many more male characters in the story than female, and they are much more active. Also, the masculine pronoun is used occasionally to refer to animals in the story. Consequently, the use of HE, HIM, HIS and HIMSELF presents more of a linguistic problem for Welty than is the case for the feminine pronouns.

As depicted in Table 1, there are, in all, 226 instances of the third person singular masculine personal pronoun. 177 (78.3%) of these refer to HIM, while 49 (21.7%) do not. The 49 instances are listed in Appendix 2. The entities which serve as referents in these sentences fall into two categories:

a) *Humans*: HE, a Negro shoeshine boy, a man sleeping in the back of a truck, a boy on a boat, a red-haired man, a priest, an old man with palm trees on his shirt, Baba, an old man with a newspaper, an old man with a colored pencil behind his ear, one or the other of three little boys, an old man with white hair like thatch, and members of a family of eight or nine people ("each ... with himself").

b) *Animals*: an alligator and a dog.

*5.3.1 The animals*

Before considering the human referents, which pose the greater potential problem in pronoun tracking, let us look at the pronouns used in connection with the two animals.

Consider first the alligator. This animal makes a brief but interesting appearance aboard the ferry that takes THEM across the Mississippi River:

6. "The boys had a surprise – <u>an alligator</u> on board. One of them pulled it by a chain around the deck, between the cars and trucks, like a toy – a hide that could walk. HE thought, Well they had to catch one sometime. It's Sunday afternoon. So they have **him** on board now, riding **him** across the Mississippi River ... 'Who want to rassle **him**? Who want to, eh?' two boys cried, looking up." (p. 11)

In this text (#6 corresponds to the number of the example in Appendix 2), the alligator is first introduced as a new "file" ("*an* alligator" rather than "*the* alligator") – to use Givón's metaphor –, then referred to once as "it", and next (three times) as "**him**". Though thus anthropomorphized, the alligator does not pose a problem for pronoun tracking. The reader easily links all three uses of "**him**" to the alligator, aided by logic, context, and the principle of topic continuity. In theory, each of the pronouns could refer to HIM, of course. But it would be quite illogical to conclude that the boys had HIM on board, are riding HIM and were asking, "Who want to rassle HIM?" Note, furthermore, that in between the use of "it" and "him" to refer to the alligator, Welty inserts "HE thought". So it is HE (rather than Welty, or the third voice) who applies the first two instances of the masculine pronoun to the alligator. Since HE is doing the thinking here, HE would have thought "So they have **me** on board now, riding **me** across the Mississippi River" – if that had been the reference intended.

Consider next the case of the dog:

20. "The dog lay sleeping on in front of the raging juke box, **his** ribs working fast as a concertina's." (p. 20)

Here we are dealing with a file which is already established and "open" ("The dog", not "A dog"). The fact that Welty assumes that this file is still open for the reader (that is, that we remember and have in mind the earlier reference to this dog) indicates that she expects a good deal of attention and alertness on the part of the reader here, since this dog was actually introduced several paragraphs earlier in the text – already somnolent ("The steady breathing THEY heard came from a big rough dog asleep in the corner", p. 18). Be that as it may, the use of "**his**" in #20 to refer to the sleeping dog follows the prescribed tracking conventions: we have an anaphoric reference to the subject of the main clause, so both anaphoric proximity and subject continuity play a decisive role here. The link to the subject is also grammatically ensured by the use of the absolute construction ("**his** ribs working fast as a concertina's"), where the absence of a finite verb dictates that the construction as a whole describes the subject of the main clause. Also the reference to the concertina movement of the ribs links the absolute construction semantically to the action described in the main clause ("sleeping").

*5.3.2 The humans*

The first few referents in our list of examples in Appendix 2 make only a fleeting appearance in the story: one sentence or short passage and these characters are gone. They are part of the passing scene, observed from the car as THEY drive south on THEIR adventure. This is true of examples #1, 2, and 3, where THEY first pass by "a small Negro" with "**his** pink-and-black hand" (#1), then "a man" (in a general sense) with "**his** shoes off" and "jolted about as **he** slept" (#2), then a "family of eight or nine people" who were "beating themselves with the wild palmettos ... like some game, each playing it with **himself**" (#3). The principle of anaphoric proximity applies in each case, while the reflexive pronoun in example #3 mandatorily links this pronoun to the common gender pronoun "each" functioning as subject of the absolute construction.

In example #7, a priest is also observed by THEM from THEIR car. Since the car is now parked rather than racing along on THEIR journey south, his appearance in the narrative is somewhat more prolonged than was the case for the topics in the first three examples. Nonetheless, the principles of anaphoric proximity and topic continuity ensure that the priest is wearing "**his** underwear", staring "as if **he** wondered what time it was", got "**his** robe off the line and **his** fish off the doorstep", and that Vespers was next, "for **him**" (#7). Theoretically, of course, the priest could be wearing HIS underwear, and HIS robe, etc., but such an interpretation would not only go against the standard tracking conventions, it would also be quite illogical.

By way of an aside, Welty has made a small, but significant, revision of the text here: where the 1955 text has "Vespers was next, for him" (p. 15), the *New Yorker* text (1952: 40) had simply "Vespers was next". The addition of "for him" in the later version ensures that the reader does not (momentarily) assume that THEY are about to attend an evening church service.

Anaphoric proximity and topic continuity also suffice in the interpretation of the pronouns in #4 about the boy on the ferry who "drew **his** initials in the dust of the [car] door", and in #5 where a red-haired man "tried to give away **his** truckload of shrimp". Logic concurs: there is no way the boy could know what HIS initials are (even the reader is not privy to this information), and HE has no truck and no shrimp to give away.

Next in the narrative comes a collection of old men:

- an old man with palm trees on his shirt (#8, 18)
- an old man with a newspaper (#9, 11)
- an old man with a colored pencil behind his ear (#10)
- an old man with white hair like thatch (#18, 21, 23, 25)

Like HIM and HER, these people are nameless. Welty keeps them apart for us by associating each with a different "object" (a shirt with palm trees on it, a newspaper, a colored pencil, and white hair like thatch).

In most of these examples, pronoun tracking can be adequately established by one or more of the conventions we have now learned to anticipate, particularly anaphoric proximity (#8, 9, 10, 11, 21), reflexivization (#8) and subject continuity (#8, 21, 25), and there is basically no real referential competition with HIM.

However, #18 requires considerable mental alertness on the part of the reader. Since two male personages, in addition to HIM, are involved in the scene depicted, pronoun tracking presents something of a challenge:

18. "What <u>the old fellow</u> wanted", said HE when HE came back at last, "was to have a friend of **his** apologize. Seems church is just out. Seems <u>the friend</u> made a remark coming in just now. **His** pals told **him** there was a lady present."
"I see you bought **him** a beer," SHE said.
"Well, <u>the old man</u> looked like **he** wanted *something*." (p. 20)

Note, first, that Welty disentangles HIM from the two other males by making use of movement: "said HE when HE *came back* at last". HE returns to HER and enters into a dialogue with HER. The result is that whenever either HE or SHE uses a masculine pronoun, the reference must be to someone other than HIM. It may also be the case that the poetic inversion, "said HE" (rather than the more prosaic "HE said") is instrumental in helping the reader identify the male speaker in the dialogue as HIM. But what about the other two males referred to in the dialogue? Here Welty adds to the general fuzziness of the setting by refusing to identify either of these two men directly. We are told only that one is an "old fellow" – but there are several such at Baba's –, and the other is "a friend of his". We have to back up three paragraphs to see who it is that HE is talking to. There we learn that "Before HE finished, one of the men who had come in beckoned from across the room. It was the old man in the palm-tree shirt" (p. 19). So the "old fellow" HE is addressing is the palm-tree man. But who is the one who should apologize? We do not learn his identity until we go forward three paragraphs – where we encounter #21, equating the apologizer with the "thatched-hair man" (p. 20):

21. "At the side of the room <u>a man with a cap on **his** white thatch</u> was trying **his** best to open a side screen door, but it was stuck fast. It was **he** who had come in with the remark considered ribald; now **he** was trying to get out the other way." (p. 20)

Note that in this text, anaphoric proximity and subject continuity ensure that all four instances of the third person singular pronoun in #21 – two instances of "his" and two of "he" – refer unambiguously to the thatched-hair man.

Having now identified the three male characters in this little drama (HE, the palm-tree man, and the thatched hair man), consider next the rather complicated play of the masculine pronouns in the exchange in #18. In addition to the first two occurrences of "he", which we have decoded as referring to HIM, there are two instances of "his", two instances of "him" and one further instance of "he". None of these pronouns refer to HIM. The first "his" refers to "the old fellow" (palm tree), while the second refers to "the friend" (thatched hair) who (ultimately) apologizes. So part of the reader confusion is due to this switch in pronoun tracking. This switch is the result of a change in subject (from "<u>the old fellow</u> wanted" to "<u>the friend</u> made"), allowing the same pronominal form ("his") to track first one subject then the next. A similar switch takes place in the case of the two instances of "him", though this switch is even harder to decipher. The first "him" ("His pals told him there was a lady present") must also refer to "the friend", because anaphoric proximity would lead us to equate the referent of "him" with the referent of "his" in "his pals". Since we have just established that "his" here refers to "the friend", so, too, does "him". The pronoun "him" in the next sentence ("I see you bought him a beer") ought logically also to refer to the apologizing friend – and this is no doubt how most readers (temporarily) interpret it. But in the sentence after this one ("Well, the old man looked like he wanted *something*"), HE makes the reference clear: the referent is the old man (palm tree) that received the beer. This identification is brought about not only by supplying the referent directly ("the old man"), but also by Welty's italicizing of the word "something" to make certain that the reader links this word to "a beer" in the preceding sentence. Note that Welty provides this clarification for the benefit of the reader, not for HER. SHE can easily see (and does see) who received the beer. Thus Welty continues to keep us, the readers, off balance, but ultimately supplies just enough information to steady our perceptions. Nonetheless, given scenes like this, one can understand why some readers find the story "opaque" and "baffling", as Pingatore (1996: 336) remarks.

Another instance of a switch in pronoun tracking is found in #19, where groups of three boys are playing slot machines:

19. "There were <u>three little boys</u> to each slot machine. The local custom appeared to be that <u>one</u> pulled the lever for the friend **he** was holding up to put the nickel in, while <u>the third</u> covered the pictures with the flat of **his** hand as they fell into place, so as to surprise them all if anything happened." (p. 20)

Let us identify the three boys in each group as follows: 1) the lever puller, 2) the nickel dropper, 3) the picture coverer. Then "he" refers to the lever puller, while "his" refers to the picture coverer. At first glance, it might appear that anaphoric proximity would dictate that "he" should refer to "the friend" (who is the nickel dropper), since "he" is preceded directly by "the friend", but a closer examination of the syntactic structure reveals that this cannot be the case. "The friend" is not the anaphoric antecedent of "he", but the object of "holding (up)", as can be seen by supplying the missing relative pronoun: "for the friend <u>whom</u> he was holding up". Since "he" is not holding himself up, "he" and "the friend" cannot be co-referential. Instead "he", being the subject of the relative clause, refers to the subject of the main clause, "one" (the lever puller) – so it is the principle of subject continuity which applies here to give us the correct tracking.

Before leaving these three boys, it should be noted that one of them is singled out earlier in the story: "One child had a live lizard on **his** shirt, clinging like a breast pin – like lapis lazuli" (#15). Here there is no problem linking "his" to the child and not to HIM, since "his shirt" clearly means "his own shirt".

In example #23 we find an instance where pronoun tracking temporarily breaks down for the main characters THEMSELVES:

23. "'I wonder what **he** called me,' SHE whispered in HIS ear.
   'Who?'
   'The one who apologized to you.'" (p. 21)

At the time of this interchange, THEY are still in Baba's, but considerable time has elapsed since HE told HER about the old man in the palm-tree shirt asking his friend to apologize to HIM (and thus indirectly to HER) for inadvertently having made some remark which might be considered rude in the presence of a lady (HER) (see #18). THEY are now dancing and SHE is mulling over that earlier conversation. Because of the considerable time gap, HE is understandably uncertain about the referential link when SHE whispers, "I wonder what **he** called me". Using Givón's "file" metaphor, we can conclude that for HIM the "file" associated with "the one who apologized" is no longer open, or no longer uniquely accessible. SHE has to re-open it with the phrase "The one who apologized to you".

The remaining instances of "he", "him", and "his" all involve Baba (#12, 13, 14, 16, 17, 22, 24). Since Baba is not simply a passing bit player in the story, there is potential linguistic trouble brewing in keeping the two male characters – Baba and HIM – apart. But pronoun tracking is quite smooth in most of these instances, due to the tracking conventions and to the lexical context. Thus anaphoric proximity ensures that "**his** friends" refers to "the owner" (Baba) in #12, and that "**his** fingers" belong to the "young man" (also Baba) in the back room where shrimp is being boiled (#13) and to "Baba himself" as he sings at the counter (#24). Similarly, the cataphorically referring "**he**" who "got ready to wait on THEM" is readily identified as Baba (#14), as is the "**him**" whom SHE greeted with the request, "Could I have some water?" (#16). In #17, "**He**" is also quite easily identified as Baba – for at least three reasons. In the first place, Baba is the subject of the immediately preceding sentence, so sentence continuity holds. Secondly, "**He**" is engaged in serving a bottle of beer and a sandwich, which is a natural activity for Baba in these circumstances, and very unlikely for HIM. Thirdly, Welty has cannily ensured that HE is out of the way by removing HIM from the scene in the preceding paragraph. ("SHE lifted HER head to watch HIM leave HER" in response to a beckoning signal from the old man in the palm-tree shirt, p. 19).

Probably the most challenging tracking problem in this collection involves the use of "**his**" in #22: "Behind **his** head there was a sign lettered in orange crayon: 'Shrimp Dance Sun. PM.'" (p. 21). But upon reflection it can be determined that it is Baba's head and not HIS head that is involved here. The evidence for this involves first of all the convention of subject continuity: Baba is the subject of the preceding clause. Further evidence comes from a mental construction of the scene itself. At the point where Baba lifts the counter flap and comes out into the room, HE has returned to his seat at the counter and "was eating another sandwich" (p. 21). Thus HE and Baba are facing in opposite directions. Consider now the location of the "Shrimp Dance" sign in relation to the counter. As we saw earlier, Welty provides us with the following setting when THEY first enter Baba's (pp. 17-18):

> The barnlike interior was brightly lit and unpainted, looking not quite finished, with a partition dividing this room from what lay behind. Midway along the partition was a bar, in the form of a pass-through to the other room, with a varnished, second-hand fretwork overhang. THEY crossed the floor and sat, alone there, on wooden stools. An eruption of humorous signs, newspaper cutouts and cartoons, razor-blade cards, and personal messages of significance to the owner or his friends decorated the overhang, framing where Baba should have been but wasn't.

If we draw the logical inference that the "Shrimp Dance" sign is part of the hodge-podge of written messages on the overhang, it follows that HE, sitting at the counter, is facing the "Shrimp Dance" sign, while Baba, facing the other direction, has the "Shrimp Dance" sign behind him. So "his" in #22 refers to Baba.

*5.4 "non-THEY" (instances of **they/them/their(s)/themselves** which do not refer to THEM)*

Unlike the third person singular personal pronouns, English third person plural pronouns are not marked for gender. Consequently, they have a much wider range of application – referring to groups of any nature, be they human, animal, inanimate entities, or abstractions. It is not surprising, therefore, to find more instances of potential conflict in the use of the plural personal pronouns than is the case for either of the singular pronouns.

A glance at Table 1 shows that there are 171 instances in all of the third person plural personal pronoun. Though this *total* is less than that for either the feminine pronoun (199 in all) or for the masculine pronoun (226 in all), the number

– and percentage – of instances referring to non-THEY (62/171 = 36.3%) is far larger than for non-SHE (5/199 = 2.5%) and considerably larger than for non-HE (49/226 = 21.7%). The 62 instances of non-THEY are listed in Appendix 3. The referents in these non-THEY instances can be grouped into three major categories:

a  Plural humans: The people in Galatoire's, girls on porches, eight or nine people on foot, the passengers on the ferry, the boys with the alligator, men at the landing, the people boiling shrimp in Baba's, the little boys in Baba's, the male guests in Baba's, the cardplayers, the girls who came to Baba's for the dance, a Negro couple.
b  Plural animals, insects: Mosquitoes and gnats, crayfish and other shell creatures, shrimp, cows.
c  Plural inanimate objects: Women's clothes, names of dead people in the churchyard, houses, pictures in the slot machines, lakes of dust, earrings.

Before we look at individual instances of these plural pronouns, it is, I believe, quite significant that all the referents are concrete visible objects. There appear to be no instances of these pronouns referring to abstractions such as ideas, thoughts, pains, grievances, rules, or traditions. Instead Welty uses these pronouns to refer to things which can be perceived and touched. These things are on the "outside", not the "inside". They are part of the landscape THEY are travelling through.

*5.4.1 Plural inanimate objects*

In Welty's text, I find six inanimate objects referred to by means of the plural pronoun:

1. "It was the wrong hat for HER, thought this Eastern businessman who had no interest whatever in women's clothes and no eye for **them**." (p. 3)
19. "HE passed between the tombs slowly but in the manner of a feat. Names took **their** places on the walls slowly at a level with the eye, names as near as the eyes of a person stopping in conversation, and as far away in origin, and in all **their** music and dead longing, as Spain." (p. 14)
20. "The houses on **their** shaggy posts, patchily built, some with plank runways instead of steps, were flimsy and alike, and not much bigger than the boats tied up at the landing." (p. 20)
27. "There were three little boys to each slot machine. The local custom appeared to be that one pulled the lever for the friend he was holding up to put the nickel in, while the third covered the pictures with the flat of his hand as **they** fell into place, so as to surprise them all if anything happened." (p. 20)

35. "In peopleless open places there were <u>lakes of dust</u>, smudge fires burning at **their** hearts. Cows stood in untended rings around **them**, motionless in the heat, in the night – their horns standing up sharp against that glow." (p. 24)
36. "<u>The earrings</u> SHE wore twinkled with **their** rushing motion in an almost regular beat. **They** might have spoken like tongues". (p. 25)

The first example also represents the first instance of "**them**" in the story. Until this point, the only other plural personal pronoun used is THEY – the first word of the story itself. Anaphoric proximity points to "women's clothes" rather than to THEM as the appropriate referent for "them" in #1. This interpretation is also grammatically motivated, since "no eye for them" is part of a compound direct object in which the phrase in question is conjoined with "no interest whatever in women's clothes". This establishes a potential equivalence between "clothes" and "them", each of which functions as part of a modifying prepositional group in the respective conjoint ("in women's clothes" and "for them"). The referential link between "them" and "clothes" is also motivated by logic, since it would be curious indeed to state that HE had no eye for THEM – it is not clear what such a statement could mean.

In example #19, the two instances of "**their**" refer to the names engraved on the tombstones (which appear as "walls" to the passengers in the car). This interpretation follows from the basic convention of topic continuity (the word, "names", appears first as the subject of the relevant sentence and is then repeated in an appositional construction) and it is supported by common logic (THEY are not on the walls). Likewise "**their**" in example #20 clearly refers, by anaphoric proximity, to "houses" and not to THEM.

Example #27 is more interesting, from a tracking point of view. We have already noted that the male pronouns "he" and "his" track two different entities in this example (neither of which is HIM). As if this were not challenge enough for the reader, Welty has constructed the passage in such a way that the pronouns "**they**" and "**them**" also track two different entities – neither of which is THEM. The first pronoun ("**they**") clearly refers to the inanimate "pictures" in the slot machine, while the second ("them") refers to the very animate three little boys. The reader deciphers these references by the use of simple logic: the phrase "as **they** fell into place" rules out a reference to both THEM and the boys; it is the pictures on the revolving wheels in the slot machine that fall into place. In the second instance, the reference clearly switches from the inanimate pictures to animate beings, since pictures cannot be surprised. But who might be surprised? In theory, the reference could be to any group of animate beings. To ensure that the reader makes the appropriate referential link, Welty supplies us with a very useful linguistic clue, namely the word "all": "so as to surprise *them all* if anything happened". This rules THEM out, since the text would then have been "so as to surprise THEM *both* if anything happened". The most logical interpretation is thus that "them all" refers to the "three little boys" (admittedly it could refer to all the people in Baba's, including THEM, but there is nothing in the context to suggest that the people in Baba's are paying any attention whatever to the boys at the slot machines). Note how helpful it is of Welty to post three rather than two little boys at each of the slot machines. Had there been only two boys, she would have had to write "them both", thereby making it unclear whether surprise would have been registered by the boys or by THEM.

The next example in this group (#35) again contains a referential switch. Here we find three instances of the plural form: **"their"**, **"them"**, and again **"their"**. We can establish that the first two pronouns refer to the inanimate "lakes of dust", while the third refers to the animate cows. None of the three pronouns refer to THEM. To see that this is true, let us look more closely at the text here. Grammatically speaking, the absolute construction ("smudge fires burning in their hearts") can only link up with "lakes of dust". These are real smudge fires – not metaphorical ones inside human breasts – as is made further evident by the fact that the horns of the cows stand out sharply "against that glow". So the referent of the first **"their"** is "lakes of dust". Similarly, the referent of the following **"them"** ("Cows stood in untended rings around them") must be "lakes of dust". Theoretically speaking, of course, "them" could refer to THEM (so that cows stood in untended rings around THEM), but the context makes this reading impossible. THEY are in a fast-moving car, driving past the lakes of dust and past the cows. So there is no way that the cows, "motionless in the heat", could stand around THEM. The final "their" switches from tracking the fires to tracking the cows. The reference is clear since there is again an absolute construction ("their horns standing up sharp against that glow") referring to the subject of the sentence ("cows"). Logic, too, plays a role, of course: cows have horns, while THEY and lakes of dust do not.

The final example in this set (#36) is also quite interesting. There is ambiguous potential in the interpretation of "their" and "they" – both of which could, in theory, refer either to the earrings or to THEM. Let us consider the larger context (p. 25):

> SHE appeared to be sound asleep, lying back flat as a child, with HER hat in HER lap. HE drove on with HER profile beside HIS, behind HIS, for HE bent forward to drive faster. The earrings SHE wore twinkled with **their** rushing motion in an almost regular beat. **They** might have spoken like tongues. HE looked straight before HIM and drove on, at a speed that, for the rented, overheated, not at all new Ford car, was demoniac.

The car is moving fast, and consequently so is everything in it. This includes both THEM and the earrings. Therefore, "their rushing motion" could refer to the motion of the earrings or, more broadly, to THEM, rushing through the night in the car. Curiously, the reference here is strongly dependent upon the amount of motion things inside the fast-moving car could be seen to have by anyone in the car itself. In a hermetically sealed car (top up, windows closed), on a smooth road, the earrings would have no visible motion at all, in which case the reference would most likely be to THEM rather than to the earrings. But this is not a hermetically sealed car; it is a convertible with the windows rolled down. The text provides ample evidence that the windows are wide open – because of the intense heat. Not only are THEY nearly eaten alive by the mosquitoes and gnats flying in and out of the car, but we also find textual references to movement of air in the car itself. Here are two examples: "By rushing through the heat at high speed, THEY brought THEMSELVES the effect of fans turned onto THEIR cheeks" (p. 7), and "HE glanced down at the map flapping between THEM" (p. 12). So the earrings are probably in motion. Standard tracking conventions then suggest that "earrings" is the intended referent for both "their" (anaphoric proximity) and "they" (subject continuity). But it is nonetheless also logically possible to view THEM as the referent, since the fast moving car would allow us to interpret "their rushing motion" as "THEIR rushing motion". A similar potential ambiguity exists in the interpretation of the second pronoun. On one reading, the moving, twinkling earrings "might have spoken like tongues". On the other reading, THEY "might have spoken like tongues". In the first instance, the twinkling of the earrings "in an almost regular beat" links motion to sound and hence points towards the "earrings" as referent. On the other hand, there could be a reference to what might have taken place between THEM (but didn't): THEY might have been more communicative during THEIR afternoon together. THEIR communication with one another might even be compared to "speaking in tongues" – that is, speaking in some unknown, and hence incomprehensible, "language" – an indirect reference to how little communication actually did take place between THEM. Since both interpretations are possible and contextually appropriate, Welty may have intended us to contemplate both readings.

*5.4.2 Plural animals and insects*

In addition to an example which we have already examined (#35, where a plural pronoun tracks some cows), the following examples illustrate the use of the plural pronouns to track animals and insects:

7. "There were thousands, millions of <u>mosquitoes and gnats</u> – a universe of **them**, and on the increase." (p. 8)
9. "More and more crayfish and other shell creatures littered THEIR path, scuttling or dragging. <u>These little samples, little jokes of creation,</u> persist-

ed and sometimes perished, the more of **them** the deeper down the road went." (p. 8)

12. "One red-haired man in a burst of wildness even tried to give away his truckload of shrimp to a man on the other side of the boat – nearly all the trucks were full of shrimp – causing taunts and then protests of 'They good! **They** good!' from the giver." (p. 9)

31. "He was counting over the platters the old woman now set out on the counter, each heaped with shrimp in **their** shells boiled to iridescence, like mounds of honeysuckle flowers." (p. 22)

33. "Going back, the ride was wordless, quiet except for the motor and the insects driving **themselves** against the car." (p. 23)

In each of these instances the reader easily establishes the referential link between the plural pronouns and the insects and shelled creatures. In #7, "a universe of **them**" can only refer to "mosquitoes and gnats". The use of "universe", meaning "countless number", plays the same role as "all" in e.g. "them all" (#27) in case there was any doubt about the reference. Similarly, in #33 the reference can only be to "the insects", since the use of the reflexive pronoun, "**themselves**" (as opposed to "them"), makes it grammatically impossible for the pronoun to refer to anything else.

In #9, we find another instance of a switch in pronoun tracking. The first plural pronoun ("their") refers to THEM, while the second one ("them") can only refer to the crayfish and other shell creatures ("these little jokes of creation"). The first referent is established by simple logic: it is more logical to conclude that the shell creatures are littering THEIR path, than that these creatures are littering their own path. In the case of the second pronoun, we again find an absolute construction ("the more of **them** the deeper down the road went") which can only refer to the subject of the sentence ("These little samples . . ."). Likewise, "**their**" in #31 can only refer to the shrimp "in **their** shells boiled to iridescence". This interpretation is dictated by anaphoric proximity and simple logic. That the reference is also to shrimp in #12 ("**They** good! **They** good!") is equally evident. Although it is grammatically possible to interpret the red-haired man's "**They** good!" as a reference to THEM, this would be illogical, since a) the context clearly refers to shrimp, and b) there has been no interaction at all between THEM and the red-haired man, so there is no way he could infer that THEY were good.

### 5.4.3 Plural humans

The rest of the instances of the plural third person pronouns involve the tracking of human referents. Consequently, the potential for conflict between these referents and THEM is heightened; but we shall see that Welty generally avoids referential ambiguity and conflict by employing one or more of the devices we have already encountered – and occasionally adding a few of her own. We begin with instances where grammar dictates that there can be no doubt about what referent the pronoun is tracking – namely, those instances involving reflexive pronouns.

*5.4.3.1 The use of reflexive pronouns*

As we have previously noted, the use of reflexive pronouns typically imposes a grammatical obligation on the pronoun to refer to something identified inside the sentence itself. The reflexive pronoun often functions as an object, and the co-referent as the subject, as in the following examples:

6. "As time passed and the distance from New Orleans grew, <u>girls ever darker and younger</u> were disposing **themselves** over the porches and the porch steps" (p. 7)
8. "<u>A family of eight or nine people</u> on foot strung along the road in the same direction the car was going, beating **themselves** with the wild palmettos." (p. 8)

Grammar dictates that the reflexive pronoun "**themselves**" must be coreferential with "girls ever darker and younger" in #6, and with "a family of eight or nine people" in #8. A reference to THEM is out of the question in these examples.

While the reflexive pronoun typically functions as the direct object, this is not necessarily the case. Consider the following example:

28. "<u>The card players</u> broke into shouts of derision, then joy, then tired derision among **themselves**; **they** might have been here all afternoon – **they** were the only ones not cleaned up and shaved." (p. 20)

Here "themselves" is part of a prepositional group ("among **themselves**"). Nonetheless, the grammatical constraints are the same as for the direct object: this reflexive pronoun can only refer to the subject of the sentence, namely "the card players". Note, additionally, that the two instances of "**they**" in this example also refer to "the card players" – not to THEM. In the first place, this interpretation accords with the principle of subject continuity. In the second place, logic rules out any reference to THEM, since THEY have not been at Baba's "all afternoon", and SHE is not likely to need a shave.

The pronoun "themselves" appears in yet another instance, but in this case the pronoun does not have a basic grammatical function in the clause (such as direct object), but rather is used for emphasis:

17. "The young boys, looking taller, had taken out colored combs and were combing **their** wet hair back in solemn pompadour above **their** radiant foreheads. **They** had been bathing in the river **themselves** not long before." (p. 12)

The second sentence in this example could be paraphrased "**They themselves** had been bathing in the river not long before" – hence the emphatic rather than the reflexive reading. As Givón remarks (1993 vol. II: 89), the difference between the reflexive and the emphatic use of e.g. "themselves" is that while "the same referent is mentioned twice in the same clause" in both instances, "the same referent participates in the clause in *two different roles*" when used reflexively, but in the same role when used emphatically. Grammatically speaking, of course, there is nothing to prevent the reader from interpreting both pronouns ("they" and "themselves") in #17 as referring to THEM. But given the context, this is not a logical interpretation. We know that THEY have not been bathing in the river at all. Consequently, the reference must be to the "young boys" – an instance of subject continuity. Similarly, the two instances of "their" in #17 must refer to the "young boys" as well. This interpretation adheres to the principle of anaphoric proximity. It is also supported by logic: THEY do not have wet hair, and even if THEY did, it would be contextually inappropriate to assume the boys were combing THEIR hair.

*5.4.3.2 Subject continuity*

As we have seen in our discussion of references to non-HER and non-HIM, subject continuity plays an important role in pronoun tracking. Here are some clear cases where the plural personal pronouns track subjects referring to non-THEM.

16. "The boys had a surprise – an alligator on board. One of **them** pulled it by a chain around the deck, between the cars and trucks, like a toy – a hide that could walk. HE thought, Well **they** had to catch one sometime. It's Sunday afternoon. So **they** have him on board now, riding him across the Mississippi River" (p. 11)

Here the convention of subject continuity renders it most likely that all three plural pronouns refer to "the boys" and not to THEM. Also the fact that these pronouns are all linked to actions involving the alligator, which the boys have captured, ensures this interpretation, as does the fact that HE is thinking about **them**. Had HE been thinking about THEM, the text would have read in part: "HE thought, Well **WE** had to catch one sometime."

24. "<u>Two little boys</u>, almost alike, almost the same size, and just cleaned up, dived into the room with a double bang of the screen door, and circled around the card game. **They** ran **their** hands into the men's pockets. ... **They** circled around and shrieked at the dog." (p. 19)
29. "<u>The original pair of little boys</u> ran in once more, with the hyphenated bang. **They** got nickels this time, then were brushed away from the table like mosquitoes, and **they** rushed under the counter and on to the cauldron behind, clinging to Baba's mother there." (pp. 20-21)

In both these examples, subject continuity leads the reader to link all instances of "they" to the "little boys". Simple logic also supports this interpretation. It would be quite out of character for THEM to be putting their hands into men's pockets, to be circling around and shrieking at the dog, to be getting nickels from the men in order to play the slot machines, and to be rushing under the counter and clinging to Baba's mother. Having thus linked all subject pronouns to **them**, it follows by the principle of anaphoric proximity that "their hands" also refers to **them** in #24. A switch in pronoun tracking at this point would lead to the illogical reading: "**They** ran THEIR hands into the men's pockets".

25. "Bringing in a strong odor of geranium talcum, <u>some men</u> had come in now – all in bright shirts. **They** drew near the counter, or stood and watched the game." (p. 19)

Once again, subject continuity makes "some men" the most likely referent for "They", and again simple logic concurs: THEY are already sitting at the counter, so it would not make sense for THEM to "draw near the counter".

32. "<u>The first arrivals of the girls</u> were coming up the steps under the porch light – all flowered fronts, **their** black pompadours giving out breathlike feelers from sheer abundance. Where **they**'d resprinkled it since church, the talcum shone like mica on **their** downy arms. Smelling solidly of geranium, **they** filed across the porch with short steps and fingers joined, just timed to turn **their** smiles loose inside the room. HE held the door open for **them**." (p. 23)

In this text – where we see HIM interacting, albeit briefly, with other people – there are six instances of the third person plural personal pronoun. Subject continuity links the two instances of "they" to "the girls" (more specifically, to "the first arrivals of the girls"), who are coming to Baba's for the evening dance. Once this link is made, topic continuity generally, and anaphoric proximity specifically, allow us also to connect the three instances of "their" to "the girls". The only tracking problem that remains, then, is identifying the referent for the final pronoun, "them" ("HE held the door open for them"). HE could, in theory, be holding the door open for the girls, or for THEM. Topic continuity suggests that the former is the appropriate interpretation. The larger context and logic support this reading. The sentence before the excerpt in #32 places THEM on the outside porch at Baba's: "Bathed in sweat, and feeling the false coolness that brings, THEY stood finally on the porch in the lapping night air for a moment before leaving" (p. 23). So the most natural conclusion is that HE is holding the door open for the girls, so that they can enter Baba's. Of course, one might argue that HE is holding the door open for THEM, so THEY could reenter Baba's after cooling off. But the sentence after "HE held the door open for them" is: "'Ready to go?' HE asked HER". So THEY do not go back in, but head for the car instead.

*5.4.3.3 Anaphoric proximity*

We have seen on numerous occasions that anaphoric proximity plays a major role in pronoun tracking, often in conjunction with other conventions. In the next four examples, anaphoric proximity plays the primary role.

4. "It was a serious, now-watch-out-everybody face, which orphaned HER entirely in the company of these Southerners. HE guessed HER age, as HE could not guess **theirs**: thirty-two" (p. 4)

It is obvious that "**theirs**" refers to "these Southerners" and not to THEM. In the first place, this interpretation links the plural pronoun to the most recently expressed plural entity, thus continuing the contrast between HER and "these Southerners". In the second place it would be quite illogical to be told that HE could not guess THEIR ages: we have just been told that he has guessed HER age, and he would presumably know HIS own.

11. "The young boys leaned on each other thinking of what next, rolling **their** eyes absently." (p. 9)

In this example anaphoric proximity links "their eyes" with "the young boys". A reading where the interpretation was "THEIR eyes" would be both macabre and textually unwarranted.

34. "Once the car lights picked out two people – <u>a Negro couple</u>, sitting on two facing chairs in the yard outside **their** lonely cabin" (p. 24)

Anaphoric proximity ensures that "their" refers to the Negro couple and not to THEM. Logic concurs: since THEY are strangers to the place and to each other, it would be nonsensical to assume that THEY held joint ownership of a cabin in Louisiana.

The last example in this section involves a double switch in pronoun tracking – first from THEM to "men in twos and threes", and then back to THEM:

21. "THEY made THEIR way on foot toward the water, where at an idle-looking landing <u>men in twos and threes</u> stood with **their** backs to THEM." (p. 16)

The sentence begins with THEIR walking down to the water after having parked the car outside Baba's Place. Thus the first two plural pronouns trace THEM. But then "men in twos and threes" are introduced, and the convention of anaphoric proximity – together with the fact that "their backs" has to mean "their *own* backs" – ensures that the third pronoun ("**their**") refers to these men. The plural pronoun thus switches from tracking THEM to tracking **them**. And since one cannot stand with one's back to oneself, it follows that the final pronoun switches back to THEM.

*5.4.3.4 The role of context and simple logic*

As we have already witnessed on numerous occasions, the grammatical conventions which aid in pronoun tracking are often supplemented by information from the wider context, combined with simple logic. Here are four examples where context and logic play a major role.

18. "Both respectable and merciful, **their** hides, SHE thought, forcing HERSELF to dwell on <u>the alligator</u> as SHE looked back." (p. 12)

Here it is clear from the larger context that the alligator is still the object being referred to. The sentence preceding the text in #18 reads as follows: "The cars and trucks, then the foot passengers and the alligator, waddling like a child to school, all disembarked and wound up the weed-sprung levee" (p. 12). The alligator has, in fact, been a topic of interest for nearly two pages at this point, so the alligator "file" is definitely "open" (but is now about to "close", as THEY leave the boat and the alligator behind). Note, furthermore, the cataphoric reference to "the alligator" in #18 itself. Admittedly, it seems at first curious to find the plural construction, "their hides", when there is only one alligator present, but SHE is generalizing from the single creature to the class as a whole. Logic, as well as context, plays a role here: had SHE been thinking not of alligator hides, but of THEIR hides, SHE would have said: "Both respectable and merciful, **our** hides".

23. "At Baba's **they** were boiling shrimp." (p. 18)

Logic dictates that "they" refers to some unspecified plural agent, since 1) at this juncture, THEY have just entered Baba's and consequently could not be in the process of boiling shrimp, and 2) since THEY do not work at Baba's, THEY would not be boiling shrimp anyway.

26. "SHE lifted HER head to watch HIM leave HER, and was looked at, from all over the room. As a minute passed, no cards were laid down. In a far-off way, like accepting the light from Arcturus, SHE accepted it that SHE was more beautiful or perhaps more fragile than the women **they** saw every day of **their** lives. It was just this thought coming into a woman's face, and at this hour, that seemed familiar to **them**." (p. 19)

This is an interesting case. Though no referent is given directly for "they", "their", and "them", we infer that the reference is to the people in the room (at Baba's) – most of whom are male. This referent is lurking as the missing agent in the first passive construction ("[SHE] was looked at, from all over the room"), and, in a more restricted sense, in the second passive construction as well ("no cards were laid down"). The corresponding active clause would be "*They* looked at her from all over the room" and "*None of the card players* laid any cards down". So the referent in all three cases is non-THEY.

30. "SHE said rapidly, as THEY began moving together too well, 'One of those clippings was an account of a shooting right here. I guess **they**'re proud of it.'" (p. 21)

Here we find two instances of "they". Logic informs us that the first refers to THEM, since the phrase, "began moving together too well", can only be interpreted as a comment on how well THEY are dancing – THEIR dancing being the topic of the three paragraphs preceding the text in #30. The second instance of "they" (in "they're proud of it") can only refer to people other than THEM. This is the only grammatically possible interpretation. Since SHE is speaking, SHE would have had to say, "I guess WE're proud of it" – were SHE to make such a curious pronouncement at all.

*5.4.3.5 The addition of "both" and "two" vs. "all"*

Besides the standard conventions employed in pronoun tracking, Welty makes use of several more specific linguistic devices to help the reader disambiguate plural pronoun reference. One of these devices is the addition of "both" or "two" when she intends the referent to be THEM rather than **them**:

- "THEY were strangers to each other, *both* fairly well strangers to the place, now seated side by side at luncheon – a party combined in a free-and-easy way when the friends HE and SHE were with recognized each other across Galatoire's." (p. 3)
- "What THEY amounted to was *two* Northerners keeping each other company." (p. 4)
- "The blades of fan shadows came down over THEIR *two* heads, as HE saw inadvertently in the mirror, with HIMSELF smiling at HER now like a villain." (p. 5)

In this way, an unambiguous duality is established, thereby removing any ambiguity or vagueness which could otherwise be associated with some of the instances of the third person plural pronouns.

In the same way that Welty employs "both" and "two" in cases where she wishes to ensure that the plural pronoun points toward THEM, she sometimes uses "all" in cases where she wishes that pronoun to point away from THEM. This allows her, at times, to make a distinction between "THEM both" and "**them** all". Logically speaking, it is quite curious that she can do this at all. One might imagine that a word like "they" would automatically include all persons present. How could the addition of "all" make it any more inclusive? And how could HE and SHE possibly be excluded from a phrase such as "they all"? We have already seen one example of how Welty manages to achieve this:

27. "There were <u>three little boys</u> to each slot machine. The local custom appeared to be that one pulled the lever for the friend he was holding up to put the nickel in, while the third covered the pictures with the flat of his hand as they fell into place, so as to surprise **them** <u>all</u> if anything happened." (p. 20)

As we saw earlier, the most appropriate interpretation of the phrase "them all" is to see it as referring to the three little boys, thereby excluding everyone else in the room, including THEM. Note that had Welty not included the word "all" here, the reader might be led to assume that it would be THEM who would be surprised if the pictures in the slot machine "fell into place".

Here is another instance:

10. "'<u>The passengers</u> walking and jostling about there appeared oddly amateurish, too – amateur travelers. **They** were having such a good time. **They all** knew each other. Beer was being passed around in cans, bets were being loudly settled and new bets made, about local and special subjects on which **they** <u>all</u> doted." (p. 9)

In this case, the use of "all", twice, irrevocably links "**they** all" to "the passengers" on the ferry. But the following question now arises: since THEY, too, are passengers on the boat, does "they all" include THEM? The answer is "no". But it takes a bit of detective work to establish this – though Welty plants enough clues to allow the reader to work out the reference. Consider first the logic involved. If "they all" included THEM, then it would follow that THEY knew each other and that THEY doted on "local and special subjects". Both inferences would be quite out of place for people who are "strangers to each other" (p. 3) and to the territory. Furthermore, the location of the protagonists on the ferry at the time relating to #10 precludes such an interpretation. HE has just driven the car onto the ferry and is still in the car, while SHE has "opened the door and stepped out" and then climbed the stairs to the "tiny bridge beneath the captain's window" (p. 9). It is from this vantage point that SHE, looking down, sees below her "the passengers walking and jostling about <u>there</u>". Consequently, neither HE nor SHE can be included in this reference to the passengers.

The same inference is relevant to the interpretation of the remaining instance of "they" in example #10: "**They** were having such a good time". The most natural and logical interpretation of the text is that here, too, "they" refers to the (other) passengers, and excludes THEM. This interpretation is in line with the principle of subject continuity: The subject of the first sentence in #10 is "the passengers". All three instances of subsequent "they" continue the reference to this subject. Note, nonetheless, a subtle achievement of Welty's here. As the reader mentally works through the intricacies of pronoun tracking in this passage, it is likely that the possibility is entertained, albeit briefly, that THEY are having a good time. When the correct referential links are ultimately grasped, the reader then rejects this interpretation. It is not that Welty is telling us that THEY are <u>not</u> having a good time; she makes no claim at all here about how THEY are doing. But she cleverly succeeds in getting the reader to consider this very question.

Turning now to another example, we find a similar use of "all" – this time in conjunction with the word, "others" – in the following instance:

5. "'I have a car here, just down the street,' HE said to HER as the luncheon party was rising to leave, <u>all the others</u> wanting to get back to **their** houses and sleep." (p. 5)

At this point in the narrative, the luncheon at Galatoire's is breaking up, and we get the first separation of THEM from other human participants in the story: HE and HER vs. "all the others". Of course, the reader must still establish the referent of "their", but this poses no problem. Anaphoric proximity makes it most natural for "**their**" to refer "all the others". At the same time it would be quite illogical for these other guests to head for THEIR houses and sleep. In the first place, people normally go to their own houses to sleep, and in the second place, THEY presumably do not own houses (in New Orleans), since THEY are only visiting.

It is not the case, however, that the use of "all" in conjunction with the plural personal pronoun necessarily always excludes THEM. The exact interpretation depends on the situation. Consider, for example, the following instance:

14. "HER shoulders dropping, HER hair flying, HER skirt buffeted by the sudden strong wind, SHE stood there, thinking **they** <u>all</u> must see that with HER entire self all SHE did was wait." (p. 10)

Here "they all" obviously excludes HER (since SHE is looking down from the ferry's bridge at the other passengers), but it may or may not exclude HIM. At this point in the narrative, HE has also removed HIMSELF from the car and has joined the other passengers on the deck below HER, so it is quite possible that HE is included in the reference of "they all". Welty leaves the question open.

In the following example, on the other hand, it appears that the phrase "them all" excludes neither HIM nor HER:

3. "It was a bold and full light, shot up under the brim of that hat, as close to **them** <u>all</u> as the flowers in the center of the table" (p. 4)

This sentence appears at the beginning of the story, when HE and SHE are seated with friends at Galatoire's. It is logical therefore to conclude that the referent of "them all" includes everyone at the table, including HIM and HER. This being the case, one might wonder why Welty added the pronoun "all" in the first place. The answer can be found by trying to delete this pronoun. The result would be a potential ambiguity: the reader would be uncertain whether "them" meant THEM, or **them**, or THEM + **them**. The addition of "all" ensures that the reader links "them" to all the people at the table (including THEM).

We find a similar instance of an inclusive "they" (this time without the addition of "all", which would be redundant) in the following example:

13. "At last a tremendous explosion burst – the whistle. Everything shuddered in outline from the sound, everybody said something – everybody

else. **They** started with no perceptible motion, but HER hat blew off."
(pp. 9-10)

At this point in the story the boat is pulling out, so everybody is moving with it. Hence "they" means everyone on the boat, including THEM. Note, incidentally, Welty's clever way of removing THEM from inclusion in the universal pronoun "everybody" in this excerpt: "everybody said something – everybody else". The use of the phrase "everybody else" is thus equivalent to the exclusive "they all". By thus excluding THEM from the referent of "everybody" in "everybody said something", Welty once again isolates the pair of THEM from the other passengers, and without making the statement herself, she forces the reader to infer that while everybody else is speaking THEY remain silent – on this occasion as on so many others.

*5.4.3.6 The use of locative adverbs*

Another technique Welty employs to distinguish THEM from **them** is to use a locative adverb to create some distance between the protagonists and other characters in the narrative. We have already noted one rather subtle instance of this, namely the use of "there" in:

10. "'The passengers walking and jostling about <u>there</u> appeared oddly amateurish, too – amateur travelers. **They** were having such a good time. **They** all knew each other. Beer was being passed around in cans, bets were being loudly settled and new bets made, about local and special subjects on which **they** all doted." (p. 9)

Recall that in this scene SHE is looking down from the bridge of the ferry and sees "the passengers walking and jostling about <u>there</u>". The adverb "there" distances these passengers from HER, with the result that the three instances of "**they**" in this passage point away from THEM. Here are two more examples of the same device:

15. "HE did after all bring the retrieved hat up the stairs to HER. SHE took it back – useless – and held it to HER skirt. What **they** were saying <u>below</u> was more polite than **their** searchlight faces." (p. 10)
22. "When SHE looked clear around, thinking **they** had a fire burning <u>somewhere</u> now, out of the heat had risen the full moon." (p. 16)

In #15, the use of the adverb "below" makes it clear that "**they**" refers to the other passengers and not to THEM. THEY are now both up on the bridge of the boat, SHE having climbed the steps up there as soon as THEY came aboard, and HE having followed shortly thereafter, bearing HER hat, which had blown off and landed on the lower deck. **They** are thus below, while THEY are above. Note that without the little adverb, the reader could easily assume that THEY (rather than **they**) were speaking, and doing so politely. Note further that once the reader has identified the referent of "**they**", it follows quite naturally (by anaphoric proximity) that "**their**" in this example also refers to the other passengers and not to THEM. This interpretation is supported by the phrase "their searchlight faces", which is Welty's way of informing us that **they** are attentively studying THEM, the two strangers.

In #22, SHE apparently mistakes the rising moon for a distant fire. The use of the indefinite locative adverb, "somewhere", leads us to conclude that "they" must refer to some general, unspecified and distant agent (= people, somebody), and not to THEM. Furthermore, this is the only logical interpretation since obviously SHE would know whether THEY had started a fire.

### 5.4.3.7 Use of HE and SHE instead of THEY

We have noted that Welty occasionally adds "both" or "two" to restrict the reference of the third person plural pronouns to the dual THEM, thereby avoiding the potential conflict between "THEM" and "**them**". A more direct way to avoid this conflict is to shun this plural pronoun altogether when the reference is to HIM and HER. This might seem to be rather difficult, since HE and SHE are not given any names. But in fact I have just used Welty's own device in the preceding sentence. By using the compound construction, "HE and SHE" (or "SHE and HE"), it is possible to refer to THEM without using the plural pronoun at all. Such a construction is rather awkward, but it does provide an unambiguous replacement for THEY. Welty employs this device at the very beginning of the story:

- "THEY were strangers to each other, both fairly well strangers to the place, now seated side by side at luncheon – a party combined in a free-and-easy way when the friends *HE and SHE* were with recognized each other across Galatoire's. The time was a Sunday in summer – those hours of afternoon that seem Time Out in New Orleans." (p. 3)

She uses it elsewhere in the text as well:

- "THEY met fishermen and other men bent on some local pursuits, some in sulphur-colored pants, walking and riding; met wagons, trucks, boats in trucks, autos, boats on top of autos – all coming to meet THEM, as though

something of high moment were doing back where the car came from, and *HE and SHE* were determined to miss it." (p. 7)
- "One more boat was coming in, making its way through the tenacious, tough, dark flower traps, by the shaken light of what first appeared to be torches. *HE and SHE* waited for the boat, as if on each other's patience." (p. 17)

In each of these cases it is clear that Welty is purposely avoiding the use of "they" so as to render the text unambiguous. This is particularly noticeable in the second example, when there is a very real candidate for the referent of a carelessly inserted "they", namely "fishermen and other men", or even "wagons, trucks, boats in trucks, autos and boats on top of autos". The use of HE and SHE in these examples is clearly an unusual construction in English, but it serves Welty's purpose well – the reader is left in no doubt as to the correct referential link.

The original *New Yorker* publication (1952) contained two additional instances of this somewhat cumbersome pairing of pronouns, but these were edited out for the 1955 publication. Here are the cases in question. In each case, Welty simply replaced the compound form "HE and SHE" or "SHE and HE" (in 1952) with "THEY" (in 1955), apparently deciding, and justifiably so, that the context was sufficient to establish the correct reference:

- "*HE and SHE* crossed the floor and sat, alone there, on wooden stools." (1952: 41) vs. "*THEY* crossed the floor and sat, alone there, on wooden stools." (1955a: 18)
- "*SHE and HE* were quite unnoticed now." (1952: 42) vs. "*THEY* were quite unnoticed now." (1955a: 21)

*5.5 Personal pronouns in the title*

We have now completed our examination of the third person personal pronouns in Welty's short story, "No Place for You, My Love". But our discussion of pronominal reference in this text would be incomplete if we ignored the challenge posed by the title itself.

In a brief biographical sketch of Eudora Welty, Nash Burger, a fellow Jacksonian, recalls some of the events he shared with Welty. One of these was entertaining Henry Miller, who had come to Jackson to visit the town's famous author. Burger (1969: 13-14) describes the encounter as follows:

> I expected to see a raffish, dissolute roué, spouting flamboyance and double-entendres. Instead I found a quiet, soft-spoken middle-aged man who had little to say and might well have been a grocer . . . I can't recall a thing he said except that he told Eudora he admired her stories but didn't think she was very good at titles – a peculiar and libelous observation I thought, then and now.

Whether one sides with Miller or Burger, there can be no denying that Welty's title for this particular story poses considerable problems of interpretation. Unlike the text itself, which involves challenges dealing with the tracking of third person pronouns, the title creates tracking problems for both first person ("my") and second person pronouns ("you"). Determining the referent of the first person pronoun (in "my love") would allow us to identify the "speaker", while the resolution of the referent for the second person pronoun would identify the addressee. But who is addressing whom? The possibilities are manifold:

1. The author could be addressing HER.
2. The author could be addressing HIM.
3. HE could be addressing HER.
4. HE could be addressing HIS wife.
5. SHE could be addressing HIM.
6. SHE could be addressing HER assumed husband.
7. SHE could be addressing HER assumed lover.
8. SHE could be addressing HERSELF.

Consider first the nature of the "speaker". It might seem logical to assume that Welty herself is the one doing the addressing here, since it is her story. However, when we recall that Welty has gone to great lengths to distance herself from the telling of the story, we must ask ourselves whether it would be reasonable to assume that she has let her own voice remain in the title.

If the answer to this question is "no" (and I am reluctant to draw this conclusion), then the title must be coming from one of the three voices which characterize the rest of the narrative. Recall that these voices belong to HIM, to HER, and to a third "observer". We can presumably rule out this third voice, because it never gets personal enough in the text to say something like "my love".

Consequently, if the voice is not Welty's own, it must be HIS or HERS. On the one hand, it would be logical to assume that HE is making a comment about HER, since much of the story involves HIS observations about HER. Recall Welty's own words: "I kept outside of her by taking glimpses of her through the curious eyes of a stranger" (1955b: 247). On the other hand, if we assume that the title is a *mental* observation rather than an *uttered* one, HE would seem to be ruled out as the "speaker" on purely grammatical grounds: nowhere in the narrative does HE ever mentally use a first or second person pronoun. Whenever we catch a glimpse of HIM from the inside, it sounds like this:

- "HE thought it was more likely that SHE would wish for HER husband if SHE had one (HIS wife's voice) than for the lover in whom HE believed." (p. 12)

Had HE used the first and second person pronouns (as found in the title), this sentence might have been formulated as follows:

- "It is more likely, HE thought, that *you* would wish for *your* husband if *you* have one (*my* wife's voice) than for the lover in whom *I* believe."

In the whole narrative, neither HE nor SHE ever mentally uses the second person pronoun. Nor do either of THEM ever mentally use "my". However, there is one instance where SHE does employ the first person pronouns "I" and "me" in a mental monologue. This is found at the very beginning of the story, when SHE senses that HE is studying HER:

- "It must stick out all over *me*, SHE thought, so people think they can love *me* or hate *me* just by looking at *me*. How did it leave *us* – the old, safe, slow way people used to know of learning how one another feels, and the privilege that went with it of shying away if it seemed best? People in love like *me*, *I* suppose, give away the short cuts to everybody's secrets." (pp. 3-4)

The use of the plural first person form, "us", in this text refers to mankind in general, rather than to HIM and HER. SHE mentally uses "us" in a similar sense in one other instance:

- "Both respectable and merciful, their hides, SHE thought, forcing HERSELF to dwell on the alligator as SHE looked back. Deliver *us* all from the naked in heart. (As SHE had been told.)" (p. 12)

Though this is very slim evidence, it would suggest that if the voice in the title is to be consistent with one of the voices in the narrative itself, then the only possible candidate for the "speaker" is HER. If this is what Welty intends us to conclude (and, again, I am not confident that it is), then there are four possible addressees, as listed above:

- SHE could be addressing HIM.
- SHE could be addressing HER assumed husband.
- SHE could be addressing HER assumed lover.
- SHE could be addressing HERSELF.

Of these four possibilities, the last one would seem the most likely. However, I find it difficult to rule out these other two interpretations:

- HE could be addressing HER.

- The author could be addressing HER.

As noted above, identifying HIM as the "speaker" would be a logical consequence of the story itself, and of Welty's own description of the relationship between the protagonists: HE is brought in by Welty to present HER to the reader.

Equally plausible, however, is the interpretation whereby Welty is the "speaker". Despite her claims about turning the narrative over to three voices other than her own, she may simply have chosen to let her own voice remain in the title itself.

I think we must conclude that we may never know for certain who is addressing whom in the title. Quite possibly this is the very effect Welty intended. The sense of generality brought about by the absence of names in the narrative is maintained in the title. And by moving from third person to first and second person, this generality is magnified many times over.

Before leaving this discussion, note that the indeterminacy we have been examining extends as well to the word "place" in the title. There are at least three natural interpretations: 1) It could refer, metaphorically, to room in the heart; 2) It could refer, concretely but locally, to the harshness and inhospitality of the landscape THEY travel through; and 3) It could refer, concretely but more globally, to the difficulties a stranger may have in adjusting to the South. The coupling of multiple readings of the word "place" with the multitude of interpretations of the pronouns "you" and "my" is fully in keeping with the "impressionistic" nature of the text itself.

## 6. Closing remarks

I hope that this examination of Welty's use of personal pronouns has resulted in a deeper understanding of "No Place for You, My Love", while simultaneously revealing her skill in solving problems which she willfully imposes upon herself by deciding to keep the protagonists (and nearly everybody else) nameless in her story. At the same time I hope that it has illuminated aspects of the nature and complexity of pronominal reference in general, while demonstrating the wide range of grammatical and logical resources which readers unconsciously employ at every turn in resolving the intricacies of pronoun tracking.

## Appendix 1: non-SHE

1. "<u>HIS wife</u> would not be at **her** most charitable if HE came bringing malaria home to the family." (p. 8)
2. "THEY caught up with an old man walking in a sprightly way in THEIR

direction, all by himself, wearing a clean bright shirt printed with a pair of palm trees fanning green over his chest. It might better be <u>a big colored woman's</u> shirt, but **she** didn't have it." (p. 15)

3. "<u>A massive back, presumably female, with a twist of gray hair on top</u>, stood with a ladle akimbo. A young man joined **her** and with his fingers stole something out of the pot and ate it." (p. 18)

4. "<u>HIS wife</u> had recommended that HE stay where HE was this extra day so that **she** could entertain some old, unmarried college friends without HIM underfoot." (p. 26)

5. "In Dickie Grogan's, as HE passed, <u>the well-known Josefina</u> at **her** organ was charging up and down with *Clair de Lune*." (pp. 26-27)


## Appendix 2: non-HE

1. "At the intersection marked Arabi, where THEIR road led out of the tangle and HE took it, <u>a small Negro</u> seated beneath a black umbrella astride a box chalked 'Shou Shine' lifted **his** pink-and-black hand and waved THEM good-by." (p. 6)

2. "There was nearly always <u>a man lying with **his** shoes off</u> in the bed of any truck otherwise empty – with the raw, red look of <u>a man sleeping in the daytime</u>, being jolted about as **he** slept." (p. 7)

3. "<u>A family of eight or nine people</u> on foot strung along the road in the same direction the car was going, beating themselves with the wild palmettos. Heels, shoulders, knees, breasts, back of the heads, elbows, hands, were touched in turn – like some game, <u>each</u> playing it with **himself**." (p. 8)

4. "<u>Another boy</u> drew **his** affectionate initials in the dust of the door on HER side." (p. 9)

5. "<u>One red-haired man</u> in a burst of wildness even tried to give away **his** truckload of shrimp to a man on the other side of the boat" (p. 9)

6. "The boys had a surprise – <u>an alligator</u> on board. One of them pulled it by a chain around the deck, between the cars and trucks, like a toy – a hide that could walk. HE thought, Well they had to catch one sometime. It's Sunday afternoon. So they have **him** on board now, riding **him** across the Mississippi River ... 'Who want to rassle **him**? Who want to, eh?' two boys cried, looking up." (p. 11)

7. "<u>The priest</u> came out onto the porch in **his** underwear, stared at the car a moment as if **he** wondered what time it was, then collected **his** robe off the line and **his** fish off the doorstep and returned inside. Vespers was next, for **him**." (p. 15)

8. "THEY caught up with <u>an old man</u> walking in a sprightly way in THEIR direction, all by **himself**, wearing a clean bright shirt printed with a pair of palm trees fanning green over **his** chest. It might be a big colored woman's shirt, but she didn't have it. **He** flagged the car with gestures like hoops. 'You're coming to the end of the road,' <u>the old man</u> told THEM. **He** pointed ahead, tipped **his** hat to the lady, and pointed again. 'End of the road.' THEY didn't understand that **he** meant, 'Take me.'" (p. 15)

9. "<u>An old man</u> up on the porch there sat holding an open newspaper, with a fat white goose sitting opposite **him** on the floor." (p. 16)

10. "Below, in the now shadowless and sunless open, <u>another old man</u>, with a colored pencil bright under **his** hat brim, was late mending a sail." (p. 16)

11. "<u>One of the four cardplayers</u> at a table in the middle of the floor was <u>the newspaper reader</u>; the paper was in **his** pants pocket." (pp. 17-18)

12. "An eruption of humorous signs, newspaper cutouts and cartoons, razor-blade cards, and personal messages of significance to <u>the owner</u> or **his** friends decorated the overhang, framing where Baba should have been but wasn't." (p. 18)

13. "A massive back, presumably female, with a twist of gray hair on top, stood with a ladle akimbo. <u>A young man</u> joined her and with **his** fingers stole something out of the pot and ate it." (p. 18)

14. "When **he** got ready to wait on THEM, <u>Baba</u> strolled out to the counter, young, black-headed, and in very good humor.
'Coldest beer you've got. And food – What will you have?'
'Nothing for me, thank you,' SHE said. 'I'm not sure I could eat, after all.'
'Well, I could,' HE said, shoving HIS jaw out. <u>Baba</u> smiled. 'I want a good solid ham sandwich.'
'I could have asked **him** for some water,' SHE said, after **he** had gone." (p. 18)

15. "<u>One child</u> had a live lizard on **his** shirt, clinging like a breast pin – like lapis lazuli." (p. 19)

16. "When <u>Baba</u> came out bringing the beer and sandwich, 'Could I have some water?' SHE greeted **him**." (p. 19)

17. "<u>Baba</u> was smiling. **He** had set an opened frosted brown bottle before HER on the counter, and a thick sandwich, and stood looking at HER." (pp. 19-20)

18. "'What <u>the old fellow</u> wanted', said HE when HE came back at last, 'was to have a friend of **his** apologize. Seems church is just out. Seems <u>the friend</u> made a remark coming in just now. **His** pals told **him** there was a lady present.'
'I see you bought **him** a beer,' SHE said.
'Well, <u>the old man</u> looked like **he** wanted *something*.'" (p. 20)

19. "There were <u>three little boys</u> to each slot machine. The local custom ap-

peared to be that <u>one</u> pulled the lever for the friend **he** was holding up to put the nickel in, while <u>the third</u> covered the pictures with the flat of **his** hand as they fell into place, so as to surprise them all if anything happened." (p. 20)

20. "<u>The dog</u> lay sleeping on in front of the raging juke box, **his** ribs working fast as a concertina's." (p. 20)
21. "At the side of the room <u>a man with a cap on **his** white thatch</u> was trying **his** best to open a side screen door, but it was stuck fast. It was **he** who had come in with the remark considered ribald; now **he** was trying to get out the other way." (p. 20)
22. "<u>Baba</u> had lifted the flap of the counter and come out into the room. Behind **his** head there was a sign lettered in orange crayon: 'Shrimp Dance Sun. PM.'" (p. 21)
23. "'I wonder what **he** called me,' SHE whispered in HIS ear.
 'Who?'
 'The one who apologized to you.'" (p. 21)
24. "In the thickening heat THEY danced on while <u>Baba</u> **himself** sang with the mosquito-voiced singer in the chorus of *'Moi pas l'aimez ça,'* enumerating the *ça*'s with a hot shrimp between **his** fingers. **He** was counting over the platters the old woman now set out on the counter" (p. 22)
25. "<u>The old thatched man</u> was again drunkenly trying to get out by the stuck side door; now **he** gave it a kick, but was prevailed on to remain." (p. 23)


## Appendix 3: non-THEY

1. "It was the wrong hat for HER, thought this Eastern businessman who had no interest whatever in <u>women's clothes</u> and no eye for **them**" (p. 3)
2. "It must stick out all over me, SHE thought, so <u>people</u> think **they** can love me or hate me just by looking at me." (p. 3)
3. "It was a bold and full light, shot up under the brim of that hat, as close to **them** <u>all</u> as the flowers in the center of the table" (p. 4)
4. "It was a serious, now-watch-out-everybody face, which orphaned HER entirely in the company of <u>these Southerners</u>. HE guessed HER age, as HE could not guess **theirs**: thirty-two" (p. 4)
5. "'I have a car here, just down the street,' HE said to HER as the luncheon party was rising to leave, <u>all the others</u> wanting to get back to **their** houses and sleep." (p. 5)
6. "As time passed and the distance from New Orleans grew, <u>girls ever darker and younger</u> were disposing **themselves** over the porches and the porch steps" (p. 7)

7. "There were thousands, millions of <u>mosquitoes and gnats</u> – a universe of **them**, and on the increase." (p. 8)
8. "<u>A family of eight or nine people</u> on foot strung along the road in the same direction the car was going, beating **themselves** with the wild palmettos." (p. 8)
9. "More and more crayfish and other shell creatures littered THEIR path, scuttling or dragging. <u>These little samples, little jokes of creation</u>, persisted and sometimes perished, the more of **them** the deeper down the road went." (p. 8)
10. "<u>The passengers</u> walking and jostling about there appeared oddly amateurish, too – amateur travelers. **They** were having such a good time. **They** <u>all</u> knew each other. Beer was being passed around in cans, bets were being loudly settled and new bets made, about local and special subjects on which **they** <u>all</u> doted." (p. 9)
11. "<u>The young boys</u> leaned on each other thinking of what next, rolling **their** eyes absently." (p. 9)
12. "One red-haired man in a burst of wildness even tried to give away his truckload of <u>shrimp</u> to a man on the other side of the boat – nearly all the trucks were full of <u>shrimp</u> – causing taunts and then protests of '**They** good! **They** good!' from the giver." (p. 9)
13. "At last a tremendous explosion burst – the whistle. Everything shuddered in outline from the sound, everybody said something – everybody else. **They** started with no perceptible motion, but HER hat blew off." (pp. 9-10)
14. "HER shoulders dropping, HER hair flying, HER skirt buffeted by the sudden strong wind, SHE stood there, thinking **they** <u>all</u> must see that with HER entire self all SHE did was wait." (p. 10)
15. "HE did after all bring the retrieved hat up the stairs to HER. SHE took it back – useless – and held it to HER skirt. What **they** were saying <u>below</u> was more polite than **their** searchlight faces." (p. 10)
16. "<u>The boys</u> had a surprise – an alligator on board. One of **them** pulled it by a chain around the deck, between the cars and trucks, like a toy – a hide that could walk. HE thought, Well **they** had to catch one sometime. It's Sunday afternoon. So **they** have him on board now, riding him across the Mississippi River" (p. 11)
17. "<u>The young boys</u>, looking taller, had taken out colored combs and were combing **their** wet hair back in solemn pompadour above **their** radiant foreheads. **They** had been bathing in the river **themselves** not long before." (p. 12)
18. "Both respectable and merciful, **their** hides, SHE thought, forcing HERSELF to dwell on <u>the alligator</u> as SHE looked back." (p. 12)
19. "HE passed between the tombs slowly but in the manner of a feat. <u>Names</u> took **their** places on the walls slowly at a level with the eye, <u>names</u> as near

as the eyes of a person stopping in conversation, and as far away in origin, and in all **their** music and dead longing, as Spain." (p. 14)

20. "The houses on **their** shaggy posts, patchily built, some with plank runways instead of steps, were flimsy and alike, and not much bigger than the boats tied up at the landing." (pp. 15-16)
21. "THEY made THEIR way on foot toward the water, where at an idle-looking landing men in twos and threes stood with **their** backs to THEM." (p. 16)
22. "When SHE looked clear around, thinking **they** had a fire burning somewhere now, out of the heat had risen the full moon." (p. 16)
23. "At Baba's **they** were boiling shrimp." (p. 18)
24. "Two little boys, almost alike, almost the same size, and just cleaned up, dived into the room with a double bang of the screen door, and circled around the card game. **They** ran **their** hands into the men's pockets. ... **They** circled around an shrieked at the dog" (p. 19)
25. "Bringing in a strong odor of geranium talcum, some men had come in now – all in bright shirts. **They** drew near the counter, or stood and watched the game." (p. 19)
26. "SHE lifted HER head to watch HIM leave HER, and was looked at, from all over the room. As a minute passed, no cards were laid down. In a far-off way, like accepting the light from Arcturus, SHE accepted it that SHE was more beautiful or perhaps more fragile than the women **they** saw every day of **their** lives. It was just this thought coming into a woman's face, and at this hour, that seemed familiar to **them**." (p. 19)
27. "There were three little boys to each slot machine. The local custom appeared to be that one pulled the lever for the friend he was holding up to put the nickel in, while the third covered the pictures with the flat of his hand as **they** fell into place, so as to surprise **them** all if anything happened." (p. 20)
28. "The card players broke into shouts of derision, then joy, then tired derision among **themselves**; **they** might have been here all afternoon – **they** were the only ones not cleaned up and shaved." (p. 20)
29. "The original pair of little boys ran in once more, with the hyphenated bang. **They** got nickels this time, then were brushed away from the table like mosquitoes, and **they** rushed under the counter and on to the cauldron behind, clinging to Baba's mother there." (pp. 20-21)
30. "SHE said rapidly, as THEY began moving together too well, 'One of those clippings was an account of a shooting right here. I guess **they**'re proud of it.'" (p. 21)
31. "He was counting over the platters the old woman now set out on the counter, each heaped with shrimp in **their** shells boiled to iridescence, like mounds of honeysuckle flowers." (p. 22)

32. "The first arrivals of the girls were coming up the steps under the porch light – all flowered fronts, **their** black pompadours giving out breathlike feelers from sheer abundance. Where **they**'d resprinkled it since church, the talcum shone like mica on **their** downy arms. Smelling solidly of geranium, **they** filed across the porch with short steps and fingers joined, just timed to turn **their** smiles loose inside the room. HE held the door open for **them**." (p. 23)
33. "Going back, the ride was wordless, quiet except for the motor and the insects driving **themselves** against the car." (p. 23)
34. "Once the car lights picked out two people – a Negro couple, sitting on two facing chairs in the yard outside **their** lonely cabin" (p. 24)
35. "In peopleless open places there were lakes of dust, smudge fires burning at **their** hearts. Cows stood in untended rings around **them**, motionless in the heat, in the night – **their** horns standing up sharp against that glow." (p. 24)
36. "The earrings SHE wore twinkled with **their** rushing motion in an almost regular beat. **They** might have spoken like tongues" (p. 25)"

## References

Binding, Paul. 1994. *The Still Moment. Eudora Welty – Portrait of a Writer.* London: Virago Press Ltd.

Burger, Nash. 1969. "Eudora Welty's Jackson". *Shenandoah – The Washington and Lee University Review*, XX: 8-15.

Carson, Barbara Harrell. 1992. *Eudora Welty: Two Pictures at Once in Her Frame.* Troy, New York: The Whitson Publishing Company.

Carter, Thomas. 1955. "Rhetoric and Southern Landscapes". *Accent*, 15: 293-297.

Elder, Walter. 1955. "That Region". *Kenyon Review*, 17: 661-670.

Evans, Elizabeth. 1981. *Eudora Welty.* New York: Frederick Ungar Publishing Co.

Givón, T. 1984. *Syntax – A Functional-Typological Introduction.* Volume I. Amsterdam: John Benjamins Publishing Company.

Givón, T. 1990. *Syntax – A Functional-Typological Introduction.* Volume II. Amsterdam: John Benjamins Publishing Company.

Givón, T. 1993. *English Grammar – A Function-Based Introduction.* Two volumes. Amsterdam: John Benjamins Publishing Company.

Gretlund, Jan. 1994. *Eudora Welty's Aesthetics of Place.* Odense, Denmark: Odense University Press.

Jones, Alun. 1969. "A Frail Travelling Coincidence: Three Later Stories of Eudora Welty". *Shenandoah – The Washington and Lee University Review*, XX: 40-53.

Mortimer, Gail L. 1994. *Daughter of the Swan – Love and Knowledge in Eudora Welty's Fiction*. Athens, Georgia: The University of Georgia Press.

Oates, Joyce Carol. 1969. "The Art of Eudora Welty". *Shenandoah – The Washington and Lee University Review,* XX: 54-57.

Pingatore, Diana R. 1996. "No Place for You, My Love". In: *A Reader's Guide to the Short Stories of Eudora Welty*. New York: G. K. Hale & Co., 334-339.

Welty, Eudora. 1952. "No Place for You, My Love". *The New Yorker* 28: 3-27.

Welty, Eudora. 1955a. "No Place for You, My Love". In: *The Bride of the Innisfallen and Other Stories*. New York: Harcourt Brace Jovanovich, 3-27.

Welty, Eudora. 1955b. "How I Write". *The Virginia Quarterly Review*, 31: 240-251.

Welty, Eudora. 1979. "Place in Fiction" [1956]. In: *The Eye of the Story – Selected Essays and Reviews*. New York: Vintage Books, 116-133.

Welty, Eudora. 1980. *The Collected Stories of Eudora Welty*. New York: Harcourt Brace Jovanovich.

# Adverbials, direct objects and the style of Carson McCullers

*John M. Dienhart*

It is a generally accepted fact of English grammar that there are strong restrictions on placing an adverbial between a transitive verb and its object; that is, the pattern PAO is a marked one in English.[1] In the words of two traditional English grammarians: "The verb is not, usually, separated from its object" (Kruisinga 1925: 291). "An adverb can freely stand in almost any position except between a verb and its direct object, where it is much less common than elsewhere" (Curme 1931: 130).

This information is also commonly passed on to Danish students of English: "An adverbial does not normally come between a verb and its object" (Steller and Sørensen 1974: 187; my translation). From a pedagogical point of view, it is useful to stress this for Danes, since in their language they can say and write things like: Jeg læser <u>aldrig</u> bøger af denne art (*I read <u>never</u> books of that kind) / De spiller <u>kun sjældent</u> støjende musik (?They play <u>only rarely</u> noisy music) / Han tømte <u>hurtigt</u> sit glas (Vestergaard 1985: 74) (*? He emptied <u>quickly</u> his glass) / Han åbnede <u>forsigtigt</u> pakken (Vestergaard 1985: 74) (*? He opened <u>carefully</u> the package).

Scattered observations by English grammarians coupled with examples like these could easily lead one to the conclusion that while PAO constructions are very common in Danish they are nearly impossible in English. Naturally, I do not wish to argue that there is no difference here between Danish and English, but I do wish in this paper to show that PAO constructions are far more common in English than one might expect from examining books on English grammar.[2]

I wish to focus in particular on the occurrence of PAO patterns in the work of Carson McCullers, a well-known and highly respected American author. Drawing on data from two of her best-known novels, *The Heart is a Lonely Hunter* (1940) and *The Member of the Wedding* (1946), I wish to propose a hierarchy of seven PAO types. For each of the seven types I shall also provide examples (in the endnotes) taken from English grammars, where they are often tucked away in obscure corners. Additional examples will be drawn from two corpus-based studies of adverbials: Jacobson (1964) and Lindquist (1989). Finally, I shall explore how McCullers' use of the PAO pattern reinforces, linguistically, certain thematic elements in her writing. Here are the seven types, illustrated with examples from McCullers' novels (abbreviated *Heart* and *Wedding*):

**TYPE I: PAO constructions involving "phrasal verbs"**[3]

She would **put on** her father's glasses with the jeweler's loupe attached (*Wedding*, p. 60) / Mick scrambled under the bed and **brought out** a large hatbox (*Heart*, p. 35).

**TYPE II: PAO constructions involving clausal objects (O:cl)**[4]

So these were the main reasons why F. Jasmine felt, in an unworded way, **that this was a morning different from all mornings she had ever known** (*Wedding*, p. 57) / She talked and did not know from one word to the next **what she would say** (*Wedding*, p. 42) / The sudden feeling was that she knew deep in her **where she would go** (*Wedding*, p. 42) / They resembled each other – they both had an anxious, questioning expression, as though they wondered every minute **if what they did was wrong** (*Wedding*, p. 61).

**TYPE III: PAO constructions involving object groups containing postmodifying clauses (O:g with DEP:cl)**[5]

Singer brought from his closet a tin box **that contained a loaf of bread, some oranges, and cheese** (*Heart*, p. 47) / Singer brought out from the closet the tin box **in which he kept crackers and fruit and cheese** (*Heart*, p. 128) / Along with the Agua Florida he found in the closet a bottle of lemon rinse **Alice had always used for her hair** (*Heart*, p. 192) / Together they made in her this feeling **that she could not name** (*Wedding*, pp. 24-25) / She took from the pocket of her shorts the package of cigarettes **she had bought the night before** (*Heart*, p. 28) / The Portuguese took from behind his ear a cigarette **which he tapped on the counter but did not light** (*Wedding*, p. 54).

**TYPE IV: PAO constructions involving an object group with non-clausal post modification**[6]

He had locked the door of the restaurant and hung on the outside a white wreath **of lilies** (*Heart*, p. 104) / She heard in the neighborhood the sound **of evening voices** and noticed the light fresh smell of watered grass (*Wedding*, p. 38) / In the noon quietness, she heard <u>again</u> the organ **of the monkey-man**, the sound that always magnetized her footsteps so that she automatically went toward it (*Wedding*, p. 61) / They passed <u>among themselves</u> a box **of bought store candy**, with chocolates set in dainty, pleated shells, and watched the winter miles pass by the window (*Wedding*, p. 30) / for when it had been decided that she and her father would share <u>with Aunt Pet and Uncle Ustace</u> a house **out in the new suburb of town**, Berenice had given quit notice and said that she might as well marry T. T. (*Wedding*, p. 149).

**TYPE V: PAO constructions involving an object consisting of a compound unit (O:cu)**[7]

She saw <u>in her mind</u> **her brother and the bride**, and the heart in her was squeezed so hard that Frankie almost felt it break (*Wedding*, p. 42) / He took <u>from his pockets</u> **the cards he carried about with him, his watch, and his fountain pen.** (*Heart*, p. 185; also Type III)

**TYPE VI: PAO constructions involving an object group with premodifier(s) but without postmodifier(s)** [8]

Most of the businesses were open, and the neon signs made a mingling of varied lights that gave <u>to the avenue</u> **a watery look** (*Wedding*, p. 126) / The telling of the wedding gathered inside her, and when it was so ready she could no longer resist, she hunted <u>in her mind</u> **a good opening remark** – something grown and off-hand, to start between them the conversation (*Wedding*, p. 54) / He crumpled some bread in a bowl and poured <u>over it</u> **hot milk** (*Heart*, p. 216) / On Sunday he got up early in the morning and took <u>from the suitcase</u> **his serge suit.** (*Heart*, p. 131) / Now, as F. Jasmine crossed her yard, she saw <u>in her mind's eye</u> **the swarming children** and heard <u>from down the street</u> **their chanting cries** – and this morning, for the first time in her life, she heard a sweetness in these sounds (*Wedding*, p. 49).

**TYPE VII: PAO constructions involving an object group without modification (other than a possible determiner)**[9]

The white man smiled at him and lighted <u>for him</u> **his cigarette** (*Heart*, p. 73) / On Saturday night she could hear the terrible music and see <u>from far away</u> **their light** (*Wedding*, p. 10) / The telling of the wedding gathered inside her, and when it was so ready she could no longer resist, she hunted in her mind a good opening remark – something grown and off-hand, to start <u>between them</u> **the conversation** (*Wedding*, p. 54).

These seven types are ordered in a rough markedness hierarchy, from unmarked to highly marked.[10]

Type I ("phrasal verbs") are so common as to be generally unmarked. Consequently, I do not take the examples in this category to be in any way "characteristic" of Carson McCullers' style.

Type II (clausal objects), though no doubt considerably less frequent than Type I, appear also to fall within the range of unmarked English constructions. I suspect, though, that many native speakers, if pressed, would probably consider them marginally more marked than Type I.

Type III (objects with clausal postmodification) is similar to Type II in that both types involve objects with subordinate clauses. The difference is that in Type II the object is itself a clause, whereas in Type III the object is a group containing a postmodifying clause. Quirk et al. seem to imply that sentences of this type are somwhat "disturbing of normal order" (1985: 499). I would agree. Though the objects are easily as long as those in Type II, the difference in object structure (group vs. clause) seems to be important in contributing to the sense of "markedness" which may be attached to Type III.

Type IV (objects with non-clausal postmodification) is more marked than type III. This may be attributable primarily to considerations of length, since postmodifiying groups are generally (though not necessarily) shorter than postmodifying clauses.

Type V (compound units as objects) is very difficult to place within the hierarchy. Clearly, compounding is a "lengthening" device, so that examples of this type could be very long indeed (longer, for example, than Type IV). Furthermore, each member of the compound unit could itself be either a single word, a group or a clause, as the examples illustrate.

Type VI (objects without postmodification) is clearly more marked than any of the previous types. This correlates well with the general fact of English sentence structure that premodification is not as "lengthening" a device as postmodification. In particular, neither subordinate clauses nor prepositional groups fit comfortably into the premodifying slot of the English nominal group (though compound units do).

Type VII (unmodified object) is the most marked type of all. Again this correlates with considerations of length, since an object without either pre- or postmodification is the shortest object of all.

It is now possible to formulate several principles which appear to be operative in PAO constructions. (Type I, being unmarked, will be ignored here.) Clearly length is an important factor. **PRINCIPLE A:** In PAO constructions the adverbial is likely to be shorter than the object. The greater the imbalance, the more marked the PAO construction is likely to be.[11]

But we have seen that semantic interpretation also plays a significant role. The clearest cases where problems can arise are those involving subordinate clauses in the object (both Type II and Type III). **PRINCIPLE B:** PAO is more likely than POA if POA might lead to the "wrong" reading (namely PO) because the adverbial could be (mis)interpreted as part of the subordinate clause in the object.

One of the important differences between the examples drawn from McCullers' novels and those taken from other sources is the preponderance of place adverbials in the former, whereas time adverbials figure more heavily in the latter. This would seem to contribute to the fact that McCullers' data appears to be rather more marked than that from other sources. **PRINCIPLE C:** An adverbial is more likely to figure in a PAO construction if it is a time adverbial than if it is a place adverbial.[12]

The last principle is one which is true of marked constructions in general. **PRINCIPLE D:** The more marked a PAO construction is, the more it lends itself to use as a stylistic device.

It seems reasonable now to ask why Carson McCullers uses so many of the marked PAO constructions. The first observation to make is that her PAO patterns are clearly only one aspect of a highly "marked" use of the English language in general. In the examples cited above we find such additional linguistic curiosities as: "a box **of bought store candy**", "Berenice had given **quit notice**", "the **heart in her** was squeezed so hard", "the **telling of the wedding**".[13] Such constructions, which abound in her work, are both lyrical and "freakish", and as such they reinforce, linguistically, important aspects of her fictional world. Fascinated by the freak shows in her hometown of Columbus, Georgia, McCullers fills her novels with "physical malformations such as giantism and dwarfism, physical asymmetry and imbalance (crossed eyes, eyes of two colors, masculine characteristics in a woman or feminine characteristics in a male)" (McDowell 1980: 16). She "became increasingly aware that one's physical aberration was but an exaggerated symbol of what she considered everyman's 'caught' condition of spiritual isolation and sense of aloneness in spite of his intense desire and effort to relate to others" (Carr 1975: 1). The very title of her first novel, *The Heart is a Lonely Hunter*, reflects this concern. A similar sentiment is expressed on the opening page of *The Member of the Wedding*: "It happened that green and crazy summer when Frankie was twelve years old. This was the summer when for a long time she had not been a member. She belonged to no club and was a member of nothing in the world." Estrangement, being different and "out of place" – these are themes in McCullers' works which are nicely reinforced by the syntactic "abnormalities" she employs. We might add that her characters are as "out of place" as the locative (place) adverbials.

But the language also pleases with its freshness, its touch of the poetical, its lyrical cadences. This is a direct reflection of McCullers' considerable musical experience and ability: "at thirteen [she] knew without a doubt that she would be a concert pianist, a career that would fulfill a destiny created for her many years earlier by a confident and enterprising mother...The discipline which she experienced through her work with Mrs. Tucker [her piano teacher] was of inestimable value to her when she began to write. She later attributed her excellent sense of form and structure to her study of music" (Carr 1975: 26).

This helps account for the fact that the locative adverbials themselves are highly repetitive, nearly formulaic. Not only do they all have the form of prepositional groups ("from the closet", "in the neighborhood", etc.), the same prepositions reoccur: in 10 cases the preposition is "from", in 7 cases "in".[14] This ties in with the sense of rhythm, timing and musical repetition which characterizes McCullers' writing in general. Here, for example is what McCullers herself writes about her first book in an outline she submitted to the publisher Houghton Mifflin in 1938:

> This book (*Heart*) is planned according to a definite and balanced design. The form is contrapuntal throughout. Like a voice in a fugue each one of the main characters is an entirety in himself – I but his personality takes on a new richness when contrasted and woven in with the other characters in the book. It is in the actual style...that the work's affinity to contrapuntal music is seen most clearly. The object...is to come as close as possible to the inner psychic rhythms of the character... (and) at the end the style expresses the inner man just as deeply as is possible without lapsing into the unintelligible unconscious" (McCullers 1971: 148).[15]

Carson McCullers thus makes good use of a stylistic device which is available to her precisely because of the restrictions which the English language imposes on PAO constructions. Despite these restrictions, however, such constructions are not as rare in English as many may have assumed.[16] This has been amply illustrated here by the data collected from various grammars. By arranging all the examples in a typological hierarchy, it is easier to get a sense of the degree of markedness that is associated with the different types. But even within the typological categories themselves, Carson McCullers pushes at the boundaries. By repositioning the locative adverbials, she makes the marked categories even more marked, and turns the PAO pattern into a characteristic feature of her writing style.

## Notes

1. The following abbreviations are used in this paper: A (Adverbial), S (Subject), P (Predicator), O (Direct Object), C (Complement), DEP (Dependent), cl (clause), g (group), cu (compound unit). Capital letters denote functions, small letters denote forms. Form and function labels are combined by means of a colon notation; thus O:cl marks an object which has the form of a clause. (See Bache, Davenport, Dienhart, and Larsen 1991).
2. While some grammars state directly that the PAO pattern is highly marked, others "condemn" the construction by not mentioning it at all. Take, for example, Quirk and Greenbaum's widely used *A University Grammar of English* (1987). The reader searches in vain under "Types of sentence structure" (1987: 16) and "Clause patterns" (1987: 166-167) for examples of PAO structure. Leech, in his modern handbook, *An A-Z of English Grammar and Usage* (1989), treats adverb(ial) position explicitly in three places (pp. 21, 24-25, 27), but he does not once mention nor give a single example of the PAO structure in these pages. The situation is similar in a recent grammar from the Netherlands: *The Student's Grammar of English* (1989), by van Ek and Robat. In their section on adverbial position (1989: 391-399) these authors treat a wide range of adverbial types and offer 90 examples of these types in various positions. Not one of these 90 examples displays the PAO structure. Greenbaum and Quirk (1990) devote a whole chapter to "The semantics and grammar of adverbials" (pp. 158-187). Of the roughly 300 examples given, only one displays PAO structure (see note 5).
3. **TYPE I: PAO constructions involving "phrasal verbs"**: Drink <u>up</u> your milk quickly (Quirk and Greenbaum 1987: 348) / Don't leave <u>out</u> anything important (Leech 1989: 358) / We'll have to pull <u>down</u> the old farm buildings (van Ek and Robat 1989: 18).

   There are two interesting issues involving "phrasal verbs": a) should such constructions be analyzed as PO or as PAO, and b) what are the constraints on movement of the "particle"? Regarding the first question, Quirk and Greenbaum (1987: 347) view examples like the above as "cases where the main verb and one or more particles seem to combine as a multi-word verb". Holders of this view are quite likely to treat such sentences as examples of PO rather than PAO structure. On the other hand, Leech (1989: 357) states explicitly that he is willing to label a verb + adverb as a "phrasal verb" only "if the adverb changes the meaning of the verb". While this looks like semantic quicksand, Leech's discussion of this point (1989: 358) suggests that he would presumably analyze "give away information" (where "give away" = "reveal") as PO, whereas "give away my shirt" would be analyzed as PAO.

   Regarding the second question, there seems to be a general feeling among grammarians who write on the subject that there is a "preference" for putting the "particle" before the object if the object is not a pronoun. Thus the three examples of "PAO" structure given above are presumably more likely than the following "POA" counterparts: Drink your milk <u>up</u> quickly / Don't leave anything important <u>out</u> / We'll have to pull the old farm buildings <u>down</u>. If the oject is a pronoun, the "particle" is nearly always placed after the object. But even here there are some exceptions, so that "PAO" structure can be found in examples like the following (taken from Kruisinga 1925: 301): I have packed <u>up</u> **everything**. / George pointed his whip at a distant pillar of smoke, rising high into the sky, and flanked by low banks of blacker smoke. "They can't put <u>out</u> **that**," said Hazel. / No one knew better than she that the labourers on the Malloring Estate were better off than those on nine out of ten estates; better paid and better housed, and – better looked after in their morals? Was she to give <u>up</u> **that**? / Little was altered, but the big hall had been re-carpeted and the boughs lopped off the great tree which shadowed the library. I pointed <u>out</u> **this**.
4. **TYPE II: PAO constructions involving clausal objects (O:cl)**: it proved <u>conclusively</u> that lightning is due to electricity (Jacobson 1964: 66) / I wonder, <u>since you're here</u>, if you'd like to write a book for us (Jacobson 1964: 94) / He urged <u>secretly</u> that she be dismissed (Quirk et al. 1985: 499) / They argued <u>categorically</u> that no changes should be implemented (Vestergaard 1985: 74) / to reveal <u>in other unmistakable ways</u> just how serious a literary fellow I was (Lindquist 1989: 63) / the woman who'd had to be told <u>on the bus</u> why everyone else was agog (Lindquist 1989: 64).

Lindquist even provides an example with two adverbials before the object: Lieberman shook from his mind like dust whatever disagreeable feelings had been gathered (1989: 59).

Whereas grammarians might quibble over how to classify the "phrasal verb" constructions (Type I), there can be no doubt about the PAO structure of these examples (Type II).

Unlike the case with the "phrasal verb", the adverbials in these examples do not have an end-position option. As Quirk et al. correctly observe (1985: 499), if the adverbial is moved to the end of the sentence it would normally be viewed as an element of the direct object clause itself. Consider their own illustration: He urged secretly that she be dismissed / He urged that she be dismissed secretly. Whereas the first example is obviously to be read as PAO, the second is more likely to be read as PO than as POA. In other words, "secretly" in the second example will be read as part of the object clause.

5. **TYPE III: PAO constructions involving object groups containing postmodifying clauses (O:g with DEP:cl)**: He presented consistently the conception that only by loyalty could the State survive (Jacobson 1964: 142) / Following Volta's discoveries many scientists soon got to work, making batteries and investigating fully the effects which could be obtained with an electric current (Jacobson 1964: 142) / The towers of the castle crown in spectacular fashion a basalt crag which appears to rise sheer out of the sea (Scheurweghs 1966: 34) / She herself interviewed with hurtful disdain the student I had turned down (Quirk et al. 1985: 499) / She keeps in the garden some of the most lovable little rabbits you ever saw (Quirk et al. 1985: 511) / I found in the kitchen the letter I thought I had burnt (Quirk et al. 1985: 511) / She put on the table a letter she had just received from her lawyer (Greenbaum and Quirk 1990: 164).

Like the clausal object constructions (O:cl) of Type II, O:g with DEP:cl constructions (Type III) tend to be "long", but length is clearly not the only determining factor. As in the case of clausal objects, the very presence of the clause itself (here as DEP:cl) can give rise to a new reading if the adverbial is moved to the end of the sentence: She keeps in the garden some of the most lovable little rabbits you ever saw / She keeps some of the most lovable little rabbits you ever saw in the garden.

6. **TYPE IV: PAO constructions involving an object group with post modification but no subordinate clauses**: He discusses admirably the development of the legend (Kruisinga 1925: 305) / He announced curtly his intention of getting rid of the rubbish (Kruisinga 1925: 305) / The words of the Bishops express faithfully the mind of the Pope (Kruisinga 1925: 306) / He retains sometimes the ordinary grammatical structure in the sentences (Jacobson 1964: 142) / To read to-day the early speeches of Lloyd George is to step into another world (Jacobson 1964: 142) / "It's not every day," he said, blithely shovelling into his pocket the change from a pound note (Jacobson 1964: 143) / He built on Inner Farne Island a small oratory with walls of unhewn stone and a roof of turf. (Scheurweghs 1966: 34) / Mr. Asquith arranged unexpectedly an exchange of offices between the First Lord and the Home Secretary (Scheurweghs 1966: 37) / We must examine carefully the meanings of the words we use (Steller and Sørensen 1974: 187) / She kept writing in feverish rage long, violent letters of complaint (Quirk et al. 1985: 499) / They want to bring into force a new regulation about passengers in buses (Quirk et al. 1985: 511) / She made into a braver man the unfortunate and terrified victim of terrorism (Quirk et al. 1985: 511) / I have examined thoroughly your reports of the last two weeks (Vestergaard 1985: 74) / studying, for the first time in his life, the business page of the morning paper (Lindquist 1989: 64)

7. **TYPE V: PAO constructions involving an object consisting of a compound unit (O:cu)**: Incidentally, we have mentioned above the Isle of Man and the Channel Islands (Jacobson 1964: 142) / Look for yourself, and you will find in the long run only hatred, loneliness, despair, rage, ruin, and decay (Jacobson 1964: 143) / Vivien could see from her bedroom window the gleam of the Thames and the spires of Oxford itself (Jacobson 1964: 143) / So she wrote, in her spare time, poems and paragraphs and ideas, and even short stories (Lindquist 1989: 64).

8. **TYPE VI: PAO constructions involving an object group with premodifier(s) but without postmodifier(s)**: Roderick heard again that same indecisive step (Jacobson 1964: 142) / A

Labour Prime Minister has, <u>formally</u>, no such strong position (Jacobson 1964: 142) / Thereby it has become deeply secularized, and has at times been in danger of losing <u>altogether</u> its spiritual vitality (Jacobson 1964: 142) / ...Peter Breughel, who is unique among painters, and whose painting never fails to produce <u>in me</u> a special thrill (Jacobson 1964: 143) / His face wore <u>habitually</u> a peevish look (Steller and Sørensen 1974: 187) / She kissed <u>on the cheek</u> her tearful and trembling mother (Quirk et al. 1985: 511) / Write on this form, <u>please</u>, your full address. (Quirk et al. 1985: 570) / She visited <u>that very day</u> an elderly and much beloved friend (Quirk et al. 1985: 1362).

9. **TYPE VII: PAO constructions involving an object group without modification (other than a possible determiner)**: The Russian prisons keep <u>well</u> their prey (Kruisinga 1925: 305) / Husband and wife remembered <u>guiltily</u> their child (Kruisinga 1925: 306) / A man of faith has <u>always</u> a son somewhere (Jakobson 1964: 142) / When he read <u>aloud</u> his translations to the merchants of Antwerp,...it was a heavenly comfort and joy to the audience (Jacobson 1964: 142) / the pioneers are learning <u>anew</u> their familiarity... (Jacobson 1964: 142).

10. Strictly speaking, Type I does not "belong" in the typology. Not only is it an unmarked category, it cuts across all the other types. Consider the following set: He had trouble making <u>out</u> where he was (Type I and Type II) / He had trouble making <u>out</u> the name she had written (Type I and Type III) / He had trouble making <u>out</u> the name of the street (Type I and Type IV) / He had trouble making <u>out</u> where he was and what the road sign meant (Type I and Type V) / He had trouble making <u>out</u> the street name (Type I and Type VI) / He had trouble making <u>out</u> the number (Type I and Type VII). The reason for this "overlap" is that, unlike Types II through VII, Type I is basically a semantic rather than a syntactic category. Nonetheless, I have chosen to set "phrasal verbs" up as a separate type for two reasons: a) it is a generally accepted (though somewhat ill-defined) category, and b) without it, examples like those given in the above set would be distributed through all the other types, with the result that Type VII would be no more marked than Type II – the marking hierarchy would be destroyed. In a rare example like the following, where a "phrasal verb" appears together with another adverbial, it is clearly this other adverbial that determines the classification (here, Type IV): Parliament in its terror and its revenge took <u>blindly</u> <u>up</u> the old weapon of repression (Kruisinga 1925: 302).

11. This observation can be found more or less explicitly in e.g. Jacobson (1964: 143), Scheurweghs (1966: 34), Steller and Sørensen (1974: 187), Quirk et al (1985: 511), Vestergaard (1985: 73-74), Greenbaum and Quirk (1990: 164). Jacobson (1964: 143) supplies the following rather remarkable example of how long an adverbial can be in a PAO construction: Fashionable taste...sees <u>in Piero's science and in the intense seriousness with which he worked out the spatial relationships (especially those that lead into the picture</u>) between the component parts of his picture a firmer basis for painting than the lyrical exquisiteness of Botticelli (1447-1510), to whom the scientific research side of the Renaissance made no appeal at all.

12. Jacobson (1964) found a total of 9,207 adverbials in his 40,000 word corpus (taken from 5 works of fiction and 5 of non-fiction). Of these, 44 (0.5%) fall into our PAO Types III through VII (Jacobson labels these collectively "E2 position"). He found only four examples (0.04%) in the most marked category, our Type VII (1964:142). Most of the 44 are time adverbials (19 examples). There are 2 examples of place adverbials (Jacobson 1964: 80).

    Lindquist's (1989) corpus of 2000 adverbials is taken from 10 works of fiction (5 by American authors, 5 by British). It consists of the first 200 adverbial occurrences in each of the 10 books. 93 of these 2000 examples (4%) appear in what he calls (following Quirk et al. 1985) "initial End" (iE) position. He defines this position as follows: "after the verb, but before an obligatory constituent in the clause (complement, obligatory adverbial or object)" (1989: 59). Position iE thus encompasses more than PAO since it includes examples like: "There was <u>still</u> half an hour to twilight" and "They had gone <u>once</u> to a bureau". But here, too, time adverbials (33 occurrences) are much more frequent than place adverbials (11).

    In the examples taken from McCullers, on the other hand, 21 of the 24 adverbials (75%) are place adverbials.

13. There are also other cases where McCullers' placement of adverbials stands out. Particularly

noticeable are locative adverbials in anticipatory-<u>there</u> constructions: **There** had been <u>in the house</u> a terrible silence, for Jarvis had turned off the radio when they came in (*Wedding*, p. 24; PAS structure) / ...**there** would come <u>over her</u> a cheated discontent (*Wedding*, p. 56; PAS structure). But the placement of the following time adverbial is also of interest: The piano tuning was <u>for a minute</u> silent (*Wedding*, p. 83; PAC structure).

14. It should be stressed that the markedness is due to the locative adverbials being prepositional groups rather than one-word forms like "in", "out", "up", "down". These latter items have been "filtered out" in our typology, since they generally participate in "phrasal verb" constructions and hence are treated as Type I. Thus, "He took <u>out</u> a cigarette" is Type I and unmarked, whereas "He took <u>from his pocket</u> a cigarette" is Type VII and marked (see note 10).

15. "Had McCullers not had a strong background in musical theory, *The Heart Is a Lonely Hunter* doubtless would have been a very different work" (Carr 1990: 18).
    "In later years, she liked to have her manuscript in progress read aloud, partially because her vision was more affected by the strokes than she let on and reading was difficult for her, but also, I think, because she listened for the rhythm and the cadence of the language – the sound as well as the meaning of the words" (McCullers 1971: 285; Editor's note).

16. The reader may have observed that I have incorporated several cases of the PAO pattern in the text of this article. If these went unnoticed during the reading of the article, they provide direct evidence that the PAO pattern is not always so marked. In order of appearance the sentences in question are: "Naturally, I do not wish to argue that there is no difference here between Danish and English, but I do wish <u>in this paper</u> to show that PAO constructions are far more common in English than one might expect from examining books on English grammar" / "I suspect, <u>though</u>, that many native speakers, if pressed, would probably consider them marginally more marked than Type I" / "While some grammars state <u>directly</u> that the PAO pattern is highly marked, others "condemn" the construction by not mentioning it at all" / "Take, <u>for example</u>, Quirk and Greenbaum's widely used *A University Grammar of English* (1987) / "On the other hand, Leech (1989: 357) states <u>explicitly</u> that he is willing to label a verb + adverb as a 'phrasal verb' only 'if the adverb changes the meaning of the verb'".

# References

Bache, Carl, Mike Davenport, John Dienhart, Fritz Larsen. 1991. *An Introduction to English Sentence Analysis*. Copenhagen: Munksgaard.

Carr, Virginia Spencer. 1975. *The Lonely Hunter: A Biography of Carson McCullers*. Garden City, New York: Doubleday.

Carr, Virginia Spencer. 1990. *Understanding Carson McCullers*. Columbia, South Carolina: University of South Carolina Press.

Curme, George. 1931. *A Grammar of the English Language* (in three volumes). Volume III: Syntax. Boston: D. C. Heath and Company.

Greenbaum, Sidney and Randolph Quirk. 1990. *A Student's Grammar of the English Language*. London: Longman.

Jacobson, Sven. 1964. *Adverbial Positions in English*. Stockholm: AB Studentbok.

Kruisinga, E. 1925. *A Handbook of Present-day English* (in three volumes). Part II,3: English Accidence and Syntax. 4th ed. (1st ed. 1911). Utrecht: Kemink en Zoon.

Leech, Geoffrey. 1989. *An A-Z of English Grammar and Usage*. London: Edward Arnold.

Lindquist, Hans. 1989. *English Adverbials in Translation: A Corpus Study of Swedish Renderings*. Lund: Lund University Press.

McCullers, Carson. 1940. *The Heart is a Lonely Hunter*. New York: Houghton Mifflin. (Page references are to the Bantam pocketbook edition, 36th printing.)

McCullers, Carson. 1946. *The Member of the Wedding*. New York: Houghton Mifflin. (Page references are to the Bantam pocketbook edition, 20th printing.)

McCullers, Carson. 1971. *The Mortgaged Heart*. (A collection of McCullers' writings edited and published posthumously by her sister, Margarita G. Smith.) Boston: Houghton Mifflin.

McDowell, Margaret B. 1980. *Carson McCullers*. Boston: Twayne Publishers.

Quirk, Randolph and Sidney Greenbaum. 1987. *A University Grammar of English*. (First published 1973.) London: Longman.

Quirk, Randolph, Sidney Greenbaum, Geoffrey Leech and Jan Svartvik. 1985. *A Comprehensive Grammar of the English Language*. London: Longman.

Scheurweghs, G. 1959. *Present-day English Syntax: A Survey of Sentence Patterns*. (First published 1959.) London: Longmans, Green and Co. Ltd.

Steller, Poul and Knud Sørensen. 1974. *Engelsk grammatik*. 2nd ed. (1st ed. 1966). Copenhagen: Munksgaard.

van Ek, Jan and Nico Robat. 1989. *The Student's Grammar of English*. (First published 1984.) London: Longman.

Vestergaard, Torben. 1985. *Engelsk grammatik*. Copenhagen: Det Schønbergske Forlag.

Zandvoort, R. W. 1965. *A Handbook of English Grammar*. 3rd ed. (1st ed. 1957). London: Longmans, Green and Co. Ltd.

# Adjectives ending in -*ly*: A study based on material from modern English literature

*John M. Dienhart*

## 1. Introduction

I have been teaching English grammar at university level for more than thirty years, and year after year students have come to my classes from secondary school with a diminishing knowledge of grammar. But one "rule" of grammar, at least, persists: many of my students are convinced that if a word ends in -*ly* it is an adverb. That is, they appear to have incorporated the following mental "rule":

Generalization 1a: "All words ending in -*ly* are adverbs."

Of course, when confronted with words such as *belly, family, fly, gully, jolly, lily, melancholy, panoply, rally, rely, silly, supply,* and *Wally*, they will agree that this is not strictly true. They may not know what a suffix is, but they can feel that in these words -*ly* is not an "ending" in the sense inherent in the "rule".

So, exposed to such data, they are eventually willing to divide -*ly* words into two basic categories: 1) those in which the -*ly* is not a true ending and hence the word in question may be something other than an adverb, and 2) the rest of the cases, which they continue to classify uncritically as adverbs. In other words, they are willing to replace Generalization 1a with Generalization 1b:

Generalization 1b: "All words ending in an -*ly* suffix are adverbs."

This is, of course, an improvement, but it is still inaccurate. It cannot be denied, however, that the generalization has wide applicability. There can be no doubt that the vast majority of words ending in an -*ly* suffix are indeed adverbs. In the opening paragraphs of this essay I have already used several such words: *strictly, eventually, uncritically.* There are, in fact, no exceptions to Generalization

1b in my own text – so far. But it is not difficult to come up with a number of exceptions. Two of the more common ones are *friendly* and *lovely*. Though these words end in an *-ly* suffix, they are adjectives, not adverbs.

In general, grammar books tend to downplay or even ignore this adjective/adverb distinction – which may be one reason for the widespread overgeneralization given above. In Quirk and Greenbaum's *A University Grammar of English* (1987), I find only one reference to an adjective in *-ly*, namely the word *cowardly* (1987: 439). In their later work, *A Student's Grammar of the English Language* (Greenbaum and Quirk 1990), I have come across only two relevant observations. The first is this: "there are some words in *-ly* that can function both as adjectives and as adverbs" (1990: 130). Two examples are given: *early* and *kindly*. Strictly speaking, this statement does not refute Generalization 1b. Instead it suggests that some adverbs in *-ly* can also be adjectives. The other reference (1990: 131) at least hints at the existence of separate adjectives bearing an *-ly* suffix:

> When we require adverbs corresponding to *-ly* adjectives such as *fiendly, lively,* and *masterly,* we normally use an adjective construction, thereby avoiding the double suffix *-lily*: *She received us in a friendly way* (not: *\*She received us friendlily.*)

A more recent grammar by Bache and Davidsen-Nielsen, *Mastering English – An Advanced Grammar for Non-native and Native Speakers* (1997), has very little to say about adjectives in **-ly**, though it does point out that the "adverb-forming suffix [*-ly*] is highly productive and much more so than the adjective-forming suffix *-ly*" (1997: 488). This observation is true enough, but it does little to warn the unwary student away from Generalization 1b.

A rich source of information is Jespersen, who, as always, provides a storehouse of relevant information (see, for example, *Part VI* of his *A Modern English Grammar on Historical Principles*, 1974: 406-417). But Jespersen's 7-volume grammar of English is not a source which is generally known to today's students of English.

It is, of course, possible to find shorter grammar books which offer clear and detailed comparisons between adjectives and adverbs bearing an *-ly* suffix. But these tend to be of older date. Here, for example, is a sensible commentary from a 1950 grammar:

> It must not be assumed ... that all adverbs must end in *-ly*, for the language has numerous adverbs formed in other ways. Nor should one assume that all words ending in *-ly* are adverbs. The words *beastly, costly, deadly, fatherly friendly, godly, homely, kingly, likely, manly, slovenly, seemly, timely, womanly, ugly*, and several others are adjectives in common use; and some words in *-ly* serve equally as adjectives and as adverbs; e.g., *daily, early, monthly, only, weekly, yearly.*" (House and Harman 1950: 158)

This is succinct and to the point. We shall see that the list of adjectives in *-ly* supplied by House and Harman is accurate as far as it goes. We shall extend this list by discovering what items are covered by the nondescript label, "several others". In addition, we shall gain a sense of the relative frequency of these adjectives, and learn something of the history of these forms.

As my data sources, I have selected eight modern literary works[1] by writers from different parts of the English-speaking world:

- *The Blind Assassin* by Margaret Atwood (Canada, 607 pages)[2]
- *The Shelters of Stone* by Jean Auel (USA, 758 pages).
- *The Unusual Life of Tristan Smith* by Peter Carey (Australia, 405 pages)
- *A World of Strangers* by Nadine Gordimer (South Africa, 247 pages)
- *Family Matters* by Rohinton Mistry (India → Canada[3], 484 pages)
- *The Enigma of Arrlval* by V. S. Naipaul (Trinidad → UK, 297 pages)
- *London* by Edward Rutherfurd (UK, 1302 pages)
- *The Fox Boy* by Peter Walker (New Zealand, 327 pages)

All in all, these sources provide a total of 4,427 pages of imaginative prose, thus constituting a solid basis for a study of the range, the frequency, and the productivity of *-ly* adjectives in modem English.[4]

## 2. Two "different" suffixes *-ly*

The basic problem (though, as we shall see, not the only one) involved here is that English uses an *-ly* suffix to form both adjectives and adverbs. Let us, for convenience, follow the *Oxford English Dictionary* (henceforth *OED*) and refer to these as Suffix 1 (adjective-forming) and Suffix 2 (adverb-forming). The fact that Suffix 1 and Suffix 2 are identical today is what causes classification problems for students of English. There being no formal difference between the two suffixed forms means that students must know something about English syntax in order to successfully and consistently make the distinction. The basic syntactic difference, of course, involves the notion of "modification": in general, adjectives modify nouns, whereas adverbs modify verbs, adjectives and other adverbs. Consider for example, the following sentence:

- "But a member of the **knightly** class did not speak treason **lightly**" (Rutherfurd 1998: 391)

*Knightly* is an adjective modifying the noun "class", whereas *lightly* is an adverb modifying the verb "speak".

Although this study focuses primarily on the adjectives themselves, and not on the differences between adjectives and adverbs, it seems appropriate to begin with a short presentation of data illustrating the two types. Consider first the adverb-forming Suffix 2, which is by far the more common. Here is one example from the beginning pages of each of the eight sources:

*Suffix 2 (adverb-forming)*
- "In reality I could **barely** get the words out; my mouth was numb; my entire face was rigid with pain" (Atwood 2001: 3)
- "People were gathering on the limestone ledge, looking down at them **warily**" (Auel 2002: 1)
- "As she crossed the Boulevard des Indiennes to the river she already felt **distinctly** uncomfortable" (Carey 1995: 7)
- "The consul and his mother were alone at meals, and I played bridge with them several times in the air-conditioned card-room, where we sat around **numbly** like so much refrigerated food" (Gordimer 1976: 11)
- "Their words had incandesced **painfully** in her mind, and she had fled to her room to weep for her dead father" (Mistry 2002: 2)
- "Winter was to me a time **mainly** of short days, and of electric lights everywhere at working hours; also a time when snow was a possibility" (Naipaul 1987: 11)
- "Under this layer of slate, deep in the Earth, pressures still more ancient had raised up a **gently** shelving ridge some two thousand feet high" (Rutherfurd 1998: 1)
- "And then there were also the bottles of Scotch on the sideboard, towards which, on that farm, thoughts turned **lightly** at the close of day" (Walker 2001: 2)

Suffix 1, though much less common, is nonetheless a recurrent feature of English. Here is one example from each of the eight texts:

*Suffix 1 (adjective-forming)*
- "The ideal sacrifice should be like a dance, was the theory: **stately** and lyrical, harmonious and graceful" (Atwood 2001: 36)
- "Ayla especially enjoyed watching the **lively**, playful calves, still quite young – the cows calved in late spring and early summer" (Auel 2002: 639)
- "He would push his freshly opened bottle of roteuse down into the already melting snow, tuck the tartan rug around his shining **shapely** brown legs, and open the first of the books in his lap" (Carey 1995: 324)
- "Would I be willing to send a **weekly** newsletter on the effects of racial segregation?" (Gordimer 1976: 35-36)
- "He realized why the flirting depressed him: it was the gulf between her coquettish words and **slovenly** appearance" (Mistry 2002: 119)

- "As long as you looked, he looked; as soon as you moved or made a gesture he was away, running at first through the reeds and tall grass and then giving the **lovely** leap that could take him clear over fences and hedges" (Naipaul 1987: 47)
- "In one comer was a rack of Indian daggers and a silver ankus, the gift of a **friendly** maharajah" (Rutherfurd 1998: 1186)
- "A Maori, thin, **elderly**, ill-looking, wearing a lady's red V-necked jumper, and his companion, a plump white woman wearing a man's tweed jacket, and with blue eyes as hard as pebbles, began to tell me about their triumphs at the races" (Walker 2001: 22)

The formal identity of Suffix 1 and Suffix 2 has a historical explanation. In Old English, adjectives were frequently formed from nouns by adding the suffix *-lic*: while adverbs were often formed by adding the suffix *-e* to adjectives, including those adjectives already ending in *-lic*. Thus *-lice* took on the nature of an adverb-forming suffix, along with *-e*. The distinction between adjectives in *-lic* and adverbs in *-lice* was thus formally marked in Old English. However, with the loss of final *-e* in the Middle English period, the formal distinction was lost, and both suffixes were reduced to what is now *-ly*. (For further details, see e.g. Jespersen 1974: 406, 408; Mencken 1979: 247, 562; Mitchell 1995: 52; *OED* 1989 IX: 129.)

In the *American Heritage Dictionary* (henceforth *AHD*) the primary meaning of the adverb-forming suffix is given as: "in a specified manner; in the manner of" (*AHD* 2000: 1043). The meaning of the adjective-forming suffix is given as "like; resembling; having the characteristics of" (*AHD* 2000: 1043). In other words, Suffix 2 is used chiefly to form manner adverbials, whereas Suffix 1 is used primarily to create characterizing adjectives.[6]

This paper is devoted primarily to exploring the nature and distribution of the adjective-forming Suffix 1. As already noted, this suffix is added primarily to nouns. So let us begin with an investigation of these forms.

## 3. -*ly* adjectives formed from nouns

Adjectives derived from nouns by adding *-ly* constitute the largest single set of counter-examples to the overgeneralization that all words ending in the suffix *-ly* are adverbs. This set of derived adjectives can, to a certain degree, be subdivided according to the nature of the noun involved.

### 3.1 From nouns referring to people

Jespersen (1974: 407) observes that "*-ly* is freely added to nouns denoting persons, particularly relatives or holders of a trade or profession". Warren (1984: 128) is more general. She calls this group simply [+human]. There can be no doubt that the people/profession category is an important subclass of -*ly* adjectives. Here are relevant examples from my data:

- "'You were just a girl when I left, now you're a beautiful woman ... just as I always knew you'd be,' he said, with slightly more than a **brotherly** glint in his eye" (Auel 2002: 2)
- "When Noake wrote to his powerful patron, he adopted not only Fox's tone of voice and attitudes but even his narrow and **clerkly** handwriting" (Walker 2001: 152)
- "For a long time ... the Dane had supposed he felt only a **fatherly** affection for her, while she, perceiving the truth far sooner, said nothing" (Rutherfurd 1998: 244)
- "The Master of Discipline was a stout, pink-faced **friendly** soul whose glasses misted over when he had to use the cane" (Walker 2001: 10)
- "Pitton's Salisbury hat! So stylish, so elegant and **gentlemanly** the gesture with which he half lifted it off his head in greeting!" (Naipaul 1987: 250)
- "He could even justify it. For were not these the ancient rules of the aristocratic, **knightly** class?" (Rutherfurd 1998: 1018)
- "The Master of the System would have clucked his **lordly** tongue not merely about my face and body, but also my voice" (Carey 1995: 70)
- "Why couldn't she accept his **manly** hobby?" (Mistry 2002: 341)
- "They were part of a great army assembled to challenge Titokowaru – the 'largest solely colonial force ever raised', according to James Belich, a historian who in 1989 published a **masterly** account of Titokowaru's war" (Walker 2001: 139)
- "The woman running the grocery store will be dark-haired and plump and **motherly**, and will talk about her thinness and the need to eat more" (Atwood 2001: 567)
- "Some of the upper sections of the panels could be opened to admit light and **neighbourly** conversations, if desired" (Auel 2002: 25)
- "He still wore the slightly vulgar sparkling suit, the lizardskin boots, but when he brought me my wine in both hands, this shining actor's garb took on a **priestly,** or even **kingly,** aspect" (Carey 1995: 365)
- "She had been something called 'household adviser' to some Indian prince who, despite Indian democracy and Nehru, seemed to have lived in all the splendour of the days of independent **princely** states" (Gordimer 1976: 20-21)
- "She gasped something to Anna about the food; and then left us, swept her **queenly** way through the guests, and disappeared, in what I gathered was the direction of the kitchen" (Gordimer 1976: 83)

- "These **saintly** impulses of hers had to be curbed, he said; he wasn't running an almshouse" (Atwood 2001: 222)
- "Like most girls of her class, she had a governess – a **scholarly** woman who told them Violet was gifted and who had taken her far beyond the standard required" (Rutherfurd 1998: 1181)
- "There was a **womanly,** sensual quality about her" (Auel 2002: 533)

All of these adjectives have existed in the English language for centuries, as witnessed by the following early entries in the *OED*: *brotherly* (1535), *clerkly* (1528), *fatherly* (1440), *friendly* (1374), *gentlemanly* (1433), *kingly* (1382), *knightly* (1375), *lordly* (1645), *manly* (1422), *masterly* (1531-32), *motherly* (1597), *neighbourly* (1558), *priestly* (1535), *princely* (1503), *queenly* (1540), *saintly* (1660), *scholarly* (1638), *womanly* (1385). This is not to say that the suffix cannot occasionally find some more modern uses in connection with people and professions. The following statement, for example, is uttered by the son of an actress, who is trying to comfort him:

- "She stroked my head, but there was something **actorly** in the way she did it and I flinched from her" (Carey 1995: 99)

The first entry for *actorly* in the *OED* is as recent as 1959 ("An actorly performance, no doubt, but at the same time genuinely felt").

It has been observed (see e.g. Jespersen 1974: 407, *OED* IX: 129) that adjectives in -*ly* tend to have positive, favorable associations (Jespersen calls them "laudatory", while the *OED* expression is "eulogistic"), and certainly this is borne out by most of the above examples. However, it would seem more appropriate to rephrase this point in the following fashion: the suffix appears to have a strong affinity for nouns with positive associations – that is, it is the base noun itself (rather than the suffix) that provides the positive connotation.

There are some cases, though, where the associations are more negative (Jespersen's word is "depreciatory"; the *OED* expression is "dyslogistic"). Again, I would prefer to say that the suffix can also attach itself to nouns with negative connotations. Two such examples occur in Jespersen's collection (1974: 407): *beggarly* and *rascally*. Here are some additional instances from my data:

- "'You're so stupid,' Roxanna said. 'You're so **cowardly**'" (Carey 1995: 158)
- "'I keep myself to myself,' she'd say. How prudent that seemed to me once. How **miserly**, now" (Atwood 2001: 83)
- "He realized why the flirting depressed him: it was the gulf between her coquettish words and **slovenly** appearance" (Mistry 2002: 119)

It may surprise some readers (as it did me) to learn that the latter example is indeed derived from a noun. The noun "sloven" is defined as "One who is habitually careless in personal appearance or work" (*AHD* 2000: 1639). According to the *OED* (XV: 741-742) the noun with this meaning can be traced back to 1530 and the corresponding adjective to 1583. The noun appears even earlier (1450) with the meaning "A person of low character or manners; a knave, rascal". The corresponding adjective based on this meaning appears in 1515. As for the other two items, the first reference to *cowardly* in the *OED* (III: 1083) is from 1576, and the earliest reference to *miserly* is from 1593 (IX: 864).

The word *surly* has shifted from a positive to a negative meaning:

- "As I have said, there was something about this woman which made one feel **surly** if one did not respond, as it was so easy to do, to the mood generated by her enthusiasms" (Gordimer 1976: 13)

According to the *OED* (XV: 550, XVII: 295) *surly* is an alternate spelling for the now obsolete *sirly*. The *OED* suggests that its original meaning may have been "lordly, majestic", which then became "masterful, imperious; haughty, arrogant, supercilious" and finally, today, "churlishly ill-humored: rude and cross" – as in the example above. The earliest *OED* instance of *surly* with this meaning is from 1670.

It should be added that we can in general move from positive to negative associations by such simple devices as the addition of a negative prefix:

- "I absolutely would not accompany her out into the **unfriendly** light of day" (Carey 1995: 185)
- "Mr Wilson, MA (St John's), 'could reprimand with great severity a boy detected in an **ungentlemanly** act,' and at the midday meal, 'it was a brave sight to see him attack a large sirloin of beef,' a pupil wrote" (Walker 2001: 135)
- "The Suffragettes had learned that the way to disarm criticism that they were **unwomanly** was to dress with great care" (Rutherfurd 1998: 1248)

These forms may be somewhat more recent than their unprefixed counterparts. The first entry for *unfriendly* in the OED is from 1425, while *unwomanly* first appears in 1529, and *ungentlemanly* in 1562.

*3.2 From nouns referring to periods of time*

Another important subclass of nouns from which adjectives in *-ly* are derived involves words denoting periods of time. This category, too, is identified by both Jespersen (1974: 407) and the *OED* (IX: 129). Jespersen apparently follows the *OED* in classifying these as items denoting "periodic recurrence". Warren (1984: 128), again, is more general. She labels this group simply [+time]. Here are some examples from my data:

- "Without the book and the **daily** act of creation I do not know how I would have gone through that difficult time" (Naipaul 1987: 154)
- "Te Whiti o Rongomai died on 18 November 1907 after being taken ill on the night following the **monthly** meeting at Parihaka, which he had addressed as usual" (Walker 2001: 323)
- "But he desisted – the **nightly** quarrels he heard while standing at the window made it clear that Manizeh was in no mood to be placated" (Mistry 2002: 341)
- "The **quarterly** session of the Supreme Court opened in Christchurch in early June 1882" (Walker 2001: 304)
- "Would I be willing to send a **weekly** newsletter on the effects of racial segregation?" (Gordimer 1976: 35-36)
- "From that day to this, when the monarch's representative comes to summon the Commons to the **yearly** opening ceremony, the door is symbolically slammed in his face" (Rutherfurd 1998: 850-851)

As with the *-ly* adjectives formed from [+human] bases, the forms denoting periods of time have all been around for a long time, as the *OED* makes clear: *daily* 1470 (IV: 216), *monthly* 1572 (IX: 1043), *nightly* 1380 (X: 415), *quarterly* 1563 (XII: 996), *weekly* 1489 (XX: 83), *yearly* 1452 (XX: 713). Unlike the [+human] subcategory, however, adjectives derived from [+time] bases do not have any particular "positive" (or "negative") associations. In fact, the semantic value of the suffix for this group of adjectives is not the same as that for the [+human] forms. The suffix does not suggest "having the characteristics of" (be those characteristics positive or negative). Thus "daily" does not mean "having the characteristics of a day", but rather "recurring on a daily basis". The general meaning for the [+time] adjectives – to use Jespersen's (1974: 407) phrase – is "denoting periodic recurrence". This leads Warren (1984: 130) to refer to members of this set as "adverbial adjectives".

*3.3 From other nouns (excluding people and time)*

Neither Jespersen nor the *OED* list any subclasses of denominal adjectives in *-ly* other than those dealing with people and time. Warren (1984: 128), however, offers one additional subclass, which she labels [+place]. In this class she includes four adjectives: *earthly*, *heavenly*, *homely*, and *worldly*. I find this set problematic, since it is highly restricted. It does not extend to such obvious "places" as city, desert, restaurant, school, store, town, university, or village. Instead, one might argue that Warren's examples carry religious overtones (at least in the case of *earthly*, *heavenly*, and *worldly*), which might link them semantically to such items as *priestly* and *saintly* from the [+human] class. Consequently, following Jespersen and the *OED*, I have divided denominal *-ly* adjectives into only three classes: a) people, b) time, and c) other.

We can now ask whether the members of the "other" subclass tend to have positive associations, as in the case of the "person" subclass, or whether they are "neutral" in this respect, like the "time" subclass.

The instances of "positive" forms supplied by the *OED* (IX: 129) all relate only to people and professions (*kingly*, *knightly*, *masterly*, *princely*, *queenly*, *scholarly*, *soldierly*). Jespersen's illustrative list (1974: 407) of "positive" forms, though much shorter (*lovely*, *masterly*, *scholarly*, *womanly*), includes the word *lovely*, thus suggesting that his notion of "positive" associations extends beyond the "person" subclass. My data tends to support this more general claim and extends the list of relevant lexical items. In each of the following examples, the adjective is derived from a noun which does not refer to people or professions, and yet there are clear positive associations:

- "The crusades had given him a religious calling; the new Continental pastime of jousting had added pageantry; now from the warm, southern, French-speaking courts of Provence and Aquitaine had come a fashion for ballads and tales of **courtly** love, together with sophisticated manners new to the northern world" (Rutherfurd 1998: 370)
- "He had little occasion to sin, but he made no great attempt to lead a **godly** life, since there was no longer any point" (Rutherfurd 1998: 928)
- "'Hop in quickly. It's **heavenly**" (Gordimer 1976: 17)
- "If Pappa stays here for a few weeks, in your happy, **homely** atmosphere, he'll soon be smiling again" (Mistry 2002: 98)
- "One **lovely** young woman with a Dresden china face under a coiffure of white hair wore a lilac chiffon cape over a full-flowing grey gown" (Atwood 2001: 427)
- "It was the hand of man, the hand of the water bailiffs and people like them, that suggested an **orderly** Nature" (Naipaul 1987: 188)
- "She had left an open space on both sides, showing a long, bare, **shapely** leg, and tied the thong low, barely over her hips, causing the fringe in front and back to sway when she walked" (Auel 2002: 99)
- "April gambolled in like a lamb this year, and taking a cue from his **sprightly** kick-up-your-heels mood, the Spring season was all aflutter with the gay bustle of arrivals and departures" (Atwood 2001: 494)

- "Kites and hawks and lammergeiers soared and dived, sometimes fighting with **stately** ravens and raucous crows" (Auel 2002: 572)
- "It occurred to her that this aristocratic young adventurer, her junior by only a few years, would soon be far more **worldly**, far wiser, far more experienced and more interesting than she would ever have the chance to be" (Rutherfurd 1998: 1162)

As with the preceding subclasses ([+person] and [+time]), we are dealing with adjectives which have been part of the English language for quite a while. Here are some early instances for each of the above adjectives – as listed in the *OED*: *courtly* (1450), *godly* (1450), *heavenly* (1382), *homely* (1366), *lovely* (1340), *orderly* (1577), *shapely* (1382), *sprightly* (1596), *stately* (1385) *worldly* (1325).

A considerably more recent adjective, apparently, is the following compound form:

- "There was a sacred quality to this place; it felt spiritual, **otherworldly**, and she didn't want to desecrate it in any way" (Auel 2002: 501)

The earliest entry in the OED for *otherworldly* is 1879. Note that in the above example the associations are, again, clearly positive.

I assume that most people would also view the following three adjectives as "positive" in some sense:

- "After a **leisurely** midday meal, further discussion revealed that the location of the bison herd was not far from a previously built surround that could be repaired and made serviceable" (Auel 2002: 198)
- "She returned with the violin and started a **lively** piece that filled the room with its energy" (Mistry 2002: 232)
- "Therefore the repairs to the house had not been carried out in what any reasonable person would consider a **timely** and satisfactory manner" (Atwood 2001: 468)

As with the other -*ly* adjectives which we have encountered, all three of these forms have been part of the English vocabulary for centuries. Here are the relevant dates from the *OED*: *leisurely* (1604), *lively* (c. 1430), *timely* (1400).

*Costly*, too, can have positive overtones in many contexts.

- "The Saxon's green cloak was trimmed with red squirrel fur, but Barnikel's blue cloak was trimmed with **costly** ermine from the Viking state of Russia, a sign that he was rich indeed" (Rutherfurd 1998: 191)

*Costly* is defined by the *OED* (III: 991) as "costs much; requiring or involving great expenditure. Of great price or value; sumptuous". An early instance is from 1494.

The following example illustrates an adjective which once had positive connotations, but now has negative associations:

- "When they opened the Maternity waiting room door they found Vincent Theroux – forty-six years old, not very tall, wide in the shoulders but now plump, even **portly** (Carey 1995: 13)

According to the *OED* (XII: 156), *portly* originally meant "Characterized by stateliness or dignity of bearing, appearance, and manner", the earliest example of which is from 1529. However, it now usually means "Large and bulky in person; stout, corpulent", as in the example given above. The earliest *OED* entry with this meaning is from Shakespeare (1596).

Similar in meaning to *portly* is the word *burly*:

- "As the elevator doors shut, I heard a walkie-talkie crackling and saw, reflected in the doors' shining surface, a **burly** man in uniform walking towards me" (Carey 1995: 333)

An entry as early as 1400 is given for *burly* by the *OED* with the meaning we see here: "stout, sturdy, massively built", but the derivational history of this word is rather obscure. The *OED* (II: 672) provides the following background:

> ME. *borlich*, northern *burli*. Usually identified with OHG. *burlîh*, MHG. *burlîch* exalted, lofty, stately, f[ormed on] *\*bur-* cogn. w. OHG *burjan* to lift up + *-lîh* = *-ly*. If this be so, the word must have existed in OE. or ON.; but it is unrecorded and no plausible etymon for the first element has yet been found in either of those langs.[8]

The *WEUD* (1996: 199) claims that *burly* is related to OE *borlice*, meaning "excellent(ly), equiv. to *bor(a)* ruler (lit. high-born one; see BEAR) + *-lice*". So it is possible that there once existed a noun from which the adjective derived, and this noun seems to have had strong positive overtones. The form *burly*, whatever its derivational history, is best viewed today as monomorphemic: the old base form is now so tightly fused to the former suffix that <ly> has become an integral part of the word.

The following *-ly* adjective appears to be rather neutral with respect to the negative-positive scale, though perhaps it could be said to have negative connotations when in a paradigmatic relation with e.g. *heavenly*:

- "A banner with a strange device, a knight sacrificing all **earthly** concerns to scale the heights" (Atwood 2001: 321)

An early entry for *earthly* in the *OED* is from 1300.

The same comments apply to *bodily*. It is rather neutral, though it can lean toward the negative in some contexts:

- "Crude references to **bodily** functions usually put a stop to Myra" (Atwood 2001: 457)

The first entry for *bodily* in the *OED* is from 1300.

I have come across the following forms which can be said to have negative connotations:

- "Was I so shallow in my emotions, so forgetful, that this 'horror made of cardboard' could erase the disgusted faces in which I had seen the effect of my own **beastly** face?" (Carey 1995: 165)
- "Several stanzas were devoted to the **dastardly** way the dark deed was perpetrated, followed by her threats and curses: a string of horrible diseases for the thieves, should they so much as taste a morsel of the stolen bird" (Mistry 2002: 403-404)
- "Cheque-books, those little purses women have, foam-rubber cushions, the **deathly** moonlight of fluorescent strips; these things came to mind confusedly" (Gordimer 1976: 101)
- "He left the shed door wide open and walked across the lawn – that part which still bore the impression, like **ghostly** shadows, of the three felled beeches – to the openness of the manor courtyard" (Naipaul 1987: 246)

These forms are as old as the positive ones. For *beastly*, the *OED* (II: 29) has an entry from 1382 in the sense "of the nature of living creatures" and from 1611 in the sense "abominable, disgusting, offensive". Early entries for *dastardly* and *deathly* stem from 1567 and 1568, respectively, while *ghostly* can be found as early as 1303.

Note, once again, that adjectives with positive associations can be made negative by the simple addition of a negative prefix:

- "Perhaps she felt it was **ungodly**" (Rutherfurd 1998: 810)
- "Yet in the days that followed, though at first he wanted to put his hand in front of his **unsightly** face whenever he saw her, he was never able to detect the revulsion he supposed the girl must feel" (Rutherfurd 1998: 265)
- " ... before the poor boy's **untimely** death, Arthur, the then heir had first been married to the Spanish princess" (Rutherfurd 1998: 638)

The following example patterns in the same way as the above instances in *un-*, though it seems somewhat forced:

- "Perversely, it was then, when he was **unlovely**, that I finally loved him freely" (Carey 1995: 365)

Even with the negative prefix, the context can determine whether the associations are negative or positive, as the following pair of examples illustrates:

- "Enough was enough, a little hammering was one thing – this kind of **unearthly** screeching at night was beyond tolerance" (Mistry 2002: 37)
- "I felt its welcoming quality, its protectiveness, and was moved by the **unearthly** beauty (as it seemed to me) of every growing thing around my cottage" (Naipaul 1987:178)

The following example involves a negative prefix which is added to the noun prior to the derivation in *-ly*:

- "William Morris appears on a charge of being **disorderly** and drunk; the bench sighs and observes that he is always **disorderly** and drunk" (Walker 2001: 109)

Whether the prefix is *un-* or *dis-*, these adjectives have been around for some time, though they tend to be somewhat more recent than the nonprefixed forms: *earthly* (1300)/*unearthly* (1611); *godly* (1450)/*ungodly* (1526); *lovely* (1340)/*unlovely* (1586); *orderly* (1577)/*disorderly* (1585); *timely* (1400)/*untimely* (1535); *unsightly* (1548).[9]

Having now examined those *-ly* adjectives in our data which derive from nouns, we turn our attention in the next section to a much smaller subset.

## 4. *-ly* adjectives formed from adjectives

Our eight texts provide nine clear instances of the adjective-forming suffix *-ly* attached to adjectives. Eight of these forms are quite common:

- " ... all I could see was Wally, his anger, his self-righteous face, the elevator rising and falling in its dark and **deadly** shaft" (Carey 1935: 394)
- "My imagination had given me a glimpse of a benign **elderly** man in a brown jacket making a shy wave from his car" (Naipaul 1987: 172)
- "But he did as he was asked, and when, two days later, the bishop and a party of ten priests and two dozen noblemen of Kent appeared, Cerdic had

- assembled a **goodly** company of some hundred people from the hamlets along the river to meet them" (Rutherfurd 1998: 164)
- "As if Faunce would ever be bothered with a minor role such as that of **kindly** uncle!" (Gordimer 1976: 40)
- "A **likely** story. But people believed it, or had to pretend they did. I suppose the Newton-Dobbses were spreading the real story around among their twenty closest friends" (Atwood 2001: 405)
- "A child, who has been wandering up and down motherless for three years or so, is found by a **lonely** woman who has always been childless" (Walker 2001: 133)
- "But none of the girls could be said to have suffered from their **lowly** Background" (Rutherfurd 1998: 1172)
- "He dismissed Nariman's explanation that Jal and Coomy's **sickly** father and their unhappy childhood was the reason for the shrine" (Mistry 2002: 26)

The ninth instance, *poorly*, is used only predicatively in English, and is rather colloquial:

- "His wife, who was often **poorly**, had always miscarried" (Rutherfurd 1998: 521)

Unlike the majority of -ly adjectives formed from noun bases, these nine adjectives formed from adjective bases are not overridingly positive. In fact, of the examples listed above, only *goodly* and *kindly* have clear positive connotations (note that in the example above, *goodly* has the sense "notable or considerable in respect of size, quantity, or number" – OED VI: 677). But like the noun-based forms, these adjectives have been around for quite a while. Here are early instances from the *OED*: *deadly* (1377), *elderly* (1660), *goodly* (1385), *kindly* (1400), *likely* (1380), *lonely* (1607), *lowly* (1374), *poorly* (1573), *sickly* (1350).

Two of these adjectives have negative counterparts: *unkindly* and *unlikely*. I found no instances of the former in my data, but the latter was quite common:

- "So in an **unlikely** way, the ideas of the aesthetic movement of the end of the nineteenth century, and the ideas of Bloomsbury, ideas bred essentially out of empire, wealth and imperial security, had been transmitted to me in Trinidad" (Naipaul 1987: 134)

The negative *unlikely* seems to be as old as its positive counterpart, *likely*: the *OED* has an entry from 1375.

Another negative form is seen in the next example:

- "'That's what these are for,' Kareja said, using the wooden supports to prop up the ungainly headdress" (Auel 2002: 231)

The *OED* informs us (VI: 315) that the form *gainly* (which does not appear in my basic data) derives from a now obsolete adjective, *gain*, plus the *-ly* suffix. *Gain* is said (VI: 312) to have meant, in Old Norse, something like "straight, direct, favourable, helpful". It is rare in Old English, but is allegedly cognate with modern German *gegen*. The adjective *gainly*, when referring to "bodily form, attitude or movement", is defined as the "reverse of ungainly; graceful, shapely". The earliest occurrence of *gainly* with this meaning in the *OED* (VI: 315) is from 1855: "The curls ... had now been displaced, and the hair twisted into the more womanly, but less gainly, protuberance at the back." The *OED* has an entry for *ungainly* from 1611, so this form seems to be older than its positive counterpart.

This completes our treatment of the small class of *-ly* adjectives derived from other adjectives. The next class is even smaller.

## 5. *-ly* adjectives formed from verbs

A few adjectives in *-ly* are constructed from a verb base, though this may not be immediately apparent:

- "The **ghastly** ritual went on: tearing anxiety of pacing and panting, climax of sobs, then panting again" (Gordimer 1976: 200)
- "For years they've bombarded me with letters, wanting Laura's own letters – wanting manuscripts, mementoes, interviews, anecdotes – all the **grisly** details" (Atwood 2001: 349)
- "The church was built of **ugly**, purplish brick and smelled of the soap with which the congregants had washed, and of the smoke with which their clothing was impregnated from their cooking fires" (Gordimer 1976: 193-194)

An early instance of the adjective *ghastly* is dated 1390 in the *OED* (VI: 389). It derives, apparently, from the now archaic verb gust + *-ly*. According to the *OED*, this verb had the meaning "to frighten, alarm, scare, terrify". The most recent instance of this verb in the *OED* is from 1616, after which it seems to have died out, while the adjective lives on. One of the *OED* examples of the verb is taken from Shakespeare's *King Lear* (1605): "Or whether gasted by the noyse I made, Full sodainely he fled".

The word *grisly* is another word with a rather mysterious history. According to the *OED* (VI: 855) this is indeed an *-ly* adjective, but it is unclear exactly where the form came from. The *OED* informs us that it is ultimately from *gris-* "a weak root" of the verb *grise*, "but the history is unknown". Part of the problem is that the history of *grise* itself is obscure (see *OED* VI: 854). The *AHD* (2000: 773, 2030) traces the word back to proto-Indo-European *\*ghrei-*, meaning "to rub". It gives the OE form as *grislic*, "terrifying", which is said to derive from Germanic *\*pis-*, "to frighten (to grate on the mind)". At any rate, *grisly* is an old form. It can be found in Chaucer's Monk's Tale around 1386 (VI: 855).

As with *ghastly* and *grisly*, the derivation of ugly is obscured by the obsolescence of the old base. According to the *OED* (XVIII: 807, 808), the adjective *ugly* arises from the addition of *-ly* to the verb *ug*, which in turn derives from Old Norse *ugga*, meaning "to fear, dread, apprehend". *Ugly*, which appears as early as 1300, is best viewed today as a monomorphemic form.

A clear instance of an *-ly* adjective from a verb base is seen in the next example:

- "He felt it would be **unseemly** to make a stronger effort, and waited for an opening" (Mistry 2002: 394)

Here the verb *seem* has attracted a negative prefix and an *-ly* suffix. Somewhat surprisingly, my basic data does not contain the word, *seemly*. According to the *OED*, both the positive form and the negative form are found as early as 1300.

Having now exhausted the list of *-ly* adjectives (in our data) derived from nouns, adjectives and verbs, the question remains: Do other word classes supply base forms for *-ly* adjectives? The answer is a qualified yes, as discussed in the next section.

## 6. *-ly* adjectives formed from bases other than nouns, adjectives, verbs

An interesting subcategory of *-ly* adjectives involves compass directions:

- "There was a bracing **easterly** wind, an open blue sky; the distant city was so clear it might have been a painting and the great curve of the river lay gleaming below" (Rutherfurd 1998: 1075)
- "Further upstream it curved in a more **northerly** direction, and the lay of the land forced the water to the wall of the cliff on the right bank" (Auel 2002: 400)
- "She looked down at the **southerly** end of the terrace of the Ninth Cave beyond a spring-fed stream that ran off the edge of the stone porch" (Auel 2002: 216)
- "'The Speedwell can't go on. She's rotten,' Captain Jones told the assembled passengers, when they had returned to the **westerly** port of Plymouth" (Rutherfurd 1998: 814)

The *OED* is rather non-committal about the derivation of these forms, though the implication seems to be that the suffix *-ly* is attached to obsolete comparative forms of the corresponding adjectives – *easter, norther, souther* and *wester* (see V: 37 for *easterly*, X: 523 for *northerly*, XVI: 71 for *southerly*, XX: 164 for *westerly*). Early dates for these forms in the *OED* are: *easterly* (1609), *northerly* (1551), *southerly* (1551), *westerly* (1577).

Another *-ly* form whose derivation is now rather obscure is *only*:

- "It was on a section of this lane that in my earliest days I had met Tack's father-in-law and exchanged the **only** words I had ever exchanged with him" (Naipaul 1987: 41)

According to the *OED* (X: 818), the adjective *only* is derived by adding *-ly* to the numeral, *one*. One of the earliest instances is from 1526. It would seem reasonable to view *only* as monomorphemic today.

Another interesting form is *early*:

- "The brightness seemed strange to me, not because I'd come from *early* winter in London, but because I'd just left the coloured twilight of the hotel" (Gordimer 1976: 38)

The *OED* (V: 23) writes: "Not found in OE., and only rarely in ME.; probably evolved from the adv[erb]." The adverb (V: 24) apparently derives from an unattested form, *\*ár*, the "positive deg[ree] of *ær* ERE + *-líce*". In Old English, *ær* had the meaning "before", and could be used as adverb, conjunction, or preposition (Mitchell 1995: 369). We see the superlative form of this archaic word in the adverb *erst* (cp. *erstwhile*). The *OED* entries leading up to the spelling *early* for the adjective are: *earlich* (1225), *erly* (1398), *erly* (1450), *early* (1594). For the adverb, the series is *ærlice* (950), *arlice* (975), *erliche* (1200), *erliche* (1225), *arli* (1300), *arliche* (1320), *orly* (1330), *erly* (1340), *airly* (1375), *eerly* (1380), *airly* (1425), *ayrly* (1513), *yerle* (1513), *early* (1535). Today *early*, as adjective and adverb, is best viewed as monomorphemic.

At this point, we have examined all the *-ly* adjectives that I have encountered in the eight selected texts. However, these texts contain several other instances of adjectives which at first glance appear to fall into this category, but which upon closer inspection prove to be "false friends". These forms are examined in the next section.

## 7. "False friends": adjectives formed by adding the suffix *-y*

The existence of the adjective-forming suffix *-y* in English can give rise to forms which may easily be mistaken for suffixed *-ly* forms. Like *-ly*, the *-y* suffix has a fondness for nouns, but it can also be appended to adjectives and verbs. In the discussion below, we shall treat these "false friends" in the order just cited: nouns, adjectives, verbs.

*7.1 -y added to nouns*

It is common knowledge that adjectives can be formed from nouns by adding the suffix *-y*:

- "No one watching her walk along the grey **sandy** path beside the river bed would have guessed at what her body was experiencing" (Carey 1995: 8)

In fact, this derivational process is extremely productive:

- "Its mission was to dish out bowls of **cabbagy** soup to the **hungry, dirty** men and boys who were riding the rails: a worthy effort, but one that was not viewed with approval by everyone in town" (Atwood 2001: 239)

Like *-ly*, this suffix can even be attached to nouns denoting persons and roles, though this usage may seem a bit forced:

- "All three had short, bright fashionable hair, not blonde and yet not brown, the blue eyes, the sunburned necks and brilliant finger-nails, the high **actressy** voices and oddly inarticulate vocabulary – vogue words, smart clichés, innuendo, and slang – of young upper-class Englishwomen" (Gordimer 1976: 50)

What is particularly relevant for the present discussion, however, is the morphology of adjectives derived from nouns which end in <l> or <le>, since in such cases it is not always easy to distinguish between the suffix *-ly* and the suffix *-y*.

*7.1.1 -y added to nouns ending in a single <l>*

Consider the following examples, all of which involve the adjectival conversion of nouns ending in <l>:

- "He had a tight knot of **curly** hair on his forehead" (Auel 2002: 569)
- "The two servants had been installed, a grouchy cook-housekeeper and a large **jowly** man who was passed off as the gardener/chauffeur" (Atwood 2001: 391)

- " ... the labour of those vegetable plots, scientific though it was, still looked brutish and underpaid, an extension of plantation life, of mud and sun and bare feet, damp huts, and **oily** or sweated felt hats folded at the back to fit the head like a visored cap" (Naipaul 1987: 205)
- "But other coastlines, those of islands at all levels near and far in the distance, emerged before and sank away into light behind us, little coastlines with a **pearly** dip of beach" (Gordimer 1976: 22)
- "He tasted his own death, not just the **steely** fact of it or its imminence or its inevitability" (Carey 1995: 347)

These are the easy cases. When a noun ends in a single <l> (*curl, jowl, oil, pearl, steel*), and this <l> is followed by <y>, it is clear that the proper morphological analysis is noun + y (*curl+y, jowl+y, oil+y, pearl+y, steel+y*) and not noun + *ly*. Whenever the suffix *-ly* is added to a noun (or any other base) ending in a single <l>, the resulting form will end in <lly>. Such forms appear to be very rare, however. I found no examples in my data, but – as noted earlier – the word *rascally* appears in Jespersen's discussion (1974: 407) of adjectives in *-ly*. Here is a supporting example from the *OED* (XIII: 198):

- "This is not the first time he has attempted a **rascally** action under cover of my name" (This instance is from 1862; the first citation for *rascally* is dated 1598)

Even without additional data relating to the formation of adjectives, the orthographic point can be illustrated by turning to the adverb-forming suffix, whose behavior in this respect parallels that of the adjective-forming suffix, as the following examples illustrate:

- "'Tristan,' she said **coolly**, 'what are you doing here?'" (Carey 1995: 335)
- "Her face was small, his hand large, and he held the jaw so hard, pressed his thumb so **cruelly**, she thought it would break through the skin" (Carey 1995: 373)

We see that when the adverb-forming suffix *-ly* is added to adjectives ending in a single <l>, the resulting adverb ends in <lly>. Other adverbial examples that come to mind are *continually, finally, generally, legally, logically, normally, optionally, originally, really, thoughtfully, usually*.

However, a word of caution is in order here: occasionally the addition of *-y* may result in a doubling of the final consonant, thereby suggesting (erroneously) that the suffix is *-ly* rather than *-y*:

- "That configuration was the distinctive feature of the great **woolly** beast, even more than its curving tusks and long trunk" (Auel 2002: 321)

According to the *OED* (XX: 522-523), the word *woolly* is derived from *wool* by the addition of *-y*. But in this case (unlike *curl, jowl, pearl* and *steel*), the suffix occasions the doubling of the <l> (though the alternative spelling, *wooly*, can also be found). Consequently, the proper analysis is *wool + (l) + y*, and not *wool + ly*.

It is reasonable at this juncture to inquire how one is to know this without access to etymological sources. A first step would be to determine when consonant doubling might take place in conjunction with the suffix *-y* (note, by the way, that a similar doubling of the <l> in *wool* occurs in *woollen*). Jespersen (1974: 213) remarks that a "consonant after a stressed vowel is doubled" before the suffix *-y*, and he illustrates with *catty, chinny, chummy* and *leggy*. Other examples that come to mind are *flabby, funny, sloppy* and *sunny*. Such a rule would appear to apply (somewhat optionally) to *woolly*, while also explaining why there is no doubling in *curly, jowly,* and *pearly,* where the stressed vowel is separated from the <l> by an intervening consonant (<r> or <w>). However, it does not explain why we find *steely* instead of \**steelly*. So the rule has its exceptions. We can improve upon the rule somewhat by adding that (normally) no doubling of the final consonant takes place if the stressed vowel is spelled with two letters (hence e.g. *greedy, meaty, moody, razny, steely*). The reason for the qualifying addition of "normally" is that *woolly* is an obvious exception.

At this point, an appeal to meaning may be useful. The *OED* (XX: 684) describes the meaning of the suffix *-y* as follows: "The general sense of this suffix is 'having the qualities of' or 'full of' that which is denoted by the sb. [= substantive] to which it is added." Although this bears a striking resemblance to the meaning of the *-ly* suffix cited earlier from the *AHD* ("like; resembling; having the characteristics of"), I think we can make a distinction here. An extension of the *OED* interpretation of the meaning of the suffix *-y* suggests a useful semantic clue: the suffix *–y* (unlike the suffix *-ly*) can be attached to nouns denoting "material" or "substance". Thus *woolly* is a derivation in *-y* (rather than *-ly*) because it derives from a noun denoting the material "wool" (so *woolly* means "having the qualities of wool", or "full of wool"). In the same fashion we have such derivations as *bloody, dirty, earthy, glassy, hairy, icy,* and *silky*. Note that I am not claiming that this is the only meaning of the suffix *–y* (contrast, for example, other items such as *mighty, needy, noisy, sexy, speedy,* and *witty*). What I am proposing is that with a problematical adjective such as *woolly*, we can – without turning to etymological sources – assume that the derivation of the adjective involves the suffix *-y* rather than *-ly*, because *wool* is a type of "material" or "substance".

*7.1.2 -y added to nouns ending in a double <ll>*

Consider next the case of nouns ending in double <ll>. Because English spelling conventions frown on a sequence of triple <lll>, the addition of the suffix *-ly* to any noun ending in <ll> will result in a reduction from *ll* + *ly* to *lly*, thereby yielding the same form as *ll* + *y*. Clearly, this could make it difficult to decide which of the two suffixes is involved.

Again, my data contains no instances of the adjective-forming suffix added to nouns ending in <ll>, but the orthographic point can once more be made by considering the formation of adverbs from adjectives ending in <ll> such as *dully* and *fully*:

- "Where coal mines had been, black mountains of coal dust glittered **dully**" (Gordimer 1976: 116)
- "Ayla didn't quite understand why the painted animals looked so lifelike, or **fully** appreciate what it had required, but she couldn't resist looking closer to see how it was done" (Auel 2002: 321)

Here are some examples of adjectives which are "false friends" of adjectives with an *-ly* suffix:

- "At slightly more than two hundred feet into the dark, damp, and **chilly** cave, the floor of the passageway ascended, not blocking the way, but making it difficult to proceed" (Auel 2002: 318)
- "The child was dressed in a stiff **frilly** frock and she wore the gilt locket I had brought as a Christmas present for her" (Gordimer 1976: 193)
- "Half a second later he was in a dark, hot, **smelly,** bustling street – the Jean Pitz Colonnade"(Carey 1995: 312)

According to the *OED*, the adjectives *chilly* (III: 119), *frilly* (VI: 199), and *smelly* (XV: 787) are derived by adding the suffix *-y* to the nouns *chill*, *frill* and *smell*, respectively. Since I have found no instances of nouns ending in <ll> which take an *-1y* suffix, the potential for confusion between the two suffixes in this case may be purely theoretical.

*7.1.3 -y added to nouns ending in <le>*

In theory, nouns ending in <le> could be as problematical as nouns ending in <ll>, since the addition of either *-ly* or *-y* yields the same orthographic result: *le* + (*l*)*y* → *ly*. This orthographic point can easily be illustrated for the suffix *-ly* by examining such adverbs as *ably, doubly, nobly, subtly,* and *terribly*. These derive, respectively, from *able, double, noble, subtle,* and *terrible*. In practice, however, it seems to be the case that an adjective ending in <*ly*> involves the suffix *-y* (and not *-ly*) if the noun from which it is derived ends in <*le*>. I have found no parallel instances of nouns ending in <*le*> which take the adjective-forming suffix *-ly*. Ljung (1970: 178) includes the form *uncly* (from *uncle*) in one of his lists of adjectives, but I have not encountered it, nor is it listed in the *OED* (though the *OED* (I: 788) does list two entries for *auntly*, both from the 19th century: "My best regards and Auntly blessing to my nephew" / "This is a very motherly and auntly tale"). Consequently, all the adjectives treated in this section are instances of "false friends". Let us start with one of the most surprising instances:

- "I stayed in my wheelchair carrying my big **knobbly** knuckles in my lap" (Carey 1995: 254)

One might be forgiven for assuming that the morphological analysis of this word is *knob* (noun) + *-ly*, and that the addition of the suffix occasions a doubling of the consonant <*b*>. But this is not the case. The *OED* informs us (VIII: 499) that *knobbly* derives from the noun *knobble* ("a small knob") + *-y*. *Knobbly* means "full of or covered with knobbles ... Esp. of knees". The first *OED* citation is from 1859 (though there is a citation for *knobble* which is much earlier: 1577). Interestingly, there is a similar adjective *knobby* (VIII: 499) which derives from *knob* + *-y* (note the consonant doubling) and means "Full of, abounding in, bearing, or covered with knobs or protuberances". So both *knobbly* and *knobby* are formed by adding the suffix *-y*, the difference in meaning depending primarily on whether the knobs are small (= *knobble*) or not. The suffix *-ly* is not involved at all.

Here are some additional examples:

- "Sparrow, who had laughed so loudly, was quiet and thoughtful in the intermission, continually passing his big hands over his cleanshaven cheeks and **bristly** neck" (Carey 1995: 166)
- "'**Bubbly** drinks at lunch have a hideous effect on people,' I said, awkwardly" (Gordimer 1976: 211)
- "Female slaves, captives from previous conquests, pour out the scarlet hang from the skin bottles in which it is fermented, and cringe and stoop and serve, carrying bowls of **gristly**, undercooked stew made from rustled thulks" (Atwood 2001: 154)
- "The final sip was signalled by a **gurgly** slurp, following which Mr. Kapur emerged with the empty cup" (Mistry 2002: 326)
- "Now they're under the **nubbly** cherry-coloured silk bedspread, the sateen sheets, drinking th scotch she's brought with her" (Atwood 2001: 308)
- "Peter was boyish-looking, with a prominent Adam's apple, a **pimply** skin, and tiny ears that seemed to participate when he talked, and lay flat back

against his head when he laughed, like a pleased animal's" (Gordimer 1976: 88)
- "The sun had come out, and she found some of the previous year's dried flower heads of teasel and used the **prickly** herb top to curry the horses' coats" (Auel 2002: 303)
- "... she took me into her bed, rocked me in her arms, bathed me, towelled me, sang to me, oiled my dry, **scaly** slun, made up my terrible face with blue and gold and silver" (Carey 1995: 235)
- "Lawns of bare earth appeared, with **spindly** saplings planted on them: weeping birches were popular" (Atwood 2001: 619)
- "He told me about abalone diving near Cape Town, angling for giant barracuda off the East African coast, riding a pony through the passes of Basutoland, and outwitting **wily** guinea-fowl in the Bushveld" (Gordimer 1976: 65)

The *OED* makes clear claims about the derivational history of *bristly* (II: 561), *bubbly* (II: 608), *gristly* (VI: 856), *gurgly* (VI: 963), *nubbly* (X: 575), *pimply* (XI:846), *prickly* (XII:461), *scaly* (MV: 369), and *wily* (XX: 357). These are all instances of the suffix -*y* added to the respective nouns ending in -*le*: *bristle, bubble, gristle, gurgle, nubble* ("a small knob or lump"), *pimple, prickle* ("a rigid sharp-pointed process developed from the bark or any part of the epidermis of a plant"), *scale,* and *wile*.

Regarding the morphology of *spindly*, the *OED* tells us only (XVI: 236) that the word derives from the noun *spindle*. There is no mention of what suffix is involved. However, a glance at the *WEUD* (1996: 1370) resolves the issue: as with the other items, this is an instance of the suffix –*y* added to a noun ending in -*le*.

As with denominal adjectives in -*ly*, denominal adjectives in -*y* can take the negative prefix *un*-, thereby extending the "false friends" into this territory as well:

- "His prominent nose and heavy browridges with **unruly** eyebrows that crossed his forehead in a single line were entirely Clan" (Auel 2002: 565)

This form is apparently to be analyzed morphologically as [*un*- + [*rule* + -*y*]]. This is the analysis given by the *OED* (XIX: 179 and IXV: 234). The first reference treats *unruly*, the second deals with *ruly* – which is said to come originally from the noun *rule* + -*y*, "but in mod [ern] use prob[ably] a backformation from *unruly*".

The spelling change, *le* + *y* → *ly*, which we find in all the examples in this section, appears to be an instance of the more general rule given by Jespersen (1974: 213) as follows: "After a consonant -*e* is generally dropped before -*y*, thus in *easy, greasy, hasty, racy, shady*, etc." We can now add: "and in words such as *bristly, bubbly, gristly, gurgly, nubbly, pimply, prickly, scaly, spindly,* and *wily*".

*7.2 -y added to adjectives*

Here are two examples where the suffix -*y* appears to be added to an adjective whose base form ends in <*le*>:

- "She had **purply** smudges under her eyes, and I guessed she'd been crying, in secret so as not to disturb anyone" (Atwood 2001: 118-119)
- "'Yes, his fur is **tickly**. It tickles him, too. He's shedding; that means some of his hair is coming out" Ayla said" (Auel 2002: 126)

In the case of *purply*, the *OED* (XII: 878) is non-committal as to whether the base form purple is an adjective or a noun. In either event, the suffix is -*y*, not -*ly*. Regarding *tickly*, it may be surprising to learn that according to the *OED* (XVIII: 61) the base form *tickle* in this derivation is an old adjective (rather than a verb or a noun), so that *tickly* = *tickle* (adj.) + -*y*. The *OED* notes (XVIII: 59) that "the use of the v[er]b-stem as adj, is unusual". The origin of *tickle* itself is unclear. It may possibly derive, by metathesis, from *kittle*, which means *tickle* (see the *OED* entries for *kittle*, VIII: 473, and the note at the end of the discussion of the verb *tickle*, XVIII: 60). The earliest entry for the adjective *tickly* in the *OED* is from 1530.

*7.3 -y added to verbs*

In addition to nouns and adjectives, the adjective-forming suffix -*y* can be added to verbs. As we have come to expect, when the verb ends in e.g. <*le*>, the <*e*> drops out and the resulting adjective could be mistaken for one with an -*ly* suffix:

- "[The cookie] was huge, the size of a cow pat, the way they make them now – tasteless, **crumbly,** greasy – and I couldn't seem to make my way through it" (Atwood 2001: 68)
- "There's something **gangly** about the stance, the placement of the hips, the feet, as if her spine is wrong for this dress – too straight" (Atwood 2001: 292)
- "Ayla climbed over the top ridge and started down, traversing at an angle along a faint trail that had been recently cleared through the hillside of dense brambles and a few **scraggly** pines" (Auel 2002: 499)
- "He made no attempt to build the picture, picking up pieces at random, tracing their **squiggly** contours with a finger" (Mistry 2002: 141)
- "The privet kept its tightness, but the rose hedge, unpruned and untrained, became wild and **straggly**" (Naipaul 1987: 35)
- "... when he tried to smile his lips were **wobbly** and misshapen" (Carey 1995: 384)

This is a very odd collection of forms, with curious histories. Let us look briefly at each in turn. The *OED* is of two minds about the derivation of *crumbly*. On the one hand, says the **OED** (IV: 82), the "16-17th c. forms *crorne-ly*, *crum-ly*, imply formation" from the noun *crumb* + *-ly*, while on the other hand, "later pronunciation associates it" with the verb *crumble* + *-y*. However, the *AHD* (2000: 437) defines crumbly as "easily crumbled", thus suggesting a derivation from the verb *crumble*, and hence with the suffix *-y*, rather than *-ly*. The *WEUD* (1996: 349) is unequivocal: *crumbly* means "apt to crumble" and derives from *crumble* + *-y*. So while we should perhaps not completely rule out the possibility that *crumbly* might be formed by suffixing *-ly* to the noun *crumb*, the evidence seems to point toward the suffix *-y* added to the verb *crumble*.

Turning our attention now to the next example, we are informed by the *OED* (VI: 356) that *gangly* is an alternate form of *gangling*, the meaning of which is "awkwardly tall or long-limbed" (*AHD* 2000: 723). And the word *gangling* itself has a curious derivation. It is apparently formed by adding the suffix *-ing* to a non-existent verb, *\*gangle* (*OED* VI: 356).

A similar fate has apparently befallen the adjective *scraggly*. The *OED* (IV: 704-705) observes that *scraggly* is constructed by adding the suffix *-y* to an imaginary verb, *\*scraggle*. *Scraggly* is defined as "irregular or ragged in growth or form".

In the case of *straggly*, whose meaning is similar to *scraggly*, there appears to be some indeterminacy. There is no doubt about the nature of the suffix, which is *-y*, but according to the *OED* (XVI: 817) the base form, *straggle*, from which it derives, could be either a verb or a noun. As a noun it means "A body or group of scattered objects; an irregular or fitful emergence (of something); a thin, lank, or untidy growth (of hair)" (XVI: 815). As a verb, the meaning is: "Of a plant, branch, etc.: To grow irregularly or loosely; to spread or shoot too far. Also, of hair: to spread in lank or untidy strands" (XVI: 815).

Regarding *squiggly* and *wobbly*, the *OED* displays no doubt: the base form is a verb. Despite the presence of corresponding nouns in each case, the *OED* derives the former from the verb *squiggle* (XVI: 417) and the latter from the verb *wobble* (XX: 475).

## 8. The resulting data set: a preliminary benchmark corpus

We have now determined what does and what does not count as a member of the class of adjectives with an *-ly* suffix. Appendix 1 provides an overview of the relevant data from our eight sources. I shall refer to this as the "preliminary benchmark corpus" (or PBMC, for short). I have excluded the following items from the appendix: *early*, *only* and *ugly*. Each of these words is best viewed today as monomorphemic, the original suffix now forming an integral part of the word. I have, however, included the following borderline cases in the chart:

*burly, ghastly, grisly* and *surly* – though they, too, are arguably monomorphemic today.

The numbers in each of the eight author columns specify the pages where the given adjective can be found in that particular text. The "Total tokens" column provides the total number of occurrences (tokens) of the associated adjective found in all eight texts, while the "Total sources" column indicates how many sources contain the given adjective at least once. The next two columns provide dates from the *OED*. The earlier date (if present) indicates the first cognate occurrence listed in the *OED* (typically with the suffix *-lic* or *-lich* rather than *-ly)*, while the second date indicates the first entry with the *-ly* (or *-li)* suffix. The penultimate column specifies the word class of the base from which the adjective is derived, while the final column indicates whether the adjective is of Germanic (G) or Romance (R) origin.

Let us consider an illustrative example. From Appendix 1 we learn that the adjective *friendly* is found a total of 86 times in 7 of the sources. It appears in a cognate Old English form as early as 900 A.D. and with the *-ly* suffix as early as 1374 A.D. It derives from the noun *friend*. Taking Appendix 1 as a whole, we can make the following observations:

- The total yield from all eight sources (4,427 pages) is 771 *-ly* adjectives (tokens). Dividing the number of tokens by the number of pages yields what we can refer to as the "token density". For the eight texts as a whole, the token density is roughly 0.17. A token density of 0.17 tokens per page corresponds to 1.7 tokens per 10 pages or 17 tokens per 100 pages. Note that Auel's book has the lowest token density (0.08), while Walker's has the highest (0.27).
- The total yield of *different -ly* adjectives (types) from all eight sources is 79. On average, each source contains about 28 different *-ly* adjectives. Naipaul's book of 297 pages has the smallest number (15), while Rutherfurd's book of 1302 pages has the largest number (53).
- Of the 79 different adjectives, 17 (22%) appear only once in the 4,427 pages: *actorly, clerkly, dastardly, deathly, easterly, goodly, neighbourly, northerly, poorly, princely, southerly, timely, ungentlemanly, unlovely, untimely, unwomanly,* and *westerly*.
- An additional 13 adjectives appear more than once, but only within a single source: *courtly, disorderly, godly, knightly, lowly, otherworldly, priestly, quarterly, queenly, scholarly, ungodly, womanly* and *yearly*.
- Thus only 49 of the 79 adjectives (= 62%) appear in more than one source. The ten most frequent are: *friendly* (86 times), *lovely* (85), *kindly* (49), *likely* (43), *daily* (38), *elderly* (35), *unlikely* (33), *lonely* (31), *worldly* (25), and *lively* (23). Together, these ten adjectives account for 448 (= 58%) of the 771 instances. The two most frequent adjectives, *friendly* and *lovely*, account for 22% of the total.
- Four of the adjectives appear in all eight sources. In order of frequency, these

are: *lovely, likely, elderly,* and *lonely*. Five appear in seven sources: *friendly, daily, unlikely, worldly* and *lively*. Two appear in six sources: *kindly* and *weekly*.

- The *-ly* suffix favors nouns, particularly those referring to people and/or professions. Of the 79 different adjectives, 61 derive from nouns (26 of which refer to people/professions), 11 derive from adjectives, and 3 derive from verbs. The remaining 4 (*easterly, northerly, southerly, westerly*) have unclear derivational histories.
- The three items which are derived from verbs (*unseemly, ghastly, grisly*) are of Germanic origin, and all three were in use by the 14th century (respectively 1390, 1386, and 1300 A.D.). The underlying verb base in two of these forms (*ghastly* and *grisly*) is no longer recognizable. It would appear, therefore, that the addition of the *-ly* suffix to verbal base forms is no longer productive.
- Of the 79 adjectives, 58 (= 73%) are of Germanic origin (note that all of the ten most frequent are Germanic). The remaining 21 are Romance in origin (most of them having entered the language through French in the Middle English period).
- The majority of these 79 adjectives have been around for a very long time. All but two of them are recorded before the 18th century – the two exceptions are *otherworldly* (1879) and *actorly* (1959). 18 of the adjectives (= 23%) go back more than a thousand years: *yearly* (725 A.D.), *kindly* and *worldly* (888 A.D.), *nightly* (897 A.D.), *friendly* (900 A.D.), *deathly, earthly* and *heavenly* (971 A.D.), *brotherly, deadly, fatherly, ghostly, knightly, lively, lordly, lovely, motherly* and *priestly* (1000 A.D.). Together these 18 "ancient" Germanic items account for 330 (= 43%) of the 771 tokens in our eight sources.

These observations all point in one direction: the adjective-forming *–ly* suffix – though firmly fixed in the English language – is not widely distributed nor highly productive. Relatively few adjectives take this suffix, and most of those that do so added the suffix a long time ago.

## 9. Testing the preliminary benchmark corpus

Having now collected 79 different *-ly* adjectives from eight literary sources of 4,427 pages, the next issue I wish to address is this: How representative, and how exhaustive is this collection? To investigate this issue, I shall let the 79 items in the PBMC serve as a basis against which to compare data from other sources. If indeed this benchmark corpus is both representative and reasonably exhaustive, we should be able to make the following predictions with respect to new texts:

- Prediction 1: New texts will add very few new types to our list of 79 adjectives, and any new type will be realized by relatively few tokens.

- Prediction 2: Whatever new types we do find will most likely be of Germanic origin.

- Prediction 3: Any new types will most likely have entered the English language prior to 1700.

- Prediction 4: More than half the tokens in any new text will derive from a subset of the 10 most frequent items in the PBMC: *friendly, lovely, kindly, likely, daily, elderly, unlikely, lonely, worldly, lively*.

- Prediction 5: It is most likely that any new types we may find will derive from base forms which are nouns. It is highly unlikely that any of them will derive from base forms which are verbs.

- Prediction 6: The token density for new texts will range from 0.08 to 0.27; the average token density will be approximately 0.17 (that is, 17 tokens per 100 pages).

To test these hypotheses, I have collected data from ten additional English prose texts – 3,315 new pages in all. To ensure maximum variation within the genre, none of the authors of these new texts are the same as the authors in the first collection. Once again, I have selected writers from different parts of the English-speaking world:

- *The Street* by Biyi Bandele (Nigeria → UK, 247 pages)
- *Red Earth and Pouring Rain* by Vikram Chandra (India, 605 pages)
- *Golden Deeds* by Catherine Chidgey (New Zealand, 264 pages)
- *Murther & Walking Spirits* by Robertson Davies (Canada, 340 pages)
- The *Enchantment of Lily Dahl* by Siri Hustvedt (USA, 273 pages)
- *Serious (The Autobiography)* by John McEnroe (USA, 321 pages)
- *Spike It* by Chris Niles (New Zealand, 343 pages)
- *Anil's Ghost* by Michael Ondaatje (Sri Lanka → Canada, 282 pages)
- *The Waiting Game* by Bernice Rubens (UK, 238 pages)
- *Cloudstreet* by Tim Winton (Australia, 402 pages)

The results of this investigation are displayed in Appendix 2 and are discussed in the next section.

## 9.1 Additional -ly adjectives

From Appendix 2 we learn that the ten new sources have provided us with an additional 454 tokens of *-ly* adjectives. Of these, 438 (96%) fall within the collection characterizing the PBMC. The remaining 16 tokens (4%) represent new data. These 16 tokens manifest 13 new types,[11] distributed as follows: *cleanly* (Chandra), *comely* (Chidgey), *comradely* (Winton), *creaturely* (Winton), *curmudgeonly* (Davies), *fleshly* (Rubens), *hourly* (Davies, McEnroe), *lawyerly* (McEnroe), *loathly* Davies), *matronly* (Rubens), *sisterly* (Chandra), *soldierly* (Davies), and *wifely* (Rubens). No new types appear in Bandele, Hustvedt, Niles or Ondaatje.

Of the 13 new types, 7 involve the people/profession category:

- "Dolly had meant it to be more friendly, more **comradely**, but she heard ridicule in her tone and watched Mrs Lamb brace up" (Winton 1996: 58)
- "Finely educated as he was, it is unlikely that John Wesley paid any attention to that **curmudgeonly** Greek sage Heraclitus who was the first, so far as we know, to point out the psychological fact that anything, if pursued beyond a reasonable point, turns into its opposite" (Davies 1992: 118)
- "Finally, I laced into him, hit him with a barrage of obscenities. It was stupid and ugly. Where once I had been **lawyerly** and careful about what came out of my mouth – even when I was furious – now the floodgates had opened" (McEnroe 2003: 206)
- "As they made their way to the car, Matron, already dressed for the occasion, appeared on the steps to wave them goodbye. She was clearly doing her **matronly** duty, for her face was without expression" (Rubens 1998: 109)
- "I was taken back to his house, and thence to tears, **sisterly** recriminations (they remembered you), hasty messages to my father, you may imagine it all" (Chandra 1996: 442)
- "His progress was stately, not marching but with **soldierly** bearing, a man proud in his profession" (Davies 1992: 41-42)
- "She did not consider him worthy of any human title. So it was 'his' suitcase she'd offered to unpack because she thought that was a **wifely** duty" (Rubens 1998: 115)

If we try to position these along the positive/negative scale, *comradely* clearly has positive connotations. So, too, does *soldierly* (in this context, at least, where it is reinforced by association with another positive *-ly* adjective – *stately*), while *curmudgeonly* is at the negative end. *Sisterly* is rather neutral – as are *matronly*, and *wifely*, being associated with the word "duty". *Lawyerly* can be either positive or negative, depending on one's view of lawyers.

Another familiar category is also represented in the new data. All the adjectives in the PBMC which denote periods of time (*daily, monthly, nightly, quarterly, weekly,* and *yearly*) also appear in the new collection. But one such form which was absent in the PBMC appears in the new collection of sources:

- "Elizabeth, who was perfectly well, was treated as an invalid for several days, and could not be expected to bail the canoe, which Anna's frequent sloppings made an **hourly** necessity" (Davies 1992: 83)

In addition to the new adjectives derived from nouns relating to people and time, two other denominal forms have appeared:

- "... [the horses] thundered around on the last turn, filling the air with sods and dust and great **creaturely** gasps of horsepower" (Winton 1996: 87)
- "With her little hobby she had no need of **fleshly** company" (Rubens 1998: 44)

Both *creaturely* and *fleshly* seem more or less neutral in terms of the positive/negative scale.

Although *-ly* adjectives are typically formed from nominal bases, recall that our PBMC does contain 11 instances of adjectival bases (*deadly, elderly, goodly, kindly, likely, lonely, lowly, poorly, sickly, ungainly, unlikely*). Our new sources provide three more:

- "In the mirror it was a good nose, straightforward and blunt, not disfigured or ugly in any manner that I knew, but she had this thing in mind, she drew it for me on a yellow pad: it was supposed to start from the brow **cleanly** and well-defined, on the thin side but not too thin, then proceed like a blade to the tilted and diamond-like tip, over nostrils sharp and hidden" (Chandra 1996: 381)[12]
- "'A **comely** bunch,' he said, looking up. 'Good genes'" (Chidgey 2000: 73)
- "He went to the washroom, bathed his face, put on his hat and coat, took up his **loathly** walking-stick and left the offices of the *Advocate*" (Davies 1992: 343)

All three of these adjectives go back to the Old English period. Both *cleanly* and *comely* are positive in meaning. According to the *OED* (III: 296), *cleanly* derives originally from the adjective for "clean" + the noun *lic* for "body". So this was once a definite compound = "cleanbodied". The word *comely* derives from an Old English adjective, *cyme*, meaning "exquisite, fine" (OED III: 530). It retains these positive associations today, with the basic sense of "pleasing in appearance" *(WEUD* 1996: 294). *Loathly*, on the other hand, is strongly negative in connotation. It derives from the adjective *loath*, which is already recorded in the Beowulf epic with the meaning "hostile, angry, spiteful" (*OED* VIII: 1071). *Loathly* itself (in its cognate form with the *-lic* suffix) is found as early as 900 A.D. The *OED* (VIII: 1072) informs us that the general meaning of the derived form is "hateful, disgusting, loathsome, repulsive, hideous, horrible". Furthermore, we are told that it was "rare in [the] 17th and 18th cent[urie]s", but that it was "revived in the 19th c[entury] as a literary word." It certainly remains rare today, appearing only once in all my sources.

The following chart provides information regarding the derivational history of the 13 new items (note that *lawyerly* is so new that it is not recorded in the 1989 edition of the *OED*).

| Adjective | OED date (lic/lich) | OED date (li/ly) | Base | Origin of base form |
|---|---|---|---|---|
| cleanly | 888 | 1340 | adj | G |
| comely | 1000 | 1300 | adj | G |
| comradely | – | 1880 | noun | R |
| creaturely | – | 1662 | noun | R |
| cumudgeonly | – | 1590 | noun | ? |
| fleshly | 888 | 1300 | noun | G |
| hourly | – | 1513 | noun | R<Gk |
| lawyerly | – | – | noun | G |
| loathly | 900 | 1300 | adj | G |
| matronly | – | 1656 | noun | R |
| sisterly | – | 1570 | noun | G |
| soldierly | – | 1577 | noun | R |
| wifely | 893 | 1385 | noun | G |

We can now determine how well our predictions have fared:

- Prediction 1: "New texts will add very few new types to our list of 79 adjectives, and any new type will be realized by relatively few tokens." Result: Four of the ten new texts (Bandele, Hustvedt, Niles, Ondaatje) contained no new types. The remaining six sources added 13 new types to our list: Chidgey added one (*comely*); Chandra and McEnroe added two each (*cleanly* and *sisterly*; *hourly* and *lawyerly*); like McEnroe, Davies also contained *hourly*, but added three additional items (*curmudgeonly*, *loathly*, *soldierly*); while Rubens added *fleshly*, *matronly* and *wifely*. The number of new tokens is – as predicted – very small: 10 of the 13 new types are realized only once (*cleanly*, *comely*, *comradely*, *creaturely*, *curmudgeonly*, *fleshly*, *loathly*, *sisterly*, *soldierly*, and *wifely*). The remaining 3 new types (*hourly*, *lawyerly*, and *matronly*) appear twice each. Only *hourly* appears in more than one source.

- Prediction 2: "Whatever new types we do find will most likely be of Germanic origin." Result: Of the 13 new types, 7 (54%) are of Germanic origin.

- Prediction 3: "Any new types will most likely have entered the English language prior to 1700." Result: 11 of the 13 new types (85%) predate 1700. The two exceptions are *comradely* (1880) and *lawyerly* (new).

- Prediction 4: "More than half the tokens in any new text will derive from a subset of the 10 most frequent items in the PBMC: *friendly, lovely, kindly, likely, daily, elderly, unlikely, lonely, worldly, lively*." Result: The following table displays the ratio of these "top 10" adjectives to the total tokens in each of the ten new sources:

| Source | Top 10 | Total tokens | Top 10/all tokens |
| --- | --- | --- | --- |
| Bandele | 9 | 22 | 41% |
| Chandra | 41 | 85 | 48% |
| Chidgey | 29 | 39 | 74% |
| Davies | 41 | 85 | 48% |
| Hustvedt | 8 | 13 | 62% |
| McEnroe | 20 | 28 | 71% |
| Niles | 18 | 24 | 75% |
| Ondaatje | 19 | 25 | 76% |
| Rubens | 36 | 68 | 53% |
| Winton | 41 | 65 | 63% |

We see that for seven of the ten texts, the "top 10" account for over half the total tokens. The ratio is lowest for Bandele (41%) and highest for Ondaatje (76%). Taking the ten texts as a whole, the frequency is 58%.

- Prediction 5: "It is most likely that any new types we may find will derive from base forms which are nouns. It is highly unlikely that any of them will derive from base forms which are verbs." Result: Of the 13 new types, 10 derive from nouns, 3 from adjectives, none from verbs.

- Prediction 6: "The token density for new texts will range from 0.08 to 0.27; the average token density will be approximately 0.17 (that is, 17 tokens per 100 pages)." Result: The lowest token density for the new texts is 0.05 (Hustvedt),[13] while the highest is 0.29 (Rubens). The average for all ten additional sources is 0.14.

On the whole, all six predictions hold up well for these ten additional sources. I believe they will hold up equally well for any other modern English prose text.

*9.2 Additional "false friends"*

In addition to new -*ly* adjectives, the new texts yielded the following supplement to our list of "false friends" – that is, adjectives which superficially resemble adjectives formed by adding an -*ly* suffix, but which upon closer inspection turn out to consist of words formed by adding the suffix -*y* to base forms ending in <*l*> or <*le*>:

- "Sam began to feel a **crawly**, exhilarating sensation in his fingers" (Winton 1996: 21)
- "The night was warm and **drizzly**" (Niles 1998: 200-201)
- "You know, Lester says, almost **giggly** with relief, we've never talked about him like this" (Winton 1996: 64-65)
- "Schoolwise I struggled to catch up, and Mrs Christiansen gave me back my **gnarly** term paper on Ethan Brand with what I think was an overly kind B+" (Chandra 1996: 206)
- "Ossie was tempted to answer in the negative, just to see what effect this might have on the boy. But before he could do so an odd, **gravelly** sound escaped from Apha's throat" (Bandele 1999: 35)
- "If everything was like the books she reads it'd be sweet, miraculous music coming down from that bookless, windowless library up there, but it's just **jangly** noise" (Winton 1996: 158)
- "With two hundred pounds in his pocket, he sits in Forrest Place with the gas-crazy Anzacs and **mealy** whingers who ask for a fag and a florin and look at you like you might be the bloke who caused all their problems in the first place" (Winton 1996: 261)
- "D'you think I'm prepared to spend one more penny on your **measly** ingratitude?" (Rubens 1998: 122)
- "He's small and hoarse, these days, **muscly** enough, but still no match for Lester who's thin and tall and angry" (Winton 1996: 241)
- "He pulled across to the narrow point of the bottleneck where the river squeezed out in a cool tea-coloured trickle to the sea and the disturbance of the two bodies meeting caused a **roily**, chopbroken channel that led out through the surf to the deep beyond" (Winton 1996: 216)
- "Lester punishes the truck up and down the bays and bluffs, getting out to blunder along **shelly** beaches and call out to his sons" (Winton 1996: 114)
- "As he came into the flat **shoaly** stretch of water he met the memory of them all down here at dusk with the fire on the beach, the lantern, the net sluicing along" (Winton 1996: 215)

- "It gave her the most marvellous, **tingly** feeling to see it going down the gurgler" (Winton 1996: 142)
- "And she laughed her tinkly laugh" (Chidgey 2000: 163)
- "The organist finds his place and gets back on his trembly way" (Winton 1996: 320)

*Crawly, gnarly, gravelly, mealy, roily* and *shoaly* all result from adding *-y* to base forms ending in <l>. Four of these words – *gnarly* (*OED* VI: 611), *gravelly* (VI: 786), *mealy* (IX: 515), and *shoaly* (XV: 292) – derive from nouns (*gnarl, gravel, meal,* and *shoal,* respectively). Regarding the remaining two – *crawly* (III: 1127) and *roily* (XIV: 39) – the *OED* is noncommittal about whether the base forms (*crawl* and *roil*) are nouns or verbs.

A special note with regard to *gravelly* is in order here. As we saw earlier in the case of *woolly,* spelling can at times be very misleading. Like *woolly, gravelly* could be mistakenly interpreted as ending in the adjective-forming suffix *-ly*. But consider the nature of the base form: like "wool", "gravel" is a kind of substance. Hence, as in the case of *woolly,* the suffix is *-y,* not *-ly,* and the doubling of the <l> is the result of a spelling convention. Consequently, the proper analysis here is *gravel + l + y* rather than *gravel + ly*.

Recall that we came up earlier with a spelling rule based on an observation of Jespersen's to explain why there was no doubling of the final consonant in words like *curly, jowly, pearly* and *steely*: No doubling of the final consonant in the base form takes place if the consonant immediately follows a stressed vowel which is not written with two letters (or, to put it in a positive form: Double the final consonant of a base form if it immediately follows a stressed vowel which is not written with two letters). This same rule applies to four of the five words given above: *crawly, mealy, roily* and *shoaly*. However, it does not explain why we find *gravelly* instead of *gravely*[14] (where the stress is on the first syllable). The spelling convention in this case appears to be rather complex. Note, for example, that we get *flowery* (with no doubling), but *Christmassy* (with doubling), even though both words, like *gravelly,* are stressed on the first syllable.

Moving on to the remaining "false friends", observe that *shelly,* involves the addition of the suffix *-y* to a base form ending in a double <ll>. The *OED* leaves no doubt (XV: 235) that the base form, *shell,* is the noun and not the verb.

The words *drizzly, giggly, jangly, measly, muscly, tingly, tinkly,* and *trembly* are all derived by adding *-y* to base forms ending in <le>. According to the *OED, giggly, measly* and *muscly* derive from the nouns *giggle* (VI: 507), *measle* (IX: 525), and *muscle* (X: 119), respectively, while *jangly* derives from the verb *jangle* (VIII: 187). Whether the remaining forms – *drizzly, tingly, tinkly,* and *trembly* – derive from base forms (*drizzle, tingle, tinkle, tremble*) that are nouns or verbs is unclear: the *OED* passes no judgement in these four cases. The relevant references are: *drizzly* (IV: 1063), *tingly* (XVIII: 124), *tinkly* (XVIII: 127), and *trembly* (XVIII: 478).

## 10. *-ly* forms that can be both adjectives and adverbs

Distinguishing between adjectives in *-ly* and "false friends" ending in *-y* involves an awareness of English morphology. There is indeed a formal difference between words such as *lovely* (*love* + *ly*) and *mealy* (*meal* + *y*), though the distinction may at times be difficult to make. On the other hand, distinguishing between adjectives in *-ly* and adverbs in *-ly* makes demands on our understanding of English grammar on a much broader scale. Consider again the first example offered in this study:

- "But a member of the **knightly** class did not speak treason **lightly**" (Rutherfurd 1998: 391)

*Knightly* and *lightly* do not overlap. The former is a member only of the adjective class, while the latter belongs only to the adverb class. If no overlap ever occurred, one might simply learn by heart those forms which are adjectives (this being by far the smaller set). All the other forms with an *-ly* suffix would then be adverbs. Unfortunately, the situation is somewhat more complicated than that. There are many words with an *-ly* suffix that can be found in both the adjective class and the adverb class (that is to say, they can take either Suffix 1 or Suffix 2). This is particularly true of those words which express periods of time (e.g. *daily, hourly, monthly, nightly, weekly, yearly*). However, it is also true of a number of other items as well, as the following doublets illustrate.

- **bodily**
  *As adjective:* "Crude references to **bodily** functions usually put a stop to Myra" (Atwood 2001: 457)
  *As adverb:* "Then he threw him **bodily** into the tunnel with the curt order: 'Work another shift'" (Rutherfurd 1998: 251)

- **cleanly**
  *As adjective:* "In the mirror it was a good nose, straightforward and blunt, not disfigured or ugly in any manner that I knew, but she had this thing in mind, she drew it for me on a yellow pad: it was supposed to start from the brow **cleanly** and well-defined, on the thin side but not too thin, then proceed like a blade to the tilted and diamond-like tip, over nostrils sharp and hidden" (Chandra 1996: 381)
  *As adverb:* " ... without protest he took the torch, opened the book and ripped off, **cleanly**, the picture of the earringed man with sad eyes" (Chandra 1996: 353)[15]

- **daily**
  *As adjective:* "We busied ourselves with **daily** life again, insofar as that was possible" (Atwood 2001: 270)
  *As adverb:* "We have fully automated credit systems in Efica. We use them **daily**, just like you do in Saarlii" (Carey 1995: 245)

- **deathly**
  *As adjective:* "Cheque-books, those little purses women have, foam-rubber cushions, the **deathly** moonlight of fluorescent strips; these things came to mind confusedly" (Gordimer 1976: 101)
  *As adverb:* "For three days he had repeatedly been sick and looked so **deathly** pale that, if she had not been used to his intense and nervous constitution, Susan might have thought that he was really ill" (Rutherfurd 1998: 629)

- **friendly**
  *As adjective:* "So there we were again, back in the cab of the Chev, with its skinny, dancing gear stick and **friendly** reek of engine oil" (Walker 2001: 15)
  *As adverb:* "Down the street Oriel Lamb met a neighbour who had some pullets for sale. They talked **friendly** for awhile and Oriel Lamb came home with four hens and a rooster for the price of a smile" (Winton 1996: 51)[16]

- **ghostly**
  *As adjective:* "Although the riverside wall built by the city's last inhabitants had badly crumbled, the original, landside wall was still standing, and within this great enclosure, across the twin hills, lay the **ghostly** ruins" (Rutherfurd 1998: 138)
  *As adverb:* "A moment later, his face **ghostly** white, his eyes larger and more solemn than ever, he faced the Norman again"(Rutherfurd 1998: 313)

- **hourly**
  *As adjective:* "I only had to pay him his **hourly** rate instead of a percentage of my earning"" (McEnroe 2003: 205)
  *As adverb:* "I watched the fire brigade on the vid screen, but I watched this catastrophe just as I had begun to watch my mother's interviews, or to listen to Rox and Wally as they moved **hourly** from rift to rapprochement and back again" (Carey 1995: 183)

- **kindly**
  *As adjective:* "Yet then, remembering Mabel's own attempt one Christmas night to lead him astray in this very cloister, the **kindly** monk had compassion" (Rutherfurd 1998: 412)

*As adverb:* "For my birthday she gave me a pair of oven gloves shaped like lobster claws. I'm sure it was **kindly** meant" (Atwood 2001: 65)

- **leisurely**
  *As adjective:* "They swam at a more **leisurely** pace back to the other side" (Auel 2002: 645)
  *As adverb:* "On the other side, a man was cycling **leisurely** along on a brand-new bicycle from the Idumota end of the bridge" (Okara 1982: 17)

- **likely**
  *As adjective:* "A **likely** story. But people believed it, or had to pretend they did. I suppose the Newton-Dobbses were spreading the real story around among their twenty closest friends" (Atwood 2001: 405)
  *As adverb:* "It gave him a hint of the effect they would very **likely** have on people when they reached the Summer Meeting" (Auel 2002: 409)

- **lively**
  *As adjective:* "Another woman whom I met sometimes at the Alexanders', a **lively** and charming woman, had been living for ten years with a man whom she admitted she could not afford to marry, because she would then lose the income of her ex-husbands' alimony" (Gordimer 1976: 165)
  *As adverb:* "I'm going to touch you up, Granny; here I come; step **lively**, Granny. Dance, Granny!" (Davies 1992: 195)

- **lowly**
  *As adjective:* "The investigative team, which included Anil in a **lowly** role as a programme assistant, had nothing left to do but get on a plane and go home" (Ondaatje 2001: 29)
  *As adverb:* "Mabel, therefore, was too **lowly** born to serve God in any formal capacity" (Rutherfurd 1998: 357)

- **monthly**
  *As adjective:* "At the **monthly** meeting at Parihaka in March, in front of an assembly of several thousand Maori and a hundred or so Europeans, the young man made a speech" (Walker 2001: 248)
  *As adverb:* "The next page told, in similar terms, of the native war dances to be seen twice **monthly** at a Mine compound near Johannesburg" (Gordimer 1976: 45)

- **nightly**
  *As adjective:* "But how to sneak past the gates? All eight of them are locked

and guarded, as is the **nightly** custom" (Atwood 2001: 328)
*As adverb:* "**Nightly**, in Chateau Felicity, the row from the Munshi flat was audible from the ground floor to the rooftop" (Mistry 2002: 239)

- **poorly**
  *As adjective:* "'I'm afraid she's very **poorly** indeed,' Matron told them. 'She has pneumonia and she's showing no signs of recovery'" (Rubens 1998: 134)
  *As adverb:* "Do you know how I come to be here? Here with you? Sitting on this **poorly** made chair?" (Davies 1992: 167)

- **untimely**
  *As adjective:* "In return she gave him the news of Dr Leigh's '**untimely** passing', as she put it, as if a piece of good news was invalid without its opposite" (Rubens 1998: 101)
  *As adverb:* "I feel a humorous relish for what I can still observe of the world from which I have been **untimely** ripped" (Davies 1992: 25)

- **weekly**
  *As adjective:* "The notion – which some of his pupils had – that he actually read our **weekly** writing was ridiculous" (Walker 2001: 10)
  *As adverb:* "In contrast we have sixteen different Dome Projection theatres whose entertainment changes **weekly**" (Carey 1995: 349)

- **yearly**
  *As adjective:* "There are many of these boxes, and they command a respectable **yearly** rental; poorer folk sit further back in the church, in free seats" (Davies 1992: 44)
  *As adverb:* "He knew that she suspected he was richer than he cared to admit; and indeed, as with many of his class, the burgeoning colonial trade and improved farming methods were **yearly** increasing his already substantial income" (Rutherfurd 1998: 994-995)

## 11. Changes in form and function

We have seen that establishing the class of adjectives in *-ly* involves a) separating these forms from similar-looking "false friends", as well as b) keeping them distinct from those adverbs which also end in an *-ly* suffix. But isolating the set involves additional factors as well, as the following discussion makes clear.

*11.1 Inflected forms*

Adjectives ending in the suffix *-ly* behave like any other type of adjective in that they can undergo changes in both form and function. One of the most common changes in form involves affixation of various types. We have already seen several instances of *-ly* adjectives taking the negative prefix *un-*: *unearthly, unfiendly, ungainly, ungentlemanly, ungodly, unlikely, unlovely, unseemly, unsightly, unwomanly*. Not surprisingly, both of the standard inflectional suffixes for adjectives, *-er* and *-est*, are available to the two-syllable forms:

- "*The Water Babies* ... must also be one of the **beastliest**, most finger-wagging books ever written for children" (Davies 1992: 251)
- "This news about the washing of the hair suggested a **lonelier** and more desperate man" (Naipaul 1987: 73)
- "She didn't know what things were coming to, but rack and ruin was the **likeliest** outcome" (Atwood 2001: 204)
- "You'd never believe it, Gil, to look at her now, but when first I set eyes on Virgie she was the **loveliest** little thing you ever saw" (Davies 1992: 172)
- "It's fine to be a Meccano boy, and that's why I want to tell you here about Meccano – the jolliest, **manliest** game ever" (Chidgey 2000: 208)
- "Chaucer was a little **portlier** of late; his goatee beard contained a few grey hairs; his face and hooded eyes were sometimes red. He looked, and was, a comfortable fellow" (Rutherfurd 1998: 608)

Since all of the above adjectives also appear in the uninflected (the so-called "positive") form in at least one of the 18 selected texts, they are, of course, included in the collection of *-ly* adjectives (that is, they figure in the number of types). However, I have chosen not to include the inflected forms in the token count, for the simple reason that they do not, strictly speaking, end in *-ly*. Thus, while both *likely* and *unlikely* are counted among the types, and all instances of their adjectival use in the 18 sources contribute to the token count, instances of *likelier* and *likeliest* are not included in the token count.[17]


*11.2 From adjective to noun*

No word class change is brought about by the affixation of either the derivational prefix, *un-*, or the inflectional suffixes, *-er* and *-est*. But like other adjectives, *-ly* forms can also change word class. A partial shift involves the use of the adjective as head in a noun group:

- "I'm a hack. A journalist on the **Daily**." (Winton 1996: 287)
- "I will not easily forget the boiling green ocean I found up that tree, or the

blustering **easterly** which swept the sea spray up the cliff face and stung my broken skin as delicately as Vincent's eau de Cologne" (Carey 1995: 74)
- "And it's always good to know where the willow grows; a decoction of the bark is so good for headaches, and the aching bones of the **elderly**, and other pains" (Auel 2002: 400)
- "Thomas could feel his heart racing: O come my **lovely**, come my heart, old friend, we are for the cliff, the precipice, come my beautiful, turn again, quick quick quickly, and now nothing impedes us" (Chandra 1996: 138)
- "You could feel the warm, salty **northerly** on your skin" (Carey 1995: 236)
- "... in the afternoons when the **southerly** blew, he could hear the kids bombing off the jetty and shrilling like gulls, setting the loose boards rattling as they ran" (Winton 1996: 18)
- "At one time he thought of entering politics, and was described then in a national **weekly** as 'a cultured man and a notable figure in Taranaki', but then nothing came of the campaign" (Walker 2001: 328)
- "Winter days now, he stands out in the **westerly** that blows down the tracks from the sea and it closes his eyes with its force" (Winton 1996: 70)

A more radical shift takes place when the adjectives move solidly into the noun class by taking a plural suffix:

- "Two **dailies** and a Sunday broadsheet, antipathetic to one another, tacitly resolved to bury the hatchet in the head of a common enemy" (Bandele 1999: 203)
- "Wendell, with all his considerable, ill-formed good will, delivered me into the safe hands of the **orderlies** at the Mater Hospital" (Carey 1995: 136)
- "For me, at least, it is pleasing to imagine that Taunoa's great grandfather, Mokena, might have sat with the child, while the **southerlies** rattled around the Hostelry and told him tales every Maori Child should know" (Walker 2001: 107)

But as is the case with adjectives in general, such a direct move from adjective to noun is rare. Much more common is to effect the move by means of a derivational suffix. A very common suffix in this category is *-ness*, which converts *-ly* adjectives into uncountable nouns:

- "People have different standards of **cleanliness**, she thought, fuming anew at Jal and Coomy" (Mistry 2002: 114)
- "... he walked towards her until he was impolitely dose, then stood absolutely still and looked into her face: he was certain that she had been beautiful, but the **comeliness** was quite irrelevant" (Chandra 1996: 366)

- "In fact, it was the one person of all the Zelandonii that he hoped he would not see, and he did like the assumed **friendliness**, but he felt he had no choice but to make the introduction" (Auel 2002: 427)
- "**Godliness** begets Industry; Industry begets Wealth; Wealth begets **Ungodliness**" (Davies 1992: 118)
- "It was imagining this that helped me overcome my phobia – the thought that my will could make him carefree, happy, not weighed down by history or **loneliness**" (Carey 1995: 281)
- "Slowly her **loveliness** was being erased by the burden upon her, and he couldn't protect her from it" (Mistry 2002: 276)
- "We had little to say, but a **neighbourliness** had been established between us, and it continued to be expressed in his shout from afar" (Naipaul 1987: 32)
- " … . the delicious lunch and the wines had, as usual, awakened in me a great respect for life lived in the exquisite **orderliness** of wealth" (Gordimer 1976: 58)
- "Winifred was a small potato too: her **sprightliness** was wasted" (Atwood 2001: 463)
- "I recognized that **surliness**, that stubbornness, that captive-princess indignation, which must be kept hidden until enough weapons have been collected" (Atwood 2001: 360)
- "For a moment, he just looked at her standing in the sun, and filled his eyes with the **womanliness** of her" (Auel 2002: 85)
- "I kept having a consciously cruel picture of him, dressed up – I thought – as he imagines a gentleman to dress, a fatuous cinema-smirk of **worldliness** on his black face" (Gordimer 1976: 149)

But nominal forms can be created by means of other derivational suffixes as well:

- "Osric had not thought much about his appearance. Nor, in a world almost without glass, was there much **likelihood** of him catching sight of himself" (Rutherfurd 1998: 265)
- "He depended for his **livelihood** on people with money; he liked the odd ways of the rich and liked to talk about these ways" (Naipaul 1987: 221)

Once again, it is clear that when the "underlying" form, with no suffixation, behaves as an adjective, it adds to the type count. However, none of the instances of -*ly* forms which behave as nouns are included in my token count. This prohibition applies whether or not a suffix is involved.

*11.3 Compounds*

On the other hand, if the *-ly* adjective participates in a compound-like construction where the adjectival nature of the *-ly* form is still discernible, then that *-ly* adjective contributes to the token count as well as to the type count. It makes no difference whether the adjective constitutes the first element of the compound, as in the following examples:

- "She sighed, wrote something down and gave it to the customer, a **burly-looking** chap in bikers' leathers" (Niles 1998: 159)
- "Square-jawed, **surly-eyed**, a man so compact he was like a boulder: everyone knew that, since the fall of Wolsey, it was Thomas Cromwell who ruled England for the king" (Rutherfurd 1998: 644)

or the second element:

- "The extraordinary scenes of government ministers personally smashing down doors and breaking open chests – even in **long-friendly** Maori settlements – will not detain us" (Walker 2001: 288)
- "Yes, he had paid, as she had paid. Two hundred pounds as the first of **ever-weekly** instalments" (Rubens 1998: 86)

In this modern computer age we are all familiar with the compound "user-friendly". But friendliness need not be directed toward users alone:

- "I told Kantarian I thought that for Davis Cup to become relevant to Americans and American players, it badly needed to be both more **fan-friendly** and more **player-friendly**"(McEnroe 2003: 319)

We have now reached the end of the discussion of what items I have included in my type and token sets of *-ly* adjectives. It is time to take stock.

## 12. Conclusion

We began with a corpus consisting of eight English prose texts (4,427 pages in all), in which we encountered 79 different adjectives with the suffix *-ly*. Treating this as a preliminary benchmark corpus, we tested it against data from 10 new texts (3,315 pages in all). This new data yielded 13 additional relevant adjectives. It seems reasonable to conclude that these combined sources (18 texts, consisting of a total of 7,742 pages), which yield 92 different *-ly* adjectives, provides a representative picture of the number and distribution of these adjectives in modem English literature.

In order best to summarize the major observations contained in this study, I have collected the data from all 18 sources into one chart, and then arranged the data in different ways for ease of interpretation. This has resulted in the following four appendices:

- Appendix 3a displays the data for all 92 adjectives in alphabetical order.
- Appendix 3b displays the same data in terms of frequency (most frequent items first).
- Appendix 3c displays the data in terms of the base form and then frequency.
- Appendix 3d displays the data in terms of chronology.

The information displayed in each of these appendices will now be briefly summarized in turn.

*The full corpus (Appendix 3a)*
The full list of types and tokens, in alphabetical order, is provided in Appendix 3a. We see that the total number of tokens found in all 18 texts is 1,225. The token density ranges from a low of 0.05 (Hustvedt) to a high of 0.29 (Rubens), the average for all 18 texts being 0.16. On average, therefore, these adjectives appear roughly 16 times in 100 pages of modem English prose.

The final column in Appendix 3a confirms that the majority of these 92 adjectives are of Germanic origin. More precisely, 65 of the 92 are Germanic, amounting to 71%.

*Frequency (Appendix 3b)*
Appendix 3b lists the 92 adjectives in terms of frequency. We see from this list that the top 10 in the full corpus are the same as for the preliminary benchmark corpus, though the relative order has changed somewhat. The revised order is: *lovely* (146), *friendly* (125), *likely* (80), *lonely* (74), *daily* (71), *kindly* (56), *unlikely* (51), *lively* (39), *elderly* (38), and *worldly* (30). Together, these 10 adjectives account for 710 of the total 1,225 tokens (= 58%). As noted earlier, all 10 of these adjectives are of Germanic origin.

At the bottom of the scale are 20 adjectives that appear only once each in all 7,742 pages: *actorly, cleanly, clerkly, comely, comradely, creaturely, curmudgeonly, dastardly, easterly, fleshly, loathly, northerly, princely, sisterly, soldierly, ungentlemanly, unlovely, unwomanly, westerly,* and *wifely.*

Appendix 3b also reveals that none of the 92 adjectives appear in all 18 texts. The most widely distributed adjectives are *likely, lonely,* and *lovely,* each of which is found in 17 of the 18 texts. 12 other adjectives appear in at least half of the texts: *daily* (15), *friendly* (15), *lively* (15), *weekly* (13), *kindly* (12), *unlikely* (12), *worldly* (11), *ghostly* (10), *deadly* (9), *elderly* (9), *orderly* (9), and *stately* (9). Observe that all of the 10 most frequent adjectives are also included in this list of the 15 most widely distributed.

*Word class of base form (Appendix 3c)*
Appendix 3c displays the 92 adjectives arranged according to a) the word class of the base form and subsequently in terms of b) frequency within that class. 71 of the 92 adjectives (= 77%) are derived from nouns, 14 (= 15%) are derived from adjectives, 3 (= 3%) from verbs, while the derivational history of the four compass directions *(easterly, northerly, southerly, westerly)* is unclear.

It is interesting to note that although adjectives supply only 15% of the base forms, the *-ly* adjectives derived from these bases account for 369 (= 30%) of the total 1,225 tokens, and 5 of these adjectives *(likely, lonely, kindly, unlikely,* and *elderly)* figure among the top 10 most frequently occurring items in the full list of 92.

The three items which are derived from verbs *(unseemly, ghastly, grisly)* account for only 15 (=1%) of the 1,225 tokens.

By far the largest class is the one derived from nouns. As we noted at the outset, two clear subclasses of noun base forms are represented: a) those relating to people and professions, and b) those relating to periods of time. The latter is the smaller subclass. It contains 6 adjectives: *daily* (71 times), *hourly* (2), *monthly* (11), *nightly* (11), *weekly* (26), and *yearly* (5). This constitutes 7% of the types (6/92) and 10% of all the tokens (126/1225).

The larger subcategory contains 32 items: *actorly* (1), *brotherly* (2), *clerkly* (1), *comradely* (1), *cowardly* (6), *curmudgeonly* (1), *fatherly* (2), *friendly* (125), *gentlemanly* (5), *kingly* (3), *knightly* (8), *lawyerly* (2), *lordly* (6), *manly* (14), *masterly* (5), *matronly* (2), *miserly* (3), *motherly* (7), *neighbourly* (2), *priestly* (5), *princely* (1), *queenly* (3), *saintly* (11), *scholarly* (7), *sisterly* (1), *slovenly* (7), *soldierly* (1), *unfriendly* (4), *ungentlemanly* (1), *unwomanly* (1), *wifely* (1) and *womanly* (6). This constitutes 35% of the types (32/92) and 20% of the tokens (245/1225). Is it pure coincidence that a large number of the adjectives in this subcategory are constructed from two-syllable base forms whose second syllable is unstressed and ends in *-er* (or in some other spelling which has the same sound)? There are 11 of these items: *actorly, brotherly, fatherly, lawyerly, masterly, miserly, motherly, neighbourly, scholarly, sisterly,* and *soldierly.* Is this perhaps why words like *fatherly* and *motherly* sound so much more "natural" than e.g. *uncly* and *auntly*? Why *daughterly* seems more probable than *sonly,* though neither occurs in my 18 sources? Could it be that a phonological factor is at work here, one so general that it also encompasses 9 other items in the set of 92: *creaturely, easterly, elderly, leisurely, northerly, orderly, quarterly, southerly,* and *westerly*? If we extend the "two-syllable" criterion to "polysyllabic", we can also include *disorderly.* Together these items constitute 23% of the full corpus (21/92).

*Chronology (Appendix 3d)*
The final appendix, Appendix 3d, arranges the list of 92 adjectives according to date, from oldest to most recent. We can see that the trend established in the PMBC is confirmed in the corpus as a whole: most of these 92 adjectives have been part of the English vocabulary for a very long time. The actual distribution of the 92 types according to date of first appearance is as follows:

| First appearance | No. of adjectives | % | Cumulative % |
|---|---|---|---|
| 700-1000 A.D. | 23 | 25.0 | 25.0 |
| 1001-1499 | 26 | 28.2 | 53.2 |
| 1500-1599 | 28 | 30.4 | 83.6 |
| 1600-1699 | 11 | 12.0 | 95.6 |
| 1700-1799 | 0 | 0 | 95.6 |
| 1800-1899 | 2 | 2.2 | 97.8 |
| 1900-present | 2 | 2.2 | 100.0 |
| Total | 92 | 100 | |

As is evident from the table, more than 95% of these adjectives were being used in the English language by the end of the 17th century. Only four of the adjectives are of more recent date: *otherworldly* (1879), *comradely* (1880), *actorly* (1959), and *lawyerly* (new).

*Parting remarks*
We have learned that identifying the class of *-ly* adjectives is much more complicated than it might seem at first. Not only is there competition from adverbs which also end in *-ly*, there is also competition from a large number of similar-looking adjectives which, to the unwary classifier, could easily be mistaken for adjectives bearing an *-ly* suffix. These are our so-called "false friends" – adjectives taking the suffix *-y*, rather than *-ly*. The troublesome cases fall into three groups, depending on the nature of the base form:
a) <y> added to base forms ending in single <l>: e.g. *crawly, curly, gnarly, gravelly, jowly, mealy, oily, pearly, roily, shoaly, steely, woolly.*
b) <y> added to base forms ending in double <ll>: e.g. *chilly, filly, shelly, smelly*
c) <y> added to base forms ending in <le>: e.g. *bristly, bubbly, crumbly, drizzly, gangly, giggly, gristly, gurgly, jangly, knobbly, measly, nubbly, muscly, pimply, prickly, purply, scaly, scraggly, spindly, squibbly, straggly, fickly, tingly, tinkly, trembly, wily,* and *wobbly.*

All of these items must be clearly distinguished from the class of adjectives with an *-ly* suffix.

We should also bear in mind that while Appendix 3a provides a complete list of the *-ly* adjectives found in the 18 sources used in this study (with the exception of *early, only* and *ugly),* this should not be viewed as a complete list of such adjectives in modern English. There can be no doubt that additional *-ly* adjectives can be found in other modern texts, though I believe it is reasonable to assume that new members will be added only sporadically to this list. Let me conclude with a couple of concrete examples. During the time I was carrying out this study, I came across a few additional instances in other sources I was reading at the time. One of these appears in a brief commentary by W. H. Auden on the jacket of a cassette containing readings of some of his own poetry:

- "In trying to think what I could say about these poems which would have any point or value, I have let myself be guided by my own experience in listening to other poets reciting their work ... If these notes sound a bit **schoolmasterly,** I am sorry, but it is very easy to ignore them" (Auden 1955)

The first *OED* entry for *schoolmasterly* is from 1865. This word thus joins our other "new-comers" – *otherworldly* (1879), *comradely* (1880), *actorly* (1959), and *lawyerly* (new) – in demonstrating that the productivity of the adjective-forming suffix has survived beyond the Middle English period.

Further evidence that the suffix is not totally moribund is provided by the following instances of *-ly* adjectives which I have also recently encountered. Like *lawyerly*, they are apparently so new that they are not recorded in the 1989 edition of the *OED:*

- "On this occasion, a veritable King Kong in the car behind sat with all his **King Kongly** might on the horn of his car, playing, no doubt, a salutation to the African sun" (Opara 1982: 43)
- "It is interesting to notice, finally, that poems in traditional formal structures all the way from Shakespeare's sonnets to Yeats's 'Sailing to Byzantium' seem to concern themselves with something like a traditional subject-matter – namely, the menace of mutability, formlessness, flux, or dissolution. This is to suggest that there is an essential **poemly** theme, one invited into poems by the formal preoccupations of the traditional poet" (Fussell 1979: 172)

With these parting remarks, this study is concluded. By examining a wide range of examples from modem English literature, I hope to have helped interested readers develop a more nuanced view of the nature and the distribution of English adjectives bearing an *-ly* suffix. I have certainly learned a good deal in the process.

## Notes

1. All the texts in this study have been selected more or less "randomly", though there were a few selectional criteria: the books should be a) ones I hadn't read before, b) of recent date, c) available from my own personal library or in the university bookstore, d) from different geographic regions, and e) at least 200 pages long. I have selected this particular literary genre because it allows for a wide range of creativity on the part of the author – and hence should provide us with some indication of the productivity of the -*ly* suffix in present-day English. It is possible that other genres, such as journalese, would contribute a different range of data, though I do not think this is likely.
2. The page count for all eight sources takes into consideration a) "late start" and b) blank pages. For example, although the last page of Atwood's novel is numbered 637, the actual text starts on page 3, and the novel contains 28 blank pages (2 for each new section). This yields 607 pages of actual text.
3. If an author has left his/her country of birth (A) to live and write in another country (B), this is noted as A → B.
4. Though there are any number of electronic texts available on CD-rom and the Internet, the range of modem copyrighted prose texts of the nature I am interested in is highly restricted. At best, recently published books are electronically available only in limited excerpts. It is clear that actually reading these texts (rather than doing a search on electronically stored data), though an enjoyable experience in itself, runs the risk of my overlooking instances of –*ly* forms. Though I have no doubt that I have missed a few instances here and there, I have done my best not to let the joy of the narrative blind me to the form of the individual words. In my estimation, the scope of the study is so broad that a few missing items will not alter the findings in any significant fashion.
5. The suffix itself apparently derives from a Germanic root (Old English *lic*) meaning "body" or "form" (*OED* IX: 129), so that the early sense of the suffix -*ly* was "having the form of". Interestingly, the noun could refer either to the living body or to a corpse. Thus we still find in English *lich-gate* (also *lych-gate*) = "The roofed gateway to a churchyard under which the corpse is set down, to await the arrival of the clergyman" (*OED* VIII: 894). Compare also the Danish and German cognates for "corpse": *lig* and *Leiche*, respectively.
6. A rather extreme position regarding the semantic value of the adjective-forming -*ly* suffix is taken by Warren (1984: 128). She argues that the suffix is "devoid of lexical meaning", though "it shows fairly clear stem preferences". As we shall see, these preferences involve, primarily, nouns relating to people and time.
7. It may be somewhat surprising to learn (*OED* VIII: 1051) that the adjective *lively* is formed by adding -*ly* to the noun *life* and not to the adjective *live* – with a consequent change in spelling and pronunciation (<f> changes to <v>). Note, however, that the same change takes place when the singular form *life* becomes the plural form *lives*.
8. ME = Middle English, OHG = Old High German, MHG = Middle High German, OE = Old English, ON = Old Norse, * = unattested reconstructed form.
9. *Sightly*, the counterpart of *unsightly*, does not appear in my collection of texts. The word does exist, however, and curiously it postdates the negative, prefixed form. According to the *OED* (XV: 447), the original meaning of *sightly* was 'visible, conspicuous'. There is an entry with this meaning from 1532. However, the first entry with the positive meaning, 'pleasing to the sight', is from 1562 – 14 years later than the first entry for *unsightly*.
10. As in the case of the sources used in establishing the preliminary benchmark corpus, the page count takes into consideration "late start" and blank pages.
11. For the sake of visibility, these 13 new items are placed at the very end of Appendix 2.
12. One can question whether *cleanly* here is to be viewed as an adverb ("start cleanly") or an adjective ("it is cleanly"). The adjective reading seems more logical, because of the coordinate construction "cleanly and well-defined". Since "well-defined" appears to be an adjectival attribute (modifying the idealized nose), "cleanly" probably is as well (compare the coordinated adjectives "sharp and hidden" at the end of the sentence). For the record, here is a clearer example, from another source: "I have before remarked that the natives of this part

of Africa are extremely **cleanly**" (Equiano 1982: 80).
13. The figure 0.05 for Hustvedt is the lowest token density for all 18 texts. The next lowest is Auel's 0.08. To be certain that I had not erred in my count, I reread Hustvedt's novel. The result was the same: in 273 pages of text, Husvedt uses only 10 -*ly* adjectives, most of them only once. As indicated in Appendix 2, these are *friendly* (3 times), *ghostly* (1), *likely* (1). *lively* (1), *lonely* (1), *neighborly* (1), *nightly* (1), *sickly* (1), *unlikely* (2), and *weekly* (1). This is the equivalent of roughly 5 -*ly* adjectives per 100 pages, or 1 in every 20 pages.
14. Note that the form *gravely* does exist, but this is an instance of the adverb-forming suffix –*ly* attached to the adjective, *grave* ("The one cannot be without the other; ask any village dotard and he will *gravely* scratch his beard, try to look wise, and tell you this" – Chandra 1996: 125).
15. As mentioned earlier, one can discuss whether *cleanly* in the first example is to be interpreted as an adjective or as an adverb. There is no doubt in the second example, where *cleanly* is clearly an adverb. It is interesting to note the unusual fact that there is a difference in pronunciation between the two forms: the first syllable of the adjective rhymes with *men*, while the first syllable of the adverb rhymes with *mean*.
16. I find the adverbial use of *friendly* quite unusual. It is also very rare. Our eighteen sources yielded 125 instances of *friendly* as an adjective, compared to this single instance of its use as an adverb. The *OED* (VI: 194) provides a few examples of *friendly* as an adverb, the most recent being from 1869.
17. I am, of course, aware that this decision can result in a slight skewing of the data. Since inflection here depends on syllable length, a construction such as "more gentlemanly" will increase the token count for *gentlemanly*, whereas *lovelier* will not increase the token count for *lovely*.

# References

*AHD = The American Heritage Dictionary of the English Language.* Fourth edition. 2000. Boston: Houghton Mifflin Company.

Atwood, Margaret. 2001 (2000). *The Blind Assassin*. London: Virago Press.

Auden, W. H. 1955 (1945). *W. H. Auden Reading His Poetry* [cassette]. London: Harper Collins Audio Books.

Auel, Jean M. 2002. The *Shelters of Stone*. London: Hodder & Stoughton.

Bache, Carl and Davidsen-Nielsen, Niels. 1997. *Mastering English – An Advanced Grammar for Non-native and Native Speakers.* Berlin: Mouton de Gruyter.

Bandele, Biyi. 1999. *The Street*. London: Picador.

Carey, Peter. 1995 (1994). *The Unusual Life of Tristan Smith*. London: Faber & Faber.

Chandra, Vikram. 1996 (1995). *Red Earth and Pouring Rain*. London: Faber & Faber.

Chidgey, Catherine. 2000. *Golden Deeds*. London: Picador.

Davies, Robertson. 1992 (1991). *Murther & Walking Spirits*. Toronto: Penguin.

Equiano, Olaudah. 1982. "Equiano on his Way to Slavery" (from *Equiano's Travels*, ed. Paul Edwards, London: Heinemann Educational Books, African Writers Series No. 10, 1967. [Note: Equiano was born in 1745/6.] In: *An Anthology of African and Caribbean Writing in English.* Ed. John J. Figueroa. London: Heinemann Educational Books, 79-88.

Figueroa, John J. 1982. *An Anthology of African and Caribbean Writing in English.* London: Heinemann Educational Books.

Fussell, Paul. 1979 (1965). *Poetic Meter and Poetic Form*. New York: McGraw-Hill.
Gordirner, Nadine. 1976 (1958). *A World of Strangers*. London: Penguin.
Greenbaum, Sidney and Randolph Quirk. 1990. *A Student's Grammar of the English Language*. Harlow, England: Longman.
House, Homer C. and Susan Emolyn Harman. 1950. *Descriptive English Grammar*. 2nd revised edition (first edition 1931). New York: Prentice Hall.
Hustvedt, Siri. 1996. *The Enchantment of Lily Dahl*. London: Hodder & Stoughton.
Jespersen, Otto. 1974 (1942). *A Modern English Grammar on Historical Principles. Part VI – Morphology*. London: George Allen & Unwin.
Ljung, Magnus. 1970. *English Denominal Adjectives*. Gothenburg Studies in English 21. Lund, Sweden: Acta Universitatis Gothoburgensis.
McEnroe, John (with James Kaplan). 2003 (2002). *Serious (The Autobiography)*. London: Time Warner.
Mencken, H. L. 1979 (1977). *The American Language – An Inquiry into the Development of English in the United States* [abridged, with annotations and new material by Raven I. McDavid, Jr.]. New York: Alfred A. Knopf.
Mistry, Rohinton. 2002. *Family Matters*. London: Faber & Faber.
Mitchell, Bruce. 1995. *An invitation to Old English and Anglo-Saxon England*. Oxford: Blackwell.
Naipaul, V. S. 1987. *The Enigma of Arrival*. Harmondsworth, Engand: Penguin.
Niles, Chris. 1998 (1997). *Spike It*. London: Pan Books.
OED = *The Oxford English Dictionary*. Second edition. Volumes I - XX. 1989. Oxford: Clarendon Press.
Ondaatje, Michael. 2001 (2000). *Anil's Ghost*. London: Picador.
Opara, Ralph. 1982. "Lagos Interlude" (from *Reflections*, ed. F. Ademole, Lagos: African Universities Press, 1962). In. *An Anthology of African and Caribbean Writing in English*. Ed. John J. Figueroa. London: Heinemann Educational Books, 42-46.
Quirk, Randolph and Greenbaum, Sidney. 1987 (1973). *A University Grammar of English*. Harlow, England: Longman.
Rubens, Bernice. 1998 (1997). *The Waiting Game*. London: Abacus Rutherfurd, Edward. 1998 (1997). London: Arrow Books.
Walker, Peter. 2001. *The Fox Boy*. London: Bloomsbury Publishing.
Warren, Beatrice. 1984. *Classifiing Adjectives*. Volume 56 in Gothenburg Studies in English. Gothenburg, Sweden: Gothenburg University.
WEUD = *Webster's Encyclopedic Unabridged Dictionary of the English Language*. 1996. New York: Random House.
Winton, Tim. 1996 (1988). *Cloudsfreet*. Ringwood, Victoria, Australia: Penguin.

# Appendix 1

## The preliminary benchmark corpus (PBMC)
## Adjectives in –ly from the first eight sources

| No. | Adjective | Atwood | Auel | Carey | Gordimer | Mistry | Naipaul | Rutherfurd | Walker | Total tokens | Total sources | OED date (lic/lich) | OED date (li/ly) | Base | Origin of base form |
|---|---|---|---|---|---|---|---|---|---|---|---|---|---|---|---|
| 1 | actorly | | | 99 | | | | | | 1 | 1 | - | 1959 | noun | R |
| 2 | beastly | | | 165 | | 110 | | | 108 | 3 | 3 | 1220 | 1611 | noun | R |
| 3 | bodily | 457 | | | | | | | 133 | 2 | 2 | - | 1300 | noun | G |
| 4 | brotherly | 267 | 2 | | | | | | | 2 | 2 | 1000 | 1535 | noun | G |
| 5 | burly | | | 333 | | | | 155, 191, 361, 461, 497, 501, 572, 730, 772, 782, 1105, 1245 | | 13 | 2 | · | 1400 | noun | G |
| 6 | clerkly | | | | | | | | 152 | 1 | 1 | - | 1528 | noun | G |
| 7 | costly | 365, 462 | | | | | | 191, 373, 515, 556, 764, 796 | 184 | 9 | 3 | - | 1494 | noun | R |
| 8 | courtly | | | | | | | 370, 404, 608, 609, 610, 692, 723, 724, 745, 786 | | 10 | 1 | | 1450 | noun | R |
| 9 | cowardly | 155, 358 | | 158 | | | | 703, 1114 | 32 | 6 | 4 | - | 1576 | noun | R |
| 10 | daily | 70, 220, 270, 498, 499, 505, 509 | 496 | 368, 382, 382 | 257 | 3, 51, 55, 81, 89, 94, 118, 119, 150 | 19, 25, 56, 154, 158, 219 | 260, 260, 268, 282, 282, 286, 323, 731, 910, 1001, 1008 | | 38 | 7 | - | 1470 | noun | G |
| 11 | dastardly | | | | | 403 | | | | 1 | 1 | - | 1567 | noun | G |
| 12 | deadly | | | 394 | | 154 | | 228, 462, 686, 1027, 1042 | 43, 75, 253, 279, 285, 289 | 13 | 4 | 1000 | 1377 | adj | G |
| 13 | deathly | | | | 101 | | | | | 1 | 1 | 971 | 1568 | noun | G |

| No. | Adjective | Atwood | Auel | Carey | Gordimer | Mistry | Naipaul | Rutherfurd | Walker | Total tokens | Total sources | OED date (lic/lich) | OED date (li/lly) | Base | Origin of base form |
|---|---|---|---|---|---|---|---|---|---|---|---|---|---|---|---|
| 14 | disorderly | | | | | | | | 109, 109 | 2 | 1 | - | 1585 | noun | R |
| 15 | earthly | 321, 375 | | | | | | 495 | | 3 | 2 | 971 | 1300 | noun | G |
| 16 | easterly | | | | | | | 1075 | | 1 | 1 | - | 1609 | ? | G |
| 17 | elderly | 72, 171, 503 | 449 | 324, 381 | 208, 256 | 58, 331 | 34, 35, 53, 138, 172 | 8, 95, 149, 176, 384, 705, 800, 938, 958, 1047, 1102, 1124, 1154 | 8, 22, 45, 122, 183, 256, 324 | 35 | 8 | - | 1660 | adj | G |
| 18 | fatherly | | | | | | | 244 | 41 | 2 | 2 | 1000 | 1440 | noun | G |
| 19 | friendly | 228, 422 | 3, 21, 22, 23, 99, 109, 125, 129, 137, 164, 218, 596 | 202 | 59, 235 | | 29, 35, 42, 66, 112, 171, 240, 262, 276 | 86, 161, 175, 186, 244, 263, 269, 353, 389, 399, 506, 535, 553, 569, 575, 586, 642, 744, 751, 764, 782, 804, 889, 928, 932, 942, 963, 977, 1003, 1008, 1047, 1130, 1184, 1186, 1193, 1243 | 10, 12, 15, 34, 56, 95, 144, 146, 151, 152, 155, 155, 157, 158, 162, 194, 231, 233, 269, 269, 269, 301, 306, 319 | 86 | 7 | 900 | 1374 | noun | G |
| 20 | gentlemanly | | | | | | | 953, 1098 | | 3 | 2 | - | 1433 | noun | R |
| 21 | ghastly | | | 32 | 200 | | | 502 | | 3 | 3 | - | 1390 | verb | G |
| 22 | ghostly | | | | | | 237, 246 | 92, 138 | 34, 34 | 6 | 3 | 1000 | 1303 | noun | G |

| No. | Adjective | Atwood | Auel | Carey | Gordimer | Mistry | Naipaul | Rutherfurd | Walker | Total tokens | Total sources | OED date (lic/lich) | OED date (li/ly) | Base | Origin of base form |
|---|---|---|---|---|---|---|---|---|---|---|---|---|---|---|---|
| 23 | godly | | | | | | | 809, 828, 828, 928, 839, 840, 863, 875, 875, 876, 876, 910, 984 | | 13 | 1 | - | 1450 | noun | G |
| 24 | goodly | 349, 396, 543 | | | | | | | | 1 | 1 | 1205 | 1385 | adj | G |
| 25 | grisly | | | | | | | 164 | 226 | 4 | 2 | 1150 | 1386 | verb | G |
| 26 | heavenly | | | | 17 | | | 83, 529, 873, 921, 943, 943 | | 7 | 2 | 971 | 1382 | noun | G |
| 27 | homely | | | | | 98 | | 789 | | 2 | 2 | - | 13... | noun | G |
| 28 | kindly | 353, 402 | | | 40, 93 | 362 | 92 | 17, 41, 76, 168, 212, 214, 237, 249, 355, 355, 379, 379, 396, 412, 430, 489, 504, 506, 556, 579, 594, 630, 669, 727, 877, 919, 949, 972, 976, 1091, 1093, 1097, 1129, 1106, 1136, 1153, 1159, 1160, 1160, 1229 | 102, 159, 293 | 49 | 6 | 888 | 1400 | adj | |
| 29 | kingly | | | 365 | | | | 352, 871 | | 3 | 2 | - | 1382 | noun | G |

| No. | Adjective | Atwood | Auel | Carey | Gordimer | Mistry | Naipaul | Rutherfurd | Walker | Total tokens | Total sources | OED date (lic/lich) | OED date (li/ly) | Base | Origin of base form |
|---|---|---|---|---|---|---|---|---|---|---|---|---|---|---|---|
| 30 | knightly | | | | | | | 370, 391, 402, 404, 418, 728, 1018, 1217 | | 8 | 1 | 1000 | 1375 | noun | G |
| 31 | leisurely | | 198, 645 | | 112 | 110 | | 427, 760, 951 | 176, 176 | 9 | 5 | - | 1604 | noun | R |
| 32 | likely | 90, 98, 145, 229, 284, 405, 491 | 205, 210 | 9, 69 | 194, 215, 233, 264 | 242, 425 | 48, 77, 276 | 94, 100, 134, 264, 298, 354 439, 515, 517, 521, 521, 610, 774, 865, 875, 902, 953, 1108, 1297 | 74, 86, 263, 290 | 43 | 8 | - | 1380 | adj | G |
| 33 | lively | 466, 467 | 328, 420, 534, 639, 681 | | 111, 165, 189, 203 | 155, 232 | 113 | 10, 202, 293, 636, 649, 809, 1085, 1234 | 122 | 23 | 7 | 1000 | 1430 | noun | G |
| 34 | lonely | 369, 581 | 238, 304, 344, 391, 418, 479 | 93, 165, 364, 384 | 99, 203 | 104, 196, 456 | 121 | 1, 74, 76, 379, 606, 621, 824, 878, 970, 1229 | 128, 133, 200 | 31 | 8 | - | 1607 | adj | G |
| 35 | lordly | | | 70 | 145 | | | 719 | 117, 184, 185 | 6 | 4 | 1000 | 1645 | noun | G |

| No. | Adjective | Atwood | Auel | Carey | Gordimer | Mistry | Naipaul | Rutherfurd | Walker | Total tokens | Total sources | OED date (lic/lich) | OED date (li/ly) | Base | Origin of base form |
|---|---|---|---|---|---|---|---|---|---|---|---|---|---|---|---|
| 36 | lovely | 49, 73, 80, 132, 190, 203, 214, 217, 230, 308, 308, 352, 391, 409, 427, 433, 442, 452, 494, 509, 558, 614 | 192, 535, 613 | 96, 182, 264, 329, 377 | 14, 65, 173, 191, 259 | 8, 14, 34, 34, 34, 60, 71, 87, 98, 121, 123, 141, 166, 167, 192, 209, 210, 271, 273, 282, 288, 305, 340, 417, 436, 440, 461, 483 | 47, 80, 122, 166 | 145, 160, 390, 495, 623, 637, 666, 835, 1145, 1175, 1186, 1238, 1281, 1293 | 2, 24, 293, 330 | 85 | 8 | 1000 | 1340 | noun | G |
| 37 | lowly | | | | | | | 327, 785, 1172 | | 3 | 1 | - | 1374 | adj | G |
| 38 | manly | | | | | 341 | | 62, 450, 717, 985, 1004, 1017, 1030, 1159, 1204 | | 10 | 2 | 1200 | 1422 | noun | G |
| 39 | masterly | | | | 173 | 71 | | 143, 408 | 139 | 5 | 4 | - | 1531 | noun | R |
| 40 | miserly | 83 | | | | | | | 100, 184 | 3 | 2 | - | 1593 | noun | R |
| 41 | monthly | 567 | 457 | | | | | 832, 1022 | 248, 323 | 4 | 2 | - | 1572 | noun | G |
| 42 | motherly | | 25 | | | | | 461, 1129 | 41, 61 | 6 | 4 | 1000 | 1597 | noun | G |
| 43 | neighbourly | | | | | | | | | 1 | 1 | - | 1558 | noun | G |
| 44 | nightly | 158, 328 | 400 | | | 341 | | | | 3 | 2 | 897 | 1380 | noun | G |
| 45 | northerly | | | | | | | | | 1 | 1 | - | 1551 | ? | G |
| 46 | orderly | 265 | 26, 52, 633 | | | | 188 | 295, 321, 638, 1119 | 125, 231, 316 | 12 | 5 | - | 1577 | noun | R |
| 47 | otherworldly | | 289, 501 | | | | | 521 | | 2 | 1 | - | 1879 | noun | G |
| 48 | poorly | | | | | | | | | 1 | 1 | - | 1573 | adj | R |
| 49 | portly | | 662 | 13 | | | | 249, 552, 1243 | | 5 | 3 | - | 1529 | noun | R |
| 50 | priestly | | | 191, 365 | | | | | | 2 | 1 | 1000 | 1535 | noun | G |
| 51 | princely | | | | 21 | | | | | 1 | 1 | - | 1503 | noun | R |

Appendix 1 · 221

| No. | Adjective | Atwood | Auel | Carey | Gordimer | Mistry | Naipaul | Rutherfurd | Walker | Total tokens | Total sources | OED date (lic/lich) | OED date (li/ly) | Base | Origin of base form |
|---|---|---|---|---|---|---|---|---|---|---|---|---|---|---|---|
| 52 | quarterly | | | | | | | | 298, 304 | 2 | 1 | - | 1563 | noun | R |
| 53 | queenly | | | | 13, 27, 83 | | | | | 3 | 1 | - | 1540 | noun | G |
| 54 | saintly | 222 | | | 32 | | | 326, 332, 361, 408, 412, 416, 653, 677, 703 | | 11 | 3 | - | 1660 | noun | R |
| 55 | scholarly | | | | | | | 559, 1181, 1204 | | 3 | 1 | - | 1638 | noun | R |
| 56 | shapely | | 99, 129, 444 | 324 | | | | | | 4 | 2 | - | 1382 | noun | G |
| 57 | sickly | 104, 312, 477, 538 | 8, 125 | 263 | | 8, 15, 26 | | 259, 259, 406, 637, 708, 1082, 1092, 1109, 1111, 1196 | | 20 | 5 | - | 1350 | adj | G |
| 58 | slovenly | 180, 547, 625 | 614 | 67 | | 119 | | 1168 | | 7 | 5 | - | 1583 | noun | G |
| 59 | southerly | | 216 | | | | | | | 1 | 1 | - | 1551 | ? | G |
| 60 | sprightly | 63, 494 | | | 208 | | | 908 | | 4 | 3 | - | 1596 | noun | R |
| 61 | stately | 36, 332, 426 | 315, 572 | | | 213 | | 59, 97, 144, 154, 319, 357, 743, 937, 1088, 1220 | | 16 | 4 | - | 1385 | noun | R |
| 62 | surly | 47 | | | 13 | | | 139, 236, 249, 283, 308, 335, 372, 644, 1064 | | 11 | 3 | - | 1670 | noun | R |
| 63 | timely | 468 | | | | | | | | 1 | 1 | 1200 | 1400 | noun | G |
| 64 | unearthly | | 342 | | 194 | 37 | 178 | | | 4 | 4 | - | 1611 | noun | G |
| 65 | unfriendly | | 458 | 185, 338 | | | | | | 3 | 2 | - | 1425 | noun | G |
| 66 | ungainly | 44 | 231 | | | | | | | 5 | 3 | - | 1611 | adj | G |
| 67 | ungentlemanly | | | | | | | 37, 813, 934 | 135 | 1 | 1 | - | 1562 | noun | R |

| No. | Adjective | Atwood | Auel | Carey | Gordimer | Mistry | Naipaul | Rutherfurd | Walker | Total tokens | Total sources | OED date (lic/lich) | OED date (li/ly) | Base | Origin of base form |
|---|---|---|---|---|---|---|---|---|---|---|---|---|---|---|---|
| 68 | ungodly | | | | | | | 625, 790, 810 | | 3 | 1 | - | 1526 | noun | G |
| 69 | unlikely | 187, 311, 390, 392, 473, 489 | 564 | 67, 243, 277 | 115, 134, 232, 237 | | 52, 96, 134, 157 | 161, 263, 551, 564, 923, 935, 966, 1001, 1008, 1032, 1208 | 33, 41, 117, 311 | 33 | 7 | - | 1375 | adj | G |
| 70 | unlovely | | | 365 | | | | | | 1 | 1 | 1377 | 1586 | noun | G |
| 71 | unseemly | 397, 636 | | 126 | | 394 | | 333 | | 5 | 4 | - | 1300 | verb | G |
| 72 | unsightly | 355 | | | | | | 265, 272 | | 3 | 2 | - | 1548 | noun | G |
| 73 | untimely | | | | | | | 638 | | 1 | 1 | - | 1535 | noun | G |
| 74 | unwomanly | | | | | | | 1248 | | 1 | 1 | - | 1529 | noun | G |
| 75 | weekly | 212, 235 | | | 36 | 225, 440 | 72, 255 | 268, 401, 1168 | 10 | 11 | 6 | - | 1489 | noun | G |
| 76 | westerly | | | | | | | 814 | | 1 | 1 | - | 1577 | ? | G |
| 77 | womanly | | 207, 301, 533, 537 | | | | | | | 4 | 1 | 1374 | 1385 | noun | G |
| 78 | worldly | 210 | | 14, 35 | 257 | 436 | 53 | 332, 332, 340, 353, 365, 411, 411, 544, 552, 636, 649, 688, 839, 839, 930, 974, 1030, 1162 | 51 | 25 | 7 | 888 | 1325 | noun | G |
| 79 | yearly | | | | | | | 393, 634, 851 | | 3 | 1 | 1050 | 1452 | noun | G |
| | Total tokens | 91 | 59 | 40 | 42 | 65 | 42 | 345 | 87 | 771 | 222 | | | | |
| | Total types | 31 | 25 | 24 | 23 | 22 | 15 | 53 | 29 | 4427 | | | | | |
| | Total pages | 607 | 758 | 405 | 247 | 484 | 297 | 1302 | 327 | | | | | | |
| | token/page | 0.15 | 0.08 | 0.10 | 0.17 | 0.13 | 0.14 | 0.26 | 0.27 | 0.17 | | | | | |

*Appendix 1* · 223

# Appendix 2

## Testing the preliminary benchmark corpus
### Adjectives in –ly from ten additional sources

| No. | Adjective | Bandele | Chandra | Chidgey | Davies | Hustvedt | McEnroe | Niiles | Ondaatje | Rubens | Winton | Total tokens | Total sources | OED date (lic/lich) | OED date (li/ly) | Base | Origin of base form |
|---|---|---|---|---|---|---|---|---|---|---|---|---|---|---|---|---|---|
| 1 | actorly | | | | | | | | | | | | | - | 1959 | noun | R |
| 2 | beastly | | | | | | | | | | | | | 1220 | 1611 | noun | R |
| 3 | bodily | 264 | 338, 345 | | 209, 336 | | 210 | | | 123 | | 8 | 6 | - | 1300 | noun | G |
| 4 | brotherly | | | | | | | | | | | | | 1000 | 1535 | noun | G |
| 5 | burly | | 33, 563 | | | | | 159 | | | | 3 | 2 | - | 1400 | noun | G |
| 6 | clerkly | | | | | | | | | | | | | - | 1528 | noun | G |
| 7 | costly | 225 | | 129, 195 | 35, 58, 144, 189, 286 | | | | | | | 8 | 3 | - | 1494 | noun | R |
| 8 | courtly | | | | | | | | 69 | | | 1 | 1 | - | 1450 | noun | R |
| 9 | cowardly | | | | | | | | | | | | | - | 1576 | noun | R |
| 10 | daily | 214, 267 | 3, 115, 141, 213, 302, 391, 515 | 157, 247, 247, 262 | 31, 55, 85, 206, 293, 293, 327, 327 | | 1 | | 30, 55 | 5, 91, 96, 99, 131 | 69, 75, 185, 394 | 33 | 8 | - | 1470 | noun | G |
| 11 | dastardly | | | | | | | | | | | | | - | 1567 | noun | G |
| 12 | deadly | | 5, 14, 14, 406, 474 | | 56, 189 | | 183, 199 | | | 15 | 340 | 11 | 5 | 1000 | 1377 | adj | G |
| 13 | deathly | 72 | 32 | | | | | 5 | | | | 3 | 3 | 971 | 1568 | noun | G |
| 14 | disorderly | 45 | | 14 | 341 | | | | | | | 3 | 3 | - | 1585 | noun | R |
| 15 | earthly | 60 | | 77, 77, 105 | | | | | | 18 | 2 | 6 | 4 | 971 | 1300 | noun | G |
| 16 | easterly | | | | | | | 46, 237, 254 | | | | | | - | 1609 | ? | G |
| 17 | elderly | | | | | | | | | | | 3 | 1 | - | 1660 | adj | G |
| 18 | fatherly | | | | | | | | | | | | | 1000 | 1440 | noun | G |

| No. | Adjective | Bandele | Chandra | Chidgey | Davies | Hustvedt | McEnroe | Niles | Ondaatje | Rubens | Winton | Total tokens | Total sources | OED date (lic/lich) | OED date (li/ly) | Base | Origin of base form |
|---|---|---|---|---|---|---|---|---|---|---|---|---|---|---|---|---|---|
| 19 | friendly | | 49, 195, 240, 489, 586, 588 | 66, 139, 200 | 67, 78, 329 | 5, 10, 200 | 20, 62, 102, 108, 110, 199, 249, 319, 319 | 120, 204 | | 44, 178, 241 | 31, 57, 58, 117, 118, 159, 280, 288, 346, 346 | 39 | 8 | 900 | 1374 | noun | G |
| 20 | gentlemanly | | 358, 567 | | | | | | | | | 2 | 1 | - | 1433 | noun | R |
| 21 | ghastly | | 351, 446 | | | | | | | | | 2 | 1 | - | 1390 | verb | G |
| 22 | ghostly | 233 | 358 | 206, 236 | 132 | 261 | | 191 | | | 90, 167, 167, 338 | 11 | 7 | 1000 | 1303 | noun | G |
| 23 | godly | | 256 | | 8, 119, 120, 124 | | | | | | | 5 | 2 | - | 1450 | noun | G |
| 24 | goodly | | | | | | | | | 162 | | 1 | 1 | 1205 | 1385 | adj | G |
| 25 | grisly | | | | | | | | | | | | | 1150 | 1386 | verb | G |
| 26 | heavenly | 267, 268, 270 | 431 | | 137 | | | | | | | 5 | 3 | 971 | 1382 | noun | G |
| 27 | homely | | | | | | | | | | | | | - | 13... | noun | G |
| 28 | kindly | 128 | 7 | | 204, 237 | | 38 | | | 32 | 95 | 7 | 6 | 888 | 1400 | adj | G |
| 29 | kingly | | | | | | | | | | | | | - | 1382 | noun | G |
| 30 | knightly | | | | | | | | | | | | | 1000 | 1375 | noun | G |
| 31 | leisurely | | 104, 359 | | | | 100 | | | 176 | | 3 | 2 | - | 1604 | noun | R |
| 32 | likely | 177 | 459, 478 | | 23, 75, 181, 243, 304, 314, 327, 354 | 126 | 249 | 41, 141, 175, 192, 322 | 82, 89, 122, 151, 274, 293, 301 | 39, 48, 71, 98, 114, 120, 142, 204 | 111, 112, 286, 310 | 37 | 9 | - | 1380 | adj | G |
| 33 | lively | 57 | 124 | 51, 68 | 22, 40, 116, 120, 159 | 167 | | 125, 233 | | 63, 72, 89 | | 16 | 8 | 1000 | 1430 | noun | G |

| No. | Adjective | Bandele | Chandra | Chidgey | Davies | Hustvedt | McEnroe | Niles | Ondaatje | Rubens | Winton | Total tokens | Total sources | OED date (lic/lich) | OED date (li/ly) | Base | Origin of base form |
|---|---|---|---|---|---|---|---|---|---|---|---|---|---|---|---|---|---|
| 34 | lonely | 25, 132, 273 | 103, 122, 127, 356, 447, 520, 520, 520, 549, 561 | 14, 82 | 208 | 171 | 109, 118, 190, 268, 277 | | 142 | 175, 214, 214 | 21, 35, 35, 60, 61, 184, 185, 212, 227, 253, 317, 317, 367, 377, 379 | 43 | 9 | - | 1607 | adj | G |
| 35 | lordly | | | | | | | | | | | | | 1000 | 1645 | noun | G |
| 36 | lovely | 248 | 97, 162, 308, 373, 377, 378, 388, 453, 463, 487, 561 | 42, 50, 50, 68, 75, 159, 160, 162, 198, 218, 227, 232, 240, 241, 242, 257, 258 | 6, 86, 103, 103, 176, 181, 231, 256, 349, 349 | | 53, 85, 309 | 53, 74, 88, 162, 238 | 35, 262 | 32, 34, 58, 58, 66, 203, 226 | 139, 139, 288, 333, 356 | 61 | 9 | 1000 | 1340 | noun | G |
| 37 | lowly | | | | 311, 312 | | | | 29 | | | 3 | 2 | - | 1374 | adj | G |
| 38 | manly | | 488, 490 | | 4 | | | | | | 167 | 4 | 3 | 1200 | 1422 | noun | G |
| 39 | masterly | | | | | | | | | | | | | - | 1531 | noun | R |
| 40 | miserly | | | | | | | | | | | | | - | 1593 | noun | R |
| 41 | monthly | 8, 129, 136 | | | | | 2 | | | 36, 96, 208 | | 7 | 3 | - | 1572 | noun | G |
| 42 | motherly | | 150 | | | | | | | | | 1 | 1 | 1000 | 1597 | noun | G |
| 43 | neighbourly | | | | | 204 | | | | | | 1 | 1 | - | 1558 | noun | G |
| 44 | nightly | | 456 | 11 | | 258 | | 67 | | 5, 96, 246 | 2 | 8 | 6 | 897 | 1380 | noun | G |
| 45 | northerly | | | | | | | | | | | | | - | 1551 | ? | G |
| 46 | orderly | | 383, 459, 473, 476 | | 72 | | | | 117, 211 | | 149, 212, 308, 339, 345, 360, 381 | 14 | 4 | - | 1577 | noun | R |
| 47 | otherworldly | | 156 | | | | | | | | | 1 | 1 | - | 1879 | noun | G |
| 48 | poorly | | | 166, 166 | | | | | | 60, 134 | | 4 | 2 | - | 1573 | adj | R |
| 49 | portly | | 214, 505 | | | | | | | | | 2 | 1 | - | 1529 | noun | R |

*Appendix 2 · 227*

| No. | Adjective | Bandele | Chandra | Chidgey | Davies | Hustvedt | McEnroe | Niles | Ondaatje | Rubens | Winton | Total tokens | Total sources | OED date (lic/lich) | OED date (li/ly) | Base | Origin of base form |
|---|---|---|---|---|---|---|---|---|---|---|---|---|---|---|---|---|---|
| 50 | priestly | | | | 193, 344 | | | | | | 319 | 3 | 2 | 1000 | 1535 | noun | G |
| 51 | princely | | | | | | | | | | | | 2 | - | 1503 | noun | R |
| 52 | quarterly | | | | 54 | | | | | 44 | | 2 | 2 | - | 1563 | noun | R |
| 53 | queenly | | | | | | | | | | | | | - | 1540 | noun | G |
| 54 | saintly | | | | | | | | | | | | | - | 1660 | noun | R |
| 55 | scholarly | | | | 18, 276, 284, 284 | | | | | | | 4 | 1 | - | 1638 | noun | R |
| 56 | shapely | | | | | | | | | | | | | - | 1382 | noun | G |
| 57 | sickly | | 278 | | | 45 | | | | 30, 32, 101 | | 5 | 3 | - | 1350 | adj | G |
| 58 | slovenly | | | | | | | | | | | 1 | 1 | - | 1583 | noun | G |
| 59 | southerly | | | | | | | 204 | 47 | | | 4 | 3 | - | 1551 | ? | G |
| 60 | sprightly | | 246, 276 | | | | | | | | 91 | | | - | 1596 | noun | R |
| 61 | stately | | 227 | | 42, 81, 123 | | | 247 | | 217 | 227 | 7 | 5 | - | 1385 | noun | R |
| 62 | surly | | 252 | | | | | | | | | 1 | 1 | - | 1670 | noun | R |
| 63 | timely | | 73 | | | | | | | 216 | | 2 | 2 | 1200 | 1400 | noun | G |
| 64 | unearthly | | 23, 74, 183, 332, 363 | | | | | | | | 270 | 6 | 2 | - | 1611 | noun | G |
| 65 | unfriendly | | | | | | | | | | | 1 | 1 | - | 1425 | noun | G |
| 66 | ungainly | | | | | | | | | | | | | - | 1611 | adj | G |
| 67 | ungentlemanly | | | | | | | | | 150 | | | | - | 1562 | noun | R |
| 68 | ungodly | | | | | | | | | | | | | - | 1526 | noun | G |
| 69 | unlikely | | | 93 | 56, 118, 304 | 20, 169 | | | 16, 21, 154, 176, 205, 230 | 18, 195, 197, 214, 229, 247 | | 18 | 5 | - | 1375 | adj | G |
| 70 | unlovely | | | | | | | | | | | | | 1377 | 1586 | noun | G |
| 71 | unseemly | | | | 148 | | | | | | | 1 | 1 | - | 1300 | verb | G |
| 72 | unsightly | | | | 323 | | | | | | | 1 | 1 | - | 1548 | noun | G |
| 73 | untimely | | | | | | | | | 96, 101 | | 2 | 1 | - | 1535 | noun | G |
| 74 | unwomanly | | | | | | | | | | | | | - | 1529 | noun | G |

228 · *The Language of Riddles, Humor and Literature*

| No. | Adjective | Bandele | Chandra | Chidgey | Davies | Hustvedt | McEnroe | Niles | Ondaatje | Rubens | Winton | Total tokens | Total sources | OED date (lic/lich) | OED date (li/ly) | Base | Origin of base form |
|---|---|---|---|---|---|---|---|---|---|---|---|---|---|---|---|---|---|
| 75 | weekly | 179 | 339 | | 202, 298, 333 | 51 | 4 | | | 37, 86, 89, 126, 169, 235 | 171, 172 | 15 | 7 | - | 1489 | noun | G |
| 76 | westerly | | | | | | | | | | | | | - | 1577 | ? | G |
| 77 | womanly | | | | 203 | | | | | | 181 | 2 | 2 | 1374 | 1385 | noun | G |
| 78 | worldly | | 203 | | 84 | | | | 83 | | 64, 230 | 5 | 4 | 888 | 1325 | noun | G |
| 79 | yearly | | | | 44, 119 | | | | | | | 2 | 1 | 1050 | 1452 | noun | G |
| 80 | cleanly | | 381 | | | | | | | | | 1 | 1 | 888 | 1340 | adj | G |
| 81 | comely | | | 73 | | | | | | | | 1 | 1 | 1000 | 1300 | adj | G |
| 82 | comradely | | | | | | | | | | | 1 | 1 | - | 1880 | noun | R |
| 83 | creaturely | | | | | | | | | 58 | | 1 | 1 | - | 1662 | noun | R |
| 84 | curmudgeonly | | | | 118 | | | | | 87 | | 1 | 1 | - | 1590 | noun | ? |
| 85 | fleshly | | | | | | | | | 44 | | 1 | 1 | 888 | 1300 | noun | G |
| 86 | hourly | | | | 83 | | 205 | | | | | 2 | 2 | - | 1513 | noun | R < Gk |
| 87 | lawyerly | | | | | | 92, 206 | | | | | 2 | 1 | - | - | noun | G |
| 88 | loathly | | | | 343 | | | | | | | 1 | 1 | 900 | 1300 | adj | G |
| 89 | matronly | | | | | | | | | 109, 165 | | 2 | 1 | - | 1656 | noun | R |
| 90 | sisterly | | 442 | | | | | | | | | 1 | 1 | - | 1570 | noun | G |
| 91 | soldierly | | | | 42 | | | | | | | 1 | 1 | - | 1577 | noun | R |
| 92 | wifely | | | | | | | | | 115 | | 1 | 1 | 893 | 1385 | noun | G |
| | Total tokens | 22 | 85 | 39 | 85 | 13 | 28 | 24 | 25 | 68 | 65 | 454 | | | | | |
| | Total types | 15 | 33 | 12 | 33 | 10 | 12 | 12 | 11 | 26 | 21 | | 185 | | | | |
| | Total pages | 247 | 605 | 264 | 340 | 273 | 321 | 343 | 282 | 238 | 402 | 3315 | | | | | |
| | token/page | 0.09 | 0.14 | 0.15 | 0.25 | 0.05 | 0.09 | 0.07 | 0.09 | 0.29 | 0.16 | 0.14 | | | | | |

*Appendix 2 · 229*

# Appendix 3a

## The full corpus – in alphabetical order
## Adjectives in –*ly* from all eighteen sources

| No. | Adjective | At | Au | Ba | Ca | Cha | Chi | Da | Go | Hu | Mc | Mi | Na | Ni | On | Rub | Rut | Wa | Wi | Total tokens | Total sources | Base | Origin of base form |
|---|---|---|---|---|---|---|---|---|---|---|---|---|---|---|---|---|---|---|---|---|---|---|---|
| 1 | actorly | | | | 1 | | | | | | | | | | | | | | | 1 | 1 | noun | R |
| 2 | beastly | | | | 1 | | | | | | 1 | 1 | | | 1 | | | | | 3 | 3 | noun | R |
| 3 | bodily | 1 | | 1 | | 2 | | 2 | | | | | | | 1 | 1 | | 1 | | 10 | 8 | noun | G |
| 4 | brotherly | 1 | | | | 2 | | | | | | | | | | | | 1 | | 2 | 2 | noun | G |
| 5 | burly | | | | | | | | | | | | 1 | | | | 12 | | | 16 | 4 | noun | G |
| 6 | cleanly | | | | | | | | | | | | | | | | | | | 1 | 1 | adj | G |
| 7 | clerkly | | | | | | 1 | | | | | | | | | | | | | 1 | 1 | noun | G |
| 8 | comely | | | | | | | | | | | | | | | | | 1 | | 1 | 1 | adj | G |
| 9 | comradely | | | | | | | | | | | | | | | | | | | 1 | 1 | noun | R |
| 10 | costly | 2 | | 1 | | | | | 2 | | | | | | | | 6 | 1 | 1 | 17 | 6 | noun | R |
| 11 | courtly | | | | 1 | | 2 | 5 | | | | | | | | | 10 | | | 11 | 2 | noun | R |
| 12 | cowardly | 2 | | | | | | | | | | | 1 | | | | 2 | | 1 | 6 | 4 | noun | R |
| 13 | creaturely | | | | | | | 1 | | | | | | | | | | | | 1 | 1 | noun | R |
| 14 | curmudgeonly | | | | | | | | | | | | | | | | | | 1 | 1 | 1 | noun | ? |
| 15 | daily | 7 | 1 | 2 | 3 | 7 | 4 | 8 | 1 | 3 | 1 | 9 | 6 | | 2 | 5 | 11 | | 4 | 71 | 15 | noun | G |
| 16 | dastardly | | | | | | | | | | | 1 | | | | | | | | 1 | 1 | noun | G |
| 17 | deadly | | | | 1 | 5 | | 2 | | | 2 | | | | | 1 | 5 | 6 | 1 | 24 | 9 | adj | G |
| 18 | deathly | | | 1 | | 1 | | | | | | | | | | | | | | 4 | 4 | noun | G |
| 19 | disorderly | | | 1 | | | 1 | 1 | | | | | 1 | | | | | | | 5 | 4 | noun | R |
| 20 | earthly | 2 | | | | | 3 | | | | | | | | | | | 2 | | 9 | 6 | noun | G |
| 21 | easterly | | | | | | | | | | | | | | | | 1 | | | 1 | 1 | ? | ? |
| 22 | elderly | 3 | 1 | | 2 | | | | 2 | | | 2 | 5 | 3 | | | 13 | 7 | | 38 | 9 | adj | G |
| 23 | fatherly | | | | | | | | | | | | 1 | | | | 1 | 1 | | 2 | 2 | noun | G |
| 24 | fleshly | | | | | | | | | | | | | | | 1 | | | | 1 | 1 | noun | G |
| 25 | friendly | 2 | 12 | | 1 | 6 | 3 | 3 | 2 | 3 | 9 | 2 | 9 | 2 | | 3 | 36 | 24 | 10 | 125 | 15 | noun | R |
| 26 | gentlemanly | | | | | 2 | | | | | | | 1 | | | | 2 | | | 5 | 3 | noun | R |
| 27 | ghastly | | | | 1 | 2 | | 1 | | | | | | | | | 1 | | | 5 | 4 | verb | G |
| 28 | ghostly | | | | | | 2 | 1 | | | | | 2 | 1 | | | 2 | 2 | 4 | 17 | 10 | noun | G |
| 29 | godly | | | | | 1 | | 4 | | | | | | | | | 13 | | | 18 | 3 | noun | G |
| 30 | goodly | | | | | | | | | | | | | | | 1 | | | | 2 | 2 | adj | G |
| 31 | grisly | 3 | | | | | | | | | | | | | | | 1 | | | 4 | 2 | verb | G |

| No. | Adjective | At | Au | Ba | Ca | Cha | Chi | Da | Go | Hu | Mc | Mi | Na | Ni | On | Rub | Rut | Wa | Wi | Total tokens | Total sources | Base | Origin of base form |
|---|---|---|---|---|---|---|---|---|---|---|---|---|---|---|---|---|---|---|---|---|---|---|---|
| 32 | heavenly | | | 3 | | 1 | | 1 | 1 | | | | | | | | 6 | | | 12 | 5 | noun | G |
| 33 | homely | | | | | | | | | | | | | | | | 1 | | | 2 | 2 | noun | G |
| 34 | hourly | | | | | | | | | | 1 | 1 | | | | | | | | 2 | 2 | noun | R < Gk |
| 35 | kindly | 2 | | 1 | | 1 | | 1 | 2 | | | 1 | 1 | 1 | | 1 | 40 | 3 | | 56 | 12 | adj | G |
| 36 | kingly | | | | 1 | | | 2 | 2 | | | | | | | | 2 | | | 3 | 2 | noun | G |
| 37 | knightly | | | | | | | | | | | | | | | | 8 | | | 8 | 1 | noun | G |
| 38 | lawyerly | | | | | | | | | | 2 | | | | | | | | | 2 | 1 | noun | G |
| 39 | leisurely | | 2 | | 2 | 2 | | 1 | 1 | | | 1 | | | 7 | 1 | 3 | 2 | | 12 | 7 | noun | R |
| 40 | likely | 7 | 2 | 1 | 2 | 2 | | 8 | 4 | 1 | 1 | 2 | 3 | 5 | | 8 | 19 | 4 | 4 | 80 | 17 | adj | G |
| 41 | lively | 2 | 5 | 1 | | 1 | 2 | 5 | 4 | 1 | 1 | 2 | 1 | 2 | | 3 | 8 | 1 | | 39 | 15 | noun | G |
| 42 | loathly | | | | | | | 1 | | | | | | | | | | | | 1 | 1 | adj | G |
| 43 | lonely | 2 | 6 | 3 | 4 | 12 | 2 | 1 | 2 | 1 | 5 | 3 | 1 | | 1 | 3 | 10 | 3 | 15 | 74 | 17 | adj | G |
| 44 | lordly | | | | 1 | | | | 1 | | | | | | | | 1 | 3 | | 6 | 4 | noun | G |
| 45 | lovely | 22 | 3 | 1 | 5 | 11 | 17 | 10 | 5 | 1 | 3 | 28 | 4 | 5 | 2 | 7 | 14 | 4 | 5 | 146 | 17 | adj | G |
| 46 | lowly | | | | | | | 2 | | | | | | | 1 | | 3 | | | 6 | 3 | adj | G |
| 47 | manly | | | | | 2 | | 1 | | | | 1 | | | | | 9 | | 1 | 14 | 5 | noun | G |
| 48 | masterly | | | | | | | | 1 | | | 1 | | | | 2 | 2 | | | 5 | 4 | noun | R |
| 49 | matronly | | | | | | | | | | | | | | | | | 1 | | 2 | 1 | noun | R |
| 50 | miserly | 1 | | | | | | | | | 1 | | | | | | | 2 | | 3 | 2 | noun | R |
| 51 | monthly | | | 3 | | | | | | | | | | | | 3 | 2 | 2 | | 11 | 5 | noun | G |
| 52 | motherly | 1 | 1 | | | 1 | | 2 | | | | | | | | | 2 | 2 | | 7 | 5 | noun | G |
| 53 | neighbourly | | 1 | | | | | | | 1 | | | | | | | | | | 2 | 2 | noun | G |
| 54 | nightly | 2 | | | 1 | 1 | 1 | | | 1 | | | 1 | | | 3 | | | 1 | 11 | 8 | noun | G |
| 55 | northerly | | 1 | | | | | | | | | | | | | | | | | 1 | 1 | ? | G |
| 56 | orderly | 1 | 3 | | 2 | 4 | | 1 | 5 | | | | 1 | | 2 | | 4 | 3 | 7 | 26 | 9 | noun | R |
| 57 | otherworldly | | 2 | | | 1 | | | | | | | | | | | | | | 3 | 2 | noun | G |
| 58 | poorly | | | | 1 | | | 2 | | | | | | | | 2 | 1 | | | 5 | 3 | adj | R |
| 59 | portly | | | | 2 | 2 | | | | | | | | | | | 3 | | | 7 | 4 | noun | R |
| 60 | priestly | | 1 | | | | | 2 | | | | | | | | | | 2 | | 5 | 3 | noun | G |
| 61 | princely | | | | | | | | 1 | | | | | | | 1 | | | 1 | 1 | noun | R |
| 62 | quarterly | | | | | | | 1 | | | | | | | | | | | | 4 | 3 | noun | R |
| 63 | queenly | | | | | | | | 3 | | | | | | | | | 2 | | 3 | 1 | noun | G |
| 64 | saintly | | | | | | | | 1 | | | | | | | | 9 | | | 11 | 3 | noun | R |
| 65 | scholarly | 1 | | | | | | 4 | | | | | | | | | 3 | | | 7 | 2 | noun | R |

232 · *The Language of Riddles, Humor and Literature*

| No. | Adjective | At | Au | Ba | Ca | Cha | Chi | Da | Go | Hu | Mc | Mi | Na | Ni | On | Rub | Rut | Wa | Wi | Total tokens | Total sources | Base | Origin of base form |
|---|---|---|---|---|---|---|---|---|---|---|---|---|---|---|---|---|---|---|---|---|---|---|---|
| 66 | shapely | | 3 | | 1 | | | | | | | | | | | | | | | 4 | 2 | noun | G |
| 67 | sickly | 4 | 2 | | 1 | 1 | | | | 1 | | 3 | | | | 3 | 10 | | | 25 | 8 | adj | G |
| 68 | sisterly | | | | | 1 | | | | | | | | | | | | | | 1 | 1 | noun | G |
| 69 | slovenly | 3 | 1 | | 1 | | | | | | | 1 | | | | | | | 1 | 7 | 5 | noun | G |
| 70 | soldierly | | | | | | | 1 | | | | | | | | | | | | 1 | 1 | noun | R |
| 71 | southerly | | 1 | | | | | | | | | | | | 1 | | | | | 2 | 2 | ? | G |
| 72 | sprightly | 2 | | | | 2 | | | 1 | | | | | 1 | 1 | | 1 | | | 8 | 6 | noun | R |
| 73 | stately | 3 | 2 | | | 1 | | 3 | | | | 1 | | 1 | | 1 | 10 | | 1 | 23 | 9 | noun | R |
| 74 | surly | 1 | | | | 1 | | | 1 | | | | | | | | 9 | | | 12 | 4 | noun | R |
| 75 | timely | 1 | | | | 1 | | | | | | | | | | 1 | | | | 3 | 3 | noun | G |
| 76 | unearthly | | 1 | | | 5 | | | 1 | | | 1 | | | | | | 1 | 1 | 10 | 6 | noun | G |
| 77 | unfriendly | | | 2 | | | | | | | | | 1 | | | | 3 | | | 4 | 3 | adj | G |
| 78 | ungainly | 1 | 1 | | | | | | | | | | | | | | | 1 | | 5 | 3 | adj | G |
| 79 | ungentlemanly | | | | | | | | | | | | | | | | | | | 1 | 1 | noun | R |
| 80 | ungodly | | | | | | | | | | | | | | | | 3 | | | 3 | 1 | noun | G |
| 81 | unlikely | 6 | 1 | | 3 | | 1 | 3 | 4 | 2 | | 4 | | | 6 | 6 | 11 | 4 | | 51 | 12 | adj | G |
| 82 | unlovely | | | | 1 | | | | | | | | | | | | | | | 1 | 1 | noun | G |
| 83 | unseemly | 2 | | | 1 | | | 1 | | | | | | | | | 1 | | 1 | 6 | 5 | verb | G |
| 84 | unsightly | 1 | | | | | | 1 | | | | 1 | | | | | 2 | | | 4 | 3 | noun | G |
| 85 | untimely | | | | | | | | | | | | | | | 2 | 1 | | | 3 | 2 | noun | G |
| 86 | unwomanly | | | | | | | | | | | | | | | | 1 | | | 1 | 1 | noun | G |
| 87 | weekly | 2 | | 1 | | 1 | | 3 | | 1 | 1 | 2 | 2 | | | 6 | 3 | 1 | 2 | 26 | 13 | noun | G |
| 88 | westerly | | | | | | | | | | | | | | | | 1 | | | 1 | 1 | ? | G |
| 89 | wifely | | | | | | | | | | | | | | | 1 | | | | 1 | 1 | noun | G |
| 90 | womanly | | 4 | | | | | 1 | | | | | | | | | | | 1 | 6 | 3 | noun | G |
| 91 | worldly | 1 | | | 2 | 1 | | 1 | | | | 1 | 1 | | | | 18 | | 2 | 30 | 11 | noun | G |
| 92 | yearly | | | | | | | 2 | | | | | | | 1 | | 3 | | | 5 | 2 | noun | G |
| | Total tokens | 91 | 59 | 22 | 40 | 85 | 39 | 85 | 42 | 13 | 28 | 65 | 42 | 24 | 25 | 68 | 345 | 87 | 65 | 1225 | | | |
| | Total types | 31 | 25 | 15 | 24 | 33 | 12 | 33 | 23 | 10 | 12 | 22 | 15 | 12 | 11 | 26 | 53 | 29 | 21 | | 407 | | |
| | Total pages | 607 | 758 | 247 | 405 | 605 | 264 | 340 | 247 | 273 | 321 | 484 | 297 | 343 | 282 | 238 | 1302 | 327 | 402 | 7742 | | | |
| | token/page | 0,15 | 0,08 | 0,09 | 0,10 | 0,14 | 0,15 | 0,25 | 0,17 | 0,05 | 0,09 | 0,13 | 0,14 | 0,07 | 0,09 | 0,29 | 0,26 | 0,27 | 0,16 | 0,16 | | | |

# Appendix 3b

## The full corpus – ordered by frequency

| No. | Adjective | At | Au | Ba | Ca | Cha | Chi | Da | Go | Hu | Mc | Mi | Na | Ni | On | Rub | Rut | Wa | Wi | Total tokens | Total sources | Base | Origin of base form |
|---|---|---|---|---|---|---|---|---|---|---|---|---|---|---|---|---|---|---|---|---|---|---|---|
| 1 | lovely | 22 | 3 | 1 | 5 | 11 | 17 | 10 | 5 | 3 | 3 | 28 | 4 | 5 | 2 | 7 | 14 | 4 | 5 | 146 | 17 | noun | G |
| 2 | friendly | 2 | 12 | | 1 | 6 | 3 | 3 | 2 | 3 | 9 | | 9 | 2 | | 3 | 36 | 24 | 10 | 125 | 15 | noun | G |
| 3 | likely | 7 | 2 | 1 | 2 | 2 | | 8 | 4 | 1 | 1 | 2 | 3 | 5 | 7 | 8 | 19 | 4 | 4 | 80 | 17 | adj | G |
| 4 | lonely | 2 | 6 | 3 | 4 | 12 | 2 | 1 | 2 | 1 | 5 | 3 | 1 | | | 3 | 10 | 3 | 15 | 74 | 17 | adj | G |
| 5 | daily | 7 | 1 | 2 | 3 | 7 | 4 | 8 | 1 | | 1 | 9 | 6 | | 2 | 5 | 11 | | 4 | 71 | 15 | noun | G |
| 6 | kindly | 2 | | 1 | | | | 2 | 2 | | | 1 | | 1 | | 1 | 40 | 3 | 1 | 56 | 12 | adj | G |
| 7 | unlikely | 6 | 1 | | 3 | | 1 | 3 | 4 | 2 | 1 | | 4 | | 6 | 6 | 11 | 4 | | 51 | 12 | adj | G |
| 8 | lively | 2 | 5 | 1 | | 1 | 2 | 5 | 4 | 1 | | 2 | 1 | 2 | | 3 | 8 | 1 | | 39 | 15 | noun | G |
| 9 | elderly | 3 | 1 | | 2 | | | | 2 | | | 2 | 5 | 3 | | | 13 | 7 | | 38 | 9 | adj | G |
| 10 | worldly | 1 | | | 2 | 1 | | 1 | 1 | | | 1 | 1 | | 1 | | 18 | 1 | 2 | 30 | 11 | noun | G |
| 11 | orderly | 1 | 3 | | | 4 | | 1 | | | | | | | 2 | | 4 | 3 | 7 | 26 | 9 | noun | R |
| 12 | weekly | 2 | | 1 | | 1 | | 3 | 1 | 1 | 1 | 2 | 2 | | | 6 | 3 | 1 | 2 | 26 | 13 | adj | G |
| 13 | sickly | 4 | 2 | | 1 | 1 | | | | 1 | | 3 | | | | 3 | 10 | | | 25 | 8 | adj | G |
| 14 | deadly | | | | 1 | 5 | | 2 | | | 2 | 1 | | 1 | | 1 | 5 | 6 | 1 | 24 | 9 | adj | G |
| 15 | stately | 3 | 2 | | | 1 | | 3 | | | | | | | | 1 | 10 | | 1 | 23 | 9 | noun | R |
| 16 | godly | | | | | 1 | | 4 | | | | | | | | | 13 | | | 18 | 3 | noun | G |
| 17 | costly | 2 | | 1 | | | 2 | 5 | | 1 | | | | | | | 6 | 1 | | 17 | 6 | noun | G |
| 18 | ghostly | | | 1 | | 1 | 2 | 1 | | | | | 2 | 1 | | | 2 | 2 | 4 | 17 | 10 | noun | G |
| 19 | burly | | | | 1 | 2 | | | | | | | | | | | 12 | | | 16 | 4 | noun | G |
| 20 | manly | | | | | 2 | | 1 | | | | 1 | | | | | 9 | | 1 | 14 | 5 | noun | G |
| 21 | heavenly | | | 3 | | 1 | | 1 | 1 | | | | | | | | 6 | | | 12 | 5 | noun | G |
| 22 | leisurely | | 2 | | | 2 | | | | | | 1 | | | | 1 | 3 | 2 | | 12 | 7 | noun | R |
| 23 | surly | 1 | | | | 1 | | | | | | | | | | | 9 | | | 12 | 4 | adj | R |
| 24 | courtly | | | | | | | | | | | | | | 1 | | 10 | | | 11 | 2 | noun | R |
| 25 | monthly | | | 3 | | | | | | | | | | | | 3 | 2 | 2 | 1 | 11 | 5 | noun | G |
| 26 | nightly | 2 | | | | | | | 1 | | | | | | | 3 | | | | 11 | 8 | noun | G |
| 27 | saintly | 1 | | | | 1 | | | | 1 | | | | | | | | | | 11 | 3 | noun | R |
| 28 | bodily | 1 | | 1 | | 2 | | 2 | | | 1 | | 1 | | | 1 | | | | 10 | 8 | noun | G |
| 29 | unearthly | | 1 | | | 5 | | | 1 | | | | | | | | | 1 | | 10 | 6 | noun | G |
| 30 | earthly | 2 | | 1 | | | | | | | | | | | | | | | 1 | 9 | 6 | noun | G |
| 31 | knightly | | | | | | 3 | | | | | | | | | | 8 | | | 8 | 1 | noun | G |

| No. | Adjective | At | Au | Ba | Ca | Cha | Chi | Da | Go | Hu | Mc | Mi | Na | Ni | On | Rub | Rut | Wa | Wi | Total tokens | Total sources | Base | Origin of base form |
|---|---|---|---|---|---|---|---|---|---|---|---|---|---|---|---|---|---|---|---|---|---|---|---|
| 32 | sprightly | 2 |   |   |   | 2 |   |   | 1 |   |   |   |   | 1 | 1 |   | 1 |   |   | 8 | 6 | noun | R |
| 33 | motherly | 1 | 1 |   |   | 1 |   |   |   |   |   |   |   |   |   |   | 2 | 2 |   | 7 | 5 | noun | G |
| 34 | portly |   | 1 |   | 1 | 2 |   |   |   |   |   |   |   |   |   |   | 3 |   |   | 7 | 4 | noun | R |
| 35 | scholarly | 3 |   |   |   |   |   | 4 |   |   |   |   |   |   |   |   |   |   |   | 7 | 2 | noun | R |
| 36 | slovenly | 2 | 1 |   | 1 |   |   |   |   |   |   | 1 |   |   |   |   | 1 |   |   | 7 | 5 | noun | G |
| 37 | cowardly |   |   |   | 1 |   |   |   | 1 |   |   |   |   |   |   |   | 2 | 1 |   | 6 | 4 | noun | R |
| 38 | lordly |   |   |   | 1 |   |   | 2 |   |   |   |   |   |   |   |   | 1 | 3 |   | 6 | 4 | noun | G |
| 39 | lowly | 2 |   |   | 1 |   |   | 1 |   |   |   |   |   |   |   |   | 3 |   |   | 6 | 3 | adj | G |
| 40 | unseemly |   | 4 |   |   |   |   | 1 |   |   |   | 1 |   |   |   |   |   |   |   | 6 | 5 | verb | G |
| 41 | womanly |   |   | 1 |   |   |   | 1 |   |   |   |   | 1 |   |   |   |   | 2 | 1 | 6 | 3 | noun | G |
| 42 | disorderly |   |   |   |   | 2 |   |   | 1 |   |   |   |   |   |   |   | 2 |   |   | 5 | 4 | noun | R |
| 43 | gentlemanly |   |   |   |   | 2 |   |   | 1 |   |   | 1 |   |   |   |   | 1 |   |   | 5 | 3 | noun | R |
| 44 | ghastly |   |   |   | 1 | 2 |   |   |   |   |   |   |   |   |   |   | 2 |   |   | 5 | 4 | verb | G |
| 45 | masterly |   |   |   |   |   |   | 2 |   |   |   |   |   |   |   |   |   | 1 |   | 5 | 4 | noun | R |
| 46 | poorly |   |   |   |   |   |   | 2 |   |   |   |   |   |   |   | 2 |   |   |   | 5 | 3 | adj | R |
| 47 | priestly |   |   |   | 2 |   |   |   |   |   |   |   |   |   |   |   |   |   | 1 | 5 | 3 | noun | G |
| 48 | ungainly | 1 |   |   |   |   |   |   |   |   |   |   |   |   |   |   | 3 |   |   | 5 | 3 | adj | G |
| 49 | yearly |   |   |   |   |   |   | 2 | 1 |   |   |   |   |   |   |   | 3 |   |   | 5 | 2 | noun | G |
| 50 | deathly |   |   | 1 |   |   |   |   |   |   |   |   |   | 1 |   |   |   |   |   | 4 | 4 | noun | G |
| 51 | grisly | 3 |   |   |   | 1 |   |   |   |   |   |   |   |   |   | 1 |   |   |   | 4 | 2 | verb | G |
| 52 | quarterly |   | 3 |   | 1 |   |   | 1 |   |   |   |   |   |   |   |   |   | 1 |   | 4 | 3 | noun | R |
| 53 | shapely |   | 1 |   | 2 |   |   |   |   |   |   |   |   |   |   | 1 |   | 2 |   | 4 | 2 | noun | G |
| 54 | unfriendly | 1 |   |   |   |   |   |   |   |   |   |   |   |   |   |   | 2 |   |   | 4 | 3 | noun | G |
| 55 | unsightly |   |   |   | 1 |   |   | 1 |   |   |   |   |   |   |   |   |   | 1 |   | 4 | 2 | noun | G |
| 56 | beastly |   |   |   | 1 |   |   |   |   |   |   | 1 |   |   |   |   |   |   |   | 3 | 3 | noun | R |
| 57 | kingly | 1 |   |   | 1 |   |   |   |   |   |   |   |   |   |   |   | 2 |   |   | 3 | 2 | noun | G |
| 58 | miserly | 1 |   |   |   |   |   |   |   |   |   |   |   |   |   |   |   | 2 |   | 3 | 2 | noun | R |
| 59 | otherworldly |   | 2 |   |   | 1 |   |   |   |   |   |   |   |   |   |   |   |   |   | 3 | 2 | noun | G |
| 60 | queenly |   |   |   |   |   |   |   | 3 |   |   |   |   |   |   |   |   |   |   | 3 | 1 | noun | G |
| 61 | timely | 1 |   |   |   | 1 |   |   |   |   |   |   |   |   |   | 1 |   |   |   | 3 | 3 | noun | G |
| 62 | ungodly |   |   |   |   |   |   |   |   |   |   |   |   |   |   |   | 3 |   |   | 3 | 1 | noun | G |
| 63 | untimely |   |   |   |   |   |   |   |   |   |   |   |   |   |   | 2 | 1 |   |   | 3 | 2 | noun | G |
| 64 | brotherly | 1 | 1 |   |   |   |   |   |   |   |   |   |   |   |   |   |   |   |   | 2 | 2 | noun | G |
| 65 | fatherly |   |   |   |   |   |   |   |   |   |   |   |   |   |   |   | 1 | 1 |   | 2 | 2 | noun | G |

| No. | Adjective | At | Au | Ba | Ca | Cha | Chi | Da | Go | Hu | Mc | Mi | Na | Ni | On | Rub | Rut | Wa | Wi | Total tokens | Total sources | Base | Origin of base form |
|---|---|---|---|---|---|---|---|---|---|---|---|---|---|---|---|---|---|---|---|---|---|---|---|
| 66 | goodly | | | | | | | | | | | | | | | 1 | 1 | | | 2 | 2 | adj | G |
| 67 | homely | | | | | | | | | | | | | | | 1 | 1 | | | 2 | 2 | noun | G |
| 68 | hourly | | | | | | | 1 | | | 1 | | | | | | | | | 2 | 2 | noun | R < Gk |
| 69 | lawyerly | | | | | | | | | | 2 | | | | | | | | | 2 | 1 | noun | G |
| 70 | matronly | | | | | | | | | | | | | | | 2 | | | | 2 | 1 | noun | R |
| 71 | neighbourly | | 1 | | | | | | | 1 | | | | | | | | | | 2 | 2 | noun | G |
| 72 | southerly | | 1 | | | | | | | | | | | | | | | | 1 | 2 | 2 | ? | G |
| 73 | actorly | | | | 1 | | | | | | | | | | | | | | | 1 | 1 | noun | R |
| 74 | cleanly | | | | | 1 | | | | | | | | | | | | | | 1 | 1 | adj | G |
| 75 | clerkly | | | | | | | | | | | | | | | | | 1 | | 1 | 1 | noun | G |
| 76 | comely | | | | | | 1 | | | | | | | | | | | | | 1 | 1 | adj | G |
| 77 | comradely | | | | | | | | | | | | | | | | | | 1 | 1 | 1 | noun | R |
| 78 | creaturely | | | | | | | | | | | | | | | | | | 1 | 1 | 1 | noun | R |
| 79 | curmudgeonly | | | | | | | 1 | | | | | | | | | | | | 1 | 1 | noun | ? |
| 80 | dastardly | | | | | | | | | | | 1 | | | | | | | | 1 | 1 | noun | G |
| 81 | easterly | | | | | | | | | | | | | | | | 1 | | | 1 | 1 | ? | G |
| 82 | fleshly | | | | | | | | | | | | | | | 1 | | | | 1 | 1 | noun | G |
| 83 | loathly | | | | | | | 1 | | | | | | | | | | | | 1 | 1 | adj | G |
| 84 | northerly | | 1 | | | | | | | | | | | | | | | | | 1 | 1 | ? | G |
| 85 | princely | | | | | | | | 1 | | | | | | | | | | | 1 | 1 | noun | R |
| 86 | sisterly | | | | | 1 | | | | | | | | | | | | | | 1 | 1 | noun | G |
| 87 | soldierly | | | | | | | 1 | | | | | | | | | | | | 1 | 1 | noun | R |
| 88 | ungentlemanly | | | | | | | | | | | | | | | | | 1 | | 1 | 1 | noun | R |
| 89 | unlovely | | | 1 | | | | | | | | | | | | | | | | 1 | 1 | noun | G |
| 90 | unwomanly | | | | | | | | | | | | | | | | 1 | | | 1 | 1 | noun | G |
| 91 | westerly | | | | | | | | | | | | | | | 1 | 1 | | | 1 | 1 | ? | G |
| 92 | wifely | | | | | | | | | | | | | | | | | | | 1 | 1 | noun | G |
| | Total tokens | 91 | 59 | 22 | 40 | 85 | 39 | 85 | 42 | 13 | 28 | 65 | 42 | 24 | 25 | 68 | 345 | 87 | 65 | 1225 | | | |
| | Total types | 31 | 25 | 15 | 24 | 33 | 12 | 33 | 23 | 10 | 12 | 22 | 15 | 12 | 11 | 26 | 53 | 29 | 21 | | 407 | | |
| | Total pages | 607 | 758 | 247 | 405 | 605 | 264 | 340 | 247 | 273 | 321 | 484 | 297 | 343 | 282 | 238 | 1302 | 327 | 402 | 7742 | | | |
| | token/page | 0.15 | 0.08 | 0.09 | 0.10 | 0.14 | 0.15 | 0.25 | 0.17 | 0.05 | 0.09 | 0.13 | 0.14 | 0.07 | 0.09 | 0.29 | 0.26 | 0.27 | 0.16 | 0.16 | | | |

*Appendix 3 · 237*

# Appendix 3c

## The full corpus – ordered by word class of base form

| No. | Adjective | At | Au | Ba | Ca | Cha | Chi | Da | Go | Hu | Mc | Mi | Na | Ni | On | Rub | Rut | Wa | Wi | Total tokens | Total sources | Base | Origin of base form |
|---|---|---|---|---|---|---|---|---|---|---|---|---|---|---|---|---|---|---|---|---|---|---|---|
| 1 | likely | 7 | 2 | 1 | 2 | 2 | | 8 | 4 | 1 | 1 | 2 | 3 | 5 | 7 | 8 | 19 | 4 | 4 | 80 | 17 | adj | G |
| 2 | lonely | 2 | 6 | 3 | 4 | 12 | 2 | 1 | 2 | 1 | 5 | 3 | 1 | | 1 | 3 | 10 | 3 | 15 | 74 | 17 | adj | G |
| 3 | kindly | 2 | | 1 | | 1 | | 2 | 2 | | | 1 | 1 | 1 | | 1 | 40 | 3 | 1 | 56 | 12 | adj | G |
| 4 | unlikely | 6 | 1 | | 3 | | 1 | 3 | 4 | 2 | | | 4 | | 6 | 6 | 11 | 4 | | 51 | 12 | adj | G |
| 5 | elderly | 3 | 1 | | 2 | | | | 2 | | | 2 | 5 | 3 | | 3 | 13 | 7 | | 38 | 9 | adj | G |
| 6 | sickly | 4 | 2 | | 1 | 1 | | | | 1 | | 3 | | | | 1 | 10 | | | 25 | 8 | adj | G |
| 7 | deadly | | | | | 5 | | 2 | | | 2 | 1 | | | 1 | | 5 | 6 | 1 | 24 | 9 | adj | G |
| 8 | lowly | | | | | | | 2 | | | | | | | | | 3 | | | 6 | 3 | adj | G |
| 9 | poorly | | | | | | | 2 | | | | | | | | 2 | 1 | | | 5 | 3 | adj | R |
| 10 | ungainly | 1 | 1 | | | | | | | | | | | | | | 3 | | | 5 | 3 | adj | G |
| 11 | goodly | | | | | | | | | | | | | | | 1 | 1 | | | 2 | 2 | adj | G |
| 12 | cleanly | | | | | 1 | | | | | | | | | | | | | | 1 | 1 | adj | G |
| 13 | comely | | | | | | | | | | | | | | | | | | | 1 | 1 | adj | G |
| 14 | loathly | | | | | | | 1 | | | | | | | | | | | | 1 | 1 | adj | G |
| 15 | lovely | 22 | 3 | 1 | 5 | 11 | 17 | 10 | 5 | | 3 | 28 | 4 | 5 | 2 | 7 | 14 | 4 | 5 | 146 | 17 | noun | G |
| 16 | friendly | 2 | 12 | | 1 | 6 | 3 | 3 | 2 | 3 | 9 | | 9 | 2 | | 3 | 36 | 24 | 10 | 125 | 15 | noun | G |
| 17 | daily | 7 | 1 | 2 | 3 | 7 | 4 | 8 | 1 | | 1 | 9 | 6 | | 2 | 5 | 11 | 3 | 4 | 71 | 15 | noun | G |
| 18 | lively | 2 | 5 | 1 | | 1 | 2 | 5 | 4 | 1 | | 2 | | 2 | | 3 | 8 | 1 | | 39 | 15 | noun | G |
| 19 | worldly | 1 | | | 2 | | | 1 | 1 | | 1 | 1 | 1 | | 1 | | 18 | 1 | 2 | 30 | 11 | noun | G |
| 20 | orderly | | 3 | | | 4 | | 1 | | | | | 1 | | 2 | | 4 | 3 | 7 | 26 | 9 | noun | R |
| 21 | weekly | 2 | | 1 | | 1 | | 3 | 1 | 1 | | 2 | 2 | | | 6 | 3 | 1 | 2 | 26 | 13 | noun | G |
| 22 | stately | 3 | 2 | | | 1 | | 3 | | | | 1 | | 1 | | 1 | 10 | | 1 | 23 | 9 | noun | R |
| 23 | godly | | | | | 1 | | 4 | | | | | | | | | 13 | | | 18 | 3 | noun | G |
| 24 | costly | 2 | | 1 | | | 2 | 5 | | | | | | | | | 6 | 1 | | 17 | 6 | noun | R |
| 25 | ghostly | | | 1 | | 1 | 2 | 1 | | 1 | | | 2 | 1 | | 2 | 2 | 2 | 4 | 17 | 10 | noun | G |
| 26 | burly | | | | | 2 | | | | | | | | | | | 12 | | | 16 | 4 | noun | G |
| 27 | manly | | | | 1 | 2 | | 1 | | | | | | | | | 9 | | | 14 | 5 | noun | G |
| 28 | heavenly | | | 3 | | 1 | | | 1 | | | | | | | 1 | 6 | | | 12 | 5 | noun | G |
| 29 | leisurely | | 2 | | | 2 | | 1 | 1 | | | 1 | | | | | 3 | 2 | | 12 | 7 | noun | R |
| 30 | surly | 1 | | | | 1 | | | | | | | | | | | 9 | | | 12 | 4 | noun | R |
| 31 | courtly | | | | | | | | | | | | | | 1 | | 10 | | | 11 | 2 | noun | R |

| No. | Adjective | At | Au | Ba | Ca | Cha | Chi | Da | Go | Hu | Mc | Mi | Na | Ni | On | Rub | Rut | Wa | Wi | Total tokens | Total sources | Base | Origin of base form |
|---|---|---|---|---|---|---|---|---|---|---|---|---|---|---|---|---|---|---|---|---|---|---|---|
| 32 | monthly | 2 | | 3 | | 1 | | | | | 1 | 1 | | | | 3 | 2 | 2 | | 11 | 5 | noun | G |
| 33 | nightly | 1 | | | | 1 | 1 | | | 1 | | | | | | 3 | | | 1 | 8 | 8 | noun | G |
| 34 | saintly | 1 | | | | | | | | | | | | | 1 | 1 | 9 | | | 11 | 3 | noun | R |
| 35 | bodily | | | 1 | | 2 | | 2 | | | 1 | | | | | 1 | | 1 | | 10 | 8 | noun | G |
| 36 | unearthly | 2 | 1 | | | 5 | 3 | | 1 | | | 1 | 1 | | | | | | 1 | 10 | 6 | noun | G |
| 37 | earthly | | | 1 | | | | | | | | | | | | | 8 | | | 9 | 6 | noun | G |
| 38 | knightly | | | | | | | | | | | | | | | | | | 1 | 8 | 1 | noun | G |
| 39 | sprightly | 2 | 1 | | | 2 | | | | | | | | 1 | | | 1 | | | 8 | 6 | noun | R |
| 40 | motherly | 1 | 1 | | 1 | 1 | | | | | | | | | | | 2 | | | 7 | 5 | noun | G |
| 41 | portly | | | | | 2 | | | | | | | | | | | 3 | 2 | | 7 | 4 | noun | R |
| 42 | scholarly | 3 | 1 | | 1 | | | 4 | | | | | | | | | 3 | | | 7 | 2 | noun | R |
| 43 | slovenly | 2 | | | 1 | | | | | | | 1 | | | | | 1 | 1 | | 7 | 5 | noun | G |
| 44 | cowardly | | | | 1 | | | | 1 | | | | | | | | 2 | | | 6 | 4 | noun | R |
| 45 | lordly | | 4 | | | | | | | | | | | | | | 1 | 3 | | 6 | 4 | noun | G |
| 46 | womanly | | | 1 | | | 1 | 1 | | | | | | | | | 2 | | | 6 | 3 | noun | G |
| 47 | disorderly | | | | | 2 | 1 | 1 | | | | | | | | | | 2 | | 5 | 4 | noun | R |
| 48 | gentlemanly | | | | | | | | 1 | | | | 1 | | | | 2 | 1 | | 5 | 3 | noun | R |
| 49 | masterly | | | | 2 | | | 2 | | | | 1 | | | | | 2 | | | 5 | 4 | noun | R |
| 50 | priestly | | | | | | | | | | | | | | | | 3 | | | 5 | 3 | noun | G |
| 51 | yearly | | | 1 | | 1 | | 1 | | | | | | 1 | | | | | 1 | 5 | 2 | noun | G |
| 52 | deathly | | | | | | | | | | | | | | | 1 | | 2 | | 4 | 4 | noun | G |
| 53 | quarterly | | 3 | | 1 | | | | | | | | | | | | | | | 4 | 3 | noun | R |
| 54 | shapely | | 1 | | 2 | | | 1 | | | | | | | | 1 | 2 | | | 4 | 2 | noun | G |
| 55 | unfriendly | 1 | | | 1 | | | | | | | | | | | | | | | 4 | 3 | noun | G |
| 56 | unsightly | | | | 1 | | | | | | | | | | | | | 1 | | 4 | 3 | noun | G |
| 57 | beastly | | | | | | | | | | | | | | | | 2 | | | 3 | 3 | noun | R |
| 58 | kingly | 1 | | | | | | | | | | | | | | | 2 | 2 | | 3 | 2 | noun | G |
| 59 | miserly | | | | | 1 | | | | | | | | | | | | | | 3 | 2 | noun | R |
| 60 | otherworldly | | 2 | | | | | | 3 | | | | | | | | | | | 3 | 2 | noun | G |
| 61 | queenly | 1 | | | | 1 | | | | | | | | | | 1 | | | | 3 | 1 | noun | G |
| 62 | timely | | | | | | | | | | | | | | | | 3 | | | 3 | 3 | noun | G |
| 63 | ungodly | | | | | | | | | | | | | | | 2 | 1 | | | 3 | 1 | noun | G |
| 64 | untimely | | | | | | | | | | | | | | | | | | | 3 | 2 | noun | G |
| 65 | brotherly | 1 | 1 | | | | | | | | | | | | | | | | | 2 | 2 | noun | G |

| No. | Adjective | At | Au | Ba | Ca | Cha | Chi | Da | Go | Hu | Mc | Mi | Na | Ni | On | Rub | Rut | Wa | Wi | Total tokens | Total sources | Base | Origin of base form |
|---|---|---|---|---|---|---|---|---|---|---|---|---|---|---|---|---|---|---|---|---|---|---|---|
| 66 | fatherly | | | | | | | | | | | 1 | | | | | 1 | | | 2 | 2 | noun | G |
| 67 | homely | | | | | | | | | | | | | | | | 1 | | | 2 | 2 | noun | G |
| 68 | hourly | | | | | | | 1 | | | 1 | | | | | | | | | 2 | 2 | noun | R < Gk |
| 69 | lawyerly | | | | | | | | | | 2 | | | | | | | | | 2 | 1 | noun | G |
| 70 | matronly | | | | | | | | | | | | | | | 2 | | | | 2 | 1 | noun | R |
| 71 | neighbourly | 1 | | | | | | | | 1 | | | | | | | | | | 2 | 2 | noun | G |
| 72 | actorly | | | | 1 | | | | | | | | | | | | | | | 1 | 1 | noun | R |
| 73 | clerkly | | | | | | | | | | | | | | | | | 1 | | 1 | 1 | noun | G |
| 74 | comradely | | | | | | | | | | | | | | | | | | 1 | 1 | 1 | noun | R |
| 75 | creaturely | | | | | | | 1 | | | | | | | | | | | | 1 | 1 | noun | R |
| 76 | curmudgeonly | | | | | | | | | | | | | | | | | | | 1 | 1 | noun | ? |
| 77 | dastardly | | | | | | | | | | | 1 | | | | | | | | 1 | 1 | noun | G |
| 78 | fleshly | | | | | | | | | | | | | | | 1 | | | | 1 | 1 | noun | G |
| 79 | princely | | | | | | | | 1 | | | | | | | | | | | 1 | 1 | noun | R |
| 80 | sisterly | | | | | 1 | | | | | | | | | | | | | | 1 | 1 | noun | G |
| 81 | soldierly | | | | | | | 1 | | | | | | | | | | | | 1 | 1 | noun | R |
| 82 | ungentlemanly | | | | | | | | | | | | | | | | | 1 | | 1 | 1 | noun | R |
| 83 | unlovely | | | | | 1 | | | | | | | | | | | | | | 1 | 1 | noun | G |
| 84 | unwomanly | | | | | | | | | | | | | | | | 1 | | | 1 | 1 | noun | G |
| 85 | wifely | | | | | | | | | | | 1 | | | | 1 | | | | 1 | 1 | noun | G |
| 86 | unseemly | 2 | | | 1 | | | 1 | 1 | | | | | | | | 1 | | | 6 | 5 | verb | G |
| 87 | ghastly | | | | 1 | 2 | | | 1 | | | | | | | | 1 | | | 5 | 4 | verb | G |
| 88 | grisly | 3 | | | | | | | | | | | | | | | | 1 | | 4 | 2 | verb | G |
| 89 | southerly | | 1 | | | | | | | | | | | | | | 1 | | | 2 | 2 | ? | G |
| 90 | easterly | | | | | | | | | | | | | | | | 1 | | | 1 | 1 | ? | G |
| 91 | northerly | 1 | | | | | | | | | | | | | | | | | | 1 | 1 | ? | G |
| 92 | westerly | | | | | | | | | | | | | | | | | | 1 | 1 | 1 | ? | G |
| | Total tokens | 91 | 59 | 22 | 40 | 85 | 39 | 85 | 42 | 13 | 28 | 65 | 42 | 24 | 25 | 68 | 345 | 87 | 65 | 1225 | | | |
| | Total types | 31 | 25 | 15 | 24 | 33 | 12 | 33 | 23 | 10 | 12 | 22 | 15 | 12 | 11 | 26 | 45 | 29 | 21 | | 407 | | |
| | Total pages | 607 | 758 | 247 | 405 | 605 | 264 | 340 | 247 | 273 | 321 | 484 | 297 | 343 | 282 | 238 | 1302 | 327 | 402 | 7742 | | | |
| | token/page | 0.15 | 0.08 | 0.09 | 0.10 | 0.14 | 0.15 | 0.25 | 0.17 | 0.05 | 0.09 | 0.13 | 0.14 | 0.07 | 0.09 | 0.29 | 0.26 | 0.27 | 0.16 | 0.16 | | | |

*Appendix 3* · 241

# Appendix 3d

## The full corpus – in chronological order

| No. | Adjective | At | Au | Ba | Ca | Cha | Chi | Da | Go | Hu | Mc | Mi | Na | Ni | On | Rub | Rut | Wa | Wi | Total tokens | Total sources | OED date (lic/lich) | OED date (li/ly) |
|---|---|---|---|---|---|---|---|---|---|---|---|---|---|---|---|---|---|---|---|---|---|---|---|
| 1 | yearly | | | | | | | 2 | | | | | | | | | 3 | | | 5 | 2 | 725 | 1400 |
| 2 | fleshly | | | | | | | | | | | | | | | | | | | 1 | 1 | 888 | 1300 |
| 3 | worldly | 1 | | | 2 | 1 | | 1 | 1 | | | 1 | 1 | | 1 | 1 | 18 | 1 | 2 | 30 | 11 | 888 | 1325 |
| 4 | cleanly | | | | | 1 | | | | | | | | | | | | | | 1 | 1 | 888 | 1340 |
| 5 | kindly | 2 | | 1 | | 1 | | 2 | 2 | | | 1 | | 1 | | 1 | 40 | 3 | 1 | 56 | 12 | 888 | 1400 |
| 6 | wifely | | | | | | 1 | | | | | | | | | 1 | | | | 1 | 1 | 893 | 1385 |
| 7 | nightly | 2 | | | | 1 | | 1 | | 1 | | 1 | | 1 | | 3 | | | 1 | 11 | 8 | 897 | 1380 |
| 8 | loathly | | | | | | | 1 | | | | | | | | | | | | 1 | 1 | 900 | 1300 |
| 9 | friendly | 2 | 12 | | 1 | 6 | 3 | 3 | 2 | 3 | 9 | | 9 | 2 | | 3 | 36 | 24 | 10 | 125 | 15 | 900 | 1374 |
| 10 | earthly | 2 | | | | | 3 | 1 | | | | | | | | 1 | 1 | | 1 | 9 | 6 | 971 | 1300 |
| 11 | heavenly | | | 3 | | 1 | | 1 | 1 | | | | | | | | 6 | | | 12 | 5 | 971 | 1382 |
| 12 | deathly | | | 1 | | 1 | | | 1 | | | | | 1 | | | | | | 4 | 4 | 971 | 1568 |
| 13 | comely | | | | | | 1 | | | | | | | | | | | | | 1 | | 1000 | 1300 |
| 14 | ghostly | | | 1 | | 1 | 2 | 1 | | 1 | | | 2 | 1 | 2 | | 2 | 2 | 4 | 17 | 10 | 1000 | 1303 |
| 15 | lovely | 22 | 3 | | 5 | 11 | 17 | 10 | 5 | | 3 | 28 | 4 | 5 | | 7 | 14 | 4 | 5 | 146 | 17 | 1000 | 1340 |
| 16 | knightly | | | | | | | | | | | | | | | | 8 | | | 8 | 1 | 1000 | 1375 |
| 17 | lively | 2 | | | 1 | 5 | 2 | 2 | | | 2 | 1 | | | | 1 | 5 | 6 | 1 | 24 | 9 | 1000 | 1377 |
| 18 | deadly | | 5 | 1 | | 1 | | 5 | 4 | 1 | 1 | 2 | 1 | 2 | | 3 | 8 | 1 | | 39 | 15 | 1000 | 1430 |
| 19 | fatherly | | | | 2 | | | 2 | | | | | | | | | 1 | | | 2 | 2 | 1000 | 1440 |
| 20 | priestly | 1 | 1 | | | | | | | | | | | | | | | | 1 | 5 | 3 | 1000 | 1535 |
| 21 | brotherly | 1 | 1 | | | 1 | | | | | | | | | | | | | | 2 | 2 | 1000 | 1535 |
| 22 | motherly | | | | | | | | 1 | | | | | | | | 2 | 2 | | 7 | 5 | 1000 | 1597 |
| 23 | lordly | | | | 1 | | | | | | | | | | | | 1 | 3 | | 6 | 4 | 1000 | 1645 |
| 24 | grisly | 3 | | | | | | | | | | | | | | | | 1 | | 4 | 2 | 1150 | 1386 |
| 25 | timely | 1 | | | | 1 | | 1 | | | | 1 | | | | | | | | 3 | 3 | 1200 | 1400 |
| 26 | manly | | | | | 2 | | | | | | | | | | 1 | 9 | | 1 | 14 | 5 | 1200 | 1422 |
| 27 | goodly | | | | 1 | | | | | | | | | | | | 1 | | | 2 | 2 | 1205 | 1385 |
| 28 | beastly | | | | 1 | | | | | | | | | | | | | | | 3 | 3 | 1220 | 1611 |
| 29 | womanly | | 4 | | | | | 1 | | | | | | | | | | | | 6 | 3 | 1374 | 1385 |
| 30 | unlovely | | | | | | | | | | | | | | | | | | 1 | 1 | 1 | 1377 | 1586 |
| 31 | godly | | | | | 1 | | 4 | | | | | | | | | 13 | | | 18 | 3 | 1380 | 1450 |

Appendix 3 · 243

| No. | Adjective | At | Au | Ba | Ca | Cha | Chi | Da | Go | Hu | Mc | Mi | Na | Ni | On | Rub | Rut | Wa | Wi | Total tokens | Total sources | OED date (lic/lich) | OED date (li/ly) |
|---|---|---|---|---|---|---|---|---|---|---|---|---|---|---|---|---|---|---|---|---|---|---|---|
| 32 | bodily | 1 | | | | | | | | | 1 | | | | 1 | 1 | | 1 | | 10 | 8 | - | 1300 |
| 33 | unseemly | 2 | | | | 2 | | 1 | | | | 1 | | | | | 1 | | | 6 | 5 | - | 1300 |
| 34 | homely | | | | | | | | | | | 1 | | | | | 1 | | | 2 | 2 | - | 1300 |
| 35 | sickly | 4 | 2 | | 1 | 1 | | | | | | 3 | | | | 3 | 10 | | | 25 | 8 | - | 1350 |
| 36 | lowly | | | | | | | | | 1 | | | | | 1 | | 3 | | | 6 | 3 | - | 1374 |
| 37 | unlikely | 6 | 1 | | 3 | 2 | | 3 | 4 | 2 | | | 4 | | 6 | 6 | 11 | 4 | | 51 | 12 | - | 1375 |
| 38 | likely | 7 | 2 | 1 | 2 | 2 | 1 | 8 | 4 | 1 | 1 | 2 | 3 | 5 | 7 | 8 | 19 | 4 | 4 | 80 | 17 | - | 1380 |
| 39 | shapely | | 3 | | 1 | | | | | | | | | | | | | | | 4 | 2 | - | 1382 |
| 40 | kingly | | | | | | | 3 | | | | | | | | | | | | 3 | 2 | - | 1382 |
| 41 | stately | 3 | 2 | | 1 | 1 | | | | | | 1 | | 1 | | 1 | 10 | | 1 | 23 | 9 | - | 1385 |
| 42 | ghastly | | | | 1 | 2 | | | 1 | | | | | | | | 1 | | | 5 | 4 | - | 1390 |
| 43 | burly | | | | 2 | 2 | | | | | | | | 1 | | | 12 | | | 16 | 4 | - | 1400 |
| 44 | unfriendly | | 1 | | | | | | | | | | | | | | | | | 4 | 3 | - | 1425 |
| 45 | gentlemanly | | | | | 2 | | | | | | | 1 | | | | 2 | | | 5 | 3 | - | 1433 |
| 46 | courtly | 1 | | | | | | | | | | | | | 1 | 1 | 10 | | | 11 | 2 | - | 1450 |
| 47 | daily | 7 | 1 | 2 | 3 | 7 | 4 | 8 | 1 | | 1 | 9 | 6 | | 2 | 5 | 11 | | 4 | 71 | 15 | - | 1470 |
| 48 | weekly | 2 | | 1 | | 1 | | 3 | 1 | 1 | | 2 | 2 | | | 6 | 3 | 1 | 2 | 26 | 13 | - | 1489 |
| 49 | costly | 2 | | 1 | | | 2 | 5 | | | | | | | | | 6 | 1 | | 17 | 6 | - | 1494 |
| 50 | princely | | | | | | | 1 | 1 | | | | | | | | | | | 1 | 1 | - | 1503 |
| 51 | hourly | | | | | | | | | | 1 | | | | | | | | | 2 | 2 | - | 1513 |
| 52 | ungodly | | | | | | | | | | | | | | | | 3 | | | 3 | 1 | - | 1526 |
| 53 | clerkly | | | | | | | | | | | | | | | | | 1 | | 1 | 1 | - | 1528 |
| 54 | portly | | | | 1 | 2 | | | | | | | | | | | 3 | | | 7 | 4 | - | 1529 |
| 55 | unwomanly | | | | | | | | | | | | | | | | 1 | | | 1 | 1 | - | 1531 |
| 56 | masterly | | | | | | | | 1 | | | | | | | | 2 | 1 | | 5 | 4 | - | 1535 |
| 57 | untimely | | | | | | | | 3 | | | 1 | | | | 2 | 1 | | | 3 | 2 | - | 1540 |
| 58 | queenly | | | | | | | | | | | | | | | | | | | 3 | 1 | - | 1548 |
| 59 | unsightly | 1 | | | | | | 1 | | | | | | | | | 2 | | | 4 | 3 | - | 1548 |
| 60 | southerly | | 1 | | | | | | | | | | | | | | | | 1 | 2 | 2 | - | 1551 |
| 61 | northerly | | 1 | | | | | | | 1 | | | | | | | | | | 1 | 1 | - | 1551 |
| 62 | neighbourly | | 1 | | | | | | | | | | | | | | | | | 2 | 2 | - | 1558 |
| 63 | ungentlemanly | | | | | | | | | | | | | | | 1 | | | | 1 | 1 | - | 1562 |
| 64 | quarterly | | | | | | | | | | | | | | | | | 2 | | 4 | 3 | - | 1563 |
| 65 | dastardly | | | | | | | 1 | | | 1 | | | | | | | | | 1 | 1 | - | 1567 |

| No. | Adjective | At | Au | Ba | Ca | Cha | Chi | Da | Go | Hu | Mc | Mi | Na | Ni | On | Rub | Rut | Wa | Wi | Total tokens | Total sources | OED date (lic/lich) | OED date (li/ly) |
|---|---|---|---|---|---|---|---|---|---|---|---|---|---|---|---|---|---|---|---|---|---|---|---|
| 66 | sisterly | | | | | 1 | | | | | | | | | | | | | | 1 | 1 | - | 1570 |
| 67 | monthly | | 3 | | | | | | | | 1 | | | | | 3 | 2 | 2 | | 11 | 5 | - | 1572 |
| 68 | poorly | | | | | | | 2 | | | | | | | | 2 | 1 | 1 | | 5 | 3 | - | 1573 |
| 69 | cowardly | 2 | | | 1 | | | | | | | | | | | | 2 | | | 6 | 4 | - | 1576 |
| 70 | westerly | | | | | | | | | | | | | | | | 1 | | | 1 | 1 | - | 1577 |
| 71 | orderly | 1 | 3 | | | 4 | | 1 | | | | | 1 | | 2 | | 4 | 3 | 7 | 26 | 9 | - | 1577 |
| 72 | soldierly | | | | | | | 1 | | | | | | | | | | | | 1 | 1 | - | 1577 |
| 73 | slovenly | 3 | 1 | | 1 | | | | | | | 1 | | | | | 1 | | | 7 | 5 | - | 1583 |
| 74 | disorderly | | | 1 | | | 1 | 1 | | | | | | | | | | 2 | | 5 | 4 | - | 1585 |
| 75 | curmudgeonly | | | | | | | 1 | | | | | | | | | | | | 1 | 1 | - | 1590 |
| 76 | miserly | 1 | | | | | | | 1 | | | | | | | | | 2 | | 3 | 2 | - | 1593 |
| 77 | sprightly | 2 | | | | 2 | | | 1 | | | | | 1 | | | 1 | | | 8 | 6 | - | 1596 |
| 78 | leisurely | | 2 | | | 2 | | | 1 | | | 1 | | | | 1 | 3 | 2 | | 12 | 7 | - | 1604 |
| 79 | lonely | 2 | 6 | 3 | 4 | 12 | 2 | 1 | 2 | 1 | 5 | 3 | 1 | | 1 | 3 | 10 | 3 | 15 | 74 | 17 | - | 1607 |
| 80 | easterly | | | | | | | | | | | | | | | | 1 | | | 1 | 1 | - | 1609 |
| 81 | ungainly | 1 | | | | | | | | | | | | | | | 3 | | | 5 | 3 | - | 1611 |
| 82 | unearthly | | 1 | | | 5 | | | 1 | | | 1 | 1 | | | | | | 1 | 10 | 6 | - | 1611 |
| 83 | scholarly | | | | | | | 4 | | | | | | | | | 3 | | | 7 | 2 | - | 1638 |
| 84 | matronly | | | | | | | | | | | | | | | 2 | | | | 2 | 1 | - | 1656 |
| 85 | elderly | 3 | 1 | | 2 | | | | 2 | | | 2 | 5 | 3 | | | 13 | 7 | | 38 | 9 | - | 1660 |
| 86 | saintly | 1 | | | | | | | 1 | | | | | | | | 9 | | | 11 | 3 | - | 1660 |
| 87 | creaturely | | | | | | | | | | | | | | | | | | 1 | 1 | 1 | - | 1662 |
| 88 | surly | 1 | | | | 1 | | | 1 | | | | | | | | 9 | | | 12 | 4 | - | 1670 |
| 89 | otherworldly | | 2 | | | 1 | | | | | | | | | | | | | | 3 | 2 | - | 1879 |
| 90 | comradely | | | | | | | | | | | | | | | | | | 1 | 1 | 1 | - | 1880 |
| 91 | actorly | | | | 1 | | | | | | | | | | | | | | | 1 | 1 | - | 1959 |
| 92 | lawyerly | | | | | | | | | | 2 | | | | | | | | | 2 | 1 | - | - |
| | Total tokens | 91 | 59 | 22 | 40 | 85 | 39 | 85 | 42 | 13 | 28 | 65 | 42 | 24 | 25 | 68 | 345 | 87 | 65 | 1225 | 407 | | |
| | Total types | 31 | 25 | 15 | 24 | 33 | 12 | 33 | 23 | 10 | 12 | 22 | 15 | 12 | 11 | 26 | 45 | 29 | 21 | | | | |
| | Total pages | 607 | 758 | 247 | 405 | 605 | 264 | 340 | 247 | 273 | 321 | 484 | 297 | 343 | 282 | 238 | 1302 | 327 | 402 | 7742 | | | |
| | token/page | 0.15 | 0.08 | 0.09 | 0.10 | 0.14 | 0.15 | 0.25 | 0.17 | 0.05 | 0.09 | 0.13 | 0.14 | 0.07 | 0.09 | 0.29 | 0.26 | 0.27 | 0.16 | 0.16 | | | |

Appendix 3 · 245

# Phonological ingenuity in "Five Songs" by W. H. Auden

*John M. Dienhart*

In this paper I wish to examine the phonological structure of five short poems by Wystan Hugh Auden (1907-1973). My interest in Auden was first kindled by a short poem in an anthology (Damrosch et al. 1985). The title of the poem, supplied by the anthologist, was "That night when joy began", taken from the first line of the poem itself.[1] The editors of the anthology noted, briefly, that "perhaps Auden's most important contribution to twentieth-century poetry is his experimentation in many verse forms and meters, combining an offhand informality with remarkable technical skill" (Damrosch et al. 1985: 819). This sounded intriguing.

The same poem is anthologized in Perrine (1969) with the following suggestion for the reader: "The rime pattern in this poem is intricate and exact. Work it out, considering alliteration, assonance, and consonance" (Perrine 1969: 181). So work it out I did. And I was amazed. Amazed at the phonological ingenuity displayed by Auden in the course of twelve short lines. This, then, is one of the five poems I shall discuss. The other four are included here because Auden himself eventually incorporated "That night when joy began" as poem number two in a poetic unity he entitled "Five Songs".

None of the individual poems in this set of five has a title, but for the sake of identification, we can use (as Auden does) the Roman numerals I through V, plus – where appropriate – the first line of each poem, thus:

## Five Songs

I  "What's in your mind, my dove, my coney"
II  "That night when joy began"
III  "For what as easy"
IV  "Seen when nights are silent"
V  "'O where are you going?' said reader to rider"

These five poems all belong to the period of Auden's early poetry, but they did not originally constitute a unit.[2] They were not even written at the same time, though they all apppear to have been composed between 1930 and 1933, when Auden was in his early twenties.[3]

Furthermore (as indicated in note 3), some of the poems were originally part of a larger text. Thus IV is taken from Auden's play, *The Dog Beneath the Skin*, which he wrote with Christopher Isherwood (probably in 1933) and published in 1935. In this play it appeared in Act II, as a song, sung by one of the female characters (see Fuller 1970: 81). Similarly, V originally appeared as the epilogue to *The Orators*, published in 1932. As Mendelson (1976: 11) has observed:

> The poems Auden wrote from the start of his career until around 1942 were subject throughout their history to elaborate reworking, cutting, and rearrangement; frequently they lost or gained stanzas between first appearance in a periodical and first book publication, then endured further transformations before being collected, or banished, or set in the larger context of a play or longer poem ...; many poems were revised or truncated; and some lyrics that had once found their way into longer works re-emerged as separate poems.

These remarks indicate quite clearly the flux that is found in Auden's poetry in general, and in his early poetry in particular. As Auden himself has remarked, "On revisions as a matter of principle, I agree with [Paul] Valery: 'A poem is never finished; it is only abandoned'" (Auden 1966: 16).

This textual flux can be attributed to the ongoing flow of the poet's imagination, which is constantly playing with new ideas and new combinations of old ones. Or, it can be seen in another light. Anthony Hecht, in his book, *The Hidden Law: The Poetry of W. H. Auden* (1993), suggests that Auden's revisions and re-combinations can be seen as part of a process of obfuscation, perhaps as much unconscious as conscious.

And what purpose could obfuscation have? For Hecht, the answer is that Auden, like many poets, wants to keep the public at a distance, especially when his poems are deeply private. Poetry is a curious game. In essence, poetry involves the public expression of private emotions. This is particularly true in the case of love poetry. And as we shall see shortly, four of the "Five Songs" are certainly love poems. Hecht (1993: 12) observes:

> The love poem always involves a not wholly assimilable mixture of strategies and motives. If, as is most often the case, it is addressed to a particular person, it ought, in the interests of the sincerity of its passion, to be read by that person alone; but since it is a "published" work, either printed or circulated in manuscript, there is in its publication, if not a violation of the intimacy it purports to convey, at least the use of the intimacy as a pretext for public and observed behavior. . .To the degree that love poems are not "con-

ventional," they invite from the reader a prurient interest in circumstances and feelings of the most private sort. And if the love is of a kind looked upon uncharitably by society in general, a good deal of covert communication may be called for.

Now the kind of love that might be "looked upon uncharitably by society" is, in Auden's case, homosexual love. Auden was quite outspoken about this aspect of his nature. In fact, it was part of his moral philosophy that man ought in all his behavior to be true to his inner nature. He was much taken by the psychosomatic theories of Homer Lane.[4] Hecht (1993: 21) gives us the Lane doctrine in one short aphorism: "There is only one sin: disobedience to the inner law of our own nature". In Lane's view, the suppression of one's own nature leads inevitably to disease. Lane's influence can be seen in much of Auden's early work, including, as we shall see, one of the "Five Songs".

Hecht argues that one way Auden could make public some of his own private feelings was by publicly disguising the participants in the private events. Using as an illustration one of Auden's best-known poems – "Lay your sleeping head, my love/Human on my faithless arm" – Hecht writes that

> the love described here is touching, vulnerable, and decently screened as regards gender. This may have been a sly and protective device, but it could just as easily be a trick Auden had learned very early from the popular song writers . . . . The Broadway musical writers he most admired had early learned a simple economic fact: though in the context of one of their shows the dramatic realities might demand that a particular song be sung by a man to a woman or vice versa, much could be so written as to be sexually indeterminate, and thus sung by either male or female vocalists for broadcast or recording purposes. Certainly the most popular and successful songs of our era observe this canny device, and Auden made handy use of it (Hecht 1993: 104).

This is an astute observation by Hecht. The avoidance of gender-marked pronouns is certainly one of the formal, generalizing devices which characterize the "Five Songs".[5]

But let us move now from grammatical form to form on another level. The main characteristic of the "Five Songs", in my view, is the variety and intricacy of the poetic structures which Auden gives us. His familiarity with and remarkably facile use of a wide range of stanza shapes and constructions is perhaps the hallmark of the Auden style. An examination of this style, as it is displayed in the "Five Songs", is the focus of my paper. In particular, I shall consider the phonological and metrical features of the poems in question.

Auden himself always stressed the importance of form in his own work – and in poetry in general. In his Inaugural Lecture as Professor of Poetry at Oxford in 1956, he informed his audience that:

> Rhymes, meters, stanza forms, etc., are like servants. If the master is fair enough to win their affection and firm enough to command their respect, the result is an orderly happy household. If he is too tyrannical, they give notice; if he lacks authority, they become slovenly, impertinent, drunk and dishonest. (Auden 1962: 22)

He has also informed us that the first question he asks himself when he reads a poem is: "Here is a verbal contraption. How does it work?" (Auden 1962: 50). Auden attributes much of his interest in the formal nature of poetry to his first "master", Thomas Hardy: "his metrical variety, his fondness for complicated stanza forms, were an invaluable training [for Auden] in the craft of making" (Auden 1962: 38).

Like Hardy, Auden was strongly influenced by early Anglo-Saxon poetry – not least, *Beowulf* – and this influence is clearly discernible in some of the "Five Songs". In the same lecture cited above, Auden tells how he came to study this poetry while he was a student at Oxford during the period 1925-1928:

> I remember one [lecture] I attended, delivered by Professor Tolkien. I do not remember a single word he said but at a certain point he recited, and magnificently, a long passage of *Beowulf*. I was spellbound. This poetry, I knew, was going to be my dish. I became willing, therefore, to work at Anglo-Saxon because, unless I did, I should never be able to read this poetry. I learned enough to read it, however sloppily, and Anglo-Saxon and Middle English poetry have been one of my strongest, and most lasting influences. (Auden 1962: 41-42)

Auden was also well-versed in, and fascinated by, the Icelandic sagas and skaldic poetry – an interest awakened early in his childhood by his father.[6] I think some of the Icelandic influence can be detected in these "Five Songs" as well.

His interests in Anglo-Saxon and Scandinavian verse were readily apparent to his fellow students at Oxford. Listen to the reminiscences of the Poet Laureate, Sir John Betjeman:

> I felt I knew as much about poetry as a schoolmaster, nearly as much as a don and certainly much more than my fellow undergraduates. Witness then my horror on being introduced to a tall milky-skinned and coltish member of 'The House' (Christ Church), who contradicted all my statements about poetry, who . . . really admired the boring Anglo-Saxon poets like *Beowulf* whom we had read in the English school; and who was a close friend of John Bryson and Nevill Coghill, real dons who read Anglo-Saxon, Gutnish, Finnish and probably Swedish and Faroese as easily as I read the gossip column of the Cherwell of which I was then an editor. (Betjeman 1975: 44)

Betjeman (1975: 45) adds that Auden would chant poetry "aloud at tea. In this he enjoyed the complicated internal rhymes in Irish hedge poetry and the alliteration of Anglo-Saxon poetry."

With this background in mind, let us now turn to an examination of the form of the poems which constitute the "Five Songs". I shall offer my own phonological and metrical analyses of each poem and, to the best of my knowledge and ability, comment where appropriate on parallels in Anglo-Saxon and Icelandic poetry.[7] Where relevant, I shall provide phonemic transcriptions of the items in question, since orthography is not always a reliable indicator of the aural links and reverberations with which Auden's poetry abounds.

## I (What's in your mind, my dove, my coney)

What's in your mind, my dove, my coney;
Do thoughts grow like feathers, the dead end of life;
Is it making of love or counting of money,
Or raid on the jewels, the plans of a thief?

5   Open your eyes, my dearest dallier;
Let hunt with your hands for escaping me;
Go through the motions of exploring the familiar;
Stand on the brink of the warm white day.

Rise with the wind, my great big serpent;
10  Silence the birds and darken the air;
Change me with terrror, alive in a moment;
Strike for the heart and have me there.

In this poem we sense immediately a number of the features of the early Germanic poetry that Auden so admired. We find alliteration, the four-stressed line, the caesura dividing each line into two half-lines (hemistichs), two stresses in each hemistich, and a natural syntactic break at the end of each line.[8] But the imitation is not labored. The alliteration is irregular, the caesuras unforced. And the poem incorporates a number of more modern features, such as stanzaic form and end-rhyme.

Consider first the metrical system. The pattern of the four-stressed line, divided into two half-lines with a caesura, is clearly recognizable. Using "–" for a stressed syllable, "x" for an unstressed syllable, and "| |" to mark the caesura, we can scan the first stanza as an example:

```
        -  x  x  -            | |       x  -  x      -  x
   x  -  x  x  -  x           | |       x  -  x  x  -
x  x  -  x  x  -               | |       x  -  x  x  -  x
   x  -  x  x  - (x)           | |       x  -  x  x  -
```

Note that the regularity consists of the presence of two stressed syllables in each half-line. The number and placement of the unstressed syllables is somewhat irregular, but this is a characteristic feature of early Anglo-Saxon poetry in general.[9]

Let us look next at the alliteration. In early Anglo-Saxon poetry, this was the main phonological device used for linking words within a line. The result was that this poetry was basically stichic (line-based) as opposed to stanzaic (also called strophic; that is, verse-based). This meant that individual lines were relatively independent of one another, end-rhyme not then being a feature of English poetry. In the absence of end-rhyme, the rules for alliteration became very highly developed, so that the repetition of alliterative patterns became an abstract device for relating one line to another. In Auden's poem, which relies for phonological unity on end-rhyme as well as on alliteration, the alliteration is not very regular, nor does it involve only major word classes (noun, verb, adjective) as in the older poetry. But it is frequent. In stanza 1 we find: *my/mine, thoughts/ (feathers)/the* (/θ/ vs. /ð/), *making/money*; stanza 2: *dearest/dallier, hunt/hands, warm/white*; stanza 3: *with/wind, me/moment, heart/have*. Strictly speaking, *open* and *eyes* (line 5) alliterate as well – in the Anglo-Saxon sense – since the onset in each of the stressed syllables can be viewed as a "zero consonant", which thus repeats. As Hamer (1970: 16) puts it: "lack of consonant counts as a consonant sound, so that two words beginning with a vowel can alliterate even if the vowel sound is not the same".

To these common features of Germanic versification Auden has added the stanza form and a rhyme scheme, *abab*. Note that the only "full rhyme" is *air/ there* – in the final stanza. The other rhymes represent varieties of "slant rhyme"; more specifically, they can be classified as examples of "consonance".[10] Cuddon, who labels this "half-rhyme", informs us (1991: 399-400) that this type of rhyme "was common in Icelandic, Irish and Welsh verse", but not common in English poetry until the time of Hopkins and Yeats. "Since then there have been many examples in the work of such poets as Wilfred Owen, John Crowe Ransom, T. S. Eliot, Emily Dickinson, Allen Tate and W. H. Auden". It can be added that the modern tendency to divide a poem into stanzas was not a feature of Old English verse, though it was (like "consonance") a common feature of Icelandic poetry (Gordon 1968: 314).

Let us now consider more closely the nature of the rhymes in this poem. The pattern *abab* is an interlocking one (rather iconic, in a love poem), also called "interlaced rhyme" (Roberts 1986: 281). The even-numbered lines (the *a*-pairs) form feminine rhymes ("–x": *coney/money, dallier/familiar, serpent/moment*), whereas the odd-numbered lines (the *b*-pairs) form masculine rhymes ("–": *life/thief, me/day, air/there*). Ignoring the final pair (*air/there*), which is a full rhyme, all the other pairs of rhymes are created by repeating what comes after the stressed vowel.

Consider first the *b*-pairs. In *life/thief* the rhyme is based on the final /f/. This is a straight-forward example of consonance. The other slant rhyme among the *b*-pairs is *me/day*. Strange as it might seem at first, this, too, is an example of "consonance", since the coda in *me* and *day* can be viewed as a "zero consonant". In the Old Icelandic formula, words or stressed syllables that ended with a vowel (that is, "repeating" a zero-consonant) were also counted as examples of "consonance" (or "half-rhymes"). This principle is obviously parallel to that which allows the "repetition" of a "zero consonant" in an onset to count as alliteration in Anglo-Saxon poetry.

The situation is a bit more complicated in the case of the *a*-pairs. If we extend the notion of "coda" to include the unstressed syllable in these pairs, these slant rhymes can also be included under the umbrella label, "consonance" (an alternative label might be "consonance with feminine ending"). The rhymes are then: /-ni/ (*coney/money*), /-ljər/ (*dallier/familiar*), and /-ənt/ (*serpent/moment*).

There is a minor inconsistency in the final pair. In all the other slant rhymes in this poem, the following generalization can be made: repeat whatever follows the stressed vowel. If this rule were followed in the last pair as well, the rhyme should have involved the repetition of /rpənt/ rather than just /ənt/. In partial defense of Auden, we should note that in his dialect *serpent* was probably /r/-less. In such non-rhotic dialects, the rhyme can be seen as /pənt/ vs. /mənt/. This is very close to the pattern established by the other pairs, since the consonants /p/ and /m/, though not identical, are closely related – they are both formed by the lips (that is, they are both bilabial).

One final phonological feature of this poem that I would like to point out is the role played by the vowel in the first syllable of each stanza: the /ʌ/ in *what* (/wʌt/; line 1); the /o/ in *open* (/opən/; line 5) and the /aɪ/ in *rise* (/raɪz/; line 9). Each of these vowels seems to set the "tone" for its stanza, in the sense that each is echoed frequently by other words in the stanza. Thus in stanza 1, /ʌ/ in *what* is echoed in *dove, love, money*, (and, to some extent, four times in *of*, though the vowel of this preposition, being unstressed, is more like /ə/ than like /ʌ/); stanza 2: /o/ in *open* is echoed in *go, motions*, and, to some extent, in *exploring*; stanza 3: /aɪ/ in *rise* is echoed in *silence, alive*, and *strike*.

We see, then, in this first poem, an Audenesque combination of old Anglo-

Saxon features with such early Scandinavian (and more modern English) features as end-rhyme, consonance, and stanzaic structure.

## II (That night when joy began)

    That night when joy began
    Our narrowest veins to flush,
    We waited for the flash
    Of morning's levelled gun.
5   But morning let us pass,
    And day by day relief
    Outgrows his nervous laugh,
    Grown credulous of peace,
    As mile by mile is seen
10  No trespasser's reproach,
    And love's best glasses reach
    No fields but are his own.

This poem is a kind of *aubaude*, or "dawn song" (see Cuddon 1991: 65), which, contrary to the lovers' expectations, does not lead to a leave-taking with the rising of the sun ("morning's levelled gun").

The poem consists of three four-line stanzas of almost perfect iambic trimeter. Unlike the first poem, then, the unstressed syllables are as regular as the stressed ones. But this straight-forward, uncomplicated meter stands in marked contrast to the system of rhyme, which displays a highly intricate and ingenious pattern of phonological repetition and variation.

The basic rhyme scheme in each stanza is *abba*, thus constituting an embedding pattern (sometimes referred to as "closed rhyme" – Roberts 1986: 276) rather than the interlocking pattern of the first poem. All the rhymes are masculine. So far, then, nothing out of the ordinary.

But now consider the nature of the rhymes. As in the first poem, they are of the slant-rhyme variety. This time, however, Auden has adopted the pararhyme (rather than "simple" consonance) for relating the rhymed pairs. Recall (from note 10) that in this type of rhyme the onsets and the codas (that is, the consonants before and after the stressed vowel) repeat, while the syllable nucleus (the vowel) is altered. This is, I think, the most difficult type of rhyme there is – and, as might be expected, it was a common feature of skaldic poetry, where the technique was called *skothending* (Schipper 1973: 13, fn. 1). Consider, for example, the word, *flush*, from the first stanza of this poem. There are many English words which could be used as the "rhyme", if consonance alone were the rhyming principle: *ash, dish, lash, mash, squash, wash, wish,* etc. Similarly, if full rhymes were sought by the poet, he could choose from such items as *blush, brush, crush, gush, hush, lush, mush, rush*. But choose pararhyme, as Auden has done, and there are only two English words that are available for the matching item: *flash* and *flesh*. In this twelve-line poem, then, Auden is faced with the "problem" of finding six pararhymes which fit comfortably into the poem. But he doesn't stop there. As an extra complication, he has chosen to establish phonological links between the pairs of pararhymes, both within and across stanzas. As we shall see, this has the effect of reducing the choices even further, so that the only permissible match for e.g. flush is *flash*. We shall also see, however, that having willingly subjected himself to these phonological shackles he nevertheless wriggles "free" of them, Houdini-like, and manipulates the English language to produce surprising pairs of rhymes.

In the first stanza, the *a*-pair is be*gan*/*gun* (/g...n/) and the *b*-pair is *flash*/*flush* (/fl... ʃ/). In the *a*-pair we see one of the techniques Auden has adopted to increase the scope of the possible rhyme: for the purpose of pararhyme, a final stressed syllable counts as well as a one-syllable word. This is, of course, standard practice in full rhyme as well (e.g. *pain/refrain, close/impose*). In stanza two the *a*-pair is *pass/peace* (/p...s/) and the *b*-pair is *relief/laugh* (/l...f/). In the third stanza there is a slight discrepancy in the pattern in both pairs. The *a*-pair is *seen*/*his own*, where /s...n/ is paired with /z...n/. In this case, *sown* is the word Auden leads us to expect as the slant rhyme for *seen*, but he "fools" us by selecting *own*, and supplying the "missing" *s* from the end of the preceding word, *his*. Here he is, of course, "guilty" of a phonological (but not orthographic) irregularity, since the final sound of *his* is voiced (/z/), rather than voiceless (/s/).[11] The *b*-pair in the last stanza is *reproach*/*reach* (/r...tʃ/). Here again Auden "fools" us: the normal syllabification of *reproach* would lead us to expect *preach*, rather than *reach*, as the second member of this pair.

The six pairs of pararhymes Auden has used in this poem are thus: be*gan*/*gun* and *flash/flush* (stanza 1); *pass/peace* and *relief*/*laugh* (stanza 2); *seen*/*his own* and *reproach*/*reach* (stanza 3). Consider now how these pairs interrelate.

In stanza 1, the vowels in the *a*-pair are /æ/ (be*gan*) and /ʌ/ (*gun*). Displaying a remarkable feat of phonological ingenuity, Auden has managed to keep the same vowels, but in reverse order (chiasmus), in the *b*-pair, where we find first /ʌ/ in *flush* and then /æ/ in *flash*. In other words, the items in the *a*-pair are related to one another by their opening and closing consonants (pararhyme), and to the items in the *b*-pair through their vowels (assonance). Another way of looking at this relationship is to observe that once the final syllables in the first two lines of the stanza are specified, the final syllables of the last two lines in the stanza are fully determined. This procedure establishes a veritable phonological strait-jacket for the poet.

To get a keener sense of this self-imposed constraint, consider again the rhymes in stanza one. From the syllable *-gan* (line 1), we can predict the consonants of the last syllable in line 4: /g/ and /n/. From the word *flush* (line 2), we can predict the vowel of the last syllable in line 4: /ʌ/. The resulting rhyme for the end of line 4 is thus fully determined by lines 1 and 2: it must be /g + ʌ + n/ = *gun*. Similarly the word *flush* (line 2) determines the consonants of the last syllable of line 3: /fl/ and /ʃ/, while the syllable *-gan* (line 1) determines the vowel of the last syllable of line 3: /æ/. The resulting rhyme for the end of line 3 is thus also fully determined by lines 1 and 2: it must be /fl + æ + ʃ/ = *flash* (this rules out the only other possible English pararhyme for *flush*, namely *flesh*).

Another way to view this phonological magic is to see the final syllables of lines 3 and 4 as "anaphones" (not anagrams, since we are dealing with phonemes rather than graphemes) of the final syllables in lines 1 and 2. Given seven phonemes (/æ ʌ f g l n ʃ/), Auden arranges them one way (/g æ n/ + /f l ʌ ʃ/) to end lines 1 and 2, and another way (/f l æ ʃ/ + /g ʌ n/) to end lines 3 and 4.

Remarkable as this achievement is in stanza one, Auden accomplishes the same legerdemain in the remaining two stanzas as well. In stanza two he uses six phonemes (/æ f i l p s/ – note that three of them are the same as in stanza one) to produce first /p æ s/ + /l i f/, and then rearranges them to give us /l æ f/ + /p i s/.

By the same token we can predict that the last syllables of the final two lines in the third stanza will be anaphones of the final syllables in the first two lines of that stanza. However, having established the pattern in the first two stanzas, Auden wriggles free of the rigid constraints he himself has imposed, and, as we saw earlier, surprises us with *reach* and *(hi)s own* instead of the predicted *preach* and *sown* (which nevertheless hover in the periphery of our minds, half-extracted from our mental lexicon by the poet-medium).

Surely, we feel, Auden must be content with this phonological *tour de force*. But no, the magician has more up his sleeve.

So far, we have seen how Auden uses end-rhyme (and anaphones) to establish an intricate relationship among the lines in any given stanza: pararhyme links the first line with the last line of each stanza ($a_1 a_2$), and the second line with the third line ($b_1 b_2$); while assonance links the first line with the third ($a_1 b_1$) and the second with the fourth ($a_2 b_2$). But Auden goes further than this: he also links the stanzas themselves to one another by means of vowel and consonant repetitions.

Consider first the vowels, which intimately bind the rhymes in the middle stanza to the rhymes of the other two stanzas: the /æ/ of lines 5 and 7 (/pæs/, /læf/) matches the /æ/ of lines 1 and 3 in the first stanza (/gæn/, /flæʃ/), while the /i/ in lines 6 and 8 (/lif/, /pis/) matches the /i/ in lines 9 and 11 in the last stanza (/sin/, /ritʃ/).

A similar but somewhat more complex relationship binds the consonants in the middle stanza rhymes to the consonants in the rhymes of the other two stanzas. The b-pair of the middle stanza relates to the b-pair in the first stanza, while the a-pair of the middle stanza relates to the a-pair of the final stanza.

Let us look first at the *b*-pairs. The final consonant (/f/) of the *b*-pair in lines 6 and 7 (/li_f_/, /læ_f_/) matches the opening consonant of the *b*-pair in lines 2 and 3 (/_fl_ʌʃ/, /_fl_æʃ/). In fact, we see that the onset (/fl/) of the *b*-pair in lines 2 and 3 splits into the two consonants /f/ and /l/, forming, in reverse order (chiasmus again), the onset and the coda of /lif/ and /læf/.

Consider next the *a*-pairs. The final consonant (/s/) of the *a*-pair in lines 5 and 8 (/pæ_s_/, /pi_s_/) matches the opening consonant of the *a*-pair in lines 9 and 12 (/_s_in/, /_z_-on/) – ignoring the slight discrepancy noted earlier, namely the voicing of the sibilant in line 12.

Observe further that the consonantal relationships are based on reversals. We have noted the reversal involved in the splitting of /fl/ into /l...f/. But observe also the more general reversal that is manifested by the fact that it is the *codas* (/s/ and /f/) in the *a*-pair and *b*-pair of the middle stanza that match the onsets in the corresponding pairs in the first and last stanzas.

The relationships are so intricate and so extensive, that the mind (except Auden's, perhaps) has difficulty in grasping them all at once.

## III (For what as easy)

    For what as easy
    For what though small,
    For what is well
    Because between,
5   To you simply
    From me I mean.

    Who goes with who
    The bedclothes say,
    As I and you
10  Go kissed away,
    The data given,
    The senses even.

    Fate is not late,
    Nor the speech rewritten,
15  Nor one word forgotten,
    Said at the start
    About heart,
    By heart, for heart.

This is perhaps the most curious of the "Five Songs". All the words are English, but some of the lines (particularly 1 and 4) do not seem to make sense in English. This has led commentators such as Thwaite (1978: 56) to remark that the lines "have a runic or cryptic quality, a curious extension of Auden's interest in Old English poetry and in the Norse sagas". Thwaite may be going a bit overboard here in attributing the complexity to Auden's love of early verse and lore, but I agree fully with the use of the word, "cryptic", a point to which I shall return after examining the basic form of this poem.

Let us first consider the meter. Each stanza consists of six lines of what is basically iambic dimeter. This can be seen by scanning the first stanza:

```
x  -  x  -  x
x  -  x  -
x  -  x  -
x  -  x  -
x  -     -  x
x  -  x  -
```

The metrical pattern is altered only twice in this stanza – in lines 1 and 5, where we find the feminine rhymes, *easy* and *simply*. Now six lines of regular iambic dimeter would yield 6 x 4 = 24 syllables per stanza. Auden (for reasons known best to him) has chosen to alter this regularity slightly but systematically, giving us 25 syllables in the first stanza, 26 in the second, and 27 in the third.

As we now expect from Auden, the rhyme scheme is intricate. It is also quite unusual, being a mix of full rhyme, slant rhyme and identical rhyme, and varying from stanza to stanza.

In the first stanza we find *abbcac*, where only the c-pair constitutes a full rhyme: *(be)tween/mean*. The other two pairs are slant rhymes. The b-pair displays consonance (*small/well*), a pattern with which we are now well familiar from the first two poems. The a-pair also shows a kind of slant rhyme in that the stressed syllables are phonologically unrelated, but the vowel of the unstressed syllable is repeated: *easy/simply* (/i/).

In the second stanza we also find three pairs of rhymes, but arranged differently: *ababcc*. This time it is the a-pair (*who/you*) and the b-pair (*say/(a)way*) which are full rhymes. Continuing the reversal of the first stanza, the c-pair is now the slant rhyme: *given/even* (/-v ə n/).

The third stanza displays yet another pattern. It seems to me that there are two ways of analyzing the rhyme scheme in this stanza, depending on how one regards the value of *late* (line 13). It forms an internal full rhyme with *fate* in the same line, as well as a slant rhyme (based on consonance) with *start* (line 16) and *heart* (lines 17 and 18). If we focus on the latter relationship, we have the pattern *abbaaa* – that is, a break with the triple pair pattern of the first two stanzas. More appropriate, I feel, is the analysis *(a)abbcc(c)c*, where I have used ( ) to mark an internal rhyme. We thus have an a-pair as an internal rhyme in the first line of the stanza: *fate/late*. This matches the internal identical rhyme (that is, repetition) of the c-pair in the last line: *heart/heart*. The c-pair shows up as a full rhyme in the two lines preceding this: *start/heart*. The b-pair is made up of the slant rhyme: *rewritten/forgotten* (/-tən/).

Auden's ingenuity thus manifests itself through the display, in three stanzas, of different ways to vary a triple rhyme scheme. Ignoring the most straight-forward pattern of *aabbcc* (which would create three unconnected "couplets"), he selects first the interlocking pattern of *abbcac*. This is followed by a different pattern, *ababcc*, which interlocks the first four lines and concludes with a couplet. Finally, he gives us a pattern which is best perceived in the form of a two-dimensional grid:

| | |
|---|---|
| a | a |
| | b |
| | b |
| | c |
| | c |
| c | c |

In this pattern, the "vertical" b-pair (slant rhyme) and the "vertical" c-pair (full rhyme) are bordered by "horizontal" pairs of internal rhymes: the a-pair (full rhyme) and another c-pair (identical rhyme). In addition, the rhyming words in all the pairs in the last stanza are interrelated by means of consonance: the coda of each stressed syllable in the rhyming words ends in /t/: *fate/late, rewritten/forgotten, start/heart*.

Let us return now to the cryptic aspect of this poem. I believe that the poem contains several examples of word and letter play, perhaps even one or more anagrams.

Consider first the role of the prepositions in the poem. Five of the six lines in the first stanza open with a preposition (*for, to, from*). Thus the first stanza makes use of three prepositions, one of them (*for*) repeated three times. The one line that does not open with a preposition (line 4) ends with one (*between*), in a very curious construction (*Because between*). The prepositions return, again three times, to close the poem (*about, by, for*). Note, in particular, that the same preposition that opens the poem (*for*), appears in its closing. In fact, if we consider the final prepositional phrase, *for heart*, we see that the two words in this phrase form a kind of border for the poem as a whole: the first word (*for*) shows up three times in the first stanza, while the last word (*heart*) shows up three times in the last stanza.

Once we begin to sense this word play, other instances can be discerned. Consider again the sequence, *for*. It appears as a prefix in line 15 (*forgotten*), and there is, I think, a direct reference to it in the next line (*Said at the start*): the "one word" (line 15) which is "said at the start" (line 16) is *for*. Consider also the last line of the first stanza, *From me I mean*. /m/ is clearly singled out for special attention, being the basis for the alliteration in *me* and *mean*.[12] But /m/ is also the last consonant in the opening preposition in this line – namely, *from*. Is it stretching the point to suggest that while the final consonant of this preposition thus links up with the alliteration in *me* and *mean*, the remaining three letters in the preposition constitute an anagram for the first word which opens the poem ("f r o" → "f o r")? Or consider the opening of the final stanza. If we look at the first word in each of the first three lines (*Fate, Nor, Nor*), we note not only that *Nor* rhymes with *For* (twice, establishing parallels between the second and third lines of the opening and closing stanzas) but also that *For* is spelled out again, by selecting, respectively, the first, second and third letters in the three words (*Fate, Nor, Nor*). *For* has indeed been "rewritten" (despite the disclaimer in line 14: *Nor the speech rewritten*). Thus, from the final stanza we learn that "Fate is not late" (which is orthographically true, since "f" is not the same as "l"), that the speech has been "rewritten", and that "for" has been "gotten"– several times.

But there is, I feel, considerably more rewriting going on in this poem – particularly, I believe, in the first stanza, which is the most cryptic of the three. Consider the clues in stanzas two and three. We have already encountered the phrase, *speech rewritten* (line 14) and *Said at the start* (line 16). Note, too, the reference to *the data given* (line 11). There is, I think, data in the first stanza which has been rewritten. But how?

A first thought is that perhaps the words in the first stanza (at least lines 1-4) have been jumbled. Maybe they can be rearranged to form a "true" English text? Careful examination of these lines suggests that this is not likely to be the case. In the first place, there is only one verb in the first four lines, and that is the relatively empty copula verb, "is" (line 3). In the second place, there are no nouns at all in these lines (nor in the stanza as a whole). In fact, we see that text of the first stanza is made up primarily of words from the lexically "less important" categories: prepositions (*between, for, from, to*), pronouns (*I, me, what, you*), and conjunctions (*because, though*). Consequently, it is amazing that Auden's stanza makes as much "sense" as it does. I certainly see no way of rearranging the words so that they make even more sense.

Let us consider, then, another approach to this text. Perhaps it is not the words that should be rearranged, but (some of) the letters. Auden may be giving us an important clue in the last three lines of the poem: *Said at the start/ About heart,/By heart, for heart*. If we take this literally, the first stanza (or perhaps the first line, since that is the real "start") says something about "heart".

Now one way for the first line (*For what as easy*) to say something about "heart" is to assume that it is an anagram for another message, perhaps one which includes the word, *heart*. And, indeed, the letters of the first line can be rearranged to spell "heart": "Fo<u>r</u> w<u>h</u>at as <u>e</u>asy". But if this is a true anagram, the rest of the letters in the line ("f", "o", "w", "a", "a", "s", "s", "y") must spell something, too – something that ties in with "heart". The best I can come up with is: "A sway of hearts" ("Ways of a heart" is better, but leaves an unused "s").[13] Not a perfect decipherment of the line, perhaps, but a step in the right direction, I feel. The actual anagrammatic reading remains elusive.[14]

## IV (Seen when nights are silent)

Seen when nights are silent,
The bean-shaped island,
And our ugly comic servant,
Who was observant.

5   O the veranda and the fruit,
The tiny steamer in the bay
Startling summer with its hoot: –
You have gone away.

Like the second of the "Five Songs", this poem has basically a three-stressed line. Unlike that poem, however, the metrical pattern is quite irregular, and hence (like the first of the "Five Songs") is an instance of an accentual meter. This can be seen from the scansion which I propose for the two stanzas:

| Stanza 1 | | | | | | | | Stanza 2 | | | | | | | |
|---|---|---|---|---|---|---|---|---|---|---|---|---|---|---|---|
|   |   | – | x | – | x | – | x |   | – | x | x | – | x | x | x | – |
| x | – |   |   |   |   | – | x | x | – | x |   | – | x | x | x | – |
| x | x | – | x | – | x | – | x |   | – | x |   | – | x | x | x | – |
|   |   | – |   | – | x | – | x |   | – |   | x | – |   |   | x | – |

The two stanzas share the accentual meter (three stresses per line) and they share the feature of being end-stopped. But otherwise they are quite different. The first stanza has 24 syllables in all – 12 stressed and 12 unstressed and each line ends with a trochee. The second stanza has 28 syllables – 12 stressed and 16 unstressed (though it is possible to read the first three lines of this stanza with an extra stressed syllable, yielding 15 stressed and 13 unstressed) – and each line ends with an iamb.

The poem thus appears to have the basic shape of an Icelandic *dróttkvætt*, the most common of the old Icelandic verse forms. The traditional *dróttkvætt* consists of 8-line stanzas or strophes, often divided into two "metrically and syntactically complete" 4-line half-strophes with 24 syllables in each strophe (Turville-Petre 1951: 166). Moreover, each line has three stressed syllables and a trochaic ending.[15] Seen in this light, the first four lines of this poem have the form of a half-strophe (or quatrain) in a dróttkvætt. One feature of the *dróttkvætt* that is not present in full force, however, is internal rhyme. Instead, Auden has adopted a very curious rhyme scheme of his own.

Note first that the rhyme pattern, like the meter, is different in the two stanzas. We find *aabb* in the first stanza and *abab* in the second. Thus the first stanza has the nature of paired couplets, whereas the second shows an interlocking pattern.[16] In addition, we find full masculine rhymes in the second stanza – *fruit/hoot* (a-pair) and *bay/(a)way* (b-pair) – contrasting markedly with the curious feminine rhymes in the first.

In fact, the rhymes in the first stanza come close to being full repetitions, but are kept from being identical primarily by a contrast in voicing. In the *a*-pair, *silent/island* (/saɪlənt/ vs. /aɪlənd/, the voicing variation is found in the final consonant of the rhyme (/t/ vs. /d/). In the *b*-pair, *servant/observant* (/sɜ(r)vənt/ vs. /(əb)zɜ(r)vənt/, the voicing variation appears in the initial consonant of the stressed syllable (/s/ vs. /z/). There is one additional feature in the *a*-pair which should be pointed out: the opening *s* of *silent* actually becomes "silent" as the first two letters are transposed to create the rhyming word, *island*.[17]

If the "s" in the first part of the word, *island*, is silent, the "and" in the second part of the word is not. Note first that it functions as a portion of the rhyming link not only to the other member of the *a*-pair (*silent*), but indeed to the members of the *b*-pair as well (*servant/observant*); all four lines of the first stanza thus end with nearly the same syllable, /ənd/ or /ənt/. Moreover, the sequence "and" can be seen as the pivotal point of the first stanza: it both ends the second line and starts the third line, thereby occupying the very middle of the stanza (like an island, "and" is surrounded by the rest of the stanza). This doubling technique is repeated in the first line of the second stanza: *O the veranda and the fruit*; this time the repetition occupies the middle of the line, rather than the middle of the stanza. Note that the repetition of *and* together with the immediately following unaccented *a* and *the* yields an internal rhyme of the form /ændə/ vs. /æn(d)ðə/.

## V ('O where are you going?' said reader to rider)

'O where are you going?' said reader to rider,
'That valley is fatal when furnaces burn,
Yonder's the midden whose odours will madden,
That gap is the grave where the tall return.'

5 'O do you imagine,' said fearer to farer,
'That dusk will delay on your path to the pass,
Your diligent looking discover the lacking,
Your footsteps feel from granite to grass?'

'O what was that bird,' said horror to hearer,
10 'Did you see that shape in the twisted trees?
Behind you swiftly the figure comes softly,
The spot on your skin is a shocking disease.'

'Out of this house' – said rider to reader,
'Yours never will' – said farer to fearer,
15 'They're looking for you' – said hearer to horror,
As he left them there, as he left them there.

This is the last of the "Five Songs". It represents a remarkable combination of features of early Anglo-Saxon poetry, of the ballad, and of skaldic rhyme technique.

Consider first, the Anglo-Saxon features. All the characteristics which we met in the first of the "Five Songs" are present in this last one: the four-line stanza, the four-stressed line, with the caesura splitting each line into two half-lines containing two stresses each, and alliteration – an alliteration which is much richer here than in the first poem.

But the ballad is here, too. It has been observed that Auden in fact modelled this poem on a folk ballad called "The Cutty Wren". Here is the first of the 11 stanzas of that ballad:[18]

O, where are you going, says Milder to Malder,
O, I cannot tell, says Festel to Fose,
We're going to the woods, says John the Red Nose,
We're going to the woods, says John the Red Nose.

Observe that the structure of this ballad is very similar to the structure of Anglo-Saxon verse. It, too, makes use of accentual meter, with four stresses per line;

and the caesura is clearly present. In Leech's view (1974: 118), the ballad (like the nursery rhyme) is, in fact, an oral survival of the old Anglo-Saxon verse form.[19]

Let us examine the metrical form of Auden's poem before considering the skaldic influence. My scansion of the first stanza is as follows:

```
x  -  x  x  -  x        ||        x  -  x  x  -  x
x  -  x  x  -  x        ||        x  -  x  x  -
   -  x  x  -  x        ||        x  -  x  x  -  x
x  -  x  x  -           ||     x  x  -        x  -
```

As in the first poem ("What's in your mind, my dove, my coney") the lines alternate between feminine (odd lines) and masculine (even lines) endings. But in this last poem, the general pattern of the unstressed syllables is considerably more regular than in the first poem, though there are still a few irregularities.

As in Anglo-Saxon poetry, there is a good deal of alliteration involving the stressed syllables. But Auden's use of alliteration is far more varied and complicated than what we find in Anglo-Saxon poetry, where the pattern is basically to have the third stressed syllable alliterate with the first (1/3), with the second (2/3), or with both the first and the second (1/2/3).

What Auden does instead is to set up a basic stanzaic pattern of 3/4 for the first and second lines, 2/4 for the third line, and 1/2 plus 3/4 for the last line. In addition to the alliteration in these syllables, Auden tends to add assonance in the odd-numbered lines. The resulting pattern is thus very similar to the skaldic technique of alternating consonant rhymes (alliteration, consonance, or pararhyme) in even-numbered lines with vowel rhymes (assonance or full-rhyme) in odd-numbered lines (Turville-Petre 1951: 166). The patterns of internal rhyme in Auden's poem can best be seen by viewing them in chart form:

| stress 1 | stress 2 | stress 3 | stress 4 | |
|---|---|---|---|---|
| | | re<u>ad</u>er | r<u>id</u>er | (line 1) |
| (<u>v</u>alley) | <u>f</u>atal | <u>f</u>urnaces | <u>b</u>urn | (line 2) |
| | mi<u>dd</u>en | | ma<u>dd</u>en | (line 3) |
| <u>g</u>ap | <u>g</u>rave | <u>t</u>all | (re)<u>t</u>urn | (line 4) |
| | | f<u>ea</u>rer | f<u>a</u>rer | (line 5) |
| | | <u>p</u>ath | <u>p</u>ass | (line 6) |
| | loo<u>k</u>ing | | la<u>ck</u>ing | (line 7) |
| <u>f</u>ootsteps | <u>f</u>eel | g<u>r</u>anite | g<u>r</u>ass | (line 8) |
| | | <u>h</u>orror | <u>h</u>earer | (line 9) |
| | | <u>t</u>wisted | <u>t</u>rees | (line 10) |
| | <u>sw</u>iftly | | <u>s</u>oftly | (line 11) |
| <u>s</u>pot | <u>s</u>kin | <u>sh</u>(!)ocking | (di)<u>s</u>ease | (line 12) |

Observe that in addition to the alliteration, which is found in every line, Auden has used pararhymes in the first and third lines (the odd-numbered lines) of each stanza: *reader/rider, midden/madden* (stanza one); *fearer/farer, looking/lacking* (stanza two); *horror/hearer, swiftly/softly* (stanza 3). In fact, the first lines of each stanza are linked by the repeated use of the suffix, *-er*, added to the verb (*ride + er*, etc.). The single exception is the word, *horror*, which fits the phonological but not the morphological pattern, thereby singling out this word for additional emphasis (and perhaps calling forth the homophonous *whorer*?).

There is an exception to Auden's alliterative "norm" in the second line of the first stanza. Here we expect the third stressed syllable to alliterate with the fourth (as in lines 6 and 10), but it alliterates with the second instead: *fatal/furnaces*. Note, however, that there is a kind of loose alliteration with both of the other stressed syllables in this line, since they all start with a labial consonant: *valley/fatal/furnaces/burn*.[20] Note also that the last two of these words are linked by internal rhyme – a rhyme involving both the stressed vowel and the consonants following it: *furnaces/burn*.[21]

We see a more extensive rhyme in the second line of the second stanza (line 6) as well. Not only do the third and fourth stressed syllables in this line alliterate, they also form a reverse rhyme (that is, alliteration plus assonance): *path/pass*. This pattern is repeated in the fourth line of this stanza (line 8) as well: *granite/grass*.

In addition to the internal rhyme, each of the first three stanzas makes use of one full rhyme at the end of the odd-numbered lines. That is, the second and fourth lines of these stanzas rhyme, yielding the pattern *abcb*. The *b*-pairs are: *burn/return, pass/grass, trees/disease*.

The first three stanzas thus display a number of parallel features involving rhyme and meter. They are also parallel in several other ways. Note that each of them asks a question, and that the question opens with the interjection, "O". Furthermore the questioner is always identified in the first line of the stanza – in a fixed pattern of dialogue mechanism: "said X to Y". Note, too, that in each of these three stanzas the questioner specifies some potential danger, and that the danger is expressed in the same form each time – "that" plus a noun: *that valley* (line 2), *that dusk* (line 6), and *that shape* (line 10). The fact that "that" is a demonstrative pronoun in two of the cases and a subordinate conjuction in the other (line 6) provides an additional example of Auden's linguistic prowess, manipulating different grammatical functions to provide parallel phonological forms.[22]

But what about the last stanza? It differs in interesting ways from the preceding three.[23] This is principally because this stanza has a different function than the others. In the first three stanzas, a cautious, passive, frightened introvert (*reader/fearer/horror*) asks questions of his bold, active extroverted counterpart (*rider/farer/hearer*). In the last stanza this active member of the pair provides answers to the questions posed in the first three stanzas. The speakers are thus reversed (each of the second hemistichs in lines 13, 14 and 15 repeats, chiasmatically, the second hemistich in lines 1, 5 and 9), so that lines 13, 14 and 15 answer, respectively, the questions posed in stanzas one, two and three.

This provides a clear function for the first three lines of the last stanza, but it gives rise to an interesting question: what role should the last line of the poem play? Auden solves this potential structural problem by using this line to depict and emphasize the departure of the active member, as the second hemistich repeats the first: *As he left them there, as he left them there*.[24] This line thus marks the end of the stanza, the end of the poem, and the end of the "Five Songs". It is also the active poet (Auden) bidding farewell to the passive reader (us).

This poem, unlike the first four, does not appear to be a love poem. Instead it seems to be advisory in nature. It issues a call for action as opposed to passivity. But what kind of action? There have been numerous suggestions. Some critics have even argued that it is a weakness of the poem, and perhaps of the poet as well, that the call is so vague. The poem was written in the 1930's, when the world was beset by economic depression, the rise of dictatorships and growing fears of a major war; in such threatening times, some critics have argued, it is the duty of good poets everywhere to point readers and listeners in the right direction, to help guide them in their choice of action. Auden's poem calls for action, but – these critics complain – it does not specify what type of action, and is therefore inadequate. This, I believe, is the wrong attitude to take toward this poem (or any poem).

First of all, Auden himself often remarked that, in his view, poetry (and poets – in fact, artists in general) can never change the world, and should not even try. Hecht (1993: 175) informs us, for example, from personal experience in Auden's company, that Auden "was fond of maintaining that art should be amusing, accessible, and without pretensions to *ultimate statements*, to solemn pomposities" [Hecht's italics]. This sentiment is the basis for the title and content of one of the chapters in Hecht's book about Auden: "Poetry Makes Nothing Happen" (Hecht 1993: 81-170). The title itself is a line from a poem Auden wrote eulogizing W. B. Yeats.

So we must look elsewhere, I think, for the "meaning" of this poem. Isherwood (1975: 76-77), I believe, is on the right track when he observes that we see in the work of Auden during this period the strong influence of

> [Homer] Lane's theories of the psychological causes of disease – if you refuse to make use of your creative powers, you grow a cancer instead. References to these theories can be found in many of the early poems, and, more generally, in *The Orators*.

So this poem, originally published as the epilogue to *The Orators*, can perhaps be seen as a call to readers and listeners to make maximum use of their creative powers. Auden concurred with Lane that failure to do so could actually lead to such "physical disorders" as "spots, coughs and cancers" (Spender 1975: 247), hence line 12: "The spot on your skin is a shocking disease".

The poem can also be seen as a call to obey the sexual dictates of one's inner psyche, an early call perhaps to "closet homosexuals" to abandon their fears and, like Auden himself, make an open declaration of their dispositions (for an interpretation that comes close to this view, see Hecht 1993: 89).

On a more general level, the poem can be seen as a call to freedom in an age of increasing unfreedom. In the words of Stephen Spender (1975: 245-246), reminiscing in his valediction at the memorial service held for Auden in Christ Church on October 27, 1973, Auden represented to his friends of this period:

> a person who was so different from ourselves . . . His poetry was unlike anything we had expected poetry to be . . . Nevertheless he did speak for the liveliest of the young at that time: who wanted to throw off the private inhibitions and the public acquiescences of a decade of censorship and dictatorship and connivance with dictatorship, those who were impassioned by freedom, and some who fought for it. He gave to them their wishes which they might not have listened to otherwise. They were grateful for that. He enabled impulses to flower in individuals. All that was life-enhancing.

This is a kind and noble tribute from a good friend. It is also an appropriate commentary, I think, on part of the meaning of this final poem.

In five short pieces from Auden's very early career as a poet we have witnessed his virtuosity and wide-ranging experimentation in the use of poetic form. From the point of view of meter, the "Five Songs" start and end with poems in the old Germanic tradition: both poems I and V consist of lines with four stresses. Poems II and IV reduce the number of stresses to three per line: the first of these (II) is in regular iambic trimeter, the other (IV) in a form which recalls the Icelandic *dróttkvætt*. The poem in the very middle (III) reduces the number of stresses further, giving us lines of iambic dimeter. Seen from this perspective, there appears to be a larger pattern of metrical form in the "Five Songs" taken as a unit: the number of stresses per line decreases and then increases to yield a nicely symmetrical system – 4 (I), 3 (II), 2 (III), 3 (IV), 4 (V).

But where Auden's virtuosity is most evident is in the intricate rhyme schemes he employs in these various verse types. His rhymes run the full gamut – alliteration, assonance, consonance, pararhyme, full rhyme, identical rhyme – in complicated patterns within lines, at the ends of lines, and across stanzas.

His interest in complicated verse forms was unabating. Even in his final year, as poet in residence at Oxford, he used to spend an hour or so each day in one of the local coffee-houses in order to discuss poetry with any aspiring student who was bold enough to sit down at his table. David Luke, a Tutor in German at Oxford recalls (1975: 207):

> He was still [in 1972-1973] curious to encounter new talent more particularly if he was told that so-and-so shared, for example, his passionate interest in the revival or importation of unusual prosodic conventions. 'Have you ever tried writing a *cywydd*?' he would ask. 'It's the classic medieval Welsh metre, consisting of ...' and he would then explain this highly complex verse-form. Or he would comment: 'At your age, what matters is not what you say in your writing but how you say it.'

Luke's reference to Auden's insistence on the importance of form captures Auden's own view very nicely. Listen to Auden himself:

> A poet has to woo, not only his own Muse but also Dame Philology, and, for the beginner, the latter is the more important. As a rule, the sign that a beginner has a genuine original talent is that he is more interested in playing with words than in saying something original; his attitude is that of the old lady, quoted by E. M. Forster – "How can I know what I think till I see what I say?" (Auden 1962: 22)

Needless to say, this attitude has led some critics to see in Auden a virtuoso more interested in form than in content. No one denies the immensity of the talent, but some have argued that the talent has left behind great lines, but no great poems. This, for example, is the view of Cox (1975: 410):

He can always be relied on to be more interesting, lively, provocative, wide-ranging, psychologically penetrating, technically skilful, and ingenious than most of his contemporaries. He has given us a small number of successful poems and a great many incidental and fragmentary brilliances. But he has never gathered up and concentrated all his powers in a major achievement, and never quite fulfilled the promise of the first volumes.

This evaluation can be contrasted with the view voiced by Fuller (1970: 8) shortly before Auden's death: "For breadth, wisdom, myth, moral power and sheer technical excitement, he is for me the greatest living poet writing in English", and "one of the most challengingly adroit versifiers there has ever been". It is hard to disagree with the last statement.

# Notes

1. Auden was often reluctant to supply titles for his own poems. In his view, it is up to the reader to determine what a poem is about; the implication that a poem can be summarized in a short title constitutes a misunderstanding of the very art of poetry.
2. The "Five Songs" first appear as a unit, so far as I have been able to determine, in Auden's *Collected Poetry* (1945). They reappear in his *Collected Shorter Poems* (1957) and in his *Collected Shorter Poems 1927-1957* (1966). Mendelson republishes them in *W. H. Auden: Collected Poems* (1976: 59-60), which is the edition I have used. I have relied on the 1976 version because Mendelson remarks (1976: 11):

   > This edition includes all the poems that W. H. Auden wished to preserve, *in a text that represents his final revisions*... Normally the decision to print an author's latest text needs no defence; and when an editor works under the final instructions of his author, he is morally obliged to respect the dead man's instructions. [My italics.]

   As an extra precaution, I have compared Mendelson's 1976 version of the "Five Songs" with Auden's own (1966: 46-48) and discovered only three small differences – all involving punctuation. In poem IV, lines 1 (*Seen when nights are silent*) and 3 (*And our ugly comic servant*) end with a full-stop in Auden 1966, whereas they end with a comma in Mendelson 1976. Quite clearly, the punctuation in Mendelson is more appropriate. Similarly, in poem V, line 7 (*Your diligent looking discover the lacking*) ends with a comma in Mendelson 1976; in Auden there is no punctuation at the end of this line. Again, the punctuation in Mendelson is an improvement.
   Auden himself has remarked that he was no good at punctuation, as Mendelson (1977: xxii) reminds us:

   > Auden's punctuation in his early years was erratic or worse. He wrote a reviewer in 1936, 'You are quite right in saying that some of the difficulties in the first book [*Poems*] were due to punctuation. I never have understood that art. Now I make someone else do it for me.'

3. For his 1977 collection of Auden's early works, Mendelson meticulously searched out the dates of composition for each text. For the record, the history of each of the five poems here under discussion is as follows:

> I: composed in November 1930 and printed in 1933, in the second edition of Auden's *Poems* (Mendelson 1977: 56, 432);
> II: composed in November 1931 and printed in 1936, in Auden's *Look, Stranger* (Mendelson 1977: 113, 433);
> III: composed in October 1931 and printed in 1932 in *New Signatures*; it did not appear in any of Auden's collections of poems until 1945 (Mendelson 1977: 113, 420);
> IV: probably composed sometime late in 1933; printed in 1935 as part of *The Dog Beneath the Skin* (Mendelson 1977: 277, 428);
> V: composed in October 1931; printed in 1932 in Auden's *The Orators* (Mendelson 1977: 110).

4. Homer Lane was an American psychologist whose theories on the origins of human illness Auden became acquainted with when he met John Layard in Berlin in 1928. Layard had been a patient and subsequent follower of Lane's. (See Carpenter 1981: 85-95.)
5. Auden does not always use this "smoke screen". See, for example, his remarkable little humorous poem called "Uncle Henry" (Auden 1966: 48-49).
6. The name, "skald", refers to the early Scandinavian poets who performed at the royal courts in Scandinavia for some 500 years (ca. 800-1300). Skaldic verse reached its peak in Iceland, where the form of poetry "became so formidable, that one is surprised that the poets succeeded in saying anything" (Auden 1968: 67).

Auden tells us that "some of the most vivid recollections of my childhood are hearing him [Auden's father] read to me Icelandic folk-tales and sagas, and I know more about Northern mythology than Greek" (Auden and MacNeice 1937: 214).

In his biography of Auden, Carpenter (1981: 7) provides additional details:

> From his father he acquired an interest in legends and stories, and in ideas. Before Wystan could read, Dr Auden, who had a sound knowledge of classical literature, entertained him with tales of the Trojan War and of quarrels among the gods of Olympus. He told Wystan about other mythological figures – Thor, Loki, and the rest of the deities of Icelandic legend. Dr Auden was particularly keen that his son should learn these tales, for not only was he deeply fond of Norse antiquities but he also believed that his own family name, Auden, showed that he himself was of Icelandic descent.
>
> He believed this because 'Auden' resembles the Icelandic name Auðunn . . . which is often found in early Norse literature and has survived as a modern Icelandic surname. George Auden apparently believed that his family was descended from or related to, a certain Auðun Skökull, who is recorded as one of the first Norse settlers in Iceland in the ninth century; and he told Wystan that before the settlement the Audens' remote ancestors had lived on the coast of the Vik, the bay to the north of modern Denmark from which the Vikings had sailed.

Carpenter (1981: 7-8) lists several other possible sources of the name, *Auden*, one of which is the Anglo-Saxon *Healfdene*, which means "half Dane".

In the summer of 1936, Auden visited Iceland with Louis MacNeice, and the two published a book about their travels the following year (*Letters from Iceland*, 1937; for later reminiscences by another member of the party, see Yates 1975: 59-68). In the book we learn that Auden was surprised to discover that many Icelanders were still endowed with the ability to create, at a moment's notice, competent stanzas of Icelandic verse. Modern Icelandic poetry, notes Auden, is technically "of a very high standard" and "rhyme, assonance, and alliteration are all expected" (Auden and MacNeice 1937: 111). He adds that they "seem to have preserved a passion for ingenuity helped by their damnably inflected language, since the days of the Scalds, . . ." As an example, he gives us the following palindrome, in which the second verse is identical to the first when read backwards (1937: 112):

>    Falla tímans voldug verk
>      varla falleg saga.
>    Snjalla ríman studla sterk
>      Stendur alla daga.
>
>    Daga alla stendur sterk
>      Studla ríman snjalla
>    Saga falleg varla verk
>      voldug tímans falla.

7. I certainly do not mean to imply that there are not other influences which it might be possible to detect. Auden was widely read and deeply influenced by all kinds of sources. As his friends, fellow Oxford students Gabriel Carritt and Rex Warner have remarked (1975: 48), during his Oxford days (1925-1928):

   > he was writing incessantly. For some weeks on end, T. S. Eliot would be the model, then Gerard Manley Hopkins or Anglo-Saxon verse. Yet even when these influences were most marked, there was always something distinctly and recognizably his own. Everything that he admired was absorbed and with increasing felicity changed according to his own image.

8. For a concise description of the most basic formal characteristics of early Anglo-Saxon poetry, see Pope (1942: 5), Fussell (1965: 75-76), Malof (1970: 88-90), and Haarder (1979: 28). A fuller description can be found in e.g. Cassidy and Ringler's chapter on "Old English Poetry" (1971: 264-288). Lehman's "The Old Germanic Verse Form" (1968) gives a clear and insightful presentation of the common features of early Germanic verse form in general, comparing the Old English forms in the south with the early Scandinavian forms in the north. Schipper's *A History of English Versification* (1973) traces the development of English verse forms from the Old English period to the end of the 19th century; particularly informative for the present topic is his chapter two, "The alliterative verse in Old English" (1973: 15-63).
   Auden himself appears to use the label, "Anglo-Saxon", in a wider sense – to include both the Old English and the old Scandinavian forms:

   > In the small extant corpus of Anglo-Saxon poetry, there is nothing as good as the best poems in the Elder Edda, but it was my first introduction to the "barbaric" poetry of the North, and I was immediately fascinated both by its metric and its rhetorical devices, so different from the post-Chaucerian poetry with which I was familiar. (Auden 1970: 22)

9. As Malof (1970: 89) remarks, the relatively unstressed syllables in Anglo-Saxon poetry "do not appear consistently enough to generalize about or predictably enough to be useful in the scansion". Nonetheless, there has been much theorizing regarding the number and nature of the various types of hemistichs. For many years, the theory of variation proposed by Eduard Sievers in 1885 was predominant, but this was challenged by John Pope in 1942. Cassidy and Ringler, writing in 1971, claim that Sievers' system "is still generally considered the 'standard' one, though Sievers himself was never fully satisfied with it". Pope's system, however, "has gradually gained ground, though without displacing that of Sievers" (Cassidy and Ringler 1971: 275). Robert Creed's "A New Approach to the Rhythm of *Beowulf*" (1966) offers a modified version of Pope's theory which Creed considers an improvement. As far as I am aware, however, the search for regularity in the maze of hemistich types in Old English poetry continues.

10. There is, in the literature, a good deal of inconsistency in the labelling of rhymes. The simplest and most consistent system with which I am familiar is the one devised by Geoffrey Leech (1974). Leech takes as his starting point the basic definition of the syllable as CVC,

where C stands for any number of consonants (including zero). Rhyme types can then be systematically labelled according to what part of the syllable is repeated in any given rhyming pair. His labels, which I shall use in this paper, are as follows (Leech 1974: 89):

| | | | | |
|---|---|---|---|---|
| a. | alliteration | <u>C</u>V(C) | <u>h</u>unt/<u>h</u>ands | /h-/ |
| b. | assonance | C<u>V</u>C | p<u>a</u>ss/l<u>au</u>gh | /-æ-/ |
| c. | consonance | CV<u>C</u> | li<u>fe</u>/thie<u>f</u> | /-f/ |
| d. | reverse rhyme | <u>CV</u>C | <u>mi</u>nd/<u>my</u> | /maɪ-/ |
| e. | pararhyme | <u>C</u>V<u>C</u> | <u>fl</u>u<u>sh</u>/<u>fl</u>a<u>sh</u> | /fl-ʃ/ |
| f. | [full] rhyme | C<u>VC</u> | f<u>ate</u>/l<u>ate</u> | /-et/ |

To Leech's list I would like to add:

| | | | | |
|---|---|---|---|---|
| g. | identical rhyme | <u>CVC</u> | <u>heart</u>/<u>heart</u> | /hɑ(r)t/ |

In this formulaic representation of the syllable, "V" is generally called the syllable nucleus; the "C" to the left of "V" is termed the syllable "onset"; and the "C" to the right of "V" is the syllable "coda". The underlining shows which part of the syllable is repeated. As illustrations for each type of rhyme I have selected examples from Auden's "Five Songs". Slashes (/ /) enclose phonemic symbols representing the sounds involved. I shall use the label "slant rhyme", where appropriate, as a general term to cover all the less standard types of rhyme, namely types b, c, d, and e. (Note, by the way, that I am following an American tradition of using /e/ and /o/ for the sounds in e.g. *fate* and *go*, respectively. I use /(r)/ to indicate that post-vocalic "r" may be audibly present for some speakers (typically American) or absent for other speakers (typically British).

11. In the Foreword to his *Collected Shorter Poems 1927-1957* (1966: 16), in which "Five Songs" appears, Auden has the following remark about his changing ear for his own poems:

> it makes me wince when I see how ready I was to treat *-or* and *-aw* as homophones. It is true that in the Oxonian dialect I speak they are, but that isn't really an adequate excuse. I also find that my ear will no longer tolerate rhyming a voiced S [that is, /z/] with an unvoiced [that is, /s/]. I have had to leave a few such rhymes because I cannot at the moment see a way to get rid of them, but I promise not to do it again.

There can be little doubt that Auden was here thinking, in part, of the last line of this poem, "That night when joy began".

12. In fact, we have here what Leech labels "reverse rhyme", since the vowel is also repeated: /mi/.
13. What I am suggesting here is that a critic like Hecht was closer to the truth than he may have realized when he wrote (1993: ix) that Auden's poems "both invite the intrusive scrutiny of the cryptographer and deny him access".
C. Day Lewis has also commented, indirectly, on Auden as a user of codes. Callan (1983: 48) informs us that in his first crime novel (1935) C. Day Lewis modelled his detective, Nigel Strangeways, on Auden. In the novel, Strangeways is told: "If you'd lived in ancient Greece the Delphic oracle would have had to go out of business. Do cut out the cryptic stuff." A more direct reference to the type of coding system under consideration here can be found in a comment of Isherwood's (1975: 75) regarding Auden's remarkable virtuosity:

> Problems of form and technique seem to bother him very little. You could say to him: "Please write me a double ballade on the virtues of a certain brand of toothpaste, which also contains at least ten anagrams on the names of well-known politicians, and of which the refrain is as follows . . ." Within twenty-four hours, your ballade would be ready – and it would be good.

Now, of course, this reference to anagrams could be purely fortuitous, but I do not think so. Isherwood knew Auden well, and having collaborated with him on a number of works (*The*

*Dog Beneath the Skin* (1935), *On the Frontier* (1938), *Journey to a War* (1939)), he had first-hand knowledge of Auden's compositional techniques.

Even more directly to the point is a short essay on anagrams by Auden himself (1970: 16-18). The essay begins with a quotation from one Dmitri Alfred Borgmann, who remarks that almost "any name with a good distribution of alphabetic letters can be turned into either a flattering or an unflattering anagram of itself"; Borgmann then illustrates with his own name, providing us with both "Grand mind, mortal fibre" and "Damn mad boring trifler". Auden also cites Galileo's anagram from the year 1610 regarding his telescopic observations of Saturn. Galileo coded his message as: *smaismrmilmepoetalevmibvnenvgttaviras*. This was an anagram for "Altissimvm planetam tergeminvm observavi" = "I have observed that the farthest planet is a triplet". Isolated, on a separate line in Auden's essay, is the (at first) curious remark: "WHY SHUN A NUDE TAG?". The reader is left to discover for himself/herself that this is one of the possible anagrammatic renditions of the poet's full name: WYSTAN HUGH AUDEN.

The problem faced by the cryptographer in trying to work out anagrams is the immensity of the number of possible permutations. For any n letters, the number of possible arrangements of the letters is n! ("n factorial"), which is short for $1 \times 2 \times 3 \times \ldots n$. Thus, if n = 3 the number of permutations is $3! = 1 \times 2 \times 3 = 6$. Now the first line of the poem under consideration ("For what as easy") contains 13 letters, so the number of possible combinations is $13! = 6{,}227{,}020{,}800$. If we assume that one of the words in the anagram is *heart*, there are "only" 8 letters remaining to be rearranged. This means there are "only" $8! = 40{,}320$ combinations to try. Of course the phonotactics and lexicon of English dictate that only a few of these combinations will be acceptable English strings, but the process of discovering the "right" one(s) is still something of a challenge.

14. Another possible clue may reside in lines 7-8: *Who goes with who/The bedclothes say*. In addition to the obvious contextual reading, "The bedclothes" may "say" something else – in the form of an anagram. This would mean either that bedclothes itself is an anagram, or that the whole line, *The bedclothes say*, is.

Some support for my suggestion that an anagram may be involved here is provided, perhaps, in the next two lines in the stanza (lines 9-10): *As I and you/Go kissed away*. "I" and "you" are, of course, the appropriate pronouns for a love poem, but they might also refer to their two homophones, the letters of the alphabet, "i" and "u". If the letters "i" and "u" "go kissed away", this could mean that they are not present in the anagram (cp. "You can kiss that raise goodbye"). And, indeed, the letters "i" and "u" are absent in the (possibly anagrammatic) line above: The bedclothes say. Interestingly, these two vowels are also absent in the first line of the poem, which I mentioned earlier as a likely anagram (*For what as easy*). Furthermore, if lines 9-10 do contain instances of homophony, this helps explain why Auden would permit himself to use the construction, *I and you*, instead of the politer *you and I*. Admittedly, there is the pressure from line 6 (*Who goes with who*), with which line 8 must rhyme, but we can add (if my hypothesis about homophony is correct) that Auden has given us the vowels ("i" and "u") in the order in which they appear in the alphabet.

One final remark on anagrams and then I'll stop (I promise): Perhaps because I've been studying this particular poem so long, I can no longer read the first three lines without seeing Auden's initials (W.H.A) in the repeated pronoun, *what*. As a result, I see a triple self-reference in the opening of the first three lines: "For w(.)h(.)a(.)"; in fact the final "t" of *what* could be incorporated, anagramatically, to produce "Fort wha" – practically impregnable.

15. The *dróttkvætt* (or "Court meter") was the favorite form of the skalds in Scandinavia. Auden (1962: 47) states that one of his "touchstones" for testing critics is to discover if he likes "complicated verse forms of great technical difficulty, such as Englyns, Drott-Kvaetts, Sestinas, even if their content is trivial".

In the second of his T. S. Eliot memorial lectures (entitled "The World of Sagas") delivered at the University of Kent in 1967, Auden (1968: 67-68) defines the *dróttkvætt* as follows:

It is a stanza of four couplets; each line has three stresses and ends on an unaccented syllable. The first line of each couplet has two alliterations, and an assonance; the second is related to the first by alliteration and also contains an internal rhyme.

He then offers an example of a *dróttkvætt* of his own devising which begins with the line: *Hushed is the lake of hawks*. This parallels very nicely the first line of the poem we are here considering: *Seen when nights are silent*. We find the three-stressed line, and the alliteration – here, in the first and third stressed syllables in both poems (Hushed . . . hawks; Seen . . . silent). In one respect the latter line is, in fact, the better example of the opening of a *dróttkvætt*, since it ends in an unaccented syllable (Auden apologizes for the missing syllable in the first example, remarking simply that he "had to ignore the unaccented ending rule"; but he does not ignore it in the poem under consideration here).

Additional information about the *dróttkvætt* can be found in Gordon (1968: 317-318). For a more general discussion of the nature of skaldic poetry as a whole, see Turville-Petre (1951: 165-174), Einarsson (1963-4), and Gordon (1968: xxxix-xliv).

16. This probably reflects the earlier form of this poem, which, according to Mendelson (1977: 277), apparently had both a different shape and a slightly different text (differences are underlined):

    Seen when night was silent,
    The bean-shaped island

    And our ugly comic servant
    Who is observant

    O the verandah and the fruit
    The tiny steamer in the bay
    Startling summer with its hoot.
    You have gone away.

    Clearly, we are witnessing here some of that poetic "flux" in Auden's poetry which I mentioned earlier. Even more of this variation is evident when we learn that Auden published a sonnet in *New Verse* in October 1933, which, as Mendelson (1977: 423-424) and Beach (1957: 134-135) have observed, is surely a precursor of this poem. The first four lines of that sonnet are:

    I see it often since you've been away:
    The island, the veranda, and the fruit;
    The tiny steamer breaking from the bay;
    The literary mornings with its hoot;

    So Auden altered the basic stanzaic form, the stress pattern, and the order of the rhymes in going from sonnet to two quatrains.

17. The island alluded to is no doubt one of the Shetland Islands. Carpenter (1981: 123) tells us that Auden spent part of his summer holiday there in 1931. It may be going too far if I suggest that the English word, *island*, calls up echoes of the orthographically identical, but phonologically dissimilar Scandinavian word for Iceland (spelled *Island*, but pronounced /islænd/, with an "s" that is definitely not silent); this would yield an indirect reference to the home of the *dróttkvætt*. Note, by the way, that while the s is silent in the English *island*, it is not silent in the rest of the poem. It is the basis of alliteration in seen (line 1), silent (line 1), servant (line 3), steamer (line 6), startling (line 7), and summer (line 7).

18. Hecht (1993: 459) informs us that "The Cutty Wren" was apparently little known until Auden himself included it in his *Oxford Book of Light Verse* in 1938. Hecht (1993: 459-463) finds Christian themes in this ballad about a small (that is, "cutty") wren, and suggests that Au-

den's poem thus contains an unconscious reference to that Christian belief which (at the time) Auden thought he had relinquished. The first stanza of the ballad which I cite here is taken from Hecht (1993: 459).

19. Malof, in his book, *A Manual of English Meters* (1970), is very informative here (though he is more cautious than Leech when it comes to historical relationships). He writes:

   > There are two main kinds of native [English] meter: The Old Native Meter, no longer a standard form in English and commonly referred to as the Anglo-Saxon Alliterative Verse, and the Folk Meter that persists to our own time and is known in various guises such as "ballad meter" or "the meter of the hymnal". Whether or not the folk meters and the alliterative verse are historically related we cannot tell for certain. But they share a number of important characteristics . . . (1970: 88)

   > Folk Meter shares some features with the Anglo-Saxon Alliterative Verse: the regularity or irregularity in the number of slacks [unstressed syllables] does not affect the basic structure: the line contains a fixed cesura that divides it metrically in half; and the full-line is best understood as consisting of two half-lines or hemistichs. It also has some features of its own: it is usually rhymed; it more sensitively distinguishes between primary and secondary stresses, which tend to alternate with each other; the number of secondary stresses may vary, while the number of primary stresses per line is fixed at four; and the hemistichs can be of unequal length, creating flexibility of line-lengths and stanza-patterns. (1970: 92)

20. We find a similar case of extensive alliteration in line 12, where the four stressed syllables are linked by the repetition of sibilants: *spot/skin/shocking/disease* (/s/, /s/, /ʃ/, /z/). Auden's poem also contains alliteration in which unstressed syllables participate. The most notable example is the repetition of /d/ in lines 6 and 7: *dusk/delay, diligent/discover*, the latter pair displaying assonance as well.

21. A more subtle repetition is found in the next line of this stanza: *Yonder's/odours* (lines 3 and 4). Here, a clever use of the contraction (for *Yonder is*) creates identity between the two unaccented syllables of these words: /də(r)z/.

22. There is, of course, a minor phonetic difference in the two forms: the demonstrative pronoun, *that*, is a "strong" form, being pronounced with an unreduced vowel, [æ], whereas the subordinate conjunction, *that*, being unstressed, is pronounced with the "weakest" of all English vowels, [ə] ("schwa"). However, since *that* is metrically unstressed in all the lines where it appears in the poem, this stress difference is barely discernible. In fact, because of the parallels established in the poem, the word *that* in line 6 is somewhat ambiguous: the most natural reading is a subordinate conjunction ("do you imagine that dusk will delay"), but the reading as a demonstrative pronoun is not impossible ("do you imagine (that) that dusk will delay").

23. Despite the differences, we should not overlook the similarities which the last stanza bears to the other three. It shares with them the basic metrical pattern, including the caesura between the hemistichs – which in stanza four is now clearly marked by punctuation in each line ( "–" and ","). Auden also masterfully parallels, orthographically, the opening interjection, "O", of the first three stanzas with the letter "O" of "Out" in the last stanza.

24. Hecht (1993: 455) has argued that this last line contains a "technical fault" – namely the conflict between the singular pronoun, *he*, and the plural *they* (as *he* left *them* there). The problem, as Hecht sees it, involves the question of how many speakers there are in this poem. It would seem that there are either two or six. If all the passive labels (*reader, fearer, horror*) refer to the same individual, and all the active labels (*rider, farer, hearer*) refer to another individual, then there are only two speakers, and the last line should have read: As he left *him* there, as he left *him* there. If, on the other hand, each label refers to a different individual, then there are three passive members, and three active members, and the last line should have read: As *they* left them there, as *they* left them there. Here is Hecht's comment:

My guess is that Auden was caught short at discovering that he had more or less boxed himself into writing "As they left them there, as they left them there," in which the repetition of third-person plural pronouns would leave everyone grammatically bewildered. His not entirely satisfactory solution was to incorporate "rider," "farer," and "hearer" into one symbolic hero-escapee while leaving the impotent and terrified enemy divided and plural.

This is not an unreasonable interpretation. It even gains some support from the fact that some 25 years after composing this poem, Auden published it in his *Selected Poetry* (1958) under the title, "The Three Companions" (Spears 1963: 57). Possibly the "three companions" are the passive questioners, and there is but one active answerer.

There is, however, an alternative explanation – namely, that there is only one active individual and only one passive individual, but that the active participant (*he*) left behind the passive one <u>and</u> the shadowy figure (or figures) alluded to in the third stanza (*that bird, that shape, the figure*). So *they* refers to the passive questioner plus one or more of these nebulous shapes. Note that on the basis of stanza three alone, it is not clear whether the three nouns (*bird, shape, figure*) refer to one object or more than one. This is, of course, irrelevant to the choice of pronoun (*they* is the necessary choice in any event, since it includes the passive individual as well). But I believe this ambiguity is resolved in line 15, where *hearer* responds to the question posed by *horror* in stanza three by replying: <u>*They*</u>*'re looking for you*. So *rider/farer/hearer* left behind *reader/fearer/horror* <u>and</u> the fearsome shapes and shadows seen by horror in stanza three. Thus <u>he</u> left <u>them</u>.

# References

Auden, W. H. 1962. *The Dyer's Hand and Other Essays*. London: Faber and Faber.

Auden, W. H. 1962. "Making, Knowing and Judging" – Inaugural Lecture delivered before the University of Oxford on June 11, 1956. In *The Dyer's Hand and Other Essays*, by W. H. Auden; London: Faber and Faber, 31-60.

Auden, W. H. 1962. "Writing". In *The Dyer's Hand and Other Essays*, by W. H. Auden, London: Faber and Faber, 13-27.

Auden, W. H. 1966. *Collected Shorter Poems 1927-1957*. London: Faber and Faber.

Auden, W. H. 1968. *Secondary Worlds*. London: Faber and Faber.

Auden, W. H. 1970. *A Certain World*. New York: The Viking Press.

Auden, W. H. and Louis MacNeice. 1937. *Letters from Iceland*. London: Faber and Faber.

Beach, Joseph Warren. 1957. *The Making of the Auden Canon*. Minneapolis: The University of Minnesota Press.

Betjeman, Sir John. 1975 (1974). "Oxford". In *W. H. Auden – A Tribute*, edited by Stephen Spender; New York: Macmillan Publishing Co., 43-45.

Callan, Edward. 1983. *Auden: A Carnival of Intellect*. Oxford: Oxford University Press.

Carpenter, Humphrey. 1981. *W. H. Auden: A Biography*. London: George Allen & Unwin.

Carritt, Gabriel, with Rex Warner. 1975 (1974). "A Friend of the Family". In *W.*

H. Auden – A Tribute, edited by Stephen Spender; New York: Macmillan Publishing Co., 45-58.

Cassidy, Frederic and Richard Ringler (eds.). 1971. *Bright's Old English Grammar & Reader*. (Third edition. The original copyright goes back to 1891), New York: Holt, Rinehart and Winston.

Cox, R. G. 1975. "The Poetry of W. H. Auden". In *The Pelican Guide to English Literature*. Volume 7: The Modern Age (Third edition. First edition 1961), edited by Boris Ford; Harmondsworth, Middlesex: Penguin Books, 395-411.

Creed, Robert. 1966. "A New Approach to the Rhythm of *Beowulf*". *Proceedings of the Modern Language Association*, 23-33.

Cuddon, J. A. 1991. *The Pengu in Dictionary of Literary Terms and Literary Theory*. (Third edtion. First published 1976). London: Penguin Books.

Damrosch, Leopold, Leonare F. Dean, William Keach, and Gerald Levin (eds.). 1985 (1980). *Adventures in English Literature*, New York: Harcourt Brace Jovanovich.

Einarsson, Stefán. 1963-4. "Anti-naturalism, Tough Composition and Punning in Skaldic Poetry and Modern Painting", *Saga-Book*, Vol. XVI, Parts 2-3, London: Viking Society for Northern Research, 124-143.

Ford, Boris (ed.). 1975. *The Pelican Guide to English Literature*. Volume 7: The Modern Age. (Third edition. First edition 1961). Harmondsworth, Middlesex: Penguin.

Fuller, John. 1970. *A Reader's Guide to W. H. Auden*. New York: Farrar, Straus & Giroux.

Fussell, Paul, Jr. *Poetic Meter and Poetic Form*. New York: Random House.

Gordon, E. V. 1965. *An Introduction to Old Norse*. (Second edition, 1968. First edition, 1927)London: Oxford University Press.

Haarder, Andreas. 1979. *Det episke liv*. Copenhagen: Berlingske forlag.

Hamer, Richard. 1970. *A Choice of Anglo-Saxon Verse*. London: Faber and Faber.

Hecht, Anthony. 1993. *The Hidden Law: The Poetry of W. H. Auden*. Cambridge, Massachusetts: Harvard University Press.

Isherwood, Christopher. 1975 (1974). "Some Notes on the Early Poetry". In *W. H. Auden – A Tribute*, edited by Stephen Spender; New York: Macmillan Publishing Co., 74-79.

Leech, Geoffrey. 1974 (1969). *A Linguistic Guide to English Poetry*. London: Longman.

Lehmann, W. P. 1968. "The Old Germanic Verse Form". In *Old English Literature: Twenty-two Analytical Essays*, edited by Martin Stevens and Jerome Mandel; Lincoln, Nebraska: University of Nebraska Press, 17-35. (Reprinted from W. P. Lehmann, The Development of Germanic Verse Form, Austin, Texas: The University of Texas Press, 1956, 23-63.)

Luke, David. 1975 (1974). "Homing to Oxford". In *W. H. Auden – A Tribute*, edited by Stephen Spender; New York: Macmillan Publishing Co., 202-217.

Malof, Joseph. 1970. *A Manual of English Meters*. Bloomington: Indiana University Press.

Mendelson, Edward (ed.). 1976. *W. H. Auden: Collected Poems*. London: Faber and Faber.

Mendelson, Edward (ed.). 1977. *The English Auden: Poems, Essays and Dramatic Writings 1927-1939*. London: Faber and Faber.

Perrine, Laurence. 1969. *Sound and Sense: An Introduction to Poetry* (Third edition. First edition 1956). New York: Harcourt, Brace & World.

Pope, John. 1942. *The Rhythm of* Beowulf: *An Interpretation of the Normal and Hypermetric Verse-Forms in Old English Poetry*. New Haven: Yale University Press.

Roberts, Philip Davies. 1986. *How Poetry Works: The Elements of English Poetry*. Harmondsworth, Middlesex: Penguin.

Schipper, Jakob. 1973. *A History of English Versification*. U.S.A.: Folcroft Library Editions. (A reprint of the 1910 Oxford edition, which itself is an English translation from the German *Grundriss der englischen Metrik*, Vienna, 1895.)

Spears, Monroe K. 1963. *The Poetry of W. H. Auden*. New York: Oxford University Press.

Spender, Stephen. 1975 (1974). "Valediction". In *W. H. Auden – A Tribute*, edited by Stephen Spender; New York: Macmillan Publishing Co., 244-248.

Spender, Stephen (ed.). 1975 (1974). *W. H. Auden – A Tribute*. New York: Macmillan Publishing Co.

Stevens, Martin and Jerome Mandel (eds.). 1968. *Old English Literature: Twenty-two Analytical Essays*. Lincoln, Nebraska: University of Nebraska Press.

Thwaite, Anthony. 1978. *Twentieth Century English Poetry*. London: Heinemann.

Turville-Petre, G. 1951. *The Heroic Age of Scandinavia*. London: Hutchinson's University Library.

Yates, Michael. 1975 (1974). "Iceland 1936". In *W. H. Auden – A Tribute*, edited by Stephen Spender; New York: Macmillan Publishing Co., 59-68.